W9-CSS-563

Haruo Aoki
Masayosi Hirose
Jean Keller
Katuhiko Sakuma

BASIC STRUCTURES IN JAPANESE

日本語の基本構造

Taishukan Publishing Company

Basic Structures in Japanese

© H. Aoki, M. Hirose, J. Keller, K. Sakuma, 1984

Exclusive Distributor in the U.S.A.
Asian Humanities Press
PO Box 4177
Santa Clara, CA 95054–0177

PRINTED IN JAPAN
ISBN 4–969–22062–0

Preface

This text was first conceived in the summer of 1975.

The notes (on dialogues, usage, and grammar) were written by Masayosi Hirose, the dialogues by Haruo Aoki, and the drills by Jean Keller and Katuhiko Sakuma. The index was prepared by Tiyuki Kumakura.

The present text is the result of revisions based on classroom experience incorporating suggestions by the following instructors: Janet Akaike-Toste, Andrew Barshay, Mary Beckman, Christalyn Brannen, David Harris, Masaharu Huzita, Akiko Inagaki, Hiroaki Inagaki, Hiromitu Kobayasi, Tiyuki Kumakura, John Mayer, Lynn Miyake, Oscar Montes, Yasuhiko Nagano, Richard Okada, Sigeko Okamoto, Betsy Olson, Kuniko Ookubo, Satosi Yamamura.

The material was prepared for the press by Christalyn Brannen assisted by Jane Okano.

Contents

Preface

Basic Structures in Japanese

by

Haruo Aoki

Masayosi Hirose

Jean Keller
Katuhiko Sakuma

Lesson 1.

A. Useful Expressions.

1. Ohayoogozaimasu.	Good morning.
2. Konnitiwa.	Hello.
3. Konbanwa.	Good Evening.
4. Oyasuminasai.	Good night.
5. Onamae wa.	What is your name?
6. Watasi wa Yamada desu.	My name is Yamada.
7. Yorosiku.	Pleased to meet you.
8. Doozo yorosiku.	Pleased to meet you.
9. Hazimemasite.	Pleased to meet you.
10. Hazimemasite doozo yorosiku.	I am pleased to make your acquaintance.
11. Tanaka san desu ka.	Are you Mr./Ms. Tanaka?
12. Hai, soo desu.	Yes, that's right (Yes, I am).
13. Iie, Watanabe desu.	No, I am Watanabe.
14. Itte kudasai.	Please say it.
15. Issyo ni itte kudasai.	Please say it all together.
16. Kore o mite kudasai.	Please look at this.
17. Moo itido itte kudasai.	Please say it again.
18. Moo itido onegaisimasu.	Would you mind (repeating it) once more?
19. Sumimasen ga moo itido onegaisi-masu.	I'm sorry, but would you mind doing it once more?
20. Itadakimasu.	[a set phrase used before beginning a meal] (Lit. "I will receive (your good food).")
21. Gotisoosama.	[a set phrase used after ending a meal] (Lit. "It was very good")
22. Itte(i)rassyai.	[a set phrase used to wish someone well when he's off to work, travel, school, etc.] (Lit. "Go and return (safely).")
23. Dotira e.	Where are you going?
24. Tyotto soko made.	Just over there (and back).
25. Siturei simasu.	I'll be leaving now. (Lit. "I am being impolite.")
26. Dewa/zya mata notihodo.	Well, see you later,
27. Dewa mata asita.	Well, see you tomorrow.
28. Dewa mata raisyuu.	Well, see you next week.
29. Doomo arigatoo gozaimasu.	Thank you very much.
30. Doo itashimashite.	You are welcome.

B. Phonology and the Writing System.

1. Vowels: There are five vowels: a, i, u, e, o.

あ　い　う　え　お

2. Consonants:

a. Single consonants: (in combination with the five vowels)

	a	i	u	e	o
k-	ka	ki	ku	ke	ko
s-	sa	si	su	se	so
t-	ta	ti	tu	te	to
n-	na	ni	nu	ne	no
h-	ha	hi	hu	he	ho
m-	ma	mi	mu	me	mo
y-	ya	—	yu	—	yo
r-	ra	ri	ru	re	ro
w-	wa	—	—	—	(w)o

Note: si, ti, tu become shi, chi, tsu respectively

	a	i	u	e	o
zero	あ	い	う	え	お
k-	か	き	く	け	こ
s-	さ	し	す	せ	そ
t-	た	ち	つ	て	と
n-	な	に	ぬ	ね	の
h-	は	ひ	ふ	へ	ほ
m-	ま	み	む	め	も
y-	や		ゆ		よ
r-	ら	り	る	れ	ろ
w-	わ				を

b.

	pa	pi	pu	pe	po
p-	ぱ	ぴ	ぷ	ぺ	ぽ

c. Voiced counterparts for k-, s-, t-, p-:

	ga	gi	gu	ge	go
g-	ga	gi	gu	ge	go
z-	za	zi	zu	ze	zo
d-	da	(zi)	(zu)	de	do
b-	ba	bi	bu	be	bo

Note: zi and di are both zi, and du becomes zu.

	a	i	u	e	o
g-	が	ぎ	ぐ	げ	ご
z-	ざ	じ	ず	ぜ	ぞ
d-	だ	ぢ	づ	で	ど
b-	ば	び	ぶ	べ	ぼ

d.

n- ん syllabic nasal

2

3. Long Vowels

aa	obaasan grandmother	おばあさん	okaasan mother	おかあさん
ii	ii good	いい	oziisan grandfather	おじいさん
ee	ee yes (informal)	ええ	oneesan elder sister	おねえさん
uu	raisyuu next week	らいしゅう	yuubinkyoku post office	ゆうびんきょく

oo (a) Write u for the second o as a rule.

	syokudoo dining hall	しょくどう	kooen park	こうえん

(b) For a handful of exceptions write o for the second o.

	ookii big	おおきい	ooi many, much	おおい

4. Double Vowels

vowel combination	Example word	English Translation
ai	hai	yes
au	au	to meet
ae	hae	fly (insect)
ao	ao	blue/green
ia	siai	tournament, match
iu	siuti	treatment
ie	ie	house
io	sio	salt
ua	guai	condition
ui	kui	stake, post
ue	ue	up, above
uo	uo	fish
ea	deau	to meet
ei	ei	ray (fish)
eu	meue	superior
eo	neon	neon
oa	doa	door
oi	oi	nephew
ou	ou	to carry on one's back
oe	koe	voice

5. Complex Consonants

a.	kya	きゃ	kyu	きゅ	kyo	きょ	kyooto Kyoto	きょうと
	sya	しゃ	syu	しゅ	syo	しょ	syokudoo dining hall	しょくどう

3

tya	ちゃ	tyu	ちゅ	tyo	ちょ	nihontya にほんちゃ Japanese tea
nya	にゃ	nyu	にゅ	nyo	にょ	nyuugaku にゅうがく entering school
hya	ひゃ	hyu	ひゅ	hyo	ひょ	hyaku ひゃく hundred
mya	みゃ	myu	みゅ	myo	みょ	myooniti みょうにち tomorrow
rya	りゃ	ryu	りゅ	ryo	りょ	ryoo りょう dormitory
pya	ぴゃ	pyu	ぴゅ	pyo	ぴょ	denpyoo でんぴょう slip, chit
bya	びゃ	byu	びゅ	byo	びょ	byooin びょういん hospital
gya	ぎゃ	gyu	ぎゅ	gyo	ぎょ	koogyoo こうぎょう industry
zya	じゃ	zyu	じゅ	zyo	じょ	zyuudoo じゅうどう judo

Note: sy, ty, zy become sh, ch, j respectively.

b. double consonants

(1) For double nasals mm, nn, write _n_ (syllabic nasal) plus m- or n- letters.

semmon	せんもん	konnitiwa	こんにちは
specialization		Hello (literally means good day.)	

(2) For pp, tt, kk, ss, (and hh) write a small _tu_ for the first consonant.

happyaku	はっぴゃく	mattaku	まったく
800	hatupiyaku	indeed	

6. Long and Short Syllables

S: a short syllable (1 beat or 1 mora) = (C) + V
   (C: consonant, V: vowel, (C) an optional consonant)
L: a long syllable (2 beats or 2 morae) = (C) + long
   vowel or S+n or S+p, t, k, s, h.

No. of syllables	No. of morae	Long or short	Examples	
1	1	S	ha tooth	me eye
1	2	L	ryoo dormitory	hon book
2	2	SS	neko cat	hito person
2	3	LS	hon-ya bookstore	tyotto a little
2	3	SL	kirei beautiful	nihon Japan

4

2	4	LL	sensei teacher	sinbun newspaper
3	3	SSS	otoko man	minami south
3	4	LSS	bungaku literature	mattaku indeed
3	4	SLS	imooto younger sister	nihontya Japanese tea
3	4	SSL	gakusei student	tosyokan library
4	4	SSSS	tatemono building	tekisuto textbook

7. Pitch Accent

a. Two morae

(1)	neko cat	ani elder brother	naka inside
(2)	hito person	kuni country	uti home

b. Three morae

(1)	naihu knife	terebi television	kamera camera
(2)	syasin photograph	mukasi long ago	rekisi history
(3)	tikaku neighborhood	hanasu to talk	taberu to eat

c. Four morae

(1)	tekisuto textbook	bungaku literature	kyanpasu campus
(2)	bihuteki beef steak	sukiyaki sukiyaki	daigaku university
(3)	hiragana hiragana	roomazi romanization	ikimasu to go
(4)	tatemono building	tosyokan library	

8. Voiceless Vowels

An unaccented i or u is devoiced between voiceless consonants.

hito person	titi father	kita north
asita tomorrow	tukue desk	rekisi history
sukiyaki sukiyaki	bihuteki beef steak	tekisuto textbook

9. Katakana

	a	i	u	e	o
zero	ア	イ	ウ	エ	オ
k-	カ	キ	ク	ケ	コ
s-	サ	シ	ス	セ	ソ
t-	タ	チ	ツ	テ	ト
n-	ナ	ニ	ヌ	ネ	ノ
h-	ハ	ヒ	フ	ヘ	ホ
m-	マ	ミ	ム	メ	モ
y-	ヤ		ユ		ヨ
r-	ラ	リ	ル	レ	ロ
w-	ワ				ヲ
n	ン				

6

かたかな stroke order

a	ア	ヤ ア	ta	タ	ノ ク タ	ma	マ	ヤ マ
i	イ	ノ イ	ti	チ	ー ニ チ	mi	ミ	ヽ ミ ミ
u	ウ	ヽ ウ ウ	tu	ツ	ヽ ツ ツ	mu	ム	ム ム
e	エ	ー エ エ	te	テ	ー ニ テ	me	メ	ノ メ
o	オ	ー オ オ	to	ト	｜ ト	mo	モ	ー ニ モ
ka	カ	ヨ カ	na	ナ	ー ナ	ya	ヤ	ヤ ヤ
ki	キ	ー ニ キ	ni	ニ	ー ニ	yu	ユ	フ ユ
ku	ク	ノ ク	nu	ヌ	フ ヌ	yo	ヨ	フ ヲ ヨ
ke	ケ	ノ ケ ケ	ne	ネ	ヽ ヲ ネ ネ	ra	ラ	ー ラ
ko	コ	フ コ	no	ノ	ノ	ri	リ	｜ リ
sa	サ	ー ナ サ	ha	ハ	ノ ハ	ru	ル	ノ ル
si	シ	ヽ ヽ シ	hi	ヒ	ノ ヒ	re	レ	レ
su	ス	フ ス	hu	フ	フ	ro	ロ	｜ フ ロ
se	セ	ヤ セ	he	ヘ	ヘ	wa	ワ	｜ ワ
so	ソ	ヽ ソ	ho	ホ	ー ナ オ ホ	(w)o	ヲ	ー ニ ヲ
						n	ン	ヽ ン

Note: × marks the strokes that are to be tapered e.g. ク. Those unmarked strokes
have blunt endings e.g. コ.

7

ひらがな stroke order

a	あ	⌐十ああ	ta	た	⌐ナたた	ma	ま	⌐二ま
i	い	いい	ti	ち	⌐ち	mi	み	みみ
u	う	⌐う	tu	つ	つ	mu	む	⌐もむ
e	え	⌐ラえ	te	て	⌐て	me	め	﹨め
o	お	⌐十おお	to	と	﹨と	mo	も	しもも
ka	か	つカか	na	な	⌐ナたな	ya	や	つゃや
ki	き	⌐ニきき	ni	に	∣ lにに	yu	ゆ	し いゆ
ku	く	く	nu	ぬ	﹨ぬぬ	yo	よ	⌐よ
ke	け	∣ l l け	ne	ね	∣ れね	ra	ら	⌐ ⸜ら
ko	こ	⌐こ	no	の	﹨の	ri	り	しり
sa	さ	⌐ささ	ha	は	∣ lには	ru	る	⸝る
si	し	し	hi	ひ	ひひ	re	れ	∣ れれ
su	す	⌐すす	hu	ふ	﹨ふふふ	ro	ろ	⸝ろ
se	せ	⌐十せ	he	へ	へ	wa	わ	オわ
so	そ	﹨ニそ	ho	ほ	∣ lにほ	(w)o	を	⌐大を
						n	ん	﹨ん

Note: × marks the strokes that are to be tapered e.g. し Those unmarked strokes
      have blunt endings e.g. い.

第 二 課

2A

スミス　　あれは私の寮です。

山田　　　そうですか。あれも寮ですか。

スミス　　いいえ，寮じゃありません。食堂です。

山田　　　あれは何ですか。

スミス　　体育館です。

山田　　　ここはどこですか。

スミス　　バークレーです。

山田　　　そうじゃありません。この建物ですよ。

スミス　　ああ建物ですか。さあ，よくわかりませんが
　　　　　図書館でしょう。

2B

スミス　　これは私たちの大学の新聞です。

山田　　　ああそうですか。

[pointing to a photograph]

山田　　　この人はだれですか。

スミス　　心理学の先生です。

山田　　　この大学のですか。

スミス　　いいえ，スタンフォードの先生です。

山田　　　ところで，御専門は何ですか。

スミス　　経済学です。

山田　　　私は社会学です。

① 例 T: あれ，寮
　　　　S: あれは寮です。

1. あれ，食堂
2. あれ，体育館
3. これ，図書館
4. それ，新聞
5. この方，田中さん
6. あの建物，図書館
7. 専門，経済学
8. この方，先生
9. これ，大学の新聞
10. 私，バークレーの学生
11. あれ，私の寮

12. これ，私のテキスト
13. あれ，スミスさんの辞書
14. 青木先生，バークレーの先生
15. これ，日本語のテキスト
16. 私の専門，文学
17. これ，私たちの大学の新聞
18. ベラー先生，バークレーの
　　　社会学の先生
19. 私，経済学
20. カーターさん，アパート

② 例 T: 図書館
　　　　{ S₁: 図書館ですか。
　　　　{ S₂: ええ，図書館です。

1. 寮
2. 食堂
3. 大学
4. 新聞
5. テキスト
6. スタンフォード
7. 経済学
8. アパート
9. 大学の新聞
10. 心理学の先生
11. スタンフォードの先生

12. 経済学の先生
13. 日本語のテキスト
14. 大学二年生
15. カーターさんの辞書
16. 田中さんの寮
17. 田中さんのテキスト
18. 私たちの大学の新聞
19. バークレーの日本語の
　　　テキスト
20. バークレーの文学の先生

③　例1　T: あれは寮ですか。（寮）

　　　　S: ええ，あれは寮です。

　　例2　T: これはテキストですか。（辞書）

　　　　S: いえ，それはテキストじゃありません。辞書です。

　　例3　T: それは田中さんの辞書ですか。（私）

　　　　S: いえ，これは田中さんの辞書じゃありません。私のです。

1.　あれは寮ですか。（食堂）

2.　これは辞書ですか。（テキスト）

3.　あれは図書館ですか。（図書館）

4.　これは新聞ですか。（新聞）

5.　あの建物は食堂ですか。（食堂）

6.　あの人は田中さんですか。（山田さん）

7.　カーターさんはバークレーの学生ですか。（スタンフォード）

8.　田中さんは大学生ですか。（大学院生）

9.　田中さんの専門は文学ですか。（文学）

10.　岡田さんは日本人ですか。（アメリカ人）

11.　それは山田さんのテキストですか。（私）

12.　ベラー先生は経済学の先生ですか。（社会学）

13.　これは図書館の本ですか。（先生）

14.　それはサンフランシスコの新聞ですか。（バークレー）

15.　学生ですか。（学生）

16.　専門は心理学ですか。（文学）

17.　御専門は文学ですか。（文学）

18.　山田さんは文学ですか。（歴史）

19.　カーターさんは寮ですか。（アパート）

20.　ここはスタンフォードですか。（バークレー）

④　例1　T: あれ

　　　　S: あれは何ですか。

例2　T:　あの人

　　　　S:　あの人は誰ですか。

1.　これ
2.　あの建物
3.　あの人
4.　あの男の人
5.　それ
6.　あの学生
7.　この建物
8.　あの女の人
9.　あの方

10.　田中さんの専門
11.　山田さんの専門
12.　その本
13.　御専門
14.　あの先生
15.　あの女の方
16.　あの建物
17.　あれ
18.　あのビル

⑤　例　T:　あれは寮です。（あれ）

　　　S₁:　あれも寮ですか。
　　　S₂:　いえ，あれは寮じゃありません。
　　　S₁:　ああ，そうですか。

1.　あれは体育館です。（あれ）
2.　これはテキストです。（それ）
3.　あの人は学生です。（あの人）
4.　あの方は先生です。（あの方）
5.　あの建物は食堂です。（この建物）
6.　カーターさんは学生です。（田中さん）

7.　岡田先生はアメリカ人です。（青木先生）
8.　この本は，図書館のです。（その本）
9.　田中さんの専門は歴史です。（山田さんの専門）
10.　カーターさんはアパートです。（ジョンソンさん）

Lesson 2 **Dialogues**

2 A

Sumisu: Are wa watasi no ryoo desu.
    are wa
    watasi no
    ryoo
    desu

Yamada: Soo desu ka. Are mo ryoo desu ka.
    Soo desu ka.
    are mo
    ka

S: Iie, ryoo zya arimasen. Syokudoo desu.
    ____ zya arimasen
    syokudoo

Y: Are wa nan desu ka.
    nan

S: Taiikukan desu.

Y: Koko wa doko desu ka.
    koko
    doko

S: Baakuree desu.

Y: Soo zya arimasen. Kono tatemono desu yo.
    tatemono

S: Aa tatemono desu ka. Saa yoku wakarimasen ga tosyokan desyoo.
    Aa
    Saa
    yoku
    wakarimasen
    ga
    tosyokan
    desyoo

Smith: That's my dorm.
    that [wa: topic marker]
    my [watasi: I]
    dormitory
    is [Copula]

Yamada: Oh, is that right?
    Is that a dormitory, too?
    Is that right?
    that too [mo: too]
    [question marker]

S: No, that's not a dormitory. That's a cafeteria.
    is not ____
    cafeteria

Y: What is that?
    what?

S: It's a gymnasium.

Y: What/where is this place?
    this place, here
    where?

S: (This) is Berkeley.

Y: That's not what I'm asking. (It's) this building (that I'm asking about).
    building

S: Oh, the building? Well, I don't know, but I guess it's a library.
    Oh
    Well
    well
    I don't know
    but
    library
    I guess

2 B

Sumisu: Kore wa watasitati no daigaku no sinbun desu.

    kore
    watasitati no
    daigaku
    sinbun

Smith: This is our college paper.

    this thing
    our ["watasi": I, "tati": pl., "no": 's]
    university, college
    newspaper

Yamada: Aa soo desu ka.

Yamada: Oh, I see.

[pointing to a photograph]

Y: Kono hito wa dare desu ka.

    kono hito
    dare

Y: Who is this person?

    this person
    who?

S: Sinrigaku no sensei desu.

S: He is a psychology professor.

Y: Kono daigaku no desu ka.

    kono daigaku

Y: At this university?

    this university

S: Iie. Sutanhoodo no sensei desu.

S: No. He is a professor at Stanford.

Y: Tokorode, gosenmon wa nan desu ka.

    tokorode
    go—
    senmon

Y: By the way, what is your major?

    by the way
    (honorific prefix)
    one's major in college

S: Keizaigaku desu.

    keizai
    —gaku

S: (I'm majoring in) economics.

    economy
    [suffix 'study,' '-ology']

Y: Watasi wa syakaigaku desu.

Y: I'm in sociology.

Lesson 2 Notes on Usage

2 A

1. そうですか。

    Soo desu ka. (with falling intonation)   Is that so. I see.

When Japanese are talking, the speaker usually pauses briefly between phrases, at which point the addressee utters such short words as ええ (ee) "Uh huh" or はい (hai) "Yes" to signal that he is following the speaker.

14

そうですか。(Soo desu ka.) with falling intonation is one of these responses. (With rising intonation it is a genuine question which means "Is that so?" or "Is that right?") These responses give the conversation a certain rhythm.

English speakers do have similar devices but Japanese use this device much more frequently than English speakers. Therefore, it is often the case that a Japanese feels uneasy when speaking to an American who just listens to him quietly.

Another important difference between Japanese and Americans that arises in conversations ought to be noted here. Americans look directly into the eyes of the person they are talking to. This is unnerving to Japanese who avoid eye-contact as a rule. It is done in Japan only when the two parties are quarreling, or when one is suspicious of what the other is saying.

2. そうじゃありません。
　　　Soo zya arimasen.

That's not what I'm asking.
That's not what I'm talking about.
That's not what I mean. etc.

3. …よ。
　　　yo.

よ (yo) is a sentence final particle which is attached to the end of a sentence providing new information that the addressee does not know. Thus, sometimes it carries with it a connotation of "I tell you."

Sometimes the speaker has to give old information as new by repeating it to the hearer when he has a hard time understanding it. よ (yo) is used in such a situation, too.

In any case, the particle should *not* get any stress, and, although it is used quite commonly among Japanese, students are advised to use it with great care because it may sound very imposing and thus rude depending on stress and intonation.

4. ああ。
　　　Aa.

Oh, ...

5. さあ，よくわかりませんが…
　　　Saa yoku wakarimasen ga...

Well, I'm not sure but...

さあ (Saa) means "Well, ..." or "Umm, ..." indicating that the speaker is not sure. よく (yoku) means "well", and わかりません (wakarimasen), "I don't know." Thus all together it means "I don't know well."

が (ga) in this case means "but."

6. …でしょう。
　　　desyoo.

It is probably ____
I guess it's ____

15

でしょう (desyoo) is used when the speaker is not sure about something. (cf. Grammar Notes for this lesson.)

2 B

1. ところで
   Tokoro de   by the way

It is used when the speaker is going to introduce a new topic of conversation. (To be discussed in Lesson 6 again.)

2. 御専門
   go-senmon   your specialty

ご (go) is an honorific prefix and せんもん (senmon) means "one's major in college" ご (go) is used to express politeness to the addressee. Thus, go-senmon cannot be used when referring to one's own major or specialty. Senmon is used when refering to the major or specialty of the speaker or a third person who requires no honorific reference.

Lesson 2 **Grammar Notes**

The main points of this lesson are:
 I. "As for ___, it is ___."
 II. Demonstratives.
 III. Possessive or descriptive relationship for nouns.
 IV. How to say "also."
 V. Negative Sentences.
 VI. Question marker ka.

I. X は Y です。   As for X, it is Y
     wa   desu

私 は 学生です。
Watasi wa gakusei desu.   I am a student

16

スミスさんは 先生 です。
Sumisusan wa sensei desu.　　　　　　　　Mr. Smith is a teacher.

Literally this pattern means, "As for X, it is Y" or "Speaking of X, it is Y" but a more idiomatic rendering should be made when translating into English.

The pattern X は Y です is often used to indicate that which is associated with X. The relationship between X and Y can only be determined by the context.

(at a restaurant)

私 は すしです。
Watasi wa susi desu.

Literally this means "As for me, (what I will have) is sushi."
but idiomatically it means
"I will have sushi."

(talking about one's major)

私 は 社会学 です。
Watasi wa syakaigaku desu.

(Lit., "As for me, (my major) is sociology.")
I am majoring in sociology.

When は (wa) is attached to a noun or phrase, this indicates that the noun or phrase has been previously introduced into the conversation either directly or by implication.

The letter は is usually read as ha when it is part of a word, but when it is used as a particle as in this pattern, it is pronounced as wa.

Katakana is conventionally used for foreign words, such as スミス (Sumisu) Smith, バークレー (Baakuree) Berkeley, etc.

さん (san) is a suffix roughly equivalent to the English Mr./Miss/Mrs. It is used with the family or given names of persons other than the speaker.

II. Demonstratives　　　　　　　　　　　　this, that etc.

When pointing out 1) objects or 2) places, the following pronoun forms are used:

	A	B	C
1) objects	これ kore	それ sore	あれ are
2) places	ここ koko	そこ soko	あそこ asoko

When the noun is specified, the following adjectival forms are used:

		A	B	C
1) objects		この kono (Noun)	その sono (Noun)	あの ano (Noun)
2) persons	(plain)	この 人 kono hito	その 人 sono hito	あの 人 ano hito
	(polite)	この 方 kono kata	その 方 sono kata	あの 方 ano kata

17

Columns A, B and C designate the proximity of the object, person, or place to the speaker and the addressee:

Column A indicates that the object/person/place is closer to the speaker.

Column B indicates that the object/person/place is closer to the addressee.

Column C indicates that the object/person/place is far from both the speaker and the addressee.

これ は 図書館 です。
Kore wa tosyokan desu.

This is a library.

それは辞書です。
Sore wa zisyo desu.

That is a dictionary.

あれは 寮 です。
Are wa ryoo desu.

That over there is a dormitory.

この 人 は 山田さんです。
Kono hito wa Yamadasan desu.

(Pointing to a man in a picture) This person is Yamada.

この 方 は 山田さんです。
Kono kata wa Yamadasan desu.

This person is Miss Yamada. (Polite form)

ここ は バークレーです。
Koko wa Baakuree desu.

This is Berkeley.

あそこは サンフランシスコです。
Asoko wa Sanhuransisuko desu.

(Pointing to S.F. from the top of the Campanile) That over there is San Francisco.

III. N₁ no N₂ (N: noun)

'N₁'s N₂, N₂ of N₁, N₂ that is N₁, etc.

これは 私 のねこです。
Kore wa watasi no neko desu.

This is my cat.

山田さん の 辞書はこれです。
Yamadasan no zisyo wa kore desu.

Yamada's dictionary is this one.

あの人はスタンフォードの先生
Ano hito wa Sutanhoodo no sensei

です。
desu.

That person over there is a professor at Stanford.

山本さん　は　経済学　の　先生
Yamamotosan wa keizaigaku no sensei
です。
desu.

Mr. Yamamoto is a professer of economics.

の (no) placed between two nouns indicates a possessive or descriptive relationship. N₁ is always the modifying noun and N₂, the noun modified.

"N の" phrases can be strung together to form a long modifying phrase.

私　の　学校　の　学生
watasi no gakkoo no gakusei

(Lit., "my school's student")
a student of my school

N₂ can be deleted when it is clear in the given context.

それは　私　の　です。
Sore wa watasi no desu.

That is mine.

これは　大学　の　です。
Kore wa daigaku no desu.

This is the university's.

山田さん　の　はあれです。
Yamadasan no wa are desu.

Yamada's is that one.

経済学　の　本　は　これです。
Keizaigaku no hon wa kore desu.

The economics book is this one.

社会学　　の　は　あれ　です。
Syakaigaku no wa are desu.

The sociology one is that one over there.

IV. も (mo)　　　　　　　　　　　　also, too

も is attached to a noun or noun with another particle (e.g. ——にも). It cannot co-occur with the particles は (wa) and が (ga).

山田さん　は　学生　です。
Yamadasan wa gakusei desu.

Yamada is a student. Smith is a student, too.

スミスさんも　学生　です。
Sumisusan mo gakusei desu.

V. Negative Sentence

X は Y ⎧では / de wa ⎫ ありません
　 wa 　 ⎩じゃ / zya ⎭ arimasen

As for X, it is not Y

あれは 食堂 ではありません。
Are wa syokudoo dewa arimasen.

That is not a cafeteria.

私 は 先生じゃありません。
Watasi wa sensei zya arimasen.

I am not a teacher.

To make Pattern I negative, change です (desu) to ではありません (de wa arimasen) or じゃありません (zya arimasen).

VI. Questions

A. か (ka)

Yes/No questions

question marker

あれは 寮 ですか。
Are wa ryoo desu ka.

Is that a dormitory?

はい，あれは 寮 です。
Hai,　are wa ryoo desu.

Yes, that is a dormitory.

これはテキストですか。
Kore wa tekisuto desu ka.

Is this a textbook?

いいえ，それはテキストじゃあり
Iie,　sore wa　tekisuto zya ari

No, that is not a textbook.

ません。
masen.

Generally speaking the so-called yes/no questions are formed by adding か (ka) to the end of declarative sentences.

The end of the sentence usually has a slightly rising intonation.

If the speaker agrees with the statement preceding the か, his answer begins with はい (hai) or ええ (ee) 'Yes'; if not, it begins with いいえ (iie) or いえ (ie) 'No.'

20

B. Questions with interrogatives:

これは 何 ですか。
Kore wa nan desu ka.   What is this?

あの 人 は 誰ですか。
Ano hito wa dare desu ka.   Who is that person over there?

ここ はどこですか。   (Lit. "What place is this?")
Koko wa doko desu ka.   Where is this?

There are three types of interrogative words that indicate 1) objects, 2) persons and 3) places:

1. object	何 nan/nani	what?, which?
2. person	誰 dare	who?
person (polite)	どなた donata	who?
3. place	どこ doko	where?

Interrogative words cannot be used before は (wa).

第三課

3 A　(Looking at the pictures on the wall)

スミス　　　　あそこに写真がありますね。

山田　　　　　あれはだれですか。

スミス　　　　私たちの学長です。

(Yamada goes up to the picture)

山田　　　　　ああ，この人が学長ですか。この写真は…

スミス　　　　これは昔のバークレーです。

山田　　　　　何もありませんね。

スミス　　　　そうですね。祖父のころです。

山田　　　　　ああ，おじいさんもバークレーですか。

3 B　山田　　　　ここは犬がたくさんいますね。

スミス　　　　そうですか。

山田　　　　　図書館にも寮の中にも…

スミス　　　　ああ，そういえば私のうちにも母の犬と妹の犬

　　　　　　　がいますよ。

山田　　　　　犬の国ですね。まったく。

1 例 T: あれ，図書館
S₁: あれは何ですか。
S₂: 図書館です。
S₁: ああ，そうですか。あれが図書館ですか。

1. あれ，ベイブリッジ
2. これ，バークレーの新聞
3. これ，日本語の辞書
4. あれ，スミスさんの寮
5. それ，山田先生の本
6. あれ，デュラント・ホール
7. あれ，社会学の図書館
8. あの方，マッカーラ先生

9. あの人，スミスさん
10. これ，スタンフォードの新聞
11. あの方，青木先生
12. あの方，父
13. あの方，母
14. あの方，兄
15. あの方，妹

2 例1 T: ここ，写真
S: ここに写真があります。

例2 T: キャンパス，犬
S: キャンパスに犬がいます。

例3 T: あそこ，先生
S: あそこに先生がいらっしゃいます。

1. あそこ，食堂
2. あそこ，山田さん
3. ここ，テキスト
4. ここ，父の写真
5. バークレーのキャンパス，犬
6. あそこ，山田さん
7. ここ，日本語の辞書
8. 山田さんのうち，ねこ
9. 山田さんのうち，ソニーのテ
レビ
10. バークレー，ヒッピー
11. デュラント・ホールの近く，
図書館
12. あの机の上，辞書
13. デュラント・ホールの二階，
図書館
14. あの建物の中，食堂
15. あの建物の中，先生

24

16. あの建物の中，学長　　　　　なり，郵便局

17. 机の上，山田さんの写真　　20. 今日の新聞，バークレーの写

18. ここ，日本語の辞書　　　　　真

19. バンク・オブ・アメリカのと

③ 例1 T: 写真　　　　　　例3 T: ねこ

S₁: 何がありますか。　　　　S₁: 何がいますか。

S₂: 写真があります。　　　　S₂: ねこがいます。

例2 T: スミス先生

S₁: どなたがいらっしゃいますか。

S₂: スミス先生がいらっしゃいます。

1. 山田さんの本　　　　　　12. スタンフォードのジョンソン

2. 山田さん　　　　　　　　　　さん

3. スミス先生　　　　　　　13. バークレーのブラウン先生

4. スミス先生の犬　　　　　14. 日本語のテキスト

5. 中国語のテキスト　　　　15. 昔のサンフランシスコの写真

6. オレンジ・ジュース　　　16. 山田さんのおとうさん

7. 母の写真　　　　　　　　17. 妹の辞書

8. 母のねこ　　　　　　　　18. スミスさんの妹さん

9. 社会学の図書館　　　　　19. 山田さんの犬

10. うちの学長　　　　　　　20. ランカスター先生

11. 大学の新聞

④ 例1 T: 写真，ここ

S₁: 写真はどこにありますか。

S₂: 写真はここにあります。

例2 T: 犬，キャンパス，寮の中

S₁: 犬はどこにいますか。

S₂: 犬はキャンパスにも寮の中にもいます。

例3　T: 先生，うち

　　　S₁: 先生はどこにいらっしゃいますか。

　　　S₂: 先生はうちにいらっしゃいます。

1.　テキスト，そこ
2.　田中さん，あそこ
3.　先生，部屋
4.　辞書，うち，図書館
5.　心理学のテキスト，ここ
6.　姉，ロサンゼルス
7.　犬，寮の中，寮の外
8.　田中さんの車，あそこ
9.　田中さんの犬，あそこ
10.　スミス先生，あそこ
11.　銀行，キャンパスの南
12.　青木先生，図書館
13.　バンク・オブ・アメリカ，

テレグラフ
14.　郵便局，バンク・オブ・ア
　　　メリカのとなり
15.　先生，あそこ
16.　昔のバークレーの写真，図書
　　　館
17.　ベラー先生，バークレー
18.　ベラー先生の本，社会学の図
　　　書館
19.　タイプライター，この部屋，
　　　あの部屋
20.　日本のレストラン，バークレ
　　　ー，サンフランシスコ

⑤　例1　T: 日本語のテキストがありますか。（日本語のテキスト）

　　　S: ええ，日本語のテキストはあります。

　　2　T: 辞書がありますか。（日本語のテキスト）

　　　S: いいえ，辞書はありません。
　　　　　日本語のテキストがあります。

1.　スペイン語のテキストがあり
　　　ますか。（日本語のテキスト）
2.　男の学生がいますか。（女の
　　　学生）
3.　図書館がありますか。（図書

館）
4.　バークレーの写真があります
　　　か。（サンフランシスコの写
　　　真）
5.　日本語の辞書がありますか。

26

（中国語の辞書）

6. 犬がいますか。（犬）

7. スミス先生がいらっしゃいますか。（ブラウン先生）

8. ビザがありますか。（マスター・カード）

9. バークレーの学生がいますか。（スタンフォードの学生）

10. 文学の学生がいますか。（言語学の学生）

11. 田中さんがいますか。（山田さん）

12. 日本語の先生がいらっしゃいますか。（中国語の先生）

13. カラーテレビがありますか。（白黒テレビ）

14. 経済学の図書館がありますか。（社会学の図書館）

15. 女の先生がいらしっゃいますか。（女の先生）

---

6 例1 T: ここに本がありますか。（ここ）

　　　 S: ええ，あります。

　 例2 T: ここに犬がいますか。（キャンパス）

　　　 S: いえ，ここにはいません，キャンパスにいます。

1. ここに本がありますか。（あそこ）

2. ここに写真がありますか。（私の部屋）

3. うちに犬がいますか。（うち）

4. ここに辞書がありますか。（アパート）

5. 先生の部屋にこの本がありますか。（図書館）

6. キャンパスにヒッピーがいますか。（キャンパス）

7. キャンパスの北は銀行がありますか。（キャンパスの南）

8. 「セイフウェイ」にしょう油がありますか。（「コオプ」）

9. この部屋に日本語の辞書がありますか。（図書館）

10. 寮の中に犬がいますか。（寮の外）

11. このページにアルファベットがありますか。（このページ）

12. このテキストに写真がありますか。（あのテキスト）

13. キャンパスの近くに本屋がありますか。（キャンパスの近く）

14. モフィット図書館にこの本が
ありますか。（東アジア図書
館）

15. 田中さんのうちにテープレコ
ーダーがありますか。（山田
さんのうち）

16. 机の上にタイプライターがあ
りますか。（机の横）

17. 図書館にこの本がありますか。

18. テレグラフにバンク・オブ・
アメリカ がありますか。
（テレグラフ）

19. ここに文学の先生がいらっし
ゃいますか。（あの建物）

20. バンクロフトにバンク・オブ・
アメリカ がありますか。
（テレグラフ）

（先生の部屋）

7 例1 T: 何かありますか。
　　　S: いいえ，何もありません。
　例2 T: 誰かいますか。
　　　S: いいえ，誰もいません。
　例3 T: どこかにありますか。
　　　S: いいえ，どこにもありません。
　例4 T: どこかにいますか。
　　　S: いいえ，どこにもいません。

1. うちに誰かいますか。
2. 何かありますか。
3. オフィスに何かありますか。
4. 図書館にどなたかいらっしゃ
いますか。
5. オフィスに誰かいますか。
6. 犬はどこかにいますか。
7. 写真はどこかにありますか。
8. クラスに誰かいますか。
9. 寮に誰かいますか。
10. 寮のへやに何かありますか。
11. 机の上に何かありますか。
12. 日本語のテキストはどこかに
ありますか。

8 例1 T: 犬がいますか。（ええ）
　　　S: ええ，たくさんいます。

28

例 2　T: 先生がいらっしゃいますか。（ええ）

　　　　S: ええ，おおぜいいらっしゃいます。

例 3　T: 本がありますか。（ええ）

　　　　S: ええ，たくさんあります。

1.　日本人がいますか。（ええ）
2.　タイプライターがありますか。（ええ）
3.　辞書がありますか。（ええ）
4.　バークレーキャンパスに犬がいますか。（ええ）
5.　部屋に机がありますか。（ええ）
6.　日本語の先生がいらっしゃい

ますか。（ええ）
7.　ねこがいますか。（ええ）
8.　アメリカ人がいますか。（ええ）
9.　うちに本がありますか。（ええ
10.　クラスに日本人がいますか。（ええ）

Lesson 3　Dialogues

3 A

Smith: There is a picture over there, isn't there?

あそこに	over there [ni: location marker]
写真が	a picture [ga: subject marker]
あります	there is, exists
ね	isn't it? you see?, etc. [sentence final particle]

Yamada: Who is he?

| あれ | that one over there [wa: topic marker] |
| だれ | who? |

Smith: He's our president.

私<ruby>私<rt>わたし</rt></ruby>たちの   our

<ruby>学長<rt>がくちょう</rt></ruby>   university president

Yamada: Oh, so this person is the president. (How about) this picture?

ああ   oh, I see

この<ruby>人<rt>ひと</rt></ruby>が   this person [ga: subject]

Smith: This is Berkeley in the past.

<ruby>昔<rt>むかし</rt></ruby>の   of the past

Yamada: There is nothing, is there?

<ruby>何<rt>なに</rt></ruby>も   anything

ありません   there is not

Smith: That's right. It was my grandfather's time.

<ruby>祖父<rt>そふ</rt></ruby>   (my) grandfather

ころ   about (that) time.

Yamada: Oh, so you grandfather is also (an alumnus of) Berkeley.

おじいさん   (your) grandfather

も   too, also

ですか   oh, I see

3 B

Yamada: There sure are a lot of dogs here, aren't there?

ここ（に）は   here [ni: location marker is deleted.]
       [wa: topic marker]

たくさん   many, much

Smith: Is that so. (Smith has been living here too long to notice it.)
Yamada: (They are) in the library, in the dorms,......

<ruby>図書館<rt>としょかん</rt></ruby>にも   at/in the library too [mo: also, too]

Smith: Oh, come to think of it, at my house too, there are my mother's dog, and my younger sister's dog.

そういえば   come to think of it

<ruby>私<rt>わたし</rt></ruby>のうち   my house

母 <ruby>母<rt>はは</rt></ruby>   (my) mother

妹 <ruby>妹<rt>いもうと</rt></ruby>   (my) younger sister

よ   [sentence final particle] I tell you

Yamada: It's a dog's country isn't it?

<ruby>国<rt>くに</rt></ruby>   country

まったく   indeed

Lesson 3 **Notes on Usage**

3 A

1. あそこに<ruby>写真<rt>しゃしん</rt></ruby>がありますね。   "There is a picture over there, you see?"

ね is a sentence final particle which is attached to the end of a declarative sentence and indicates that the speaker wants the addressee to agree with what he is saying.

<ruby>何<rt>なに</rt></ruby>もありませんね。   There is nothing, isn't there?

そうですね。   That's right, isn't that?

ここは<ruby>犬<rt>いぬ</rt></ruby>がたくさんいますね。   There are many dogs, aren't there?

<ruby>犬<rt>いぬ</rt></ruby>の<ruby>国<rt>くに</rt></ruby>ですね。   It's a dog's country, isn't it?

2. ああこの<ruby>人<rt>ひと</rt></ruby>が<ruby>学長<rt>がくちょう</rt></ruby>ですか。   (with falling intonation)
"Oh, this is the president."

This is a question in form, but in this case with falling intonation, it is not a question. It is used to express acknowledgement of something not known before. "So this person is the president of the university." Also, see the next example.

ああおじいさんもバークレー   So your grandfather went to CAL, too.

ですか。

3. おじいさんもバークレーですか。

Literally, the sentence means "Your grandfather is Berkeley," but the addressee is able to decipher what is missing from the context of the sentence. In this case this means:

31

"Oh, so your grandfather ('s Alma Mater) is Berkeley, too."
  (cf. GN L. 2)

御専門は何ですか。   What is your major?

私は社会学です。   I'm in sociology.

3 B

1. たくさん (functions as an adverb and can be used for people)   many, much

  犬がたくさんいますね。   There are many dogs, aren't there?

  "Many" for people is おおぜい, but たくさん is also used for people.

2. そういえば   Come to think of it,
                               Now that you mentioned it,

  図書館がたくさんありますね。   There are many libraries, aren't there?

  そういえば，この建物にもあり   Come to think of it, there are some in

  ますよ。   this building, too.

3. 祖父, おじいさん

  そふ is my/our grandfather, and おじいさん is someone else's grandfather. When the speaker is talking to someone who is not a member of his family, he uses そふ to refer to his own grandfather. When the speaker is talking about the addressee's grandfather, or when the speaker is talking to his own family member, he uses おじいさん, the polite form.
  These distinctions apply to all kinship terms, i.e.

	Plain form	Polite form
grandfather	祖父	おじいさん
mother	母	おかあさん
younger sister	妹	妹 さん

  (Other forms will be introduced later. (Notes on Usage L. 8))

4. 犬の国ですね。   It's a country of dogs isn't it?

  The topic of the sentence (ここは "here") is not mentioned because it is obvious from the previous sentence.

5. まったく

Literally, it means "entirely." In this case, however, it means something like "indeed," "really," etc.

The normal word order is ここはまったく犬の国ですね。

However, in order to show emphasis, especially in exclamations, the most important part of the sentence tends to be uttered first, then followed by elements of less importance.

Emphatic sentences	Normal sentences
犬の国ですね。ここは。	ここは 犬 の 国 ですね。
	Koko wa inu no kuni desu ne.
	This is a country of dogs, isn't it?
たくさんいますね。犬が。	犬 がたくさんいますね。
	Inu ga takusan imasu ne.
	There are many dogs, aren't there?
大勢いますね, まったく。	まったく大勢いますね。
	Mattaku oozei imasu ne.
	There are many people, indeed.

Lesson 3 **Grammar Notes**

The main points of this lesson are:
I. Existential verbs and topic marker <u>wa</u> and location marker <u>ni</u>.
II. Negative existential verbs.
III. How to list things exhaustively (<u>to</u>).
IV. How to say "something" "nothing," "somewhere" and "nowhere."
V. subject marker <u>ga</u>.

I. Existential Verbs

A. $\underline{\text{X}\atop\text{LOCATION}}$ に $\underline{\text{Y}\atop\text{SUBJECT}}$が $\begin{cases}\text{あります}\\\text{います}\\\text{いらっしゃいます}\end{cases}$ There is/are <u>Y</u> at <u>X</u>

ここに本があります。   There is a book here.
そこに犬がいます。   There is a dog there (near you).

33

The verb does not change for singular or plural subjects.

There are two different verbs for expressing the existence of animate and inanimate subjects. When the subject is animate います (imasu) is used. Otherwise, あります is used. Here animate means a human being, an animal, (or occasionally something that is or appears to be capable of moving itself, e.g. a bus, a taxi, etc.)

に (location marker) indicates where the object/animal is.
が (subject marker)

The normal word order of "existential sentences" is:

＿＿＿＿に＿＿＿＿が あります/います/いらっしゃいます

B. $\underset{\text{TOPIC}}{\underline{\text{Y}}}$ は $\underset{\text{LOCATION}}{\underline{\text{X}}}$ $\underset{\text{ni}}{\text{に}}$ $\begin{cases} \text{あります} \\ \text{います} \\ \text{いらっしゃいます} \end{cases}$ (Lit. "As for Y," it is at X")
Y is at X

しんぶん
新聞はここにあります。   The newspaper is here.
はは
母はあそこにいます。   My mother is over there.
せんせい
先生はニューヨークにいらっし   The teacher is in New York.

ゃいます。

To indicate the location of something (or someone) which has already been introduced into the conversation, the pattern ＿＿は＿＿にあります/います is used. Thus, it literally means something like "As for the newspaper (that we have been talking about/that you are looking for, etc.), it is here." or "As for my mother, she is over there." In other words, は marks old information.

C. $\underset{\text{LOCATION}}{\underline{\text{X}}}$ (に)は $\underset{\text{wa}}{}$ $\underset{\text{SUBJECT}}{\underline{\text{Y}}}$ が $\begin{cases} \text{あります} \\ \text{います} \\ \text{いらっしゃいます} \end{cases}$

しんぶん
ここには新聞があります。   There is a newspaper here.
いぬ
ここ(に)は犬がたくさんいます。   There are many dogs here.
きゃんぱす   がくせい
キャンパスには学生がおおぜい   There are many students on campus.

います。

せんせい
バークレーには先生がおおぜい   There are many teachers in Berkeley.

いらっしゃいます。

To indicate what is at the location which has already been introduced into the conver-

34

sation, the above pattern is used. In this case the location is the topic of the sentence. に may be dropped.

II. Negative Sentences

ありません		あります
いません	negative form of	います
いらっしゃいません		いらっしゃいます

私の本がありません！   My book is missing! (My book is not here.)

時間がありません。   We don't have time. (There is no time.)
(time)

先生がいらっしゃいません。   No teacher is here.

本はここにありません。   The book is not here.

ここは犬がいませんね。   There is no dog here, is there?

犬がいません。   There is no dog.

犬はいません。   The dog is not here.

III. N と N

N and N (と is used to list things exhaustively.)

ここに本と新聞があります。   There are a book and a paper here.

山田さんとスミスさんがいます。   Yamada and Smith are here.

IV.

何かありますか。   Is there something?

いいえ，何もありません。   No, there is nothing.

何かいますか。   Is there some animal?

いいえ，何もいません。   No, there is no animal.

誰かいますか。／いらっしゃい   Is there anyone?
ますか。

いいえ，誰もいません。／いらっしゃいません。	No, there is no one.
どこかにありますか。	Is it somewhere?
いいえ，どこにもありません。	No, it is nowhere.
どこかにいますか。	Is he/she somewhere? Is the animal somewhere?
いいえ，どこにもいません。	No, he/she is nowhere. No, the animal is nowhere.
あそこには何もありません。	There is nothing over there.
この部屋には何もいません。	There is no animal in this room.
きょうは誰もいません。	Today, there is no one here.
その本はどこにもありません。	I cannot find the book anywhere. (The book does not exist anywhere.)

V. <u>X</u> が <u>Y</u> です。　　　　　<u>X</u> is the <u>Y</u> (that's in question)

ここに田中さんがいますか。	Is there a Mr. Tanaka here?
はい，わたしが田中です。	Yes, I am Tanaka.
あれは誰ですか。	Who is he?
私たちの学長です。	He is our president.
ああこの人が学長ですか。	Oh, this person is the president.

In this pattern, <u>Y</u> is old information and <u>X</u> is new information about <u>Y</u>.
<u>X</u> が in this pattern carries with it a connotation of <u>X</u> and only <u>X</u> is the <u>Y</u> in question. Thus, in the first example, "I and only I (in this group) am Tanaka." Also, in the second example, "This person is the president."
が can be stressed in this usage. This が can be called the exhaustive listing が.

第三課　漢字

一	二	三	四	五
いち	に	さん	し／よん	ご
一月	二月	三月	四月　四十	五月

六	七	八	九	十
ろく	しち／なな	はち	く／きゅう	じゅう
六月	七月　七十	八月	九月　九十	十月

第　四　課

4A　図書館で

スミス　　明日も図書館へ来ますか。

山田　　　いいえ，明日はヨセミテへ行きます。

スミス　　バスでですか。

山田　　　ええ，車がありませんから…

スミス　　ヨセミテで何を見ますか。

山田　　　そうですね，　やっぱりあの滝やハーフドームなど
　　　　　を見るつもりですが…

4B　スミス　　山田さんのクラスはいつはじまりますか。

山田　　　英語のですか。

スミス　　まだほかに勉強しますか。

山田　　　アメリカ文学をとるつもりですがどうですか，ス
　　　　　ミスさん。

スミス　　さあ，あのうちょっと…

山田　　　そうですか。あ，英語のクラスは十月二日にはじ
　　　　　まります。

① 例 T: 行く
    ⎧S₁: 行きますか。
    ⎨S₂: ええ，行くつもりです。

1. 来る
2. 行く
3. 見る
4. 勉強する
5. 帰る

6. 読む
7. 食べる
8. 買う
9. 話す
10. する

② 例 T: 田中さん，ヨセミテ，行く
    S: 田中さんはヨセミテへ行きます。

1. 山田さん，ニューヨーク，行く
2. 田中さん，うち，帰る
3. スミスさん，キャンパス，行く
4. 田中さんとスミスさん，サンフランシスコ，行く

5. ブラウン先生，ニューヨーク，行く
6. スミスさん，日本，行く
7. 山田さん，日本，帰る
8. 田中さんと山田さん，ヨセミテ，行く
9. 岡田さん，図書館，行く
10. 山田さん，国，帰る

③ 例 T: 田中さん，滝，見る
    S: 田中さんは滝を見ます。

1. 田中さん，本，読む
2. テキスト，買う
3. 映画，見る

4. 山田さん，日本語のクラス，とる
5. 日本語の辞書，買う

40

6. スミスさん，英語，話す
7. スミスさん，英語と日本語，話す
8. 私たち，日本語のテキスト，買う
9. 田中さん，ビール，飲む
10. 山田さん，新聞，読む
11. 父と母，英語，話す
12. 私たち，日本語1，とる
13. ヨセミテの滝とハーフドーム，見る
14. 青木さん，英語の新聞，読む
15. ブラウンさん，日本語と中国語，勉強する

④ 例　T: 図書館，本，読む
　　　　S: 図書館で本を読みます。

1. バー，ビール，飲む
2. クラス，日本語，話す
3. うち，英語，話す
4. サンフランシスコのバー，ウイスキー，飲む
5. サンフランシスコ，映画，見る
6. バークレー，日本文学，勉強する
7. 日本，カラー・テレビ，買う
8. 食堂，新聞，読む
9. ラボ，日本語，勉強する
10. 日本，日本文学，勉強する

⑤ 例1　T: 車，サンフランシスコ，行く
　　　　S: 車でサンフランシスコへ行きます。
　　例2　T: バス，サンフランシスコ，見る
　　　　S: バスで，サンフランシスコを見ます。

1. バス，ヨセミテ，行く
2. バート，うち，帰る
3. 車，スタンフォード，行く
4. バス，サンフランシスコ，行く
5. はし，すきやき，食べる
6. ナイフとフォーク，ビフテキ，食べる
7. ひらがな，名前，書く
8. ローマ字，名前，書く

9. ボールペン，名前，書く　　10. バス，ニューヨーク，行く

6 例 T: ニューヨーク，行く
　　　{ S₁: ニューヨークへ行きますか。
　　　{ S₂: いえ，行きません。

1. 新聞，読む　　　　　　　　10. テキスト，買う
2. 朝ごはん，食べる　　　　　11. テキスト，読む
3. 日本，行く　　　　　　　　12. 日本語，勉強する
4. ヨセミテ，行く　　　　　　13. 社会学のコース，とる
5. テレビ，見る　　　　　　　14. 辞書，買う
6. サンフランシスコ，行く　　15. 辞書，ある
7. 映画，見る　　　　　　　　16. 犬，いる
8. ブラウン先生，いらっしゃる　17. フランス語，話す
9. テレビ，買う　　　　　　　18. サンフランシスコ，行く

7 例1 T: ヨセミテ，行く
　　　　{ S₁: どこへ行きますか。
　　　　{ S₂: ヨセミテへ行きます。
　例2 T: 滝，見る
　　　　{ S₁: 何を見ますか。
　　　　{ S₂: 滝を見ます。
　例3 T: 図書館，本を読む
　　　　{ S₁: どこで本を読みますか。
　　　　{ S₂: 図書館で読みます。

1. ニューヨーク，行く　　　　4. ビール，飲む
2. ヨセミテ，滝を見る　　　　5. サンフランシスコ，ビールを
3. テレビ，見る　　　　　　　　　飲む

42

6. 友達のアパート，勉強する
7. 日本，カメラを買う
8. カメラ，買う
9. 映画，見る
10. スタンフォード，日本語を勉強する
11. ブック・ストアー，社会学のテキストを買う
12. 社会学のテキスト，買う
13. 日本語，話す
14. 日本語のクラス，日本語を話す
15. ニューヨーク，行く
16. ニューヨーク，スミスさん，本を買う
17. ニューヨーク，映画を見る
18. サンフランシスコ，行く
19. サンフランシスコ，映画を見る
20. バークレー，日本語のコースをとる

Lesson 4 **Dialogues**

4 A

At the library

図書館で   [de: location marker of action]

Smith: Are you coming to the library tomorrow?

明日   tomorrow

図書館へ   to the library [e: direction marker]

Yamada: No. Tomorrow I am going to Yosemite.
Smith: By bus?

バスで   by bus [de: instrument marker (by means of)]

Yamada: Yes, Because there is no car. [I don't have a car.]

ええ   Yes. (colloquial form)

| ——から | because ____ |

Smith: What are you going to see at Yosemite?

ヨセミテで	at/in Yosemite [で: location marker of action]
何を なに	what [を: object marker]
見ますか み	do you see?

Yamada: Well, let's see. Just like everybody else does, I plan to see such things as the waterfalls, and Half Dome.

そうですね	Well, let's see…[an idiomatic expression]
やっぱり	as one may think/expect
あの	that (that famous; that you know)
滝やハーフドームなど たき	the waterfalls and Half Dome, etc.
見るつもりです み	(I) intend to see

4 B

Smith: When do your classes start?

| クラス | courses, classes |
| いつ | when |

Yamada: (you mean) The English one?
Smith: Are you going to study something else besides (it)?

| まだ | yet, more |
| ほかに | other (than this) |

Yamada: I am thinking about taking American literature, but what (do you think) about it, Mr. Smith?

アメリカ文学 ぶんがく	American literature
——をとる	take ____
どうですか	How about it? [what do you think]

Smith: Umm, It's a little bit [difficult]…

| さあ，あのう… | Umm… |

44

ちょっと	a little bit

Yamada: I see. Oh, (by the way) the English class begins on October 2nd.

あ	Oh,
十月	October
二日 ふつか	the 2nd (day of the month)
にはじまります	begins on/at [time]

Lesson 4 Notes on Usage

4 A

1. 車がありませんから…   Because I don't have a car.

くるま

から essentially means "from," i.e. the point of departure. (To be introduced in L. 5.) When attached to the end of a sentence, it means "That's why.", i.e. the preceding part is the explanation for what follows. Here, in this particular sentence, the latter part of the sentence is missing because it is obvious from the context. That is バスで行きます "I will go by bus."

In Japanese the parts of a sentence which are obvious from the context tend to be left unsaid. Therefore, sentences like this one are extremely common.

2. そうですね。   Let's see..., Hmmmm....

そうです。 basically means "What you just said is correct.", i.e. "That's right, isn't it?" Therefore, it indicates agreement with the other person's statement. This same form, when spoken rather slowly, may be used to indicate that the speaker is looking for an appropriate answer. It is a device used to gain time to think. Its English equivalent would be "Let's see..." The distinction will be clear from the context.

Why this particular form is used for the latter purpose is left for further investigation, but one possible explanation would be that it presumably shows that the speaker does not want to **antagonize the addressee while he** is taking time to gather his thoughts.

3. やっぱり   just as one thinks/expects

S: ヨセミテで，何を見ますか。   What are you going to see at Yosemite?

み

45

Y: そうですね。やっぱりあの滝や
ハーフドームなどを見るつもり
ですが。

Let's see. Just like everybody else does (just as you expected me to do), I plan to see such things as the waterfalls and Half Dome, (but what do you think about my plan?)

4. あの

The basic meaning is "that over there." Here it means "that famous," "that everybody knows, is talking about," etc.

あの滝やハーフドームなど

such things as those (famous) waterfalls and Half Dome

5. が

が after a sentence means "but" as in the second utterance by Yamada in 4B.

Yamada: アメリカ文学をとるつも
りですが，どうですか，
スミスさん。

I am thinking about taking American literature, but what do you think (about it), Mr. Smith?

The part that follows が, i.e. どうですか。 "What do you think (about it)?," is often left unsaid unless the speaker specifically wants to get the addressee's opinion. In such a case, が at the end of a sentence makes the statement somewhat softer because it implies "What do you think about my opinion?"

(See the example in Section 3 above.)

4 B

1. まだほかに

まだ

in this case means "still more."

ほかに

other than this/that

まだほかに勉強しますか。

Will you be studying something else besides that?

2. どうですか

What do you think about it?

どう literally means "how." But the whole phrase means "What do you think about it?"

46

3. さあ，あのう…ちょっと…   Well, Umm (That's) a little....

あのう means "Ummm...," "Well." It indicates that the speaker has something to say but for some reason he hesitates. (It's also used to cut in on a conversation.)

ちょっと is a colloquial form of すこし which means "little," or "a little."

The unuttered part of the above sentence would be something like "(That might be a little) too difficult for you." Generally speaking, in Japanese it is considered to be polite to say things indirectly by implications because it shows discretion and modesty.

4. そうですか。   I see.

Here Yamada understands what Smith wanted to say even though he did not say it, namely "I'm afraid it might be a little too difficult for you."

5. そうですか。あ，英語のクラスは十月二日に始まります。   あ Oh, by the way,

I see. Oh, by the way, my English class starts on October 2.

Lesson 4   Grammar Notes

The main points of this lesson are:
I. Object marker o, location marker de, instrument marker de, direction marker e, time marker ni.
II. Verb conjugation.
III. How to give a partial listing.
IV. How to say "I intend ＿＿"

I. In the preceding lessons the terms Topic, Subject, and Location of existence were introduced. In this lesson some more terms will be introduced.

A. を   Object marker

山田さんは英語を勉強します。   Miss Yamada will study English.
私はハーフドームを見ます。   I will see Half Dome.

ブラウンさんは日本語を話します。 Mr. Brown speaks Japanese.

山田さんはビールを飲みます。 Miss Yamada drinks beer.

As the English translation indicates, the tense of the verb (represented by -masu) is either future or habitual present. (See Section II below for more discussion on various verb forms.) For this reason, this tense is called non-past.

B. で Location marker for action verbs

私は図書館で勉強します。 I will study at the library.

ヨセミテで滝を見ます。 (I) will see the waterfalls at Yosemite.

ウィスキーはバーで飲みます。 (As for whisky, I drink it at a bar.) I drink whisky at a bar.

うちではビールを飲みます。 At home I drink beer.

(cf. に：location marker for verbs of existence)

C. で Instrument marker: "with," "by," "by means of," "using____"

何で手紙を書きますか。 What are you going to write the letter with?

ペンで書きます。 I will write it with a pen.

これは英語で言います。 I will say this in English.

日本人ははしで食べます。 Japanese eat with chopsticks.

私はバスで行きます。 I will go by bus.

D. へ Direction marker "to," "toward" (に can also be used as a direction marker)

山田さんはヨセミテへ行きます。 Ms. Yamada is going to Yosemite.

私はバスで学校へ行きます。 I go to school by bus.

図書館へ来ます。 I will come to the library.

48

E.　に　　　　　　　　　　　　　　　　Time marker "at," "on," "in (point in time)"

as in the days of the week.

月曜日	火曜日	水曜日	木曜日	金曜日	土曜日	日曜日
げつようび	かようび	すいようび	もくようび	きんようび	どようび	にちようび
Monday	Tuesday	Wednesday	Thursday	Friday	Saturday	Sunday

as in the months of the year.

一月	二月	三月	四月	五月	六月
いちがつ	にがつ	さんがつ	しがつ	ごがつ	ろくがつ
January	February	March	April	May	June

七月	八月	九月	十月	十一月	十二月
しちがつ	はちがつ	くがつ	じゅうがつ	じゅういちがつ	じゅうにがつ
July	August	September	October	November	December

日曜日に図書館へ行きますか。　　　Do you go to the library on Sunday?

日本語のクラスは九時に始まり　　　The Japanese class starts at 9 o'clock.
ます。

英語のクラスは十月二日に始ま　　　The English class starts on October 2.
ります。

に is used for absolute time expressions like the ones given above. It is not used for relative time expressions like the ones below.

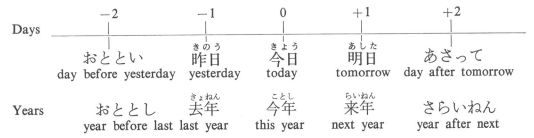

Days		−2	−1	0	+1	+2
		おととい	昨日	今日	明日	あさって
		day before yesterday	yesterday	today	tomorrow	day after tomorrow
Years		おととし	去年	今年	来年	さらいねん
		year before last	last year	this year	next year	year after next

The terms given above and the ones introduced before may be schematically lined up like this:

[Topic は] [Time に Location で Subj. が Instr. で Direc. へ Object を Verb].
　　　　　　　　　　　　　　　　(action)

[Topic は] [Location に (Existence verbs) Subj. が Verb].

When an element in the right hand brackets [ ] above is the same as the Topic in the left hand brackets, it is deleted.

［山田さんは］　［あした（山田さんが）ヨセミテへ行きます。］

［この本は］　［スミスさん（この本を）が読みます。］

49

Usually 行<ruby>行<rt>い</rt></ruby>きます and 来<ruby>来<rt>き</rt></ruby>ます correspond to English "go" and "come" respectively. There are cases, however, where they do not correspond.

e.g. ちょっと待<ruby>待<rt>ま</rt></ruby>ってください。　　Just a minute. I'm coming.

今行<ruby>行<rt>い</rt></ruby>きます。

II. Verb Conjugation (non-past).

Japanese verbs conjugate in terms of style (Plain/Polite), tense (Non-Past/Past) and affirmativeness/negativeness.

In this lesson, three forms are introduced: the Plain Non-Past Affirmative, the Polite Non-Past Affirmative, and the Polite Non-Past Negative forms. Here "Present" means "Non-Past" or "Non-complete," thus it includes "Future" as well.

There are two classes of verbs: 1) RU-verbs and 2) U-verbs.

A. RU-verbs:

RU-verbs comprise a verb class in which the Plain Non-Past Affirmative form (or the so-called Dictionary form) is formed by the addition of ru to a root which ends in a vowel (either i or e).

見<ruby>見<rt>み</rt></ruby>　　る：　mi -ru (to see, to look, to watch)

食<ruby>食<rt>た</rt></ruby>べる：　tabe-ru (to eat)

The underlining indicates the root of the verb.

The Polite Non-Past Affirmative form is formed by adding -masu to the root.

見<ruby>見<rt>み</rt></ruby>ます：　mi-masu

食<ruby>食<rt>た</rt></ruby>べます：　tabe-masu

The Polite Non-Past Negative form is formed by adding -masen to the root.

見<ruby>見<rt>み</rt></ruby>ません：　mi-masen

食<ruby>食<rt>た</rt></ruby>べません：　tabe-masen

B. U-verbs:

U-verbs comprise a second verb class in which the Plain Non-Past Affirmative form (dictionary form) is formed by the addition of u to a root which ends in a consonant (s, k, g, t, r, w, b, m or n)

50

貸 す： kas-u (to lend)

話 す： hanas-u (to talk)

書 く： kak-u (to write, to paint, to draw)

泳 ぐ： oyog-u (to swim)

打 つ： ut-u (to hit, strike) [pronounced "utsu"]

帰 る： kaer-u (to return home)

取 る： tor-u (to take)

始 まる： hazimar-u (to begin)

買 う： ka-u (to buy) [w drops from kaw-u]

遊 ぶ： asob-u (to play)

読 む： yom-u (to read)

飲 む： nom-u (to drink)

死 ぬ： sin-u (to die)

The Polite Non-Past Affirmative form is formed by adding -imasu to the root.

貸 します： kas-imasu [pronounced 'kashimasu']

話 します： hanas-imasu

書 きます： kak-imasu

泳 ぎます： oyog-imasu

打 ちます： ut-imasu [pronounced 'uchimasu']

始 まります： hazimar-imasu

取 ります： tor-imasu

帰 ります： kaer-imasu

買 います： ka-imasu [w drops from kaw-imasu]

遊 びます： asob-imasu

読 みます： yom-imasu

飲 みます： nom-imasu

死 にます： sin-imasu

The Polite Non-Past Negative form is formed by adding -imasen to the root.

e.g. 貸<ruby>か</ruby>しません：　<u>kas-imasen</u>

The w of the root automatically drops except before a. Thus, 買う kaw- : ka-u, ka-imasu, ka-imasen.

C. Irregular Verbs

There are three irregular verbs: する (su-ru) "to do" 来る (ku-ru) "to come" and 行く (ik-u) "to go."

Non-Past

する	Plain	Polite
Affirmative	する	します
Negative	しない	しません
来る	Plain	Polite
Affirmative	来る	来ます
Negative	来ない	来ません
行く	Plain	Polite
Affirmative	行く	行きます
Negative	行かない	行きません

D. Verbs of Existence:

Non-Past

ある	Plain	Polite
Affimative	ある	あります
Negative	ない	ありません
いる	Plain	Polite
Affirmative	いる	います
Negative	いない	いません
いらっしゃる	Plain	Polite
Affirmative	いらっしゃる	いらっしゃいます
Negative	いらっしゃらない	いらっしゃいません

III. <u>Noun</u> や (<u>Noun</u> や) <u>Noun</u> など　　　<u>N</u> (<u>N</u>) <u>N</u>, etc. や "and" is used for partial listing. など can be omitted. (cf. と "and" for complete, exhaustive listing)

あそこに本や鉛筆などがあります。

There are such things as books and pencils over there.

私は，ビールやウィスキーや酒などを飲みます。

I will drink (such things as) beer, whiskey and sake.

IV. Verb (Plain Non-Past) つもりです   intend to V, plan to V

   つもり tumori occurs only with verbs of controllable action. Therefore, it may occur with 見る，する，取る and so on, but not with 始まる，開く(to open)，(おなかが)すく (to get hungry)，混む (to get crowded)，(あめが)ふる (to rain) and so on.

ヨセミテで滝やハーフドームなどを見るつもりです。

I plan to see the waterfalls and Half Dome at Yosemite.

アメリカ文学を取るつもりです。

I plan to take American literature (class).

第四課　漢字

何	曜　日	日
なに／なん	よう　び	にち
何がありますか　何日	何曜日	日曜日

月	火	水	木	金	土
げつ／がつ	か	すい	もく	きん	ど
月曜日　何月	火曜日	水曜日	木曜日	金曜日	土曜日

昨　日	今　日	明　日	今
きのう	きょう	あした	いま
昨日	今日	明日	今

第　五　課

5 A　スミス　　　　日曜日はどこかへ行きますか。

山田　　　　　ええ。 サンフランシスコへ行くつもりです。

　　　　　　　ゴールデンゲートがまだですから…

スミス　　　　橋ですか，公園ですか。

山田　　　　　ああ公園があるんですか。どちらもまだです。

スミス　　　　橋は船からがきれいですよ。

山田　　　　　どこから出るんですか。

スミス　　　　フィッシャーマンズウォーフからです。 橋のす

　　　　　　　ぐ下まで行きますよ。

山田　　　　　そうですか。いろいろありがとうございました。

5 B　スミス　　　　こちらはベイリーさんです。

山田　　　　　よろしくおねがいします。

ベイリー　　　ベイリーです。どうぞよろしく。

スミス　　　　ベイリーさんはこの十二月に日本へ行くんです。

山田　　　　　あ，そうですか。

ベイリー　　　ええ， 十一月にハワイまで行きます。 一か月ほ

　　　　　　　どホノルルの友だちのうちにいるつもりです。

山田　　　　　日本ははじめてですか。

ベイリー　　　はい，はじめてです。 弟は去年行きましたが。

① 例 T: 読む
　　 S: 読みました。

1. 大学，行く
2. あの映画，見る
3. バー，ビール，飲む
4. 図書館，勉強する
5. 買物する
6. 社会学の本，読む
7. 箸，食べる
8. ゴールデンゲート，見る
9. 日本，船，行く
10. ヨセミテの滝，見る
11. うち，晩ごはん，食べる
12. 山田さん，国，帰る
13. スミス先生，会議，いらっしゃる
14. ニューヨーク，車，行く
15. 日本，カメラ，買う
16. うち，宿題，する
17. 昨日，車，買う
18. キャンパス，映画，見る
19. リンさん，うち，帰る
20. 公園，遊ぶ

② 例 T: 宿題，する
　　 S₁: 宿題をしましたか。
　　 S₂: いいえ，しませんでした。

1. 日本，行く
2. ヨセミテの滝，見る
3. 買物，する
4. 晩ごはん，食べる
5. 昨日，来る
6. ビール，飲む
7. 社会学のクラス，行く
8. 日本語，とる
9. フイッシャーマンズ・ウォーフ，行く
10. 昨日，サンフランシスコ，行く
11. 漢字，書く
12. 山田さん，うち，帰る
13. 日本語の宿題，する
14. ベラー先生，会議，いらっしゃる
15. 日曜日，映画，見る
16. 社会学のテキスト，買う
17. キャンパス，車，来る

56

18.　バークレーのキャンパス，見
　　る

19.　大学，経済学，とる
20.　日本，カメラ，買う

3　例　T:　大学へ行く
　　　　S:　大学へ行かない

1.　ゴールデンゲートを見る
2.　日本語の辞書を買う
3.　先生はニューヨークへいらっ
　　しゃる
4.　バークレーの昔の写真を見る
5.　サンフランシスコで買物をす
　　る

6.　山田さんはうちにいる
7.　アメリカ文学のクラスをとる
8.　ヨセミテへバスで行く
9.　図書館で勉強する
10.　大学の食堂で食べる

4　例　T:　日本へ行く
　　　　S₁:　日本へ行きますか。
　　　　S₂:　いいえ，行かないつもりです。

1.　新聞を買う
2.　明日うちにいる
3.　宿題をする
4.　ニューヨークへ行く
5.　今日は映画を見る
6.　明日図書館へ行く
7.　その本を読む
8.　ヨセミテへ行く

9.　明日来る
10.　公園へ行く
11.　車を買う
12.　テレビを見る
13.　あさっては行く
14.　今日は晩ごはんを食べる
15.　クラスで英語を話す

5　例　T:　このバス，バークレー，サンフランシスコ，行く
　　　　S:　このバスはバークレーからサンフランシスコまで行きます。

1. あのバス，リッチモンド，オークランド，行く

2. このバス，バークレー，スタンフォード，行く

3. バート，イースト・ベー，デイリー・シティー，行く

4. 今日，十ページ，二十ページ，読む

5. あの飛行機，サンフランシスコ，ロス，行く

6. このバス，ゴールデンゲート公園，橋，行く

7. 今日，九時，十二時，勉強する

8. T.W.A. サンランシスコ，ニューヨーク，行く

9. 昨日，フィッシャーマンズ・ウォーフ，ベイブリッジのすぐ下，行く

10. 明日，一時，三時，クラスがある

11. 月曜日，金曜日，勉強する

12. 九月，六月，大学へ行く

6 例1 T: 明日，ヨセミテ，行く

$\{$ S₁: 明日どこへ行きますか。

S₂: ヨセミテへ行くつもりです。

2 T: 日本，テレビ，買う

$\{$ S₁: 日本で何を買いますか。

S₂: 日本でテレビを買うつもりです。

1. 日本，カメラ，買う
2. 大学，心理学，とる
3. ヨセミテ，滝，見る
4. 今，図書館，行く
5. サンフランシスコ，ゴールデンゲート，見る

6. 今日，食堂，食べる
7. 日本，日本文学，勉強する
8. サンフランシスコ，カラー・テレビ，買う
9. 図書館，宿題，する
10. バークレー，日本語，とる

7 例 T: 山田さんは行きますか。

   S: さあ，よくわかりませんがたぶん行くでしょう。

1. キャンパスに食堂があります
   か。
2. ブラウン先生は今日いらっし
   ゃいますか。
3. あの建物は寮ですか。
4. スミスさんはお酒を飲みます
   か。
5. 大学の近くに郵便局があり
   ますか。

6. 「コープ」にしょう油があり
   ますか。
7. あの建物は図書館ですか。
8. 明日試験がありますか。
9. ジョンソンさんはアメリカ人
   ですか。
10. 山田先生はあしたクラスへい
   らっしゃいますか。

8 例1 T: あさって，サンフランシスコ，行く

   S₁: あさって，どこかへ行きますか。
   S₂: ええ，サンフランシスコへ行きます。

例2 T: 今日，本，買う

   S₁: 今日，何か買いますか。
   S₂: ええ，今日本を買います。

例3 T: 昨日，スミスさん，来る

   S₁: 昨日，誰か(が)来ましたか。
   S₂: ええ，スミスさんが来ました。

1. 今日，学校，行く
2. 昨日，すきやき，作る
3. 明日，日本語の辞書，買う
4. 昨日，すし，食べる

5. 今日，ワイン，飲む
6. 日曜日，てんぷら，作る
7. おととい，ブラウンさん，来
   る

8. 昨日，テレビ，買う

10. 今日，スミスさん，来る

9. 去年，日本，行く

Lesson 5 **Dialogues**

5 A

Smith: Are you going somewhere on Sunday?

日曜日 (に) (on) Sunday

どこか some/anywhere

Yamada: Yes, I'm planning to go to San Francisco. Since I haven't been to the Golden Gate yet.

まだ not yet

Smith: You mean the bridge or the park?

Yamada: Oh, you mean there is a Golden Gate Park (too). I haven't been to either one.

ああ Oh

——んです (lit. "it is the case")

どちらも either one (with Neg.)

Smith: The bridge looks beautiful from a boat.

よ Yo: sentence final particle

Yamada: Where does it leave from?

どこ where

Smith: (It leaves) from Fisherman's Wharf. It goes out to (just under) the bridge.

すぐ immediately

Yamada: Is that right? Thank you very much for everything.

5 B

Smith: This is Mr. Bailey

こちら (このかた) this person here

60

Yamada: How do you do.
Bailay: I am Bailey. How do you do.
Smith: Mr. Bailey is going to Japan this December.

<ruby>十二月<rt>じゅうに がつ</rt></ruby>　　　　　　　　　December

Yamada: Oh, is that so?
Bailey: Yes, I will be going to Hawaii in November. I plan to stay at my friend's in
　　Honolulu for about a month.

<ruby>十一月<rt>じゅういちがつ</rt></ruby>　　　　　　　November
まで　　　　　　　　　　as far as
<ruby>一か月<rt>いっ げつ</rt></ruby>　　　　　　　　one month
ほど　　　　　　　　　　about, or so
うち　　　　　　　　　　house

Yamada: Is this your first time to Japan?
Bailey: Yes, it is (for me). But my younger brother went last year.

Lesson 5　Notes on Usage

5 A

1.　どこかへ　　　　　　　　　　　to some place

2.　いろいろ

　いろ means "color" but いろいろ means "various, all kinds of, several, diverse, many, etc."
　ありがとうございました　(in the Past Tense) is used to thank the addressee for what he has done for the speaker.
　All together the phrase means "Thank you for all you have done for me."

5 B

1.　スミス：こちらはベイリーさんです。

やまだ：よろしくおねがいします。

ベイリー：ベイリーです。どうぞよろしく。

こちら literally means "this side," but when it is used to introduce someone it means "this person." In this situation このひと is too blunt and impersonal, and is never used. このかた, a polite form of このひと, can be used but there is a touch of the impersonal about it. So the best choice would be こちら.

When よろしく, which literally means "treat things appropriately" or "be nice to me" is followed by おねがいします, which means "I ask a favor of you," the phrase means "I ask that you be so kind as to treat me well." However, the basic meaning has been virtually lost and the phrase is used much as "How do you do?" or "Hi, nice to meet you," when we meet people for the first time.

どうぞ meaning "please" is merely added to the よろしく with the おねがいします deleted.

The following are other variations of "How do you do?":

よろしく。

はじめまして。

どうぞよろしくおねがいします。

はじめまして，どうぞよろしく。

2. 一か月ほど "for about a month." ほど "approximately," is a suffix

一時間ほど勉強しました。　　　　　I studied for about one hour.

Lesson 5　**Grammar Notes**

The main points of this lesson are:
  I. How to say "from/to."
 II. How to say "I have no intention to/of."
III. Past tense forms of verbs.
 IV. How to say "not yet" and "already."
  V. A pattern used to provide an explanation or facts.
 VI. How to say "probably."
VII. How to say "something" "nothing," "someone"/"no one," "somewhere"/"nowhere."
VIII. Plain Past Negative and Polite Past Negation of verbs.

I. <u>A</u> から <u>B</u> まで　　　　　　　　from <u>A</u> to/as far as <u>B</u>

から　indicates the starting point, point of departure, source;

まで indicates up to a point, to, as far as, etc.

船<ruby>ふね</ruby>はフィッシャーマンズウォーフから橋<ruby>はし</ruby>のすぐ下<ruby>した</ruby>まで行きます。	The boat goes from Fisherman's Wharf to right below the bridge.
船<ruby>ふね</ruby>はフィッシャーマンズウォーフから出ます。	The boat leaves from Fisherman's Wharf.
ベイリーさんはこの十二月に日本へ行きます。十一月にハワイまで行きます。	Mr. Bailey will go to Japan this December. He will go to (as far as) Hawaii in **November**.

II. Verb (root)-(a)-ないつもりです

have no intention of V-ing
intend not to V

See the verb conjugation table for the-(a)nai forms (or the Plain Non-Past Negative form).

(cf. **Verb (Plain Non-Past)** つもりです) (L.4)

今日はうちにいないつもりです。	I intend not to be/stay home today.
わたしは，何も買<ruby>か</ruby>わないつもりです。	I have no intention of buying anything today.
明日も，どこにも行かないつもりです。	I have no intention of going anywhere tomorrow either.
何もしないつもりです。	I have no intention of doing anything.
あした図書館<ruby>としょかん</ruby>へ来ないつもりですか。	Do you intend not to come to the library tomorrow?

III. Past Tense Forms of Verbs

See the verb conjugation table at the end of this lesson.

Polite Past Affirmative: V- ました。　e.g. 行きました　　　(went)
　　　　　　　　　　　　　　　　　 見ました　　　　(saw)

Polite Past Negative: V- ませんでした。 e.g. 買いませんでした (did not buy)

山田<ruby>やまだ</ruby>さんはヨセミテへ行きました。	Yamada went to Yosemite.
ヨセミテで滝<ruby>たき</ruby>やハーフドームなどを見ました。	She saw the waterfalls and Half Dome at Yosemite.

何も買いませんでした。   She did not buy anything.

IV. まだ / もう   (not) yet/already

「スターウォーズ」を見ましたか。   Have you seen "Star Wars"?
いいえまだです。   ...No, not yet.
（バスの停留所で）   (at a bus stop)
バスはもう来ましたか。   Has the bus come (and gone) yet?
いいえまだです。   ...No, not yet.

V. Plain form of verb＋のです/んです (no desu/n desu) is used to provide an explanation or facts. It is therefore frequently used in questions which elicit explanations or facts from the addressee. Usually it is not translated into English. The slash (/) indicates "or." のです or んです follows a sentence ending in the plain form.

あしたはサンフランシスコへ行きます。ゴールデンゲートを見るんです。   I am going to San Francisco tomorrow. I am going to see the Golden Gate (bridge). (＝that's why)

橋ですか，公園ですか。   Do you mean the bridge or the park?

（ああ，公園があるんですか。）   Oh, (is it that) there is a park?

船はどこから出るんですか。   Where does the boat leave from?

ベイリーさんは日本へ行くんです。   Mr. Bailey is going to Japan.

VI. Plain form of verb＋でしょう "probably," "I guess," "It seems to me that." This form replaces です. It is often used with たぶん which means "maybe, perhaps."

行くでしょう。   Probably he/she will go.

食べるでしょう。   He/she will probably eat.

さあ，よくわかりませんがたぶん図書館でしょう。   Well, I don't know but I guess it's a library.

64

VII.

何か   something, anything

誰<ruby>だれ</ruby>か   someone, anyone

どこか   somewhere, anywhere

どちらか   either one

何も	nothing,	誰<ruby>だれ</ruby>も	no one
どこにも	no where (existence)	どこでも	nowhere (action)
どこへも	no where (direction)	どちらも	neither one

cf. GN IV L. 3.

日曜日はどこかへ行きますか。	Are you going somewhere on Sunday?
ええ，タホへ行きます。	Yes, I am going to Tahoe.
いいえ，どこへも行きません。	No, I am not going anywhere.
昨日誰<ruby>だれ</ruby>か(が) 来ましたか。	Did someone come yesterday?
ええ，山田さんが来ました。	Yes, Yamada came.
いえ，誰<ruby>だれ</ruby>も来ませんでした。	No, no one came.
きょう，何か(を) 買うつもりですか。	Are you planning to buy something today?
ええ，豆腐<ruby>とうふ</ruby>と野菜<ruby>やさい</ruby>を買<ruby>か</ruby>うつもりです。	Yes, I plan to buy some tofu and vegetables.
いえ，何も買わないつもりです。	No, I have no intention of buying anything.

Both が (subject marker) and を (object marker) are optional after these words: 何か, 誰<ruby>だれ</ruby>か, どこか, etc.

Compare these words with 何, 誰<ruby>だれ</ruby>, どこ, etc.

どこへ行きますか。	Where are you going?
日本<ruby>にほん</ruby>へ行きます。	I am going to Japan.
どこへも行きません。	I am not going anywhere.

However, particles へ (direction marker), で (location marker for action verbs), に (location marker for existential verbs) are not optional.

どこかへ行きましたか。	Did you go somewhere?

どこかにありますか。	Is it somewhere?
いいえ，どこにもありません。	No, it is nowhere.
どこかで見ましたか。	Did you see it somewhere?

VIII. Verb Conjugation

In the preceding lesson three forms were introduced: Plain Non-Past Affirmative (or the Dictionary form), Polite Non-Past Affirmative and Polite Non-Past Negative.

In this lesson three more forms are introduced: A. Plain Non-Past Negative, B. Polite Past Affirmative and C. Polite Past Negative.

A. Plain Non-Past Negative forms: See also Section 2 above.

RU-verbs: Attach -nai to the root.

いる	いない	does not exist (animate)
見る	見ない	does not see
寝る	寝ない	does not sleep
食べる	食べない	does not eat

U-verbs: Attach -anai to the root.

貸す：	貸さない	does not lend
書く：	書かない	does not write
買う：	買わない	does not buy [w does not drop]

(See the table on the next page for other examples.)

Irregular verbs:

する：	しない	does not do
来る：	来ない	does not come
行く：	行かない	does not go [The irregular feature does not show here.]

Plain Past Negative forms are made by adding -katta after dropping *i*.
    kasu kasanai (Plain Non-past Neg.) kasanakatta (Plain Past Neg.)
Polite Past Negative forms are made by adding -desita to -masen.
    kasu kasimasen (Polite Non-Past Neg.) kasimasen desita (Polite Past Neg.)
いらっしゃる, the polite way of saying:
    いる "to be," 行く "to go," and 来る "to come"

先生はニューヨークへいらっしゃいます。	The teacher is going to New York.

66

			Non-Past		Past	
			Plain	Polite	Plain	Polite
V	RU-verb たべる	Af.	たべる	たべます	たべた	たべました
		Neg.	たべない	たべません	たべなかった	たべませんでした
	U-verb かく	Af.	かく	かきます	かいた	かきました
		Neg.	かかない	かきません	かかなかった	かきませんでした
	Ir. する	Af.	する	します	した	しました
		Neg.	しない	しません	しなかった	しませんでした
	Ir. いく	Af.	いく	いきます	いった	いきました
		Neg.	いかない	いきません	いかなかった	いきませんでした
	Ir. くる	Af.	くる	きます	きた	きました
		Neg.	こない	きません	こなかった	きませんでした
	Ir. ある	Af.	ある	あります	あった	ありました
		Neg.	ない	ありません	なかった	ありませんでした
	Ir. いる	Af.	いる	います	いた	いました
		Neg.	いない	いません	いなかった	いませんでした
A	うるさい	Af.	うるさい うるさい Noun	うるさいです	うるさかった	うるさかったです
		Neg.	うるさくない	うるさ｛くありません（くないです）｝	うるさくなかった	うるさ｛くありませんでした（くなかったです）｝
AN	しずかだ	Af.	しずかだ しずかな Noun	しずかです	しずかだった	しずかでした
		Neg.	しずかじゃない	しずかじゃありません	しずかじゃなかった	しずかじゃありませんでした
N	がくせい	Af.	がくせいだ がくせいの Noun	がくせいです	がくせいだった	がくせいでした
		Neg.	がくせいじゃない	がくせいじゃありません	がくせいじゃなかった	がくせいじゃありませんでした

行 く
い　　く
行く

来 る
く
来る

帰 る
かえ
帰る

見 る
み
見る

読 む
よ
読む

話 す
はな
話す

食 べる
た
食べる

飲 む
の
飲む

大 学
だい　がく
大学

学 生
がく　せい
学生

先 生
せん　せい
先生

第 六 課

6A　ブラウン　　もしもし，ブラウンですが。

　　　山田　　　あ，ブラウンさん，この間はどうも。

　　　ブラウン　　ところで部屋はどうですか。

　　　山田　　　立派な部屋ですよ。広くて，明るくて，ただ
　　　　　　　　ここはうるさい時がありますねえ。

　　　ブラウン　　ルームメートはもういますか。

　　　山田　　　ええ，ジョンソンさんという人ですがまじめで
　　　　　　　　よく勉強します。

　　　ブラウン　　山田さんとは大分違いますね。

　　　山田　　　まあ，ひどいですねえ。

6B　渡辺　　　もしもし，山田さんですか。

　　　山田　　　はい。あ，渡辺さんですね。

　　　渡辺　　　はい，渡辺です。寮の部屋はいかがですか。

　　　山田　　　うるさいですねえ。

　　　渡辺　　　勉強することができますか。

　　　山田　　　朝はしずかですから本を読むことができますが
　　　　　　　　夕方はちょっと…

　　　渡辺　　　そうですか。私のアパートは静かですよ。試験
　　　　　　　　の前はうちで勉強しませんか。

　　　山田　　　ありがとうございます。

1　例1　T:　バークレー，うるさい

　　　{S₁:　バークレーは，いかがですか。
　　　{S₂:　うるさいです。

　　例2　T:　バークレー，きれいだ

　　　{S₁:　バークレーは，いかがですか。
　　　{S₂:　きれいですねえ。

1.　バークレー，にぎやかだ
2.　寮，うるさい
3.　ゴールデンゲート，きれいだ
4.　第六課，やさしい
5.　日本語，おもしろい

6.　この本，難しい
7.　日本の車，安い
8.　スミスさんの部屋，しずかだ
9.　カリフォルニア，明るい
10.　日本のカラーテレビ，いい

2　例1　T:　この部屋，明るい

　　　{S₁:　この部屋は明るいですねえ。
　　　{S₂:　ええ，ほんとうに明るい部屋ですね。

　　例2　T:　この部屋，静かだ

　　　{S₁:　この部屋は静かですねえ。
　　　{S₂:　ええ，ほんとうに静かな部屋ですね。

1.　このテレビ，いい
2.　このアパート，高い
3.　このアパート，静かだ
4.　このキャンパス，広い
5.　このキャンパス，きれいだ
6.　この本，難しい
7.　このビール，おいしい
8.　このビール，高い
9.　あの子供，うるさい

10.　この車，きれいだ
11.　この車，いい
12.　この車，りっぱだ
13.　このタイプライター，やすい
14.　この部屋，せまい
15.　この部屋，静かだ
16.　あの人，きれいだ
17.　あの人，りっぱだ
18.　あの人，まじめだ

3 例1 T: 英語，やさしい
S₁: 英語はやさしいですか。
S₂: いいえ，やさしくありません。
例2 T: 寮，静かだ
S₁: 寮は静かですか。
S₂: いいえ，静かじゃありません。

1. 田中さんのアパート，高い
2. 文学のクラス，難しい
3. その部屋，広い
4. 中国語，やさしい
5. スタンフォードのキャンパス，にぎやかだ
6. 寮，うるさい
7. ブラウンさん，まじめだ
8. 日本語の辞書，安い
9. あの本，新しい
10. 日本語，難しい
11. この犬，小さい
12. この建物，古い
13. 田中さんの車，高い
14. 田中さんの車，新しい
15. その犬，大きい
16. ソニーのカラー・テレビ，安い
17. 日本語，やさしい
18. 日本の車，いい
19. スミスさんの部屋，明るい
20. スミスさんの部屋，きれいだ
21. 田中さんの部屋，静かだ

4 例1 T: 私のアパート，静かだ，安い
S: 私のアパートは静かで安いです。
例2 T: 私のアパート，広い，安い
S: 私のアパートは広くて安いです。

1. 私のアパート，便利だ，安い
2. この部屋，きれいだ，明るい
3. 山田さんの本，高い，立派だ
4. キャンパス，広い，きれいだ

71

5. 田中さん，静かだ，まじめだ
6. 寮の部屋，せまい，うるさい
7. 私の車，小さい
8. このおかし，古い，まずい
9. テレグラフ，にぎやかだ，おもしろい
10. スミスさん，まじめだ

5 例 T: 寮，勉強します
     S: 寮で勉強することができます。

1. 日本語，話します
2. 明日，サンフランシスコ，行きます
3. 今，帰ります
4. 明日，来ます
5. 日本語，書きます
6. 日本語の新聞，読みます
7. アメリカ，ソニーのテレビ，買います
8. 寮，テレビを見ます
9. ハンバーガー，作ります
10. アラビア語，話します

Lesson 6 Dialogues

6 A

Brown: Hello. This is Brown.

もしもし　　　　　　　　　　Hello. [on the telephone]

Yamada: Oh, Mr. Brown. Thank you for the other day.

この間　　　　　　　　　　　the other day

どうも　　　　　　　　　　　Thanks.

B: Say, how's your room?

72

ところで	By the way, Say
どうですか	How is it? How do you like it?

Y: It's a great room. It's roomy and there is a lot of light. But it sure is noisy here sometimes.

立派だ	splendid, excellent
広い	roomy
明るい	bright
ただ	only, but
うるさい	noisy
時	time
ねえ	[variation of ね]

B: Have you got a roommate yet?

ルームメート	roommate
もう	already

Y: Yes. Her name is Johnson. She is really serious and studies a lot.

＿＿という人	a person called＿＿
まじめだ	serious
よく	well (adv.)

B: She is quite different from you, isn't she?

＿＿と(は)違う	different from＿＿
大分	quite

Y: Oh, how can you say that?

ひどい	terrible

6 B

Watanabe: Hello. Is this Yamada?
Yamada: Yes. Oh, this is Watanabe, isn't it?
W: Yes, this is Watanabe. How do you like your room in the dorm?

いかがですか。   How do you like it?

Y: It sure is noisy.

W: Can you study (there)?

Y: The mornings are quiet so I can read, but the evenings are a little...

朝 (あさ)   morning

静かだ (しず)   quiet

夕方 (ゆうがた)   evening

ちょっと   a little

W: Is that so? My apartment is quiet. Why don't you study at my place before exams?

アパート   apartment

試験 (しけん)   examination

Y: Thank you.

Lesson 6   **Notes on Usage**

6 A

1. もしもし   Hello. (over the telephone)

This is the very first greeting used in making or answering a telephone call.

This form is also used to call the attention of someone on the street whose name the speaker does not know.

もしもし，何か落ちましたよ。 (お)   Sir! (Miss!) You dropped something. (lit. Something dropped.)

2. ブラウンですが。   This is Brown. (over the telephone)

While こちらはブラウンですが (Lit. "This side (of the line) is Brown.") is used, これはブラウンですが is never used.

Here が "but" is used as a softening device. Literally, the speaker is saying "This is Brown but do you have time to talk with me now?" or "This is Brown but do you think that I can talk with him?" but he leaves the phrase after the が, which is already understood by the addressee, unsaid.

74

In Japanese implying things or leaving things unsaid shows discretion and modesty thus acting as a softening device. In this situation it would sound strange if the が were left out.

3. この間はどうも。　　　　　　　　　Thank you for the other day.

It is customary to thank a person for what he did for you the last time you met him. ありがとうございました is left unsaid after どうも in this quasi-polite style of speech. It should be used in a more formal situation that requires a more polite style of speech. いいえ，どういたしまして，"No, not at all" "Don't mention it" or "That was nothing" would be an appropriate reply to this.

4. ところで

This is a signal that the speaker is going to introduce a new topic into the conversation. ところで is used much more frequently than the English "By the way." In English we often launch into a new topic without using any set phrase, but in Japanese ところで or some other such phrase is necessary in changing the topic.

5. どうですか。/いかがですか。

How do you like ____?
How is ____?
How/What about ____?

Both mean the same thing, but いかがですか is polite.

部屋はどうですか。　　　　　　　　　How do you like your room?

いかがですか。　　　　　　　　　　　How are you? (In Japanese this cannot be asked of a healthy person whom you meet everyday because you know how he is.)

アイスクリームはいかがですか。　　　How about some ice cream?

6. ただ

It means "but (the only thing that contradicts the preceding statement is) ____"
Thus, depending on the context it means: "but (the only drawback is) ____" "but (the good thing is) ____"

田中さんはきれいで頭がいいです。ただ体が弱いですね。

Tanaka is pretty and smart. But she is sickly. (But the only drawback is that she is physically weak.)

うちの子はばかできれいでも何でもありませんがただ体は丈夫です。

My kid is dumb and isn't pretty or anything, but she is healthy (but the good thing is that her body is strong (healthy)).

75

7. 山田さんとは大分違いますね。 　　You are quite different from Mr. Yamada, aren't you?

バークレーは大分違いますね。 　　Berkeley is quite different, isn't it?

バークレーは，東京とは大分違 　　Berkeley is quite different from Tokyo, isn't it?
いますね。

8. まあ，ひどいですねえ。 　　Oh! How mean! What a horrible thing to say! How can you say that!

まあ is an exclamation expressing surprise and can be translated as "Why!" "My!" etc. This form is used by women only. (The form that can be used by both men and women is わあ.)

　　ひどい 　　　　　　　　　means "terrible" or "awful"

The sentence means "What a terrible thing to say!", but the ねえ at the end of the sentence, a variation of ね ("isn't it?" or "don't you think so?"), indicates that Yamada is not really angry at Brown.

6 B

1. 本を読むことができます。 　　one can read a book

In English one can say, "one can read," and it implies that "one can read a book." In Japanese, however, ほんを, the object of reading must be said or the sentence sounds incomplete.

2. ちょっと 　　　　　　　　　little, a little

Here the full statement is ゆうがたは，ちょっとできません, that is, "In the evening it is a little impossible (difficult) to study." Although ちょっと means "little" or "a little," the sentence actually means that is almost totally impossible to study, which would literally be とてもできません. Some people tend to understate situations.

e.g. 試験はどうでしたか。 　　How was your exam?

——ええ。ちょっとむずかしか 　　...Oh, it was a little difficult, just as you
　　　（とても）
ったですね，やはり。 　　may expect (I had expected).
　　　　　　　　　　　　　　　(very)

3. うちで勉強しませんか。 　　How about studying at my place?
　　　　　　　　　　　　　　　Would you like to study at my place?

76

The negative question form is often used as an offer or as a suggestion.

ちょっとそこで，コーヒーを飲みませんか。	Why don't we stop off for a cup of coffee there?
こんばん一緒に映画を見ませんか。	How about going to the movies tonight?
——そうですね。今何をやっていますか。	...Well, let's see... What's playing?
——せっかくですがまたにしてくださいませんか。	...Thanks for asking, but can I take a rain check? (Maybe next time.)

It can also be interpreted as a simple negative question: Aren't you going to study at home? But in that case の（ん）ですか tends to be included.

勉強しないんですか。	Is it the case that you're not going to study?

Lesson 6 **Grammar Notes**

The main points of this lesson are:
  I. Sentence final forms (affirmative and negative) for adjectives.
 II. Sentence final forms (affirmative and negative) for adjectival nouns.
III. Pre-noun forms
 IV. Multiple adjectives and adjectival nouns
  V. How to say "to be able to _____."
 VI. How to say "how do you like _____?" "how is _____?"

I. Sentences ending with an Adjective

Topic は **A** です	As for _____, (it) is **A**
Topic は Subj. が **A** です	As for _____, (its) _____ is **A**
寮の部屋はうるさいです。	The dorm room is noisy.
この大学は古いです。	The university is old.
私の車は安いです。	My car is cheap.
山川さんは目が大きいです。	As for Yamakawa, her eyes are big.

です following an adjective makes the sentence end in the polite form. The negative form of adjectives in the sentence final position is as follows:

Adjective (root) ＋ くありません。　　　　is not A

The root form of the adjective is the plain form minus the final い。

わたしの部屋はうるさくありま　　My room is not noisy.
せん。

この本は古くありません。　　　This book is not old.

私の車は安くありません。　　　My car is not cheap.

There is a variant form A (root) くないです。 This is a little too blunt, so we will not practice this pattern here.

II. Sentences ending with an Adjectival Noun

Topic は AN です　　　　　　　As for ＿＿＿, (it) is AN
Topic は Subj が AN です　　　As for ＿＿＿, (its) ＿＿＿ is AN
私の部屋はきれいです。　　　　My room is nice (clean, attractive)
あなたのアパートは静かですか。　Is your apartment quiet?
山川さんは目がきれいです。　　Yamakawa has pretty eyes.

The negative form of adjectival nouns in the sentence final position is as follows:

Adjectival Noun ＋ {では / じゃ} ありません　　is not AN

では is used in formal speech or writing, じゃ in colloquial speech.

私のアパートは静かではありま　　My apartment is not quiet.
せん。

山田さんの部屋はきれいじゃあ　　Yamada's room is not clean/pretty.
りません。

III. Pre-noun forms

A modifier always precedes the noun that it modifies and is in its plain form.

A. Adjectives

大きい箱　　　　　　　　　　a large box

78

広い部屋 (ひや)   a big (roomy) room

Adjectives end with い when the tense is non-past. Hence, they are often called
い-adjectives.

B. Adjectival Nouns

きれいな部屋 (ひや)   a nice (clean, attractive) room
静かな部屋 (しず) (ひや)   a quiet room

Adjectival nouns are semantically like adjectives but syntactically they behave very much
like nouns. Unlike regular nouns, which take の when they modify another noun, adjectival
nouns take な when they modify a noun. Hence, they are often called な-adjectives.
Note that きれい is an adjectival noun even though it ends with い.

IV. Multiple Adjectives and Adjectival Nouns

A. When Modifier₁ is an Adjective

広くて明るい部屋 (ひや)   a big and bright room
古くて立派なうち (ふる) (りっぱ)   an old and splendid house

The て form of an adjective is formed by dropping the い and adding くて.

B. When Modifier₁ is an Adjectival Noun

静かできれいなアパート   a quiet and nice (clean) apartment
きれいでかわいい女の子 (おんな)   a pretty and adorable girl

The て form of an Adjectival Noun is formed by adding で

V. <u>Verb (Plain Non-Past Aff.)</u> ことができ   be able to <u>V</u>

ます

静かですから勉強することが (しず) (べんきょう)   Because it is quiet, I can study.
できます。

本を読むことができます。   I can read books.

フィッシャーマンズウォーフ   One can board (take) a boat from (at)

から船に乗ることができます。   Fisherman's Wharf.

Literally こと means "thing" or "event." Here it nominalizes a verb. That is, 見ること,
for example, means "to see," or "seeing."
できます means "be able," "possible."

VI. ＿＿は { どうですか   How do you like ＿＿? 'How is ＿＿?

        いかがですか   How about ＿＿? What about ＿＿?

部屋はどうですか。   How do you like your room?

おばあさまはいかがですか。   How is your grandmother?

日曜日はどうですか。   How about Sunday?

いかがですか is a polite form of どうですか.

Various forms of Adjectives, Adjectival Nouns, and Nouns.

Sentence final form or predicate form in the Non-Past and past tenses.

		Non-Past tense		Past tense	
		Plain form	Polite form	Plain form	Polite form
A あかるい Af.	あかるい	あかるいです	あかるかった	あかるかったです
bright	Neg.	あかるくない	あかる { くありません (くないです) }	あかるくなかった	あかる { くありませんでした (くなかったです) }
AN きれいだ Af.	きれいだ	きれいです	きれいだった	きれいでした
beautiful (clean)	Neg.	きれい { ではない じゃない }	きれい { ではありません じゃありません }	きれい { ではなかった じゃなかった }	きれい { ではありませんでした じゃありませんでした }
N 先生 Af.	先生だ	先生です	先生だった	先生でした
teacher	Neg.	先生 { ではない じゃない }	先生 { ではありません じゃありません }	先生 { ではなかった じゃなかった }	先生 { ではありませんでした じゃありませんでした }

Pre-noun forms in the present and past tenses.

			Non-Past tense	Past tense
A	広い spacious	Af.	広いアパート	広かったアパート
		Neg.	広くないアパート	広くなかったアパート
AN	きれいだ beautiful	Af.	きれいなアパート	きれいだったアパート
		Neg.	きれい{ではない / じゃない}アパート	きれい{ではなかった / じゃなかった}アパート
N	学生 student	Af.	学生の山田さん	学生だった山田さん
		Neg.	学生{ではない / じゃない}山田さん	学生{ではなかった / じゃなかった}山田さん

第六課　漢字

大きい
おお
大きい

小さい
ちい
小さい

安い
やす
安い

高い
たか
高い

新しい
あたら
新しい

古い
ふる
古い

広い
ひろ
広い

明るい
あか
明るい

買う
か
買う

書く
か
書く

私
わたし
私

本
ほん
本

車
くるま
車

第 七 課

7A　（食堂で）

ウェートレス　　　　いらっしゃいませ。

高木　　　　　　　　レモン・ティーをください。

ブラウン　　　　　　私はコーヒーお願いします。

7B　高木　　　　　　　　ここはにぎやかですね。

ブラウン　　　　　　ええ，ちょっとうるさいですね。

　　　　　　　　　　でもコーヒーはおいしいです。

高木　　　　　　　　そうですか，私のレモン・ティーはまあまあ

　　　　　　　　　　です。

7C　ブラウン　　　　　　あそこにいる人はきれいですね。

高木　　　　　　　　あの人は男の人じゃありませんか。

ブラウン　　　　　　そうじゃありませんよ。あの男の人のとなり

　　　　　　　　　　にいる人ですよ。

高木　　　　　　　　ああ，あの人ですか。あれは私の妹ですよ。

ブラウン　　　　　　そうですか。

高木　　　　　　　　じゃ，紹介しましょうか。

1 例 T: この建物は古い

　　{S₁: この建物は古いですか。
　　{S₂　いいえ，新しいです。

1.　田中さんのアパート，せまい
2.　この本，高い
3.　テレグラフ，静かだ
4.　田中さんのアパート，便利だ
5.　先生のうち，小さい
6.　日本語のクイズ，やさしい
7.　あの車，安い
8.　このおかし，おいしい（まずい）
9.　寮の部屋，広い（せまい）
10.　寮，不便だ
11.　田中さんのアパート，新しい
12.　明日のクイズ，難しい

2 例 T: 山田さん，目，きれいだ

　　{S₁: 山田さんは目がきれいですね。
　　{S₂: ええ，ほんとうに（山田さんの目は）きれいですね。

1.　あの人，鼻，大きい
2.　このねこ，耳，大きい
3.　スミスさん，手，小さい
4.　この店，ハンバーガー，おいしい
5.　この部屋，窓，小さい
6.　この大学，キャンパス，きれいだ
7.　あの大学，図書館，立派だ
8.　この犬，足，大きい

3 例 T: スミスさん（目，大きい）

　　{S₂: スミスさんはどんな人ですか。
　　{S₂: （スミスさんは）目 {が／の} 大きい人です。

1.　山田さん（手，きれいだ）
2.　ジミー（＝ねこの名前）（耳，大きい）
3.　「姿」（＝店の名前）（すし，おいしい）
4.　スミスさんの犬（足，大きい）

84

5. ジョンソンさん(頭、いい)

6. ブラウンさん(＝学生の名前)
   (日本語，上手だ)

7. 大山さん(歌，下手だ)

8. 山田さん(テニス，上手だ)

4 例 T: 山田さんは中国語を話します。
　　　S: 山田さんは中国語を話す人です。

1. あのバスはサンフランシスコ
   へ行きます。

2. スミスさんはあそこにいます。

3. ジョンソンさんはバスで来ま
   す。

4. 山田さんは毎日図書館で勉強

します。

5. 大山さんはお酒を飲みません。

6. ブラウンさんは肉を食べませ
   ん。

7. あの船は十時半に出ます。

5 例 T: サンフランシスコへ行きます，バス(あれ)
　　　{ S₁: サンフランシスコへ行くバスはどれですか。
　　　{ S₂: あれです。

1. フランス語を話します，人(ス
   ミスさん)

2. 寮で漢字を勉強します，人(ブ
   ラウンさん)

3. 成田へ行きます，飛行機（こ
   れ)

4. 明日うちへ帰ります，人(ジョ
   ンソンさん)

5. あそこにあります，建物（食
   堂)

6. あそこにいます，人（田中さ
   ん)

7. リノへ行きます，バス(これ)

8. 食堂の北にあります，建物(図
   書館)

6 例 T: 私は昨日本を買いました。(難しい)
  S: 私が昨日買った本は難しいです。

1. ブラウンさんは本を書きました。(やさしい)
2. 青木先生はすきやきを作りました。(おいしい)
3. スミスさんはペンを使いました。(よくない)
4. 私は車を買いました。(安い)
5. 私は昨日映画を見ました。(おもしろい)

6. 私は漢字を勉強しました。(むずかしい)
7. ゴッホは絵を描きました。(きれいだ)
8. 先生は試験を作りました。(まあまあ)
9. 私は昨日セーターを買いました。(大きい)

7 例 T: 今日テニスをする
  S₁: 今日は何をしましょうか。
  S₂: テニスをしましょう。

1. 明日，ビールを飲む
2. 今晩アイスクリームを買う
3. 今日，サンフランシスコへ行く
4. 今晩，映画を見る
5. 今晩，日本町で食べる
6. 来年，社会学のクラスを取る
7. 今日，中華料理を作る
8. 今週末，ヨセミテへ行く
9. 明日，ピクニックをする

10. 今日，プールで泳ぐ
11. 今晩，キップスでピザを食べる
12. 土曜日，図書館で勉強する
13. 来年，日本へ行く
14. 金曜日，ロスへ車で行く
15. 明日，ワイン・カントリーへ行く
16. 今日，日本の映画を見る

86

Lesson 7 **Dialogues**

7 A

(At a cafeteria)

Waitress: Welcome.

いらっしゃいませ   A standard greeting which shops and restaurants use when a customer enters.

Takagi: Please give me some lemon tea.

ください   please give me

Brown: I'll have some coffee.

お願いする   to request

7 B

Takagi: It's really bustling with activity here, isn't it?

にぎやかだ   active and noisy

Brown: Yes, It is a little noisy, isn't it? But the coffee is good.

ちょっと   a little

うるさい   noisy (unpleasant connotation)

でも   but

Takagi: Oh, really? My lemon tea is only so-so.

そうですか   Is that so?

まあまあ   so-so, ok.

7 C

Brown: That person over there is pretty, isn't she?

あそこ	over there
きれいだ	beautiful or pretty

Takagi: Isn't that person a guy?

| 男の人 おとこ ひと | man (person who is a man) |

Brown: That's not what I mean. The person next to the guy.

| よ | !, I tell you. |
| となり | beside or next to |

Takagi: Oh, that person? That's my younger sister.

| 妹 いもうと | younger sister |

Brown: Oh, really?

| そうですか | |

Takagi: Then, shall I introduce you?

じゃ	then or well then
紹介する しょうかい	to introduce
ましょう	(I/we) shall, let us

Lesson 7 **Notes on Usage**

7 A

1. お願いします。
ねが

   Lit. "Please do me a favor." (cf. L. 13 GNI)

お願いします or ください are often used when ordering at restaurants.

   コーヒー(を)お願いします。

   コーヒーをください。

7 B

2.　ここはにぎやかですね。　　　　　　It's really bustling with activity here, isn't it?

　　ね at the end of a sentence asks the addressee for agreement. (cf. Notes on Usage 3A L. 3)

3.　でも　　　　　　　　　　　　　　but/however

　　でもコーヒーはおいしいです。　　But the coffee is good.

　　山田：　　あのアパートはい　　That apartment is nice, isn't it?
　　　　　　　いですね。

　　ブラウン：　えぇ，でも高くて　　Yes, but it's expensive and inconvenient.
　　　　　　　ふべんです。

4.　まあまあ　　　　　　　　　　　so-so

e.g.　スミス：　映画はどうでしたか。　How was the movie?

　　山田：　　まあまあでした。　　It was so-so.

7 C

　　じゃ　　　　　　　　　　　　　well/well then, In that case,

　　じゃ，紹介しましょうか。　　　If that's the case, shall I introduce you?

　　山田：　　図書館へ行きます　　Are you going to the library?
　　　　　　　か。

　　ブラウン：　えぇ，行くつもり　　Yes, I intend to go.
　　　　　　　です。

　　山田：　　じゃ，この本を返　　Well then, would you please return this
　　　　　　　してくださいませ　　book for me?
　　　　　　　んか。

Lesson 7 Grammar Notes

The main points of this lesson are:
 I. Pre-noun forms for Nouns, Adjectives, Adjectival Nouns.
 II. Noun modification: sentence modifying a noun (relative clause)
III. How to say "Let's do ____."

I. Pre-noun forms

A. Noun modifying a Noun
   Noun の Noun (cf. L. 2)

男の子	a boy (male child)
音楽の本	a music book
ピカソの絵	Picasso's picture
学生の山田さん	Yamada who is a student

B. Adjective modifying a Noun
   Adjective (plain form) Noun

うるさいアパートです。	It is a noisy apartment.
これは古い本です。	This is an old book.
かわいい子供です。	He/She is a cute child.

C. Adjectival Noun modifying a Noun
   Adjectival noun な Noun

しずかなアパートです。	It is a quiet apartment.
きれいな目ですね。	What pretty eyes! (aren't they?)
りっぱな家です。	It is a splendid (grand) house.

90

II. Noun modification: Sentence modifying a Noun (=relative clause)

S(=relative clause)　Noun　(S=sentence)
　　　　|_____↑

A noun can be modified by a sentence. In this case, the verb in the sentence modifying the noun must 1) be in its plain form, and 2) must immediately precede the noun being modified. (The form itself is the same as that which precedes つもりです or ことができます patterns.)

The subject marker in the relative clause is either が or の.

The Topic は may not be used in a relative clause. It is always the topic of the main sentence.

あれはヨセミテへ行くバスです。　　That is the bus that goes to Yosemite.

私のいるアパートは静かです。　　The apartment in which I live is quiet.
が

あれは私が昨日見た映画です。　　That is the movie I saw a yesterday.

ジョンソンさんはまじめでまいにち勉強する人です。　　Johnson is a person who is diligent and studies every day.

When the modifying phrase ends with a noun, an adjective, or an adjectival noun, their forms are the same as the ones introduced in the Section I.

Noun: (e.g. 学生)

学生の山田さんはあそこにいます。　　Yamada, who is a student, is over there.

Adjective: (背が高い)
背が高い山本さんは東京へ行きます。　　Yamamoto, who is tall, is going to Tokyo.

Adjectival Noun: (e.g. きれいだ)

目のきれいな田中さんは, 私の友だちです。　　Tanaka, with the pretty eyes, is my friend.

91

III. <u>Verb (Pre-masu)</u> ましょう。　　　　　Let's <u>V</u>!

きょうは何をしましょうか。　　What shall we do today?
テニスをしましょう。　　　　　…Let's play tennis.
日本語のクラスのパーティーを　Let's have a Japanese class party.
しましょう。

第七課　漢字

手	足	目	耳	口	名前
て	あし	め	みみ	くち	な　まえ
手	足	目	耳	口	名前

上	下	中	外	山田	田中
うえ	した	なか	そと	やま　だ	た　なか
上	下	中	外	山田	田中

上手だ　　　　　　　下手だ　　　　　　静かだ
じょうず　　　　　　へ　た　　　　　　しず

　　上手だ　　　　　　　下手だ　　　　　　静かだ

第八課

8A 山田　　　ブラウンさんは御兄弟が何人ありますか。

　　ブラウン　兄が一人と妹が二人あります。山田さんのおう
　　　　　　　ちは何人家族ですか。

　　山田　　　両親と祖母の四人です。

　　ブラウン　おばあさんは何年生まれですか。

　　山田　　　明治四十年ごろです。　もっと前かも知れません
　　　　　　　が…

　　ブラウン　ああ，明治十四年ですか。まだお元気ですか。

　　山田　　　ええ，でも歯がありませんので食事に時間がか
　　　　　　　かります。

8B 山田　　　飛行機は何時ですか。

　　ベイリー　午後一時です。

　　山田　　　ホノルルまで何時間かかりますか。

　　ベイリー　四時間半ぐらいです。

　　山田　　　チャーターですか。

　　ベイリー　いえ日航ですから往復で千四百ドルかかります。

　　山田　　　高いですね。ひとりで行くんですか。

　　ベイリー　いえ，ガールフレンドと行きます。

　　山田　　　あ，そうですか，じゃ，日本からうめぼしを送っ
　　　　　　　てくださいませんか。

① 例1 T: 紙かみ，五

$\begin{cases} S_1: & 紙が何まいありますか。 \\ S_2: & 紙は五まいぐらいあります。 \end{cases}$

例2 T: ビール，十一

$\begin{cases} S_1: & ビールが何ぼんありますか。 \\ S_2: & ビールは十一ぽんぐらいあります。 \end{cases}$

例3 T: くるま，六

$\begin{cases} S_1: & くるまが何だいありますか。 \\ S_2: & くるまは六だいぐらいあります。 \end{cases}$

1. えんぴつ，七
2. チョーク，八
3. シーツ，四
4. タイプライター，四
5. バス，九
6. 紙かみ，十
7. 万年筆まんねんひつ，四
8. ワイン，一

9. 酒さけ，八
10. 車，三
11. タオル，二
12. ビール，十四
13. 車，六
14. シーツ，一
15. ペン，三

② 例1 T: お兄さん，一人ひとり

$\begin{cases} S_1: & ご兄弟が何人ありますか。 \\ S_2: & 兄が一人ひとりあります。 \end{cases}$

例2 T: お金，一ドル

$\begin{cases} S_1: & お金がありますか。 \\ S_2: & ええ，一ドルあります。 \end{cases}$

1. 妹さん，一人
2. お金，二ドル
3. お兄さん，二人，妹，一人
4. お金，千ドル
5. お兄さん，二人，弟さん，一人

6. お姉さん，一人
7. 時間，ある
8. お金，十ドル
9. お姉さん，一人，弟さん，一人
10. お金，一ドル

③ 例1 T: サンフランシスコ，ホノルル，四時間半
　　　｛S₁: サンフランシスコからホノルルまで何時間かかりますか。
　　　｛S₂: 四時間半ぐらいです。
　　 例2 T: 映画，三ドル
　　　｛S₁: 映画はいくらかかりますか。
　　　｛S₂: 三ドルぐらいです。

1. 心理学の本，十ドル
2. うち，大学，一時間
3. 古い車，千ドル
4. 新しい万年筆，五ドル
5. 中国語の辞書，十五ドル
6. 日本のカメラ，三百ドル
7. バークレー，ヨセミテ，車，三時間半
8. うち，公園，車，二時間
9. ロス，カタリナ，船，一時間
10. サンフランシスコ，ニューヨ

　 ーク，飛行機，四時間
11. スタンフォード，バークレー，一時間
12. バークレー，サンフランシスコ，バス，一時間
13. 日本語のテキスト，三十ドル
14. サンフランシスコ，日本，千ドル
15. ハワイ，日本，飛行機，八時間

④ 例 T: 本　ください
　　　S: 本をください。

1.　えんぴつ
2.　酒（さけ）
3.　手紙（てがみ）

4.　てんぷら
5.　すし
6.　日本語の辞書（にほんご　じしょ）

5　例　T: 行く
　　　　S:　行ってください。

1.　カメラを買う
2.　社会学をとる（しゃかいがく）
3.　手紙を書く（てがみ）
4.　この本を読む
5.　日本語で話す（にほんご）
6.　ここにいる
7.　ここへ来る
8.　うちで勉強する（べんきょう）
9.　うちへ帰る
10.　レコードを聞く

11.　橋の下まで行く（はし）
12.　アイスクリームを食べる
13.　体育館のプールで泳ぐ（たいいくかん　およ）
14.　黒沢の映画を見る（くろさわ　えいが）
15.　図書館で宿題をする（としょかん　しゅくだい）
16.　コープで買物をする（かいもの）
17.　うちでビールを飲む
18.　近くの公園で遊ぶ（ちか　こうえん　あそ）
19.　お金を貸す（か）
20.　いらっしゃる

6　例1　T: 本，読みます
　　　　　S:　本を読んでくださいませんか。

1.　漢字，書きます（かんじ　か）
2.　山田さん，送ります（やまだ　おく）
3.　田中さん，話します
4.　えんぴつ，書きます
5.　食べます

6.　田中さん，お金，貸します（か）
7.　山田さん，言います（い）
8.　買物，します（かいもの）
9.　てんぷら，作ります（つく）
10.　今日，テニス，します

11. 山田さん，カメラ，買います
12. 大学，来ます
13. 万年筆，包みます
14. 英語，話しません
15. 日本語，話します
16. 山田さん，言いません
17. 銀行，行きます
18. 新聞，買います
19. 本，送ります
20. 母，手紙，書きます

7 例1 T: 行く
        S: 行ってください。
  例2 T: 行かない
        S: 行かないでください。

1. 食べる
2. 買う
3. 包まない
4. 使う
5. 本を見ない
6. えんぴつで書く
7. 急がない
8. ビールを飲まない
9. 日本語で話す
10. 明日，うちに来る
11. 漢字で書く
12. お金を貸す
13. まだ帰らない
14. ここで勉強しない
15. カメラを買う
16. 買物をする
17. 日本語のクラスで英語を話さない
18. 明日も学校へ来る
19. この手紙を出す
20. 英語の宿題をする

8 例 T: 行く，ガールフレンド
    {S₁: 一人で行きますか。
    {S₂: いいえ，ガールフレンドと行きます。

1. 勉強する，田中さん
2. 遊ぶ，友だち
3. アパートに住む，ブラウンさん
4. 映画を見る，ガールフレンド
5. ニューヨークへ行く，父
6. スタンフォードへ行く，山田
   先生
7. ヨーロッパへ行く，兄，妹
8. 買物をする，母
9. テニスをする，田中さん，山
   田さん，スミスさん
10. 文学のクラスをとる，スミス
    さん

9 例1 T: 明日雨がふりますか。（いいえ）
     S: いいえ，ふらないかもしれません。
 例2 T: 明日雨がふりますか。（ええ）
     S: ええ，ふるかもしれません。

1. 明日スタンフォードへ行きま
   すか。
2. 日本でカメラを買いますか。
3. あの方は先生ですか。
4. あのレストランは混んでいま
   すか。
5. 先生は今日いらっしゃいませ
   んか。
6. 明日雨がふりませんか。
7. 寮はにぎやかですか。
8. 山田さんはもう帰りましたか。
9. ブラウンさんはあした来ませ
   んか。
10. あれはスミスさんの本ですか。
11. レストランはすいていました
    か。
12. ジョンソンさんは時間があり
    ますか。
13. ルームメートは文学のクラス
    をとりませんか。
14. あの方は日本人ですか。
15. 今日はテニスをしませんか。
16. 山田さんは飛行機で帰りませ
    んか。
17. ベイリーさんはあの映画を見
    ましたか。
18. ジョンソンさんはアメリカ人
    ですか。

19. あの辞書はよくありませんか。
20. スミスさんはもう食事をしま
    したか。

Lesson 8 **Dialogues**

8 A

Yamada: How many brothers and sisters do you have?

御 (ご)   [honorific prefix]

兄弟 (きょうだい)   brothers (and sisters)

何人 (なんにん)   how many [people]

Brown: I have an older brother, and two younger sisters. How many are there in your family?

兄 (あに)   (my) older brother

一人 (ひとり)   one (person)

妹 (いもうと)   (my) younger sister

二人 (ふたり)   two (people)

おうち   (your) family, house, home

家族 (かぞく)   family

Y: There are four of us, including my parents and my grandmother.

両親 (りょうしん)   (my) parents

祖母 (そぼ)   (my) grandmother

B: In what year was your grandmother born?

おばあさん   (your) grandmother

何年 (なんねん)   what year

生まれ (うまれ)   birth

Y: Around Meiji 40 (1907), but it might have been earlier.

明治（めいじ）	Meiji era (1868-1912)
ごろ	around (time)
もっと	more
かも知（し）れません	may, might

B: Wow, Meiji 14 (1881). Is she (still) in good health?

ああ	Oh, Wow
まだ	still
お	[honorific prefix]
元気（げんき）	good health

Y: Yes, but since she does not have any teeth, it takes her a long time to eat a meal.

でも	but, however
歯（は）	**tooth**
ありません	**does not exist**
ので	because
食事（しょくじ）	meal
時間	time (duration)
かかります	**take (time, money)**

8 B

Yamada: What time is your plane?

飛行機（ひこうき）	airplane
何時（じ）	what time?

Bailey: (It leaves) at one p.m.

午後（ごご）	afternoon
一時（じ）	one o'clock

Y: How many hours does it take to Honolulu?

まで	to, as far as
何時間	how many hours

100

B: About four and a half hours.

半 _{はん}   half (suffix)

ぐらい   about (quantity)

Y: Are you taking a charter flight?

チャーター   charter flight

B: No, Japan Airlines, so it'll cost a thousand four hundred dollars round trip.

日航 _{にっこう}   Japan Airlines

往復 _{おうふく}   round trip

——で   with/for____

千   one thousand

四百   four hundred

ドル   dollar

かかる   cost, take (time, money)

Y: That's expensive. Are you going alone?

高い   expensive, high

ひとりで   alone

B: No, I'm going with my girlfriend.

ガールフレンド   girlfriend

と   with, together with

Y: I see. Well, won't you please send me some umebosi.

送る _{おく}   to send

うめぼし   pickled plum

Lesson 8 Notes on Usage

8 A

1. 御兄弟 _{ごきょうだい}   your brothers and sisters

101

ご is an honorific prefix which usually attaches to words of Chinese origin. The character for きょう means "older brother," and that of だい, "younger brother." Together, however, it means your or another person's brothers and sisters.

2. ありますか。

When words like "brothers" and "sisters" or other family members are used in an abstract sense as a member of a group or category called family members rather than as individual people, あります is used rather than います.

Recently, however, among young people this usage of あります has been replaced by います. This probably shows that they regard their family as specific individuals rather than members in a group or category.

3. 兄・妹
あに　いもうと

あに means "my older brother" and いもうと means "My younger sister." There are two different forms for each kinship term, depending on whether the speaker is referring to his own or someone else's family. When speaking to someone outside his own family, the speaker refers to his own family member using the forms listed in the left hand column below and when referring to his adressee's or someone else's family he uses the forms listed in the right hand column.

	plain form (my own family)	polite form (someone else's)
father	ちち（父）	おとうさん
mother	はは（母）	おかあさん
older brother	あに（兄）	おにいさん
older sister	あね（姉）	おねえさん
younger brother	おとうと（弟）	おとうとさん
younger sister	いもうと（妹）	いもうとさん
grandfather	そふ（祖父）	おじいさん
grandmother	そぼ（祖母）	おばあさん

Yamakawa is speaking to Johnson about his family.

Johnson: 山川さんには御兄弟があ
りますか。

J: Do you have any brothers and sisters?

Yamakawa: ええ兄と 妹 が一人ずつ
あります。

Y: Yes, I have an older brother and a younger sister (one of each). 〔ずつ：____ of each〕

J: お兄さんは何をしていらっしゃ
(honorific "do")

いますか。学生ですか。

Y: ええ，兄は，この大学の三年生で
(3rd year)

す。

J: 妹さんは。

Y: 妹はまだ高校生です。

J: かわいいでしょうね。

Y: いいえ全然！

J: What does your brother do? Is he a student?

Y: Yes, he's a junior at this university.

J: How about your sister?

Y: She is still a high school student.

J: She must be cute.

Y: No, not at all!

When speaking to his own family member, the speaker uses the polite forms in the right hand column.

Yamakawa: お兄さんはどこにいる。

Y's sister: さあ，知らないわ。

Y: Where is big brother?

S: Gee. I don't know. [わ is a sentence final particle used only by females.]

4. おうち   your home, your house, your family

お is an honorific prefix used for Japanese indigenous words. うち means "inside" but here it means "house, home, or family." "My house, home, or family" is うち; the お prefix is used only to refer to other people's house, home or family.

5. 何人家族

何人 "How many people" and 家族 "family" all together means "a family of how many people?"

6. 両親

りょう means "both" and しん means "parent(s)." 両親 means "my parents" but your/ someone else's parents is 御両親 with 御, the honorific prefix used with Chinese words.

7. 祖母

"my grandmother" See the section on 兄 and 妹.

8. 何年生まれ

103

何年 means "what year" and 生まれ means "born". All together it means "born in what year?"

9. でも, 歯がありませんので, 食事に時間がかかります。

でも	but
歯	tooth/teeth
歯がありません	There are no teeth.
ので	therefore
食事	meal
食事に	for meal
時間	time
時間がかかります	it takes time.

8 B

1. 日航

"JAL" is an abbreviation of 日本航空 "Japan Airlines."

2. 往復で

おうふく means "round trip." で essentially means "with" but here it means as a whole "for a round trip."

Other examples of this usage of で：

このりんごはいくらですか。	How much are these apples?
——三つで二百円です。	____ 3 for 200 yen.

3. 一人で   alone

Lesson 8 **Grammar Notes**

The main points of this lesson are:
   I. Numbers and classifiers.

II. How to say "approximately" for quantity or degree.
III. How to say "about" "around" for time.
IV. How to request objects.
V. Indirect object marker <u>ni</u>.
VI. A. How to request an action to be done.
    B. How to request an action not to be done.
VII. How to say "it takes."
VIII. How to say "to have."
IX. How to say "possibly" or "might be."
X. How to say "with."
XI. How to say "when."

I. Numbers and classifiers

There are two systems: (1) the Japanese system and (2) the Chinese system.

The Japanese system		The Chinese system	
1. ひとつ	6. むっつ	1. いち	6. ろく
2. ふたつ	7. ななつ	2. に	7. しち
3. みっつ	8. やっつ	3. さん	8. はち
4. よっつ	9. ここのつ	4. し, よ, よん	9. く, きゅう
5. いつつ	10. とお	5. ご	10. じゅう

When one wants to ask "how many," using the Japanese system, いくつ is used.

The Chinese system is used in mathematics and in counting things that require certain classifiers.

The Japanese system is usually used to count things that have roughly the same height, width, and length, such as apples, potatoes, candies, balls, boxes, etc. or to count things that do not have specific classifiers, like watches, briefcases. It is also used to count children's ages.

For numbers over ten, only the Chinese system is used.

11 じゅういち   12 じゅうに   13 じゅうさん

20 にじゅう   21 にじゅういち   22 にじゅうに

30 さんじゅう   100 ひゃく   101 ひゃくいち

260 にひゃくろくじゅう   1000 せん

1400 せんよんひゃく   2000 にせん

9875 きゅうせんはっぴゃくななじゅうご   10000 いちまん

38746 さんまんはっせんななひゃくよんじゅうろく

The numbers 4 and 7 in the Chinese system have alternative forms, which are in fact the Japanese forms. し '4' is often avoided because it sounds exactly like the word for "death" and なな is used for しち "7" to avoid confusion with いち "1" which sounds very much like it. よ is used with classifiers only.

Some classifiers:

A.　～時 [for telling time, ～o'clock]

　　何時 — what time

1.　一時　　　　　　　　6.　六時
2.　二時　　　　　　　　7.　七時
3.　三時　　　　　　　　8.　八時
4.　四時　　　　　　　　9.　九時
5.　五時　　　　　　　10.　十時

B.　～時間 [for counting hours, duration]

　　何時間 — how many hours

1.　一時間　　　　　　　6.　六時間
2.　二時間　　　　　　　7.　七時間
3.　三時間　　　　　　　8.　八時間
4.　四時間　　　　　　　9.　九時間
5.　五時間　　　　　　10.　十時間

C.　～年 [for counting years]

　　何年 — how many years

1.　一年　　　　　　　　6.　六年
2.　二年　　　　　　　　7.　七年
3.　三年　　　　　　　　8.　八年
4.　四年　　　　　　　　9.　九年
5.　五年　　　　　　　10.　十年

〜年間
二年間 means for the length of two years.

D. 〜月 [for counting months]
何か月 — how many months

1. 一か月
2. 二か月
3. 三か月
4. 四か月
5. 五か月

6. 六か月
7. 七か月
8. 八か月
9. 九か月
10. 十か月

E. 〜ドル [for counting American dollars]
何ドル — how much (how many dollars)

1. 一ドル
2. 二ドル
3. 三ドル
4. 四ドル
5. 五ドル

6. 六ドル
7. 七ドル
8. 八ドル
9. 九ドル
10. 十ドル

F. 〜円 [for counting Japanese yen]
何円 — how much (how many yen)

1. 一円
2. 二円
3. 三円
4. 四円
5. 五円

6. 六円
7. 七円
8. 八円
9. 九円
10. 十円

107

G. 〜人 [for counting people: for counting one or two people, the Japanese system is used. For counting three or more people, the Chinese system is used.]

何人 — how many people

1. 一人
2. 二人
3. 三人
4. 四人
5. 五人

6. 六人
7. 七人
8. 八人
9. 九人
10. 十人

H. 〜枚 [for counting flat things such as sheets of paper]

何枚 — how many sheets)

1. 一枚
2. 二枚
3. 三枚
4. 四枚
5. 五枚

6. 六枚
7. 七枚
8. 八枚
9. 九枚
10. 十枚

I. 〜台 [for counting vehicles or machines such as cars]

何台 — how many (vehicles)

1. 一台
2. 二台
3. 三台
4. 四台
5. 五台

6. 六台
7. 七台
8. 八台
9. 九台
10. 十台

J. 〜本 [for counting long cylindrical objects such as pencils]

何本 — how many (cylindrical objects)

1.	いっぽん 一本	6.	ろっぽん 六本
2.	にほん 二本	7.	ななほん 七本
3.	さんぼん 三本	8.	はちほん／はっぽん 八本
4.	よんほん 四本	9.	きゅうほん 九本
5.	ごほん 五本	10.	じっぽん／じゅっぽん 十本

K. ～分 [for telling minutes]
なんぷん
何分

1.	いっぷん 一分	6.	ろっぷん 六分
2.	にふん 二分	7.	ななふん 七分
3.	さんぷん 三分	8.	はっぷん／はちふん 八分
4.	よんぷん 四分	9.	きゅうふん 九分
5.	ごふん 五分	10.	じっ／じゅっぷん 十　分

Generally, no particles are used after classifiers.

1. あそこに人が三人います。 There are three people over there.
2. あそこに三人，人がいます。

II. ぐらい   approximately (quantity or degree)

ホノルルまで何時間ぐらいかか
ります。

四時間半ぐらいです。

いくらぐらいかかりますか。

150 ドルぐらいでしょう。

About how many hours does it take to Honolulu?

It's about four and a half hours.

About how much does it cost?

It's about 150 dollars, I guess.

III. ごろ   about (time)

It is used to show approximate time, day, month, season, year, etc. It cannot be used to show approximate duration of time. In such cases, ぐらい is used.

祖母(そぼ)は明治(めいじ)四(よん)十(じゅう)年(ねん)ごろに生(う)まれました。

My grandmother was born around Meiji 40 (1907).

三時(じ)ごろ，うちに帰ります。

I will go home around three o'clock.

明治　Meiji: (1868-1912)　To convert M.40 to the Western calendar, add 40 to 1867. (=1907)

大正　Taisho: (1912-1926)　To convert T.12, add 12 to 1911. (=1923)

昭和　Shōwa: (1926-1989)　To convert S.35, add 35 to 1925. (=1960)

平成　Heisei: (1989-　)　To convert H.6, add 6 to 1988. (=1994)

IV. Requesting an object

ください。

Please give me.

くださいませんか。

Would you please give me (polite request).

Object をください。

Please give me the object.

Object をくださいませんか。

Would you please give me the object.

レモン・ティーをください。

Please give me some lemon tea.

えんぴつをくださいませんか。

Would you please give me the pencil.

V. に   Indirect Object marker

この万年筆(まんねんひつ)は，東京(とうきょう)の友(とも)だちに送(おく)ります。

I am going to mail this fountain pen to a friend in Tokyo.

今日母(はは)に手紙(てがみ)を書くつもりです。

I plan to write a letter to my mother today.

山田さんに電話(でんわ)をしてください。

Please telephone Mr. Yamada.

Indirect Object に Object をください	"Please give I.O. Obj."
(私に)さしみをください。	Please give me some sashimi.
(私に)万年筆をください。	Please give me a fountain pen. (At a store, said to a clerk, it means, "I would like to buy a fountain pen.")

Request sentences with classifiers
Classifiers follow the noun phrase that they modify, and they do not take particles.

(私に)紙を一枚ください。	Please give me a sheet of paper. (one)
(私に)万年筆を一本ください。	Please give me a fountain pen. (one)
(私に)りんごを五つください。	Please give me five apples.

VI. A. Requesting an action

V てください V てくださいませんか	Please Verb./Would you please Verb.
食べてください。	Please eat.
ケーキを食べてください。	Please eat the cake.
読んでくださいませんか。	Would you please read?
本を読んでくださいませんか。	Would you please read the book?
行ってください。	Please go.
バスで行ってください。	Please go by bus.
来てくださいませんか。	Would you please come?
田中さんと来てくださいませんか。	Would you please come with Mr. Tanaka?

B. Verb ないでください
Plain Non-Past Neg. | Please do not V. |

Verb ないでくださいませんか	Would you please not V?
これを食べないでください。	Please don't eat this.
明日は来ないでくださいませんか。	Would you please not come tomorrow.

111

VII. かかります   takes (time, cost, manpower)

See examples in II. above.
その仕事は三人かかります。   It takes three people to do the job.

VIII. あります   to have. (This is an extended usage of the
                                        pattern presented in Lesson 2.)

私には兄弟が三人あります。   I have three siblings.

あの人にはお金があるんですか。   Does that person have money?

さあ，あるかどうかわかりませ   Gee, I don't know if he does or doesn't.
ん。

今お時間がありますか。   Do you have time now?

いいえ，今はちょっと…   No, right now I'm a little (busy)....

あとにしてくださいませんか。   Could you make it later?

どうしたんですか。元気があり   What's the matter? You look wiped out.
ませんね。   (Lit. You don't have much energy.)

ええ，お金を落したんです。   ...Yeah, I dropped some money.

IX. Sentence(plain form)かもしれません   possibly, may or might be

V: 行く/行った

A: 高い/高かった

A.N.: きれい/きれいだった

N: 学生/学生だった

Negative: ない/なかった

今日は雨がふるかもしれません   It may rain today, don't you think?
ね。

112

ベイリーさんはもう日本へ行っ
たかもしれませんね。

Mr. Bailey might have already gone to Japan, don't you think?

あの時計はスイス製ですね。

That watch is Swiss-made, isn't it?

ええ。高いかもしれませんね。

...Yes, and it might be expensive.

このアパートはきたないですが，
前はきれいだったかもしれませ
ん。

This apartment is dirty, but it may have been attractive before.

あの人は先生かもしれません。

That person may be a teacher.

明日は来ないかもしれません。

I might not come tomorrow.

X. と

with, together with

と一緒に

ひとりで行きますか。

Are you going alone?

いいえ，友だちと行きます。

No, I am going with a friend.

誰かと行くんですか。

Are you going with someone?

ええ，田中さんと(一緒に)行き
ます。

Yes, I'm going with Tanaka.

XI. いつ

when?

いつ日本へ行きますか。

When are you going to Japan?

明日行くつもりです。

I am going tomorrow.

第八課　漢字

父	母	両親	兄	弟	兄弟
ちち	はは	りょう しん	あに	おとうと	きょう だい
父	母	両親	兄	弟	兄弟

家族	男	女	人
か ぞく	おとこ	おんな	ひと／じん
家族	男	女	女の人　アメリカ人

か	月	半	人	円	百	千
	げつ	はん	にん	えん	ひゃく	せん
一か月		十時半	十人	十円	百円	千ドル

お金	時間	外国人
かね	じ かん	がい こく じん
お金	時間	外国人

第九課

9A　スミス　　大山さんは今日来ていますか。

小山　　いいえ，今サンフランシスコへ行っています。

スミス　　山村さんは来ていますか。

小山　　来ていますが今クラスに行っています。

スミス　　田中さんは来ていますか。

小山　　田中さんは今日来ません。

スミス　　今日は誰もいないんですね。

9B　ブラウン　　山田さんは最近何か本を読んでいますか。

山田　　例の「ルーツ」というのを買ったんですが宿題が多くてまだ読んでいません。

ブラウン　　宿題って英語のですか。

山田　　ええ，多いですね。ここは宿題が。

ブラウン　　日本の大学ではパチンコばかりしていたんでしょう。

山田　　ひどいですね。もう。じゃブラウンさんは何か読んでいるんですか。

ブラウン　　ええ，読んでいますよ。ＴＶガイドとか…

1　例1　T: 何か食べましたか。

　　　　　S: いえ，何も食べませんでした。

　　例2　T: だれ/どなたか行きましたか。

　　　　　S: いいえ，だれも/どなたも行きませんでした。

　　例3　T: どこかへ行きますか。

　　　　　S: いいえ，どこへも行きません。

1.　何かありますか。　　　　　　6.　どこかへ行きましたか。

2.　何か飲みますか。　　　　　　7.　何か勉強しましたか。

3.　どこかへ行きますか。　　　　8.　だれか行きますか。

4.　何か飲みますか。　　　　　　9.　だれかいましたか。

5.　どなたかいらっしゃいますか。　10.　どなたかいらっしゃいますか。

2　例1　T: スミスさん，来る。

　　　　　S: スミスさんは来ています。

1.　スミスさん，寮に住む　　　　6.　おなか，すく

2.　山田さん，サンフランシスコ　7.　バート，混む
　　へ行く　　　　　　　　　　8.　図書館，あく

3.　クラス，始まる　　　　　　　9.　田中さん，結婚する

4.　ブラウンさん，日本へ行く　　10.　スミスさん，田中さんの本を

5.　まど，あく　　　　　　　　　　　借りる

3　例　T: 本を読みますか。

　　　　S: ええ，今，読んでいます。

1.　勉強しますか。　　　　　　　3.　飲みますか。

2.　テレビを見ますか。　　　　　4.　書きますか。

116

5. 練習しますか。

6. コーヒーを飲みますか。

7. ジャズを聞きますか。

8. 遊びますか。

9. テープを聞きますか。

10. 復習しますか。

11. てんぷらを作りますか。

12. ペンを使いますか。

4 例1 T: 新聞を読みますか。

S: ええ，新聞ばかり読んでいます。

例2 T: バーへ行きますか。

S: ええ，バーへばかり行っています。

1. テレビを見ますか。

2. ビールを飲みますか。

3. レコードを聞きますか。

4. 英語を話しますか。

5. アパートで勉強しますか。

6. 映画を見ますか。

7. 図書館へ行きますか。

8. 図書館で勉強しますか。

9. 本を読みますか。

10. 日本語の勉強をしますか。

5 例 T: あそこに山田さんがいます。

S₁: あそこにいるのはだれですか。

S₂: あそこにいるのは山田さんです。

1. 机の上に辞書があります。

2. アパートで日本語を勉強しました。

3. 昨日テキストを買いました。

4. バーでスコッチを飲みました。

5. スタンフォードで文学を勉強しました。

6. 昨日黒沢の映画を見ました。

7. 田山先生がいらっしゃいました。

8. スミスさんが社会学を勉強しています。

9. 山田さんが小説を読んでいます。

10. ブラウンさんがブック・スト
   アーでテキストを買いました。

⑥ 例 T: 本，読む
   { S₁: 本を読みましたか。
   { S₂: いいえ，まだ読んでいませんが読むつもりです。

1. 宿題，する
2. テキスト，買う
3. ラボのテープ，聞く
4. ヨセミテ，行く
5. 京都，行く
6. 京都，見る

7. ゴールデン・ゲート・ブリッジ，見る
8. すきやき，食べる
9. 今日の新聞，読む
10. 結婚する

⑦ 例1 T: あそこ，本，ある
   { S₁: あそこに何かありましたか。
   { S₂: ええ，本がありました。
   例2 T: 図書館，山田先生，いらっしゃる
   { S₁: 図書館にどなたかいらっしゃいましたか。
   { S₂: ええ，山田先生がいらっしゃいました。
   例3 T: クリスマス，ハワイ，行く
   { S₁: クリスマスにどこかへ行きましたか。
   { S₂: ええ，ハワイへ行きました。

1. 部屋の中，スミスさん，いる
2. 今日，サンフランシスコ，行く
3. ブック・ストアー，文学のテキスト，買う

4. ブック・ストアー，新しい辞書，買う
5. そこ，山田さん，いる
6. 日本，空手，勉強する

118

7. きのう，バークレー，行く 9. 今，クラス，行く

8. コーヒー，飲む 10. クリスマス，日本，行く

⑧ 例 1 T: ここにある本を読む

S: ここにある本を読んでください。

2 T: ここにある本を読まない

S: ここにある本を読まないでください。

1. あそこにあるノートを読まない 5. テーブルの下にあるケーキを食べない

2. 私が読む雑誌を取る 6. 私が歌う歌を歌う

3. 山田さんが飲むワインを買う 7. 私が作ったすしを食べる

4. 私が描いた絵を見る 8. 私が勉強する部屋で話さない

Lesson 9 Dialogues

9 A

Smith: Is Mr. Ooyama here today?
Koyama: No. He's gone to San Francisco now.

来ている	to have come
今	now
行っている	has gone
サンフランシスコへ	to San Francisco

S: How about Mr. Yamamura, has he come ?
K: He is here, but he is in class now.
S: How about Mr. Tanaka, has he come ?
Y: He is not coming in today.
S: There is no one here today, is there ?

<ruby>誰<rt>だれ</rt></ruby>も	no one
いない	is/are not

9B

Brown: Have you been reading anything lately ?

山田さんは	You
<ruby>最近<rt>さいきん</rt></ruby>	recently, these days
何か	some/anything
読んでいる	be reading

Yamada: I bought "Roots" (the one everybody is talking about) but I am swamped with homework and have not read it yet.

<ruby>例<rt>れい</rt></ruby>の	that (the one that you know)
——というの	the one called ____
買った	bought
<ruby>宿題<rt>しゅくだい</rt></ruby>	homework
多い	much/many
まだ	not yet, still
読んでいない	have not read

B: Is the homework for English ?

——って	____ that you say [informal]
英語	English

Y: Yes. They sure give a lot of it here, don't they ?

多い	much/many

B: You must have been playing <u>pachinko</u> all the time when you were in college in Japan.

パチンコ	<u>pachinko</u>, a pinball game
——ばかり	nothing but____
していた	was doing
でしょう	probably

Y: Oh, come on. What about you ? Are you reading anything ?

ひどいですね。もう。	How awful!

じゃ   then

B: Sure I am. There's TV Guide, and...

——とか   ____ and... (etc.)

Lesson 9 **Notes on Usage**

9B. (Nothing on 9 A)

1. 例の
<small>れい</small>

例 literally means "an example," but here it means "the one that everyone is talking about," "the one that everyone knows." It can be substituted by あの "that."

ねえ，山川さん。例のことですが，
<small>やまかわ</small> <small>れい</small>
どう思いますか。
<small>おも</small>

Say, Yamakawa-san. You know that thing we were talking about. What do you think about it?

2. 「ルーツ」というの   the one called Roots

Here の is equivalent to English "the one," "the one that's called Roots." In much the same way that the pronoun "one" replaces the word "book" in English (i. e. "the book called Roots"), の is a pronoun that replaces 本 (i.e. 「ルーツ」という本).
<small>ほん</small>
↓   ↓
one   の

の is used when its referent is obvious from the context, where the repetition of the same word needs to be avoided. (See drill 5)

3. 宿題が多くてまだ読んでいません。   I have a lot of homework, and I haven't
<small>しゅくだい</small>   read it yet.

て is used to connect two sentences. The semantic relationships between the two sentences vary. It could be sequential: "A" happens and then "B" happens after it (e.g. 朝，起きて，顔をあらいました。 "I got up in the morning and washed my face.") It could be simple listing of events or situations: e.g. この部屋は広くて明るいです。 "This room is spacious and light." or 中村さんは，日本人で背が低いです。 "Nakamura is a Japanese and he is short." It could also be a cause-effect relationship, which includes reason: e.g. 宿題が多くて，まだ読んでいません。 "There is a lot of homework, so (therefore) I have not read it yet," or 寮は夕方うるさくて，全然勉強できません。 "The dorm is noisy in the evening and so I cannot study at all."

4. 宿題って英語のですか。 By homework do you mean English homework?

って is a shortened colloquial form of ____ というのは which means "what you say/ call ____."

山川さんって誰。 Who's Yamakawa?

MIT って何。 What's MIT?

5. 多いですね。ここは宿題が。 There sure is a lot isn't there of homework here.

The normal word order is ここは宿題が多いですね。 Here Yamada is emphasizing the enormous amount of homework by reversing the normal order.

あついですね。今日は。 It's hot today, isn't it?

きれいですね。あなたの字は。 It's beautiful!···your handwriting.

6. ひどいですね。もう。 How mean!

もう means "already." It also means "any more" in a context like もう知りません. (lit. "I don't know any more!, i.e., I don't care any more!").

Here, one possible implication of もう is "I am not going to let you do any more to me."/"I am not going to tolerate this kind of treatment any longer." もう indicates that the speaker is pretty upset. Here Yamada is still friendly but at least in the style of the sentence she is pretending that she is angry and she turns the tables on Brown by saying じゃブラウンさんは,何か読んでいるんですか. ("Well, what about you? Are you reading anything?")

7. 「TV ガイド」とか… TV Guide, and...

とか is similar to や. That is, it is used when giving a partial random listing. (cf. と, exhaustive listing.) とか is used when the speaker is recalling things from his memory one by one.

テレグラフには,銀行とか,くつ屋とか,レストランなどがあります. On Telegraph there is a bank, some shoe stores, restaurants, and things like that.

Lesson 9 **Grammar Notes**

The main points of this lesson are:
  I. The V-teimasu construction form (stative and progressive meanings)
 II. The negative forms of V-teimasu construction.
III. Past tense of V-teimasu construction.
 IV. V-teimasu in relative clauses.
  V. How to say "something/nothing," "someone/no one," "somewhere/no where."
 VI. How to say "nothing but."
VII. How to say "already", "not yet."

I. Verb (te-form) ています

The て form of the verb is made just like the plain past tense except the final vowel, i.e. た or だ, is replaced by a て or で. Consult the table in L.5 Grammar Notes.

This pattern means either 1) the state resulting from a completed action exists, or will exist, over a period of time, or 2) an action is now or will be taking place over a period of time.

All verbs can have the first meaning, but only the action verbs, such as 書く (to write), 話す (to speak), 見る (to see), 食べる (to eat), etc., can have the second meaning, too.

The verbs of motion, which indicates motion from one place to another, 行く (to go), and 来る (to come), for example, can have only the first meaning.

A. Verbs that have only stative meaning in the V-teimasu construction

1. 行く	to go	6. 始まる	(something) begins
2. 来る	to come	7. 開く	(something) opens
3. 帰る	to return	8. 結婚する	to get married
4. いらっしゃる	to go/come/be	9. 混む	to get/become crowded
5. 住む	to live	10. おなかがすく	to get/become hungry

田中さんはサンフランシスコに行っています。

Tanaka has gone to San Francisco (and he is in S.F. now).

123

上田さんは学校に来ています。　Ueda has come to school. (So he is at school now.)

Here, the location marker for existence, に, is used as a direction marker because the person has arrived at a place and he is still there. (i.e. as a result of his going/coming he ended up being in/at the place.)

社会学のクラスは始まっています。　The sociology class has begun.

寮に住んでいます。　I am living in the dorms.

山田さんは大分飲んでいますね。　Yamada has had quite a bit to drink, hasn't he?

田中先生は，いろいろな本を読んでいます。　Professor Tanaka has read various books.

今日，図書館はあいていますか。　Is the library open today?

B. Verbs that have both stative and progressive meanings in the V-teimasu construction : Action Verbs

1. 取る	to take	11. 食べる	to eat
2. 飲む	to drink	12. 使う	to use
3. 書く	to write	13. 読む	to read
4. 作る	to make	14. 遊ぶ	to play
*5. 借りる	to borrow	15. 待つ	to wait
*6. 貸す	to lend	16. 話す	to speak
7. 見る	to see	17. 泳ぐ	to swim
8. 勉強する	to study	18. 聞く	to listen
9. 練習する	to practice	19. 買う	to buy
10. 復習する	to review		

* 借りている and 貸している can have both the stative and progressive meanings; they are most often used to describe a state.

山田さんは今本を読んでいます。　Yamada is reading a book now.

ほら，子どもたちがあそこで遊　Look. The children are playing over there.

んでいますよ。

ルームメートは，今図書館で勉強しています。 My roommate is studying at the library now.

雨がふっていますよ。 It's raining.

スミスさんはビールを飲んでいます。 Smith is drinking beer.

II. Negative forms of the stative and progressive forms

Verb (te-form) ていません

山川さんはまだ来ていません。 Yamakawa has not come yet.

私はその音楽を聞いていません。
1) I have not heard that music. (negation of "state")
2) I am not listening to that music. (negation of "action of progress")

III. Past tense forms of the above patterns

V (te-form) ていました

V (te-form) ていませんでした

昨日は一日中，雨がふっていました。 It was raining all day yesterday.

私は音楽を聞いていませんでした。
1) I had not heard that music. (stative)
2) I was not listening to that music. (progressive)

cf. わたしは音楽を聞きませんでした。 I did not listen to that music.

IV. V ている form in a relative clause

In a relative clause only the plain forms are used.

テレビを見ている人は田中さんです。 — The man who is watching TV is Tanaka.

新聞を読んでいた人は山田さんです。 — The man who was reading a paper is Yamada.

In multiple modification of a Noun

あそこで新聞を読んでいる，耳の大きい人はスパイです。 — That man with the big ears who is reading a paper over there is a spy.

When speaking, usually there is a slight pause between the modifying clauses.

V.　何か : something/anything

何も : not anything, nothing (always in a negative sentence)

誰か : someone/anyone

誰も : not anyone, no one (in negative)

どこか : somewhere

どこへも/どこにも : nowhere (in negative)

These forms are introduced in Lesson 3.

何か読んでいますか。 — Are you reading something ?

ええ，「エデンの東」を読んでいます。 — Yes, I am reading East of Eden.

いいえ，何も読んでいません。 — No, I am not reading anything.

誰か(を)待っているんですか。 — Are you waiting for someone ?

ええ，友だちを待っています。 — Yes, I am waiting for my friend.

いえ，誰も待っていません。 — No, I am not waiting for anyone.

VI. ばかり　　　　nothing but, exclusively

N ばかり V "V nothing but N"

新聞ばかり読んでいます。 — I read nothing but newspapers.

126

山田さんはレコードばかり聞い
ています。

Yamada listens to nothing but records.

<ruby>最近<rt>さいきん</rt></ruby>バーへばかり行っています。

Recently, I am going to nothing but bars.

<ruby>毎日<rt>まいにち</rt></ruby><ruby>図書館<rt>としょかん</rt></ruby>でばかり<ruby>勉強<rt>べんきょう</rt></ruby>してい
ます。

Everyday he is studying only at the library.

が and を disappear when ばかり is used with the noun.

VII. もう   already

まだ "not yet, still" (cf. GN 4, L. 5)

「ルーツ」はもう読みましたか。

Have you already read Roots?

いいえ，まだ読んでいません。

No, I have not read it yet.

いいえ，まだです。

No, not yet.

			ている form			
			Non-Past		Past	
			Plain	Polite	Plain	Polite
V	Ru-Verb たべる	Af.	たべている	たべています	たべていた	たべていました
		Neg.	たべていない	たべていません	たべていなかった	たべていませんでした
	U-Verb かく	Af.	かいている	かいています	かいていた	かいていました
		Neg.	かいていない	かいていません	かいていなかった	かいていませんでした
	Ir. する	Af.	している	しています	していた	していました
		Neg.	していない	していません	していなかった	していませんでした
	Ir. いく	Af.	いっている	いっています	いっていた	いっていました
		Neg.	いっていない	いっていません	いっていなかった	いっていませんでした
	Ir. くる	Af.	きている	きています	きていた	きていました
		Neg.	きていない	きていません	きていなかった	きていませんでした

127

第九課　漢字

英語　　　　語　　　　日本　　　　中国　　　　国
えい ご　　　ご　　　　に ほん　　　ちゅう ごく　　くに

英語　　　　フランス語　　日本　　　　　中国　　　　　国

新聞　　　　住む　　　　使う　　　　作る　　　　多い
しん ぶん　　す　　　　　つか　　　　つく　　　　おお

新聞　　　　住む　　　　使う　　　　　作る　　　　多い

聞く　　　　開く　　　　　　　祖父　　　　祖母
き　　　　　あ　　　　　　　　そ ふ　　　　そ ぼ

聞く　　　　開く　　　　　　　祖父　　　　　祖母

128

第　十　課

10 A

ウェイトレス	いらっしゃい。
スミス	何がいいですか。
山田	そうですね。私はうなぎにします。うなぎはすきですか。
スミス	一度日本から来た友だちのうちで食べたことがありますが，あまりすきじゃありません。私はさしみにします。

(to the waitress)

山田	じゃあ，さしみとうなぎをください。
ウェイトレス	さしみは上と並がありますが…
山田	並にしてください。
ウェイトレス	並は切れています。
スミス	山田さん出ましょうか。

10 B

店員	いらっしゃいませ。
山田	万年筆をください。
スミス	山田さんが使うんですか。
山田	いえ，東京の友だちに送るんです。
店員	これはいかがでしょう。
山田	あ，これはいいですね。これを一本ください。すみませんが早くつつんでくださいませんか。急いでいますから…
店員	はい，承知いたしました。

1 例1 T: 部屋，しずかだ
         S: 部屋はしずかでした。
   例2 T: あの映画，いい
         S: あの映画はよかったです。
   例3 T: 食堂，食べる
         S: 食堂で食べました。   ⎫
                                      ⎬ 第四課の復習
   例4 T: 山田さん，学生   ⎪
         S: 山田さんは学生でした。 ⎭

1. 英語の試験，難しい
2. あの建物，りっぱだ
3. これ，妹の部屋
4. きのう，日曜日
5. バス，ヨセミテ，行く
6. 山田さんのアパート，広い
7. 寮，にぎやかだ
8. うち，テレビ，見る
9. あれ，私のアパート
10. 山田先生，アメリカ，いらっ
    しゃる

11. この車，高い
12. ここ，犬，いる
13. スミスさん，元気だ
14. この公園，きれいだ
15. この辞書，やすい
16. 昔のバークレー，しずかだ
17. この本，おもしろい
18. きのうの宿題，やさしい
19. あの店のすきやき，まずい
20. あの店，おいしい

2 例1 T: 文学のクラス，難しい
         ⎧S₁: 文学のクラスは難しかったですか。
         ⎨
         ⎩S₂: いえ，難しくありませんでした。
   例2 T: 公園，きれいだ
         ⎧S₁: 公園はきれいでしたか。
         ⎨
         ⎩S₂: いえ，きれいじゃありませんでした。

130

1. その辞書，高い
2. あのレストランのビフテキ，おいしい
3. 図書館，しずかだ
4. きのうの宿題，やさしい
5. この車，やすい
6. あの映画，おもしろい
7. ヨセミテ，滝，見る
8. 京都，見る
9. その人，アメリカ人
10. 寮，うるさい
11. ブラウンさん，まじめな学生
12. ブラウンさん，まじめだ
13. 昨日の新聞，読む
14. 宿題，多い
15. アパート，しずかだ
16. スミスさん，ハンサムだ
17. スミスさん，元気だ
18. 昔のテレグラフ，にぎやかだ
19. その本，難しい
20. その本，便利だ

③ 例1 T: さしみ，好きだ

$\begin{cases}\text{S}_1: & \text{何が好きですか。} \\ \text{S}_2: & \text{さしみが好きです。}\end{cases}$

例2 T: テニス，する，好きだ

$\begin{cases}\text{S}_1: & \text{何が好きですか。} \\ \text{S}_2: & \text{テニスをするのが好きです。}\end{cases}$

1. うなぎ，好きだ
2. ヨセミテ，好きだ
3. 犬，きらいだ
4. 日本語，上手だ
5. 山田さん，好きだ
6. クラス，行く，きらいだ
7. 田中さん，中国語，うまい
8. 漢字，書く，きらいだ
9. 映画，見る，好きだ
10. スミスさん，フランス語，うまい
11. 山田さん，テニス，する，好きだ
12. 日曜日，ゴルフ，する，好きだ
13. 漢字，下手だ
14. スミスさん，箸，食べる，上手だ
15. 日本風のレストラン，食べる，

　　　　好きだ　　　　　　　　　　む，好きだ

16.　ブラウンさん，スポーツ，下　　18.　田中さん，漢字,書く,上手だ
　　　手だ　　　　　　　　　　　　19.　寮，きらいだ
17.　サンフランシスコのバー，飲　　20.　漢字，好きだ

④　例1　T:　ヨセミテへ行ったことがありますか。（ヨセミテ）
　　　　　S:　ええ，行ったことがあります。
　　例2　T:　心理学をとったことがありますか。（社会学）
　　　　　S:　いえ，心理学はとったことがありませんが，社会学はとっ
　　　　　　　たことがあります。

1.　このレコードを聞いたことが　　　　ますか。（ドイツ）
　　　あります。（このレコード）　　7.　箸で食べたことがありますか。
2.　日本語をとったことがありま　　　　（箸）
　　　すか。（中国語）　　　　　　8.　バートでサンフランシスコへ
3.　日本へ行ったことがあります　　　　行ったことがありますか。
　　　か。（日本）　　　　　　　　　　（バス）
4.　ゴールテンゲートパークを見　　9.　ヨセミテの滝を見たことがあ
　　　たことがありますか。（橋）　　　りますか。（ニューヨークの
5.　中国の映画を見たことがあり　　　　滝）
　　　ますか。（日本の映画）　　　10.　日本のビールを飲んだことが
6.　フランスへ行ったことがあり　　　　ありますか。（ドイツの）

⑤　例　T:　ウイスキー
　　　　{S₁:　私はウイスキーにします。ウイスキーが好きですか。
　　　　{S₂:　ええ，きらいじゃありません，私もウイスキーにします。

1. うなぎ
2. コーヒー
3. クールズ
4. コーラ
5. 日本茶(ちゃ)

6. ワイン
7. アイスクリーム
8. スープ
9. お酒(さけ)
10. すきやき

6　例1　T: 早い，包(つつ)む
　　　　　S: 早く包んでくださいませんか。
　　例2　T: 静かだ，する
　　　　　S: 静かにしてくださいませんか。

1. いい，読む
2. 早い，行く
3. やさしい，する
4. 静かだ，する
5. きれいだ，包(つつ)む

6. きれいだ，書く
7. にぎやかだ，する
8. 安い，する
9. いい，見る
10. 早い，来る

7　例　T: 友だちとあのレストランで食べました。
　　　　S: 友だちと食べたのはあのレストランです。

1. 昨日あの映画(えいが)を見ました。
2. 第三課(だいかしけん)の試験は難しかったです。
3. 山田さんは漢字(かんじ)が下手でした。
4. この本はおもしろかったです。
5. ブラウン先生は歌(うた)が上手でした。
6. あの二人は今週(こんしゅう)クラスに来ま

せんでした。
7. あの人はどこへも行きませんでした。
8. あの建物(たてもの)は食堂(しょくどう)でした。
9. 岡野(おかの)さんは何も食べませんでした。
10. 今年(ことし)，田中さんは日本へ帰りました。

133

⑧　例 1　T: ヨセミテ, 行く, 明日

　　　{S₁: いつヨセミテへ行きますか。

　　　{S₂: 明日行くつもりです。(controllable) (cf., L. 4, GN IV)

　　例 2　T: 英語のクラス, 始まる, 二日

　　　{S₁: 英語のクラスはいつ始まりますか。(uncontrollable)

　　　{S₂: 二日に始まります。

1.　映画を見る, 明日
2.　日本語の辞書, 買う, 今日
3.　うち, 帰る, 今
4.　日本語のクラス, 始まる, 二日
5.　国, 帰る, 十月
6.　文学のクラス, 始まる, 午後一時
7.　銀行, 開く, 午前十時
8.　映画, 始まる, 午後七時
9.　カメラ, 買う, 昨日
10.　ヨセミテ, 行く, あさって
11.　ヨーロッパ, 行く, きのう
12.　宿題, する, 今
13.　ゴールデンゲート, 見る, 日曜日
14.　社会学のクラス, 始まる, 午後二時
15.　「セイフウェイ」, 開く, 午前八時

Lesson 10　Dialogues

10 A

Waitress: Welcome!

　いらっしゃい　　　　　　　　　　Welcome!

Smith: What are you going to have?

　いい　　　　　　　　　　　　　　good

Yamada: Let's see. I'll have the <u>unagi</u>. Do you like <u>unagi?</u>

うなぎ	eel
すき	like, fond of

S: I had it once at the house of a friend from Japan, but I don't care much for it. I'll have the sashimi.

一度 (いちど)	once
友だち	friend
食べた	have eaten, ate
＿＿ことがある	have an experience of <u>V</u>-ing
あまり	not so much
さしみ	sashimi

Y: Well, we'll have the sashimi and the unagi.

＿＿をください	Please give (me/us)＿＿

W: The sashimi comes in deluxe or regular.

上 (じょう)	deluxe, better
並 (なみ)	regular

Y: The regular, please.

＿＿にしてください	Please make (it) ＿＿

W: We're all out of the regular.

切れている (き)	cut, out of stock

S: Yamadasan, let's leave? shall we ?

出ましょう	Let's leave, get out.

10 B

Clerk: Welcome. (may I help you)

いらっしゃいませ

Yamada: I want to buy a fountain pen. (please give me a fountain pen)

万年筆（をください）(まんねんひつ)	fountain pen (please show me)

Smith: Are you going to use it?

使う   use

Y: No, I'm going to send it to a friend in Tokyo.

送る   send

C: How about this one?

Y: This one is fine. I'll take one. Could you do me a favor and wrap it up right away? I'm in a hurry.

一本 （いっぽん）   one (long thing)

すみませんが…   Excuse me, but could you do me the favor of...

早く   quickly

つつむ   to wrap

急いでいます   I'm in a hurry.

C: Yes, certainly

Lesson 10   Notes on Usage

10 A

1. いらっしゃい "Welcome!" A greeting to a visitor, a guest, or a customer.
   e.g. At Smith's house: Yamakawa is at the door.

   Y: ごめんください。   Y: Hello.

   S: はあい (He opens the door.)   S: Yes. (Just a minute.)

   Y: こんにちは。   Y: Hello!

   S: ああ，山川（やまかわ）さん。いらっしゃい。   S: Oh, Yamakawa-san. Welcome! Please come in.
   さあどうぞ，おはいりください。

   Y: じゃ，ちょっとしつれいします。   Y: Well, then, excuse me.

   e.g. At a restaurant: A customer walks in.

136

Waiter: いらっしゃい。   W: Welcome!
Customer: (nods)

いらっしゃいませ is the more polite form of the above.

2. 何がいいですか。

Literally it means "What is good?" or "What do you think is good?" At a restaurant it is often used by one restaurant goer to another. i.e. "What do you like?" or "What are you going to have?"

When a customer wants to ask the waitress what is good at the restaurant, he would say 何がおいしいですか。 that is, "What is delicious?"

3. あまり   (not) so much

スペイン語はあまり上手じゃあ   I'm not very good at Spanish.
りません。

映画はあまり見ません。   I don't see movies very much/often.

山川さんはあまり食べません。   Yamakawa does not eat much.

昨日あまり勉強しませんでした。 I didn't study much yesterday.

4. 上, 並

上 means "up" or "above" and 並 means "regular". Here じょう means "deluxe" or "super" though the term usually refers to quality rather than quantity. In the case of sashimi, じょう is the one that has more varieties of fish than the なみ, which consists of only one kind of fish, tuna.

5. 切れています。

Literally, it means that it is "cut." Here it means that the sashimi is "out of stock." Since the なみ sashimi requires fewer kinds of fish than the じょう, it does not make sense to say that the なみ is out of stock when they can serve the じょう.

6. 出ましょうか。

Smith is suggesting that they leave the restaurant because the restaurant does not want to serve the cheaper regular sashimi.

10 B

1. これはいかがでしょう。

How about this one?
How do you like this one?

The question marker か is often unsaid when it is obvious that the speaker is asking a question. So the full sentence of the above is これはいかがでしょうか.

でしょう literally means "probably" or it indicates uncertainty, but when it is used in a question it makes the question sound soft, hence polite.

これは本でしょうか。（↘）

Is this a book? (a more polite form of これは本ですか)

これは何でしょうか。（↘）

What is this?

あの方はどなたでしょうか。（↘）

Who is that person?

2. すみませんが…

Excuse me but (could I ask a favor of you...?) (cf. Useful Expressions L. 1)

すみません means "I'm sorry" or "Excuse me." Here, however, it means "I am sorry to trouble you, but...," hence it means "Could I ask a favor of you?" or "Could you do me a favor?"

3. 承知^{しょうち}いたしました。

Literally it means "I (humbly) understand it," or "I am aware of it." Hence in this context it means "Certainly!," "All right!," or "Very well!" It is used in a formal situation by a sales clerk to a customer, or to his boss.

Lesson 10 **Grammar Notes**

The main points of this lesson are:
  I. Past tense of Adjectives, Adjectival Nouns and Nouns.
 II. How to say "I decide on____."
III. Adverbs.
 IV. How to say "X likes/dislikes Y," "X is good/bad at Y."
  V. How to say "There was a time when" "I have (had the experience of)."

138

I. Past tense of Adjectives, Adjectival Nouns and Nouns: (See chart in Lesson 5 Grammar Notes.)

Adjectives: (e.g. 大^{おお}きい)

-て form	Affirmative		Negative	
	おおきくて		おおきくなくて	
	Plain form	Polite form	Plain form	Polite form
Non-Past	おおきい	おおきいです	おおきくない	おおき {くありません／(くないです)}
Past	おおきかった	おおきかったです	おおきくなかった	おおき {くありませんでした／(くなかったです)}

Adjectival Nouns: (e.g. しずかだ)

Nouns: (e.g. 学生)

-で form	しずかで がくせいで		しずかで(は)なくて／じゃなくて がくせいで(は)なくて／じゃなくて	
	Plain form	Polite form	Plain form	Polite form
Non-Past	しずかだ (しずかなＮ) がくせいだ (がくせいのＮ)	しずかです がくせいです	しずか {で(は)／じゃ} ない がくせい {で(は)／じゃ} ない	しずか {では／じゃ} ありません がくせい {では／じゃ} ありません
Past	しずかだった がくせいだった	しずかでした がくせいでした	しずか {で(は)／じゃ} なかった がくせい {で(は)／じゃ} なかった	しずか {では／じゃ} ありませんでした がくせい {では／じゃ} ありませんでした

よい／いい： good

いい is a variation of よい used in conversation. It is restricted to the Non-Past affirmative forms only.

	Affirmative		Negative	
	Plain form	Polite form	Plain form	Polite form
Non-Past	よい いい	いいです	よくない	｛よくありません （よくないです）
Past	よかった	よかったです	よくなかった	｛よくありませんでした （よくなかったです）

Just like other adjectives, the plain forms are used to modify a noun.

e.g. ｛よい
　いい｝本　　よくない本

II. Noun にします　　　　　　　　　　　　　decide on N

何にしますか。　　　　　　　　　　　What will you have?
　　　　　　　　　　　　　　　　　　　(Lit. "What will you decide on?")

（私は）さしみにします。　　　　　　I will have sashimi.
　　　　　　　　　　　　　　　　　　　(Lit. "I will decide on sashimi.")

何がいいですか。　　　　　　　　　　What would you like?

（私は）コーヒーにします。　　　　　I will have coffee.

This pattern is used when choosing from several alternatives, whether specified or unspecified.

Note: this can also be used to say:

（私は）さしみです。　　　　　　　　"I will have sashimi." (cf. L. 2)

III. Adverbs

A. Adverbs derived from Adjectives:

早い……早く　　　　　　　　　　　Drop the final い of an adjective and add く to the root.

安い……安く

いい……よく

早くつつんでください。	Please wrap it up quickly.
今日は早く起きました。	Today, I got up early.
安くしてください。	Please make it cheaper.
よく勉強してください。	Please study hard. (Lit. "a lot," "well")
よく勉強しましたか。	Did you study well?

B. Adverbs derived from Adjectival Nouns:

静かだ……静かに	Drop the だ, then add に.
きれいだ……きれいに	
子供が寝ていますから静かにしてください。	The child is sleeping so please be quiet.
きれいにしてください。	Please make it nice. Please clean (this) up.
きれいにつつんでください。	Please wrap it nicely.

IV. Topic は Object が

好きです	Topic likes Object
嫌いです	____ hates/dislikes _____
上手です	____ is good at _____
下手です	____ is bad at _____
うまいです	____ is good at _____

The verbs that indicate one's emotion, ability, or desire (see lesson 13), such as すきだ like, きらいだ dislike or hate, じょうずだ skillful, へただ unskillful, etc., usually take が as their object marker. Note: うまい good, is frequently used in colloquial speech.

私はさしみが好きです。	I like sashimi.
山本さんは，犬が嫌いです。	Yamamoto hates dogs.
ブラウンさんは日本語が上手です。	Brown is good at Japanese.
ブラウンさんはテニスがうまいです。	Ms. Brown is good at tennis.

The object slot may be filled by a verb, which takes the form of <u>Verb (Plain form)</u> + の.

田中さんはテニスをするのが下   Tanaka is poor at (playing) tennis.
手です。

わたしは，日曜日に勉強する   I hate studying on Sunday.
のが嫌いです。

V. <u>Sentence (Plain Past tense)</u> ことがあります

    V—た
    A—かった   There was a time when ＿＿＿
    AN—だった   I have had the experience of ＿＿＿
    N—だった

This pattern means "There was a time ＿＿＿" Hence, when the subject is a person it can mean "Have the experience of ＿＿＿."

ニューヨークへ行ったことがあ   Have you ever been to New York?
りますか。

ドルが高かったことがあります。   There was a time when the dollar was worth more.

山田さんは先生だったことがあ   Yamada was once a teacher.
ります。

聞いたことはありますが，見た   I have heard about it but I have never
ことはありません。   seen it.

142

第十課　漢字

東京
とう　きょう
東京

手紙
て　がみ
手紙

友達
とも　だち
友達

貸 す
か
貸す

借 りる
か
借りる

出 す
だ
出す

出 る
で
出る

送 る
おく
送る

急 ぐ
いそ
急ぐ

早 い
はや
早い

便 利 だ
べん　り
便利だ

不 便 だ
ふ　べん
不便だ

難 しい
むずか
難しい

好 き だ
す
好きだ

第　十　一　課

11　A　本田先生　　スミスさんは日本語のほかに何を勉強しました
　　　　　　　　　　か。

　　　　スミス　　　スペイン語を勉強しました。

　　　　本田　　　　どうしてスペイン語にしたんですか。

　　　　スミス　　　高校の時ガールフレンドがメキシコ人だったか
　　　　　　　　　　らです。

　　　　本田　　　　あ，そうですか。で，日本語とスペイン語とど
　　　　　　　　　　ちらがむずかしいですか。

　　　　スミス　　　それはスペイン語の方がずっとやさしいと思い
　　　　　　　　　　ます。スペイン語は漢字がありませんから。

11　B　ブラウン　　山田さん，ちかごろ勉強はどうですか。

　　　　山田　　　　それはもちろん朝から晩まで勉強ばかりしてい
　　　　　　　　　　ますよ。

　　　　ブラウン　　じゃＡばかりでしょう。

　　　　山田　　　　それが実はＣばかりなんです。Ｄもあるんです。

　　　　ブラウン　　どうしてですか。また机の前で寝てばかりいる
　　　　　　　　　　んでしょう。

　　　　山田　　　　ブラウンさんじゃありませんよ。でもほんとう
　　　　　　　　　　はちょっとホームシックなんです。東京の彼か
　　　　　　　　　　ら手紙が来ないんです。

1　例1　T:　スペイン語，日本語，やさしい

　　　　　S₁:　スペイン語と日本語とどちらがやさしいですか。

　　　　　S₂:　スペイン語の方が（日本語より）やさしいです。

　　例2　T:　スポーツをします，映画を見ます，楽しい

　　　　　S₁:　スポーツをするのと映画を見るのとどちらが楽しいですか。

　　　　　S₂:　スポーツをする方が（映画を見るより）楽しいです。

1.　バート，バス，便利だ

2.　寮，アパート，好きだ

3.　サンフランシスコ，バークレー，大きい

4.　映画を見ます，レコードを聞きます，楽しい

5.　日本語，中国語，難しい

6.　キャデラック，ベンツ，たかい

7.　サンフランシスコ，バークレー，すずしい

8.　お茶，コーヒー，好きだ

9.　泳ぎます，山登りをします，楽しい

10.　学校へバスで行きます，車で行きます，速い

2　例1　T:　日本語，スペイン語，フランス語，難しい

　　　　　S₁:　日本語とスペイン語とフランス語の中でどれが一番難しいですか。

　　　　　S₂:　日本語が一番難しいです。

　　例2　T:　レコードを聞く，テレビを見る，映画を見る，好きだ

　　　　　S₁:　レコードを聞くのとテレビを見るのと映画を見るのとではどれが一番好きですか。

　　　　　S₂:　レコードを聞くのが一番好きです。

1.　心理学，社会学，経済学，おもしろい

2.　日本料理，フランス料理，中華料理，おいしい

3.　スキーをする，テニスをする，ゴルフをする，好きだ

4. ビール，ウイスキー，ワイン，
　　好きだ

5. 日本語を書く，日本語を読む，
　　日本語を話す，やさしい

6. 寝る，遊ぶ，食べる，好きだ

7. 山田さん，ブラウンさん，ス
　　ミスさん，まじめだ

8. 泳ぐ，山登りをする，のんび
　　りする，楽しい

9. 日本料理を作る，フランス料
　　理を作る，中華料理を作る，
　　難しい

10. 学校へバスで行く，バートで
　　行く，車で行く，速い

③ 例1 T: 行く
　　　　 S: 行ってばかりいます。

　　 例2 T: 本を読む
　　　　 S: 本ばかり読んでいます。

1. 話す
2. 遊ぶ
3. 映画を見る
4. テニスをする
5. 来る
6. テレビを見る
7. 勉強する
8. 行く

9. 宿題をする
10. 食べる
11. バーボンを飲む
12. うちにいる
13. 急ぐ
14. レコードを聞く
15. パンを食べる
16. 飲む

④ 例 T: まだ起きています，明日試験があります
　　　 S₁: どうしてまだ起きているんですか。
　　　 S₂: 明日試験があるからです。

1. 行きません，お金がありません。

2. ドイツ語を取りません，難しいです。

3. 遅刻した，朝ねぼうした。

4. 今日クラスへ行きません，風邪を引いています。

5. パンばかり食べている，お金がない。

6. うなぎにしませんでした，きらいです。

7. このアパートを借りました。しずかです。

8. 中国語を取りませんでした，難しいです。

9. 数学ばかり取っています，専門にしました。

10. アスピリンを飲んでいます，頭が痛いです。

11. 遅刻しました，車の事故がありました。

12. ピクニックをしませんでした，雨が降っていました。

13. 部屋を掃除しています，お客が来ます。

14. 古い車を買いました，新しい車を買うお金がありませんでした。

15. 食事しません，時間がありません。

---

5 例1 T: 山田さんは行きますか。（はい）

　　 S: はい，行くと思いますが……

　 例2 T: この本は難しいですか。（いいえ）

　　 S: いいえ，難しくないと思いますが……

1. ブラウンさんの車は新しいですか。（はい）

2. スペイン語は難しいですか。（いいえ）

3. あの方は先生ですか。（いいえ）

4. 山川さんはもう帰りましたか。（はい）

5. 郵便はもう来ていますか。（はい）

6. バートは便利ですか。（いいえ）

7. 山田さんは今日テニスをします
か。（はい）

8. 先生は今日いらっしゃいます
か。（はい）

9. あのレストランは今混んでい
ますか。（いいえ）

10. 銀行は今日開いていますか。
（はい）

11. あの建物は寮ですか。（はい）

12. 山田さんは日本語が上手です
か。（いいえ）

13. あのレストランは高いですか。
（いいえ）

14. 寮の部屋はせまいですか。
（はい）

15. スミス先生はもういらっしゃ
っていますか。（はい）

16. 田中さん新しいテレビを買い
ますか。（はい）

17. 会話のクラスは二日に始まり
ますか。（はい）

18. スミスさんはもうゴールデン
ゲートを見ましたか。（はい）

19. あそこにいらっしゃる方はブ
ラウン先生ですか。（はい）

20. 山田さんはもう買物をしまし
たか。（はい）

6 例 T: フランス，行く

S₁: どこへ行きましたか。

S₂: フランスへ行きました。

S₁: そのほかにどこかへ行きましたか。

S₂: いいえ，フランスだけです。

1. 文学，とる
2. 新聞，読む
3. テニス，する
4. 数学，とる
5. てんぷら，食べる

6. ニューヨーク，行く
7. ワイン，飲む
8. 和英辞典，買う
9. 公園，行く
10. ゴルフ，する

Lesson 11 **Dialogues**

11A

Prof. Honda: What did you study besides Japanese?
Smith: I studied Spanish.
H: Why did you decide on Spanish?

> どうして   why

S: Because my girlfriend in high school was Mexican.

> 高校   high school
>
> メキシコ人   Mexican

H: Oh, I see...Incidentally, which is more difficult, Japanese or Spanish?

> で   a variant of それで, "and"
>
> どちら   which

S: Of course I think Spanish is much easier. Because Spanish doesn't have any <u>kanji</u>.

> 方   Lit., "side"
>
> ずっと   by far, considerably
>
> …から   because

11B

Brown: How are your studies going these days?

> 近ごろ   these days, recently

Yamada: Well, naturally all I do is study from morning till night!

> 晩   late evening, night

B: Then you must be getting straight A's.

> じゃ   a variant of それじゃ, "well then."

Y: Well, actually, all I'm getting is C's. I even have some D's.

ばかり	only

B: I wonder why. You must be dozing off at your desk as usual.

また	again
寝る	to sleep

Y: I'm not like you, you know! Actually I'm a little homesick. I haven't gotten a letter from my boyfriend in Tokyo in a while.

でも	a variant of けれども, "however," "but."
ほんとうは	actually
ホームシック	homesick
彼	my boyfriend (Lit., "he")

Lesson 11 Notes on Usage

11A

1. 日本語のほかに "other than (or besides) the Japanese language"

   1) 日本語のほかに何を勉強しましたか。　What did you study besides Japanese?

   2) 山本さんのほかに誰もいません。　There is no one other than Yamamoto.

2. どうしてスペイン語にしたんですか。　Why did you study Spanish? (Lit. "Why did you decide on (choose) Spanish?")

した is the plain past tense form of する (します). See Notes on Usage for Lesson 10 for the explanation of にする (にします).

3. ガールフレンド Here this means "girlfriend." But in Japanese, ガールフレンド simply means a boy's female friend, (and not his steady) or a girl's female friend.

4. あ，そうですか。で 日本語とスペイン語とどちらが難しいですか。
で is a shortened form of それで "and" or ところで "by the way." Here it means "By the way."
e.g.

Yamada:	昨日はバートが来なくてこまりました。	Y: Yesterday BART was late and inconvenienced me. (Lit., "BART didn't come and I was in trouble)
Brown;	ああバートはあてになりませんね。で どうしたんですか。	B: Oh, BART is so unreliable. And what did you do?
Y:	しかたがないから来るまでまちました。	Y: There was nothing I could do so I waited till it finally came.

5. それは

それは literally means "that" but here it means "of course," or "needless to say."

スペイン語と日本語とどちらがやさしいですか。   Which is easier, Spanish or Japanese?

それはスペイン語の方がやさしいですよ。   Of course Spanish is easier.

6. ずっと

It has two meanings: (1) "by far" and (2) "continuously, without interruption." In ずっとやさしい it means "by far."

e.g. ずっとやさしいです	It's much easier.
ずっと難しいです	It's much harder.
ずっと大きいです	It's much bigger.

7. と思います   I think ____.

This does not mean he is not sure. It is just a matter of style. Thus, even though the speaker is sure of what he is saying, it still sounds better to say と思います. (This may explain why many Japanese say "I think ____" in English.)

11B

1. ちかごろ   recently

最近 means the same thing but is a Chinese word, and so sounds a little formal. (cf. Dialogue B L. 8)

2. 朝から晩まで   from morning till night

朝から晩までテレビばかり見ています。   I do nothing but watch T.V. from morning to night.

3. じゃ（では）   Well, then, in that case etc.

朝から晩まで勉強ばかりしています。   I've been studying from morning till night.

じゃＡばかりでしょう。   Well, then, you must be getting all A's.

4. それが It is usually followed by 実は "actually."

5. 実は Literally, this means "the fact is," "to tell the truth." In English the phrase, "to tell the truth" is usually used to clarify a given situation. In the following example, 実は has the same meaning.

e.g. それが実はＣばかりなんです。   Actually, to tell the truth, I've been getting all C's.

However, 実は is most often used to mark the beginning of the real topic of conversation as in the following example:

e.g. Yamada is visiting Tanaka. After a routine exchange of greetings and unimportant comments on what is happening in the world, they begin to speak about what brought Yamada to see Tanaka.

T: で　御用件は。   T: And what brings you here today?

Y: はあ，実はこの六月に娘が結婚いたしますので…   Y: Well, my daughter is getting married in June, so...

153

6. また寝てばかりいるんでしょう。 Literally, また means "again," but here it does not really have any great significance and merely carries the connotation of "as usual."

Some examples of the usage of また：

山川さんはまた変なことを言っています。

Yamakawa is saying something strange (again) as usual.

またつくえの前で寝てばかりいるんでしょう.

You must be dozing off at your desk as usual.

Brown does not seriously mean that Yamada is sleeping all the time.

7. ブラウンさんじゃありませんよ。 "I'm not you (Brown さん)," or "I'm not like you." Here, the implication is that you (Brown) may be taking naps at the desk, but I am not like you.

8. でも   but, however
でも is an informal variant of けれども。

でも　ほんとうはちょっとホームシックなんです。

But really (the fact is) I'm a little home-sick.

9. ほんとうは   the truth is
While 実は, "the fact is," can be used to mark the beginning of the real topic of conversation, ほんとうは, "the truth is," cannot be used in this manner. ほんとうは is closer in meaning to "to tell the truth" and is used to correct misconceptions and/or to reveal the true facts of a given situation.

10. 彼   he

This means a girl's boyfriend or sweetheart. A boy's girlfriend or sweetheart is 彼女 (かのじょ)

Lesson 11 Grammar Notes

The main points of this lesson are:
I. Comparisons

154

I. Comparisons

A. Nouns

Question: <u>A</u> と <u>B</u> と （では） どちら （の方） が <u>X</u> ですか。

Which is <u>X</u>-er, <u>A</u> or <u>B</u>?

ねこと犬とではどちら（の方）が
かわいいですか。

Which is cuter, a cat or a dog?

フットボールはバークレーと
UCLA と （では） どちらが強い
んですか。

Who is stronger in football, Cal or
UCLA?

Answer or Statement: (<u>A</u> と <u>B</u> とでは) <u>A</u> の方が (<u>B</u> より) <u>X</u> です。

(As for <u>A</u> and <u>B</u>,) <u>A</u> is <u>X</u>-er (than <u>B</u>).

When it is obvious from the context, the elements in the parentheses may be omitted.

ねこの方がかわいいです。

Cats are cuter.

UCLA の方が強いです。

UCLA is stronger.

フットボールは (バークレーと
UCLA とでは) UCLA の方が
バークレーより強いです。

As for football, UCLA is stronger than
Cal.

B. Verbs

When comparing two actions or states, it is necessary to first change them into nominal
phrases.

Question: <u>Verb₁ (Plain form)</u> のと <u>Verb₂</u> のと （では） どちら（の方）が <u>X</u> で
すか。

Which do you <u>X</u> more <u>V₁</u> or <u>V₂</u>?

155

スポーツをするのと映画を見る
のとではどちらが楽しいですか。

Which do you enjoy more, (playing) sports or (going to the) movies?

Answer or Statement: V_1 (Plain form) 方が (V_2 より), X です。

I X V_1 more than V_2.

スポーツをする方が（映画を見
るより）楽しいです。

I enjoy (playing) sports more than (going to the) movies.

II. Superlatives (three or more) the best of, the most ____

A. Nouns

Question:

A と B と C の中で $\begin{cases} \text{どれが一番 } X \text{ ですか。} \\ \text{だれが} \\ \text{どこが} \end{cases}$
（とでは）

Which is the most X, (X-est) A, B, or C?'

――の中で   among ____

一番   the most, the best

一番大きい   the largest

一番おいしい   the most delicious

これは大学で一番大きい図書
館です。

This is the largest library in the university.

スミスさんはクラスで一番よく
できます。

Smith is the best student in the class.

ねこと犬と象の中でどれが一番
好きですか。

Which do you like best, cats, dogs, or elephants?

ねこが一番好きです。   I like cats best.

Answer or Statement: A が一番 X です。 I X A the best!

ねこが一番好きです。   I like cats best.

156

B. Verbs

As with comparisons three or more actions or states must be changed into nominal phrases in a superlative structure.

Question: <u>V₁</u> (plain form) のと <u>V₂</u> のと <u>V₃</u> のとではどれが一番 <u>X</u> ですか.
Which is the most <u>X</u>, <u>V₁</u>, <u>V₂</u> or <u>V₃</u>?

スキーをするのとテニスをする のと泳ぐのとではどれが一番好 きですか。
Which do you like the most, skiing, playing tennis, or swimming?

Answer or Statement: <u>V₁</u> (<u>V₂</u>/<u>V₃</u>) のが一番 <u>X</u> です。
I <u>X</u> <u>V₁</u> (<u>V₂</u>/<u>V₃</u>) the most

スキーをするのが一番好きです。
I like skiing the most.

III. Reasons and Causes

Question: どうして/なぜ <u>Sentence (Plain form)</u> { の / ん } ですか. Why _____ ?

どうして
Why?! (Colloquial, informal. Used among friends.)

どうしてですか。
Why is that? (formal)

どうしてスペイン語にしたんで すか。
Why did you take Spanish? (Lit. Why did you decide on Spanish?)

どうしてそんなに食べるんです か。
Why do you eat so much?

どうしてねこの方が好きなんで すか。
Why do you like cats (better than other animals?)

Answer: <u>Sentence (Plain form)</u> からです。
Because _____ .

から basically means "from," that is, the explanation or reason comes from _____ or "because of this reason." Here it means "because" or "the reason is." から is used to make the reasons explicit by spelling them out. Thus, から has the nuance of "This is the reason why" whereas のです is used to give reasons covertly. のです does not mean "this is the reason why" but rather "it is the case that _____ ."

157

どうしてスペイン語にしたんですか。	Why did you take Spanish ?
ガールフレンドがメキシコ人だったからです。	…Because my girlfriend was a Mexican.
どうしてまだ起きているんですか。	Why are you still up ?
明日試験があるからです。	…(Because) I've got an exam tomorrow. (on a rainy day)
どうして学校へ行かないんですか。	Why aren't you going to school ?
かさがないからです。	…Because I don't have an umbrella.

While のです can be used in questions such as どうしてそらは青いんですか ("Why is the sky blue?") or あたまがいたいんですか ("Is it the case that you have a headache?"), etc., からです cannot be used in the same way. Of course it can be used in a question like "Is it because you came by Bart?", バートで来たからですか, which asks whether the speaker is correct in assuming that the reason why the addressee was late for class is because he came by Bart.

IV. Verb (te-form) てばかりいます。   Do nothing but V

主人は近ごろ寝てばかりいます。	My husband is always sleeping these days.
うちでは食べてばかりいます。	I do nothing but eat at home.
あの人はさっきから笑ってばかりいます。	That person has done nothing but laugh for the last few minutes.
うちの人はテレビを見てばかりいるんですよ。	All my husband does is watch TV. (complaining to a friend)
この夏は日本語を勉強してばかりいます。	This summer all I've been doing is studying Japanese.

V. Sentence (Plain form) と思います。　　　I think that _____

あしたもここに来ると思います。　　I think I'll come here tomorrow, too.

あの建物は寮だと思います。　　I think that building is a dormitory.

あの人はまだ若いと思います。　　I think that person is still young.

この本は別に難しくないと思います。　　I don't think that this book is particularly difficult.

Note that in Japanese, Example 4 literally means "I think that this book is not particularly difficult," but in English it is better to say "I don't think that...." It is also possible to say in Japanese この ほんは別に難しいとは思いません which has the same translation as above, "I don't think that...." 思います is somewhat stronger than 思いません in asserting that the book is not difficult.

第十一課　漢字

朝 あさ	晩 ばん	漢 字 かん じ	映 画 えい が
朝	晩	漢 字	映 画

試 験 し けん	思 う おも	方 ほう
試 験	思 う	方

一 番 いち ばん	楽しい たの	泳 ぐ およ
一 番	楽しい	泳 ぐ

起きる お	寝 る ね	宿 題 しゅく だい
起きる	寝 る	宿 題

159

第十二課

12 A

スミス　今ちょっとよろしいですか。
本田（ほんだ）　どうぞ。
スミス　失礼（しつれい）します。
本田　スミスさん元気がありませんね。
スミス　風邪（かぜ）を引（ひ）いて少し熱（ねつ）があるんです。
本田　それはいけませんね。
スミス　あのう宿題はあさって出してもいいですか。それともあした出さなくてはいけないでしょうか。
本田　まあそんな心配はしなくてもいいですよ。来週（らいしゅう）でもいいです。
スミス　できるだけやってみますが……
本田　無理をしてはいけませんよ。

12 B

山田　ここはいろんな人が食べていますね。
スミス　あそこには食べなから字引をひいている人がいますよ。
山田　そんなに勉強（べんきょう）しなくてはいけないんですか。
スミス　今とっているサンスクリット語のクラスは一日に（いちにち）少（すく）なくとも四時間字引をひかなくてはいけません。
山田　じゃ，スミスさんも食（た）べながら字引をひくことがあるんですね。
スミス　はい時々（ときどき）あります。

① 例　T:　これ
　　　{ S₁:　これでもよろしいですか。
　　　{ S₂:　ええ，それでもいいですよ。

1.　明日
2.　えんぴつ
3.　この本
4.　来週
5.　安い辞書

6.　せまいアパート
7.　サンドイッチ
8.　安いカメラ
9.　古本
10.　日曜日

② 例　T:　和英辞典，使う
　　　{ S₁:　あのう，ちょっと和英辞典を使ってもいいですか。
　　　{ S₂:　はい，どうぞ。

1.　テレビ，見る
2.　英語，話す
3.　辞書，借りる
4.　新聞，読む
5.　たばこ，吸う
6.　電話，使う
7.　テープ・レコーダー，借りる

8.　写真，見る
9.　レコード，聞く
10.　カメラ，見る
11.　車，使う
12.　日本語のテキスト，見る
13.　タイプライター，使う
14.　この本，借りる

③ 例1　T:　テキストを買いません。
　　　{ S₁:　あのう…テキストを買わなくてもいいでしょうか。
　　　{ S₂:　いいえ，買わなくてはいけません。

162

1. 会議に出ません。
2. 本を読みません。
3. クラスへ行きません。
4. ペンで書きません。
5. 広くありません。
6. 勉強しません。

7. 心理学のテキストを買いません。
8. きれいじゃありません。
9. しずかじゃありません。
10. 日本語で書きません。

④ 例1 T: 本を読みます。
  $\begin{cases} S_1: & 本を読まなくてはいけないでしょうか。 \\ S_2: & いいえ、読まなくてもいいですよ。 \end{cases}$

1. 明日来ます。
2. これを食べます。
3. きれいです。
4. タイプします。
5. 安いです。

6. シャワーを浴びます。
7. 部屋を掃除します。
8. 図書館へ行きます。
9. 学生です。
10. 明るいです。

⑤ 例 T: たばこを吸う、新聞を読む
  S: たばこを吸いながら新聞を読みます。

1. レコードを聞く、宿題をする
2. 歌を歌う、シャワーを浴びる
3. 新聞を読む、食べる
4. テレビを見る、のんびりする
5. 歌を歌う、晩ごはんを作る

6. たばこを吸う、勉強する
7. レコードを聞く、部屋を片付ける
8. コーヒーを飲む、本を読む
9. ビールを飲む、テレビを見る

163

10. 歩く，本を読む
11. 食事する，漢字を覚える
12. 歩く，アイスクリームを食べ
13. 勉強する，ごはんを作る
14. ビールを飲む，運転する

6　例1　T: テレビを見る，たまに
　　　　{ S₁: テレビを見ますか
　　　　{ S₂: ええ，たまにテレビを見ます。
　　例2　T: 図書館で勉強する，めったに
　　　　{ S₁: 図書館で勉強しますか。
　　　　{ S₂: いいえ，めったに図書館で勉強しません。

1. 授業に遅刻する，めったに
2. 寮はうるさい，たまに
3. バークレーは寒い，ほとんど
4. サンフランシスコへ行く，時時
5. 映画を見る，めったに
6. テレグラフはにぎやかだ，いつも
7. 朝早く起きる，たまに
8. オークランドで買物をする，いつも
9. 寮の食べ物はまずい，時々
10. 風邪を引く，あまり
11. 学校へバスで来る，ほとんど
12. スミスさんの部屋はきれいだ，全然
13. 宿題をしない，時々
14. 日本料理を食べる，たまに

7　例　T: サンフランシスコへ行きますか。
　　　S: はい，行くことがあります。

1. 日本の映画を見ますか。
2. 日本語で話しますか。
3. プールでおよぎますか。
4. 図書館で勉強しますか。

164

5. てんぷらを作りますか。
6. ラボでねますか。
7. 授業にちこくしますか。
8. たばこをすいますか。
9. お酒を飲みますか。
10. テニスをしますか。

Lesson 12 **Dialogues**

12 A

Smith: May I speak with you for a moment?

よろしい   would it be all right?

Prof. Honda: Certainly. Have a seat.

どうぞ   Lit., "Please"

S: Thank you.

失礼します   Lit., "I am being impolite"

H: You don't look very well.

元気がない   to have no spirits, energy

S: I've caught a cold and have a slight fever.

風邪をひく   to catch a cold

少し   a bit, a little

熱   fever

H: I'm sorry to hear that.

それはいけませんね。   Lit., "That won't do, will it?"

S: Umm...Would it be all right if I turn in my homework the day after tomorrow? Or should I turn it in tomorrow?

あのう   Umm...

宿題を出す   to turn in homework

165

H: Don't worry so much about it. Next week would be fine.

心配する   to worry

来週   next week
(らいしゅう)

S: I'll try my best.

できるだけ   as much as possible

やってみる   try to do

H: Don't kill yourself over it.

無理をする   to overwork
(むり)

12 B

Yamada: There are all sorts of people eating here, aren't there?

いろんな   A variant of いろいろな, "various"

Smith: Look, there's somebody looking up something (in a dictionary) while he's eating.

字引   dictionary

字引をひく   look up words in a dictionary

Y: Do you suppose he has to study that hard?

S: Well, I have to spend at least four hours a day looking up words for my Sanskrit class.

サンスクリット語   Sanskrit

少なくとも   at least
(すく)

一日   a day
(いちにち)

四時間   four hours

Y: Then you must occasionally look things up in a dictionary while you're eating, right?

S: Yes, I do every now and then.

時々   every now and then
(ときどき)

Lesson 12 **Notes on Usage**

12 A

1. スミス： 今ちょっとよろしいで
   　　　　　すか。

   本田（ほんだ）　： どうぞ。

   スミス： 失礼（しつれい）します。

   S: May I speak with you for a minute?

   H: Certainly. Have a seat. (Lit., "certainly" or "sure")

   S: Thank you. (Lit., "Excuse me for entering.")

Smith is speaking to a professor, so he is using very polite language. 失礼します literally means "I'll be impolite," hence, "Excuse me." This form can be used when entering or leaving someone's room.

2. 風邪（かぜ）を引（ひ）いて少し熱（ねつ）があるんです。　I've caught a cold and have a bit of a fever.

風邪を引く means to "catch a cold," and 熱がある means "to have a temperature or fever." "I have a cold" is 風邪を引いています.

3. それはいけませんね。　　　That's too bad.

4. あのう　　　　　　　　　Umm...

Although あのう basically indicates hesitation, it does not necessarily mean that the speaker is reluctant to speak. It is often used as a device to soften the impact of what the speaker wants to say.

5. それとも
   宿題はあさって出してもいいで
   すか，それとも明日出（だ）さなくて
   はいけませんか。

   or (connecting two sentences)
   May I turn in my homework the day after tomorrow? Or do I have to turn it in tomorrow?

167

12 B

1. ここはいろんな人が食べています
   ね。

   There are all sorts of people eating here,
   aren't there.

いろんな is a contracted form of いろいろな which means "various." It is only used
in colloquial speech.

バークレーにはいろんな人がい
ます。

There are all kinds of people in Berkeley.

このごろどんなことをしている
んですか。

What have you been doing these days?

いろんな本を読んでいます。

I've been reading all kinds of books.

2. 字引をひいています。

(He) is using a dictionary.

The verb ひく literally "to pull," is used in many ways. Here it means to consult or
use (a dictionary), but in 風邪_{かぜ}をひく, it means "to catch a cold."

3. そんなに

   that much, to that extent

   そんなに勉強_{べんきょう}しなくてはいけ
   ないんですか。

   Do you have to study that much?

   どうしてそんなに高いんですか。

   Why is it so expensive?

4. 一日_{いちにち}に少なくとも四時間字引をひ
   かなくてはいけません。

   (I) have to consult a dictionary at least
   four hours a day.

一日 means "one day" and 一日に means "in a day." 一日に四時間字引をひく, thus,
means "(I) consult a dictionary for four hours a day." に is often deleted as in the above
example. 少なくとも means "at least." Literally, it means "even if (it is) a little."

少なくとも一日_{いちにち}四時間は勉強_{べんきょう}
してください。

(Please) study at least four hours a day.

少_{すく}なくともこれだけは覚えてく
ださい。

At least memorize this.

168

5. 時々 (ときどき)　　　　　　　　　　sometimes

Some expressions used to indicate frequency of an action:

いつも	always
よく	often
時々 (ときどき)	sometimes
たまに	once in a while
あまり　　ない/ありません	not very, not much
ほとんど　ない/ありません	hardly ever
めったに　ない/ありません	rarely
全然 (ぜんぜん)　　ない/ありません	never

e.g.

大山(おおやま)さんはいつもバーへ行きます。	Ooyama always goes to bars.
大山さんはよくバーへ行きます。	〃　often　〃　〃　〃
大山さんは時々バーへ行きます。	〃　sometimes 〃　〃　〃
大山さんはたまにバーへ行きます。	Ooyama goes to bars once in a while.
大山さんはあまりバーへ行きません。	Ooyama doesn't go to bars much.
大山さんはほとんどバーへ行きません。	〃　hardly ever goes to bars.
大山さんはめったにバーへ行きません。	〃　rarely　〃　〃　〃.
大山さんは全然バーへ行きません。	〃　never　〃　〃　〃.

Lesson 12 **Grammar Notes**

The main points of this lesson are:
- I. Expression for granting permission.
  - A. "may"
  - B. "need not"
- II. Expression for indicating prohibition and obligation.
  - A. "must not"
  - B. "have to"
- III. An expression used to describe a situation where a person does two things simultaneously.
- IV. A pattern used to say, "There are/are not times when _____."

I. Expressions for granting permission.

A. <u>Verb (te-form)</u> てもいいです

It's all right if you <u>V</u> / You may <u>V</u>

宿題は明日出してもいいです。

You may turn in your homework tomorrow.

テレビを見てもいいです。

You may watch TV.

たばこをすってもいいですか。

Is it all right if I smoke?

ええ、どうぞ。

Be my guest. (Sure, go ahead.)

Often more than two <u>V</u> てもいい phrases are strung together.

テレビを見ても酒を飲んでも何
をしてもいいですよ。

You may watch TV or drink sake or whatever you want.

Actually the pattern is a part of the pattern <u>Sentence</u> てもいいです, which literally means "It's all right if (you) <u>Sentence</u>." When the sentence in <u>Sentence</u> てもいいです ends with a verb, it means "It's all right if (you) do <u>Verb</u>." Hence it is often translated as "(You) may do <u>Verb</u>."

The <u>Sentence</u> may also end in a Noun, Adjective, or Adjectival Noun.

N	明日でもいいです	Tomorrow is all right.
N	だれでもいいです	Anyone would be okay.
A	高くてもいいです	It's all right (even) if it's expensive.

170

A:	まずくてもいいです	It' all right (even) if it tastes terrible.
AN:	下手でもいいです	It's all right (even) if you're not good at it.

B. <u>Verb (Plain, Non-Past, Neg.)</u> なくてもいいです

It's all right if (you) don't <u>V</u>.
(You) don't have to <u>V</u>.

宿題はあした出さなくてもいいですよ。	You don't have to turn in your homework tomorrow.
こんどの試験は受けなくてもいいですよ。	You don't have to take the next exam.
この本は読まなくてもいいですね。	We don't have to read this book, do we?

As in the previous pattern, this pattern may follow a Noun, an Adjective, or an Adjectival Noun as well.

N:	アパートでなくてもいいです。	It doesn't have to be an apartment.
N:	山川さんでなくてもいいです。	It doesn't have to be you, Yamakawa.
A:	安くなくてもいいです。	It doesn't have to be cheap.
A:	赤くなくてもいいです。	It doesn't have to be red.
AN:	静かでなくてもいいです。	It doesn't have to be quiet.
AN:	りっぱでなくてもいいです。	It doesn't have to be splendid.

II. Expressions for indicating prohibition and obligation.

<u>Verb (te-form)</u> てはいけません

(You) must not do <u>V</u>
(It is not good if <u>V</u>)

無理をしてはいけません。	You mustn't push yourself too hard.
たばこをすってはいけません。	You must not smoke.
寝てはいけませんよ。	You must not sleep!

Nouns, Adjectives, or Adjectival Nouns may also be used.

	えんぴつで書いてもいいですか。	Is it all right if I write with a pencil?
N:	いいえ，えんぴつではいけません。	No, a pencil won't do.
	少し古くてもいいですか。	Is it all right if it's a bit old?
A:	いいえ，古くてはいけません。	It can't be old. (Lit., "No, it's not good if it's old.")
AN:	車はあまりりっぱじゃいけません。	A car shouldn't be too splendid.

では can be contracted to じゃ, and ては to ちゃ in an informal situation.

そんな変なものを食べては／ちゃいけません。You shouldn't eat such strange things.

B. Verb (Plain, Non-Past, Neg.) なくてはいけません

You must do $\underline{V}$ or You have do $\underline{V}$ (Lit., "It's not all right if you don't $\underline{V}$")

宿題は明日出さなくてはいけませんか。	Do I have to turn in my homework tomorrow?
ペンで書かなくてはいけません。	You must write with a pen.
部屋をそうじしなくてはいけません。	I must clean the room.

なくてはいけません can also be used with Nouns, Adjectives, or Adjectival Nouns.

N:	日本語でなくてはいけません。	It has to be in Japanese.
N:	山田でなくてはいけません。	It has to be Yamada.

172

A:	安くなくてはいけません。	It has to be cheap.
A:	アパートは大学に近くな くてはいけません。	The apartment has to be close to campus.
AN:	静かでなくてはいけませ ん。	It has to be quiet.

The contracted form of なくては is なくちゃ, which is used in informal conversation.

もっと食べなくちゃいけません よ。	You must eat more than that.

III. (Subject が) V₁ (pre-masu) ながら V₂   doing two things simultaneously

The same subject does two actions (V₁ and V₂) simultaneously with an emphasis on V₂ (V₂ is the main action). V₁ should be a verb which designates an action which lasts over a period of time. For this reason, a verb which is not durative such as 違う, 結婚する, 遅刻する, かかる, or 切れる, cannot be used as V₁.

レコードを聞きながら部屋をそ うじしました。	I cleaned my room, listening to records.
飲みながら書きましたから字を まちがえました。	I made some mistakes because I wrote it drinking sake.
私は歌を歌いながらふろにはい ります。	I (always) sing while taking a bath.

IV. V (Plain, Non-Past) ことがあります   There are times when/that____

バークレーで雪がふることがあ ります。	There are times when it snows in Berkeley. (Once in a while it snows in Berkeley.)
私は図書館で眠ることがありま す。	There are times when I sleep at the library.
何も食べないことがあります。	There are times when I don't eat anything.

173

第十二課　漢字

姉	妹	字引	電話
あね	いもうと	じびき	でん わ
姉	妹	字 引	電 話

心配	元気	少し	覚える
しんぱい	げん き	すこ	おぼ
心 配	元 気	少 し	覚 え る

料理	分かる
りょうり	わ
料 理	分 か る

第 十 三 課

13 A　ジョンソン　　　　山田さん「七人の侍」を見たことがありま
　　　　　　　　　　　　すか。

　　　山田　　　　　　　いいえ，まだです。見たいですねえ。今どこ
　　　　　　　　　　　　かに来ているんですか。

　　　ジョンソン　　　　あしたから始まります。姉も姉のボーイフレ
　　　　　　　　　　　　ンドも見たがっていますから一緒に行きませ
　　　　　　　　　　　　んか。

　　　山田　　　　　　　お二人とも時代劇がお好きなんですか。

　　　ジョンソン　　　　ええ，「座頭市」はいつも見ています。

13 B　店員　　　　　　　いらっしゃいませ。

　　　山田　　　　　　　「文芸春秋」の二月号が欲しいんですが
　　　　　　　　　　　　もう来ていますか。

　　　店員　　　　　　　はい，来ております。

　　　山田　　　　　　　もう一人友達が欲しがっていますから二冊お
　　　　　　　　　　　　願いします。いくらですか。

　　　店員　　　　　　　二冊で七ドルでございます。

　　　山田　　　　　　　アメリカは高いですね。

① 例1 T: カメラ
    { S₁: 今何が一番欲しいですか。
    { S₂: そうですね。やっぱりカメラが欲しいですね。

   例2 T: 山田さん，カメラ
    { S₁: 山田さんは今何を一番欲しがっていますか。
    { S₂: そうですね。カメラを欲しがっています。

1. お金
2. 新しい車
3. いい友だち
4. ブラウンさん，レコード
5. 「アイビーエム」のタイプライター
6. 山田さん，自転車
7. 和英辞典
8. スミスさん，計算器
9. ルームメート，英和辞典
10. 木村さん，カラーテレビ
11. ブラウンさん，ガールフレンド
12. 漢和辞典
13. ルームメート，テープ・レコーダー
14. いい辞書

② 例1 T: 今晩，あの映画を見る
    { S₁: 今晩何か見たいものがありますか。
    { S₂: ええ，あの映画が見たいと思います。

   例2 T: 明日，ヨセミテへ行く
    { S₁: 明日どこか行きたいところがありますか。
    { S₂: ええ，ヨセミテへ行きたいと思います。

   例3 T: 今日，テニスをする
    { S₁: 今日何かしたいことがありますか。
    { S₂: ええ，テニスがしたいと思います。

1. 今日，ワイン・カントリーへ行く
2. 今晩，ビールを飲む
3. 来年，車を買う

4. 今晩、時代劇を見る
5. 今年、日本語を習う
6. 週末、ゴルフをする
7. 明日、おすしを食べる
8. 明日、ステレオを買う
9. 今日、勉強する

10. 来年、フランス語を取る
11. 水曜日、黒沢の映画を見る
12. 週末、テニスをする
13. 明日、サンフランシスコへ行く
14. 日曜日、ロスへ行く

③ 例　T: 「七人の侍」を見る
　　　S₁: 「七人の侍」を見たことがありますか。
　　　S₂: いいえ、まだ見たことがありません。ぜひ見たいと思います。

1. うなぎを食べる
2. ヨーロッパへ行く
3. お酒を飲む
4. 中国へ行く
5. 日本茶を飲む
6. フランス語を取る
7. さしみを食べる
8. 日本の小説を読む

9. 「文芸春秋」を見る
10. 中国語を勉強する
11. 黒沢の映画を見る
12. ヨセミテの滝を見る
13. 三島由紀夫の小説を読む
14. 日本の時代劇を見る
15. ゴールデンゲート公園を見る

④ 例　T: 田中さん、行く
　　　S₁: 田中さんは行きたがっていますか。
　　　S₂: いいえ、行きたがっていません。

1. 山田さん、テニス、する
2. ベイリーさん、映画、見る
3. 田村さん、自転車、欲しい
4. スミスさん、ウイスキー、飲む

5. 田中さん、ステレオ、買う
6. ベイリーさん、ガールフレンド、欲しい
7. 田村さん、すきやき、食べる
8. ジョンソンさん、カメラ、買

　　　　う

9. ブラウンさん，カラーテレビ，
　　ほしい

10. 山田さん，アメリカ文学，取
　　　る

5　例　T: 今晩，いい映画がある
　　　S₁: 今晩いい映画があるんですが，一緒に行きませんか。
　　　S₂: ありがとうございます。ぜひ行きたいと思います。

1. 今晩，パーティーがある
2. 明日，サンフランシスコへ行
　　く
3. 今晩，レストランで食べる
4. 来週，ヨセミテへ行く
5. 今，図書館へ行く

6. 今日，買物をする
7. 明日，コンサートがある
8. 今日，海岸へ行く
9. 来年，ヨーロッパへ行く
10. 来週，ディズニーランドへ
　　行く

6　例　T: 雑誌，二冊，七ドル
　　　S₁: 雑誌を二冊お願いします。
　　　S₂: はい，二冊で七ドルです。(になります)

1. えんぴつ，十本，一ドル
2. テキスト，一冊，十ドル
3. ビール，二本，一ドル
4. ボールペン，一本，二ドル
5. 雑誌，四冊，十四ドル
6. 辞書，二冊，十五ドル

7. ノート，二冊，十二ドル
8. ハンバーガー，一つ，二ドル
9. 絵葉書，五枚，五十セント
10. ビッグマック，一つ，八十五
　　セント

178

Lesson 13 **Dialogues**

13 A

Johnson: Have you ever seen <u>Seven Samurai</u>?
Yamada: No, not yet. I sure would like to see it though. Is it playing somewhere now?

     どこか   somewhere

J: It starts tomorrow. My older sister and her boyfriend want to see it, so would you
like to come with us?

     一緒に   together

Y: Do they both like <u>samurai</u> movies?

     お   an honorific prefix
     時代劇   films with historical settings, "samurai" films

J: Yes, they're always going to see <u>Zatooichi.</u>

13 B

Clerk: May I help you?
Yamada: Yes. I'm looking for the February issue of <u>Bungei Shunjuu.</u> Has it come in
yet?

     文芸春秋   a literary magazine
     号 （ごう）   issue

C: Yes it has.

     おる   humble form of verb いる

Y: I'd like to have two copies of it, since I have a friend who wants one.
C: Two copies will come to $7.00.

     でございます   to become, come out to (humble form)

Y: It's sure expensive here in America, isn't it?

Lesson 13　Notes on Usage

13 A

1.　山田さん「七人の侍」を見
　　たことがありますか。

Have you ever seen The Seven Samurai, Yamada?

The Japanese tend to avoid calling the addressee あなた "you." Either あなた is deleted (left unsaid) or the addressee's title or name is used instead. Calling someone by his first name is considered to be very informal and only occurs among family members or among close friends. Usually people call each other by their family names even when they are very close friends. Since calling someone by the first name is considered to be very casual, one never calls someone whom one respects by the first name. In such a case the person's title is used. Furthermore, if someone has ever been your teacher, he remains your teacher even if he no longer teaches you. And even if you get to know him very well, 先生 is used to address him at all times and honorific language is used to refer to him.

(Smith to Prof. Honda)

スミス：先生ちょっとよろしい
　　　　ですか。

本田：どうぞ。

S: May I speak with you for a moment?

H: Certainly. Have a seat.

(Prof. Honda and Prof. Shimizu)

本田：清水先生！

清水：ああ本田先生よく降りま
　　　すね。

本田：いやあ，まったく，ところ
　　　で今ちょっとよろしいで
　　　すか。

H: (Good morning,) Professor Shimizu.

S: Oh, (Good morning,) Professor Honda. It's certainly raining, isn't it?

H: It sure is. By the way, do you have a minute?

「七人の侍」　The Seven Samurai is one of Kurosawa's best known films. The Magnificent Seven is a Hollywood version of this Japanese movie.
「座頭市」　The Blind Swordsman is a series of movies about a blind masseur who is a fantastic swordsman. They are rather bloody, but they have many exciting swordfighting scenes.

180

時代劇 is a play or a movie placed in the historic past. 時代 means "period" and 劇, "drama."

2. お二人とも時代劇がお好きなん　Do both of them like <u>samurai</u> movies?

ですか。

お is an honorific prefix. 二人 means "two people." Since Yamada is asking about Johnson's sisters, she uses the honorific forms to be polite. とも means "both (or all) of them." お好き is the honorific form of "like, to be fond of."

3. いつも mean "always, all the time." (cf. Notes on Usage L. 11 for other words that indicate frequency of an action.)

13 B

1. 「文芸春秋」is the name of a magazine that specializes in literature and essays of general interest. Its readers are mostly middle-and upper-middle class intellectuals. 文芸 means "literature or literary art" and 春秋 means "spring and autumn," in other words, "years." The four seasons are:

春(はる)　　spring　　　　　　　　秋(あき)　　autumn

夏(なつ)　　summer　　　　　　　　冬(ふゆ)　　winter

しゅん and じゅう（しゅう）are 音 (Chinese) readings for the characters 春 and 秋, respectively.

2. 二月号 is the "February issue." 二月 is "February" and 号 means "number" or "issue."

3. もう来ていますか。　　　　　　Has it arrived yet?

…はい，来ております。　　　…Yes, it has.

おります is the humble form of います. Thus, it literally means "It has arrived and (humbly) is here." Since the store clerk has to show respect to the customer, she/he uses the honorific (exalted) forms when referring to the customer and the humble forms when referring to the goods and services affiliated with himself/herself or the store.

4. 二冊お願いします。

冊 is the classifier for books and notebooks.

一冊（いっさつ）　　　　　六冊（ろくさつ）

二冊（にさつ）　　　　　　七冊（ななさつ）

三冊（さんさつ）　　　　　八冊（はっさつ）

四冊（よんさつ）　　　　　九冊（きゅうさつ）

五冊（ごさつ）　　　　　　十冊（じゅっさつ／じっさつ）

The object marker を never occurs after the classifier. Therefore, the object plus を must come before the classifier: 本を二冊お願いします。

5.　二冊で七ドルでございます。　　　That's seven dollars for the two (books).

でございます is the humble form of です。This form is often used by store clerks.

ちょっとすみませんが… これ（を）お願いします。	Excuse me, (but...). Could I have these, please?
いらっしゃいませ。はい，かしこまりました。千五百円でございます。	Welcome! Right away sir. (Lit., "Yes, certainly.") That will be ￥1500.
はい。じゃこれでお願いします。	Fine. Here you are. (Lit., "Well, with this please.")
二千円お預かりします。	Thank you. (Lit., "I received ￥2000.")

(The clerk goes to get the change.)

お待たせいたしました。五百円のおつりでございます。ありがとうございました。	Sorry to have kept you waiting. Your change. (Lit., "Your change of ￥500".) Thank you very much.

Lesson 13 **Grammar Notes**

The main points of this lesson are:

I. Expressions used to indicate desire of the speaker or the addressee ("you," the second person) in questions and answers:

"What do you want?"   I want____

"What do you want to do?"   I want to____

II. Desire of a third person:

"What does Mary want?"   She wants____

"What does Mary want to do?"   She wants to____

III. The year, month, and day.

I. A: （私は） <u>Noun</u> がほしいです   (I) want <u>N</u>
         Object

   （私は） <u>Noun</u> がほしくありません   (I) don't want <u>N</u>
         Object

Here the subject can only be the speaker. "You" can be used with ほしいです only
in questions. Just as with すき，きらい，上手 etc. introduced in Lesson 10, the object
marker is が.

私は水^{みず}がほしいです。   I want some water.

何がほしいですか。   What do you want?

ベンツがほしいです。   I want a Mercedes-Benz.

「文芸春秋^{ぶんげいしゅんじゅう}」の二月号^{ごう}がほしい   I want the February issue of Bungei
んです。   Shunjuu.

私は今何もほしくありません。   I don't want anything right now.

去年^{きょねん}の誕生日^{たんじょうび}に何がほしかっ   What did you want for your birthday last
たですか。   year?

何もほしくありませんでした。   I didn't want anything.

B. （私は） <u>Noun</u> が（を） <u>Verb (pre-masu)</u> たいです   I want to <u>V</u>
         Object

   （私は） <u>Noun</u> が（を） <u>Verb (pre-masu)</u> たくありません   I don't want to <u>V</u>
         Object

何かしたいことがありますか。   Is there anything that you want to do?

今晩^{こんばん}映画が見たいんですが…   I want to see a movie tonight, but...

暑いですね。ビールが飲みたい   It's hot, isn't it? I sure would like to
ですね。   have a beer.

暑くてどこへも行きたくありま   It's so hot that I don't want to go
せん。   anywhere.

II. Desire of third person.

A. (3rd person は) <u>Noun</u> をほしがっています   (He/She) wants <u>N</u>
                 Object

     (3rd person は) <u>Noun</u> をほしがっていません   (He/She) doesn't want <u>N</u>
                   Object

When the subject of "want" is the third person, ほしがる has to be used instead of ほしい. The suffix がる is conjugated like a U-verb. Since ほしがる is a verb, its stative form ほしがっています must be used to indicate the state of desiring something. In other words, "He wants a car" can only be expressed as 車をほしがっています. Notice also that the object marker is を rather than が.

友達が「文芸春秋」をほしがっています。	A friend of mine wants the Bungei Shunjuu.
メリーさんは何をほしがっていますか。	What does Mary want?
いいカメラをほしがっています。	She wants a good camera.
赤ちゃんはミルクをほしがっていました。	The baby wanted milk.
あの人は何もほしがっていませんでした。	That person didn't want anything.

B. (3rd person は) <u>Noun</u> を <u>Verb (pre-masu)</u> たがっています   He/She wants to <u>V</u>
                Object

     (3rd person は) <u>Noun</u> を <u>Verb (pre-masu)</u> たがっていません   He/She doesn't
                Object   want to <u>V</u>

Like ほしがる, when the third person wants to do something たがる is used instead of たい, and the object marker is を.

スミスさんは何をしたがっていますか。	What does Smith want to do?.
メキシコへ行きたがっています。	He wants to go to Mexico.
ベイリーさんはおすしを食べたがっています。	Bailey wants to eat sushi.

184

弟はまだ帰りたがっていません。　　My younger brother doesn't want to go home yet.

兄はパーティーに来たがっていませんでした。　　My older brother didn't want to come to the party.

III. The year, month and day

In Japanese June 6 1980 is written 千九百八十年六月六日 <ruby>せんきゅうひゃくはちじゅうねんろくがつむいか</ruby> (the order is the year, the month, the day).

The days of the month are:

*1st	一日	ついたち		13th	十三日	じゅうさんにち
*2nd	二日	ふつか		*14th	十四日	じゅうよっか
*3rd	三日	みっか		15th	十五日	じゅうごにち
*4th	四日	よっか		16th	十六日	じゅうろくにち
*5th	五日	いつか		17th	十七日	じゅうしちにち
*6th	六日	むいか		18th	十八日	じゅうはちにち
*7th	七日	なのか		19th	十九日	じゅうくにち
*8th	八日	ようか		*20th	二十日	はつか
*9th	九日	ここのか		21th	二十一日	にじゅういちにち
*10th	十日	とおか		22nd	二十二日	にじゅうににち
11th	十一日	じゅういちにち		23rd	二十三日	にじゅうさんにち
12th	十二日	じゅうににち		*24th	二十四日	にじゅうよっか

*Irregular. Everything following 24th is regular.

（お）誕生日はいつですか。　　When is your birthday?

四月一日です。　　It is April first.

第十三課　漢字

春
はる
春

夏
なつ
夏

秋
あき
秋

冬
ふゆ
冬

冊
さつ
冊

お願い
ねが
お願い

始まる
はじ
始まる

会う
あ
会う

習う
なら
習う

降る
ふ
降る

暑い
あつ
暑い

寒い
さむ
寒い

生まれる
う
生まれる

第 十四 課

14 A　山田　　　　　　　ジョンソンさん，御両親はどちらですか。

ジョンソン　　　ノースダコタです，寒い所ですよ。

山田　　　　　　　でも日本の北海道ほど寒くはないでしょう。

ジョンソン　　　北海道の冬は知りませんが去年のクリスマス
に帰った時にはずっと零下三十度でしたよ。
雪が深くて二階の窓から出入りしなければな
りませんでした。

山田　　　　　　　じゃ，多分ノースダコタの方が寒いですね。

14 B　山田　　　　　　　バークレーは暖かいですね。　ここの二月も
これぐらいの暖かさですか。

ジョンソン　　　大体そうですね。

山田　　　　　　　冬がないんですね。雨は一月と二月とどちら
が多いですか。

ジョンソン　　　多分二月も一月と同じくらいでしょう。よく
知りませんが。

山田　　　　　　　そう言えばきのうも寮を出た時に降ってい
ましたね。

1 例 T: スペイン語，イタリア語，難しい
   S₁: スペイン語はイタリア語と同じぐらい難しいですか。
   S₂: ええ，同じぐらいだと思います。

1. 日本語，英語，難しい
2. サンフランシスコ，オークランド，雨が降る
3. 今日，きのう，暑い
4. ロスのスモッグ，東京の，ひどい
5. 日本料理，中華料理，おいしい
6. スミスさん，ジョンソンさん，飲む
7. オークランド，サンフランシスコ，大きい
8. ミシガン，バークレー，お金がかかる
9. 田中さん，ブラウンさん，たばこを吸う
10. トヨタ，ニッサン，する

2 例 T: フランス語，ロシア語，難しい
   S₁: フランス語はロシア語と同じぐらい難しいですか
   S₂: いいえ，フランス語はロシア語ほど難しくないと思います。

1. このビール，ハイニケン，高い
2. 山田さん，田中さん，食べる
3. クールズ，ハイニケン，高い
4. 日本，メキシコ，広い
5. ブラウンさん，山田さん，テニスが上手だ
6. カリフォルニア，ハワイ，雨が降る
7. アパート，寮，うるさい
8. 本州，北海道，雪が降る
9. お茶，コーヒー，たかい
10. ジョンソンさん，山田さん，まじめだ
11. バート，バス，便利だ
12. このレストラン，あのレストラン，おいしい
13. バークレー，サンフランシスコ，人が多い
14. 東京，京都，古い
15. ニューヨーク，東京，人が多い
16. 中国語，日本語，難しい

17. ノース・サイド，サウス・サイド，しずかだ

18. バークレー，オークランド，あぶない

19. 日本人，中国人，英語が上手だ

20. すきやき，てんぷら，おいしい

3　例　T:　日本へ行きます，カメラを買います
　　　　S:　日本へ行った時にカメラを買います。

1. 日本へ行きます，カメラを買います

2. 山田さんが来ます，話します

3. 子供が寝ます，新聞を読みます

4. 授業が終わります，先生に聞きます

5. バートに乗ります，新聞を読みます

6. ベイリーさんに会います，言います

7. うちへ帰ります，宿題をします

8. 朝起きます，シャワーを浴びます

9. サンフランシスコへ行きます，買います

4　例　T:　日本へ行きます，スーツケースを買います
　　　　S:　日本へ行く時にスーツケースを買います。

1. 日本へ行きます，英和辞典を買います

2. 学校へ行きます，手紙を出します

3. 日本へ行きます，日本語を習います

4. 寝ます，ラジオを聞きます

5. ロスへ行きます，車を借ります

6. デートをします，めがねをかけません

7. 新聞を読みます，めがねをかけます

8. うちへ帰ります，スミスさん

に電話をかけます

9. ホンコンへ行きます，計算器を買います

10. ホンコンに着きます，手紙を書きます

5 例 T: 行きます。
　　 S: 行かなければなりません。

1. 毎朝早く起きます。
2. 宿題をします。
3. ラボへ行きます。
4. 今日早く帰ります。
5. テキストを買います。
6. 仕事を探します。
7. 洗濯をします。

8. 親に手紙を書きます。
9. 今日買物をします。
10. 明日宿題を出します。
11. 論文を書きます。
12. 公害問題を考えます。
13. 図書館へ本を返します。
14. エネルギー問題を考えます。

6 例 T: 雪が深い，二階の窓から出入りする
　　 S: 雪が深くて二階の窓から出入りしなければなりませんでした。

1. 遠い，車で行く
2. 頭が痛い，今日クラスを休む
3. お金がない，二時間歩く
4. 分らない，五回読む
5. まずい，捨てる
6. 車が動かない，バートで来る
7. きたない，書きなおす
8. 寒い，セーターを着る

9. 英語の宿題が難しい，スミスさんに聞く
10. 漢字が分らない，大きい辞書を引く
11. 歯が痛い，アスピリンを飲む
12. 頭がわるい，日本語の勉強を止める

Lesson *14* **Dialogues**

14 A

Yamada: Where do your parents live?

どちら Where, lit., "which side"

Johnson: In North Dakota. It's really cold there, you know.

Y: But it's not as cold as Hokkaido, is it?

ほど extent, as much as

J: Well, I don't know about Hokkaido winters, but last Christmas when I went home, it was around 30° below zero the whole time. The snow was so deep we had to go in and out from the second story window.

知る to know

ずっと the whole time

零下（れいか） below 0° C.

三十度（さんじゅうど） 30°

雪 snow

深い（ふか） deep

出入りする（で はい） to go out and in

Y: Gee, then North Dakota's probably colder, isn't it?

14 B

Yamada: Berkeley's warm isn't it? Is February here always this warm?

暖かい（あたた） warm

これぐらい this much

暖かさ（あたた） warmth

191

Johnson: Yes, for the most part.

大体(だいたい)   for the most part

Y: There really isn't a winter to speak of, is there? Does it rain more in January or February?

J: I'm not sure, but they're probably about the same. I think...

Y: Oh, yes, come to think of it, it was raining when we left the dorm yesterday, wasn't it?

そう言えば   now that you mention it

Lesson 14   Notes on Usage

14 A

1. ジョンソンさん, 御両親はどちら   (Johnson,) where do your parents live?
   ですか。

   どちら (which?) can be used to mean "Where?" in a polite situation.

   お生まれはどちらですか。   Where were you born?

   (どちらのお生まれですか)   (Lit., "Where is your place of birth?")

   お住まいはどちらですか。   Where do you live? (Lit., "Where is your house?")

2. ジョンソン：ノースダコタです,   J: North Dakota. It's a really cold place!
   寒い所ですよ。

   山田：でも北海道ほど寒くない   Y: But it's probably not as cold as Hok-
   でしょう。   kaido.

   でしょう "probably" or "I guess" can be also used with a rising intonation to mean "It must be____, right?" or "I guess it is____. Am I wrong?"

   山田さん, あしたも学校へ来る   Yamada, you're coming to school to-
   んでしょう。   morrow, aren't you (Lit., "right")?

   ロサンジェルスはスモッグがひ   The smog is pretty bad in LA, right?
   どいんでしょう。

192

Compare this でしょう (↗) with Johnson's statement in 14B: 多分二月も一月と同じぐらいでしょう (↘) with falling intonation which is a statement.

3. ずっと零下三十度でした。   It was thirty degrees below zero the whole time (literally, "continuously").

ずっと means "continuously" or "by far." Here it means "continuously."

山田さんは朝からずっと図書館で勉強しています。   Yamada has been studying in the library straight through since this morning.

零 is the number "zero." 下 means "below" or "under." 度 means "degree." 零下三十度 means "30 degrees below zero" (in Celsius).

4. 雪が深くて二階の窓から出入りします。   The snow is so deep that (literally, "and") we go in and out through the second floor window.

雪が深い means "the snow is deep." 二階 is the "second floor." 階 is the classifier for "floors."

1st (street) floor	一階 いっかい		6th floor	六階 ろっかい	
2nd	〃	二階 にかい	7th 〃	七階 ななかい	
3rd	〃	三階 さんがい（さんかい）	8th 〃	八階 はちかい	
			9th 〃	九階 きゅうかい	
4th	〃	四階 よんかい	10th 〃	十階 じゅっかい（じっかい）	
5th	〃	五階 ごかい			

The basement is 地下, and the underground floors are called 地下一階, 地下二階, etc. The roof floor of a building is called 屋上, (The roof of a house is 屋根).

出入りする means to "go in and out (lit., "to go out and in")." 出 is the pre-ます form of the verb 出る "to go out" and 入り, that of the verb 入る "to go in."

このドアから出入りしないでください。   Please do not use this door. (Lit., "Please do not go out and in from this door.")

窓から出入りする literally means "to go out and in from the window," but a more idiomatic translation would be "to go in and out through the window."

14 B

1. 大体そうですね。

   <ruby>大体<rt>だいたい</rt></ruby>

   大体 means "approximately" or "roughly," so the phrase means "It's about that."

2. よく知りませんが…

   I'm not very sure, but... (Lit., "I don't know very well, but...")

   It is quite common to use <ruby>多分<rt>たぶん</rt></ruby> "perhaps," …でしょう "I guess," and よく知りませんが "I don't know very well, but..." together. The presence of a great number of these phrases does not necessarily reflect the speaker's degree of uncertainty. The speaker may feel safer if he uses various words denoting uncertainty to indicate that he does not want to make any assertive statement.

3. 寮を出た時に

   <ruby>寮<rt>りょう</rt></ruby>

   When we left the dorm

   The point of departure of the verbs of "leaving" is marked by を rather than から. (Although it is true that some verbs of this group may also take から in spite of this rule, for the present it is best to use を.)

   けさ七時にうちを出ましたがやっぱり遅刻しました。バートが来なかったんです。

   <ruby>遅刻<rt>ちこく</rt></ruby>

   I left home at seven this morning and (as you might have expected) I was late. Bart didn't come.

   ことし大学を出てアイビーエムに就職しました。

   <ruby>就職<rt>しゅうしょく</rt></ruby>

   I graduated from the university and got a job with IBM.

Lesson 14 **Grammar Notes**

The main points of this lesson are:
  I. Comparisons
     A. "X is as _____ as Y."
     B. "X is not as _____ as Y."
 II. A pattern to express obligation.
III. A pattern to express: "When X took place, Y."
IV. The use of a suffix to change adjectives into nouns.

I. Comparisons

A. <u>X</u> は <u>Y</u> と同じぐらい <u>A/AN</u> です   <u>X</u> is as <u>A/AN</u> as <u>Y</u>

今日は昨日と同じぐらい寒いで
す。   Today is as cold as yesterday.

山田さんはスミスさんと同じぐ
らいまじめです。   Yamada is as diligent as Smith.

B. <u>X</u> は <u>Y</u> ほど <u>A</u> くありません   <u>X</u> is not as <u>A/AN</u> as <u>Y</u>

         AN じゃありません

アパートは寮ほどうるさくあり
ません。   Apartments are not as noisy as the dorms.

バートはバスほど便利じゃあり
ません。   Bart is not as convenient as the bus.

II. <u>Verb (Plain Non-Past, Neg.)</u> なければ なりません。   Have to do <u>V</u>. (Lit., "should or ought to")

雪が深くて二階の窓から出入り
しなければなりません。   The snow was so deep that we have to go in and out through the second floor window.

お金がありませんから仕事をし
なければなりません。   I don't have any money so I have to work. (due to my own decision)

仕事をしなくてはいけません。   I have to work. (due to outside pressure)

III. <u>Sentence (Plain Past)</u> 時に <u>X</u>   When <u>S</u>, <u>X</u>

去年のクリスマスに帰った時に   When I went home last Christmas, the

195

はずっと零下三十度でした。   entire time it was 30 degrees below zero.

きのう寮を出た時に雨が降っ   When we came out of the dorm, it was
ていましたね。   raining, wasn't it?

わたしが来た時にはまだ誰もい   When I came nobody was here yet.
ませんでした。

小さかった時にはよく泣きまし   When I was little I cried a lot.
た。

学生だった時にはよく飲みまし   I drank a lot (often) when I was a stu-
た。   dent.

When the verb in the main sentence is in the past tense as in the above examples, the sentence describes an action that took place in the past. When the tense of the verb in the main sentence is in the Non-Past, however, the sentence describes an event that will take place in the future.

カメラは日本へ行った時に買い   I will buy the camera when I go to Japan.

ます。

行った is the Plain Past form of the verb 行く (to go), but the action described in this sentence has not occurred yet because the verb of the main clause is in the Non-Past. The Past tense is often used in this way (行った時…買います。) to describe one future event which is to be followed by another. In the example above the speaker indicates that the action of buying (the camera) will take place after the action of going to (and arriving in) Japan, so the verb 行く is in its past tense form 行った. Compare the above with the following example:

カメラは日本へ行く時に買いま   I will buy the camera when I go to Japan
す。   (before going to Japan).

In this case the use of Non-Past has the implication of "at the time (or just about the time) that I go (in the future)."

IV. 暖かさ   warmth

さ is a suffix that changes an Adjective into a Noun.

暖かい → 暖かさ   warmth

寒い　 → 寒さ　 coldness

大きい → 大きさ   size, largeness

196

いい（よい） → よさ　　　　　　　　quality

It can also be attached to an Adjectival Noun.

きれいだ　 →	きれいさ	cleanliness; attractiveness or beauty
立派だ　　 →	立派さ	grandeur, splendor
静かだ　　 →	静かさ（静けさ）	silence, tranquility
にぎやかだ →	にぎやかさ	liveliness

第十四課　漢字

遊 ぶ
あそ
遊　ぶ

時
とき
時

考 え る
かんが
考　え　る

所
ところ
所

雨
あめ
雨

雪
ゆき
雪

同 じ
おな
同　じ

近 い
ちか
近　い

遠 い
とお
遠　い

辞 書
じ　しょ
辞　書

知 る
し
知　る

第　十　五　課

15 A　　山田　　　　スミスさん，ちょっといいですか。

スミス　　　はい，どうぞ。

山田　　　　この単語の意味が分からないんですが……

スミス　　　字引をひいてみましたか。

山田　　　　ええ，あしたクイズがあって単語を三百覚え なければならないのですがこの単語が一つだ けどうも……

スミス　　　あ，この単語はどんな字引にもありませんよ。 ミスプリントです。

15 B　　ジョンソン　岡村さんは昨日いらっしゃったんですね。

岡村　　　　ええ，英会話の勉強をしに来ました。

ジョンソン　あ，そうですか。じゃ，一緒にコーヒーでも 飲んでからあのカンパニーレに上がってみま せんか。

岡村　　　　ええ，そうしましょう。あそこに上がるのに はお金がいりますか。

ジョンソン　ええ，十セントです。

岡村　　　　あのう十セントは大きい方ですか。

ジョンソン　いいえ，小さい方ですよ。さあ，行きましょう。

① 例　T:　今日，テニスをする

　　　　　　{S₁:　今日は何をしましょうか。
　　　　　　{S₂:　テニスをしましょう。

1. 明日，ビールを飲む
2. 今晩，アイス・クリームを買う
3. 今日，サンフランシスコへ行く
4. 今晩，映画を見る
5. 今晩，日本町で食べる
6. 来年，社会学のクラスを取る
7. 今日，中華料理を作る
8. 今週末，ヨセミテへ行く
9. 明日，ピクニックをする
10. 今日，泳ぐ
11. 今晩，キップスでピザを食べる
12. 土曜日，図書館で勉強する
13. 来年，日本へ行く
14. 金曜日，ロスへ車で行く
15. 明日，ワイン・カントリーへ行く
16. 今日，日本の映画を見る

② 例　T:　来る，本を借りる

　　　　　　{S₁:　何（を）しに来たんですか。
　　　　　　{S₂:　本を借りに来たんです。

1. 行く，本を返す
2. 出かける，食事する
3. 行く，映画を見る
4. うちへ帰る，本を取る
5. 行く，ビールを飲む
6. 来る，スミスさんに会う
7. 行く，えんぴつを買う
8. 行く，手紙を出す
9. 出かける，レコードを借りる
10. 郵便局へ行く，切手を買う
11. 山田さんのうちへ行く，本を借りる
12. 海岸へ行く，泳ぐ
13. うちへ帰る，ごはんを食べる
14. 日本へ行く，日本語を習う
15. 図書館へ行く，勉強する
16. サンフランシスコへ行く，買物をする

③ 例　T:　食べる

　　　　　　S:　食べてみませんか。

1. 行く
2. 来る
3. 勉強する
4. 買う
5. 話す
6. 読む
7. 食べる
8. 飲む

9. 見る
10. 遊ぶ
11. 作る
12. 練習する
13. 復習する
14. 結婚する
15. 使う
16. 送る

4 例 T: コーヒーを飲む，カンパニーレに上がってみる。
  { S₁: コーヒーを飲んでから何をしますか。
  { S₂: カンパニーレに上がってみるつもりです。

1. うちへ帰る，寝る
2. 図書館へ行く，宿題をする
3. 日本語を勉強する，日本へ行く
4. ヨーロッパへ行く，ドイツ語を習う
5. ごはんを食べる，テレビを見る
6. 大学を出る，セイフウェイで働く
7. 試験が終わる，メキシコへ行く
8. 晩ごはんを食べる，映画を見に行く

9. 授業が終わる，うちへ帰る
10. 宿題をする，コンサートへ行く
11. うちへ帰る，昼寝をする
12. 授業が終わる，プールへ泳ぎに行く
13. 大学を出る，旅行する
14. 日本語をマスターする，ビジネス・スクールに入る
15. ニューヨークの会議が終わる，ワシントンでスミスさんに会う

5 例 T: 授業が終わる，ビールを飲む
  { S₁: 授業が終わってからビールでも飲みませんか。
  { S₂: ええ，いいですね。飲みましょう。

1. キャンパスを見る，コーヒーを飲む
2. 宿題をする，テレビを見る
3. 試験が終わる，パーティーをする
4. 食事する，映画を見に行く
5. 授業が終わる，コーヒーを飲みに行く
6. 部屋を片付ける，アイス・クリームを食べる
7. 買物をする，お茶を飲む
8. お風呂に入る，テレビを見る
9. 勉強する，お茶を飲みに行く
10. 試験が終わる，おすしを食べに行く

6　例　T: この単語の意味，分からない
　　　　S₁: 分かりません。
　　　　S₂: 何が分からないんですか。
　　　　S₁: この単語の意味が分からないんです。

1. この漢字，分からない
2. この漢字の読み方，分からない
3. 新しい辞書，欲しい
4. もっと大きい辞書，欲しい
5. すきやき，食べたい
6. 文法，難しい
7. 「七人の侍」，見たい
8. ここの文法，分からない
9. ここのパラグラフ，分からない
10. ここのロー・スクール，入りたい
11. あの映画，見たい
12. 三船，好きだ

Lesson 15　Dialogues

15A

Yamada: Do you have a minute?
Smith:　 Sure.

いいですか   lit., "Is it O.K.?"

Y: Well, I'm not sure about the meaning of this word.

単語   word

意味   meaning

S: Did you look it up in the dictionary?

Y: Yes, I did. I've got a quiz tomorrow, and I have to learn 300 words. But somehow I just can't find this one word.

だけ   only, just

どうも   No matter how much I try.…

S: Well, you're never going to find this word in any dictionary. It's a misprint.

15B

Johnson: You just arrived yesterday, didn't you?

いらっしゃる   honorific for 来る here

Okamura: Yes, I came to study English conversation.

英会話   English conversation

J: Oh, well, would you like to go have some coffee or something and then go up to the top of the Campanile?

O: Yes, I'd like that. Does it cost anything to go up there?

上がる   go up, climb

いる   to need

J: Yes, it's a dime.

O: Umm, is a dime the larger coin?

大きい方   the larger one

J: No, it's the smaller one. Shall we go then?

小さい方   the smaller one

さあ   well, come on

Lesson 15 **Notes on Usage**

15A

1. 山田：すみません。ちょっといい　　Y: Do you have a minute, Smith?
    いですか。

    スミス：はい，どうぞ。　　　　　　S: Sure (What's up?)

Compare this dialogue with the one in 12A. Yamada and Smith are friends so Yamada says いいですか, whereas in 12A Smith is talking to her professor so she uses the more formal よろしいいですか.

2. 意味が分からないんですが。　　　　I don't know what this means, but...
    　　　　　　　　　　　　　　　　　(Lit, "I don't understand the meaning of
    　　　　　　　　　　　　　　　　　this but...')

The verb 分かる "to understand" is a verb that indicates the ability to understand and its object is marked by が and not を.

    フランス語が分かりますか。　　　　Do you understand French?

    この漢字が分かりません。　　　　　I don't know this character. (Lit., "I don't
    　　　　　　　　　　　　　　　　　understand this character.")

3. 字引 ＝ 辞書　　　　　　　　　　a dictionary

4. 単語　　　　　　　　　　　　　　words or vocabulary items

単 means "single" and 語 means "word." ことば means "words" as well as "languages."

5. この単語がひとつだけどうも

だけ means "only," "exclusively." どうも is a part of a longer phrase どうも分かりません "I cannot understand or make sense out of this."

6. この単語はどんな字引にもあり　　This word is not in any kind of a dic-
    ませんよ。　　　　　　　　　　　tionary.

204

どんな "what kind?" is used with ____ にも to mean "whatever kind of ____." (cf. こんな "this kind," そんな "that kind," あんな "that kind")

| この話はどんな本にも書いてありませんよ。 | This story is not (written) in any (kind of a) book. |
| こんなにやさしいことはどんな子供にもできます。 | Any child can do something as easy as this. |

15B

1. 岡村さんはきのういらっしゃったんですね。 / You arrived here yesterday, didn't you, Okamura? (Lit., "You came yesterday, didn't you, Okamura?")

いらっしゃる is an honorific verb which means "to come," "to go," or "to be." It is a U-verb and is conjugated as follows: いらっしゃる, いらっしゃらない. いらっしゃった, いらっしゃいます (cf. L.5).

Here, Johnson is being very polite because he does not know Okamura very well yet.

| きょうどこかへいらっしゃいますか。 | Are you going somewhere today? |
| 山川さんはこのあいだのパーティーにいらっしゃいましたね。 | Yamakawa, you came to (were at) the party the other day, did (were)n't you? or You were at the party the other day weren't you? |

2. 英会話の勉強をしに来ました。 / I came to study English conversation.

英 in 英会話 stands for "English" as in 英語 and 会話 means "conversation." Thus, the word means "English conversation (or conversational English)."

Compound verbs like 勉強する can be used in two ways:

As a compound verb: 勉強する (to study), 掃除する (to clean up), 買物する (to go shopping).

As an object and a verb: 勉強をする (to do (my) studies), 掃除をする (to do the cleaning), 買物をする (to do the shopping).

Therefore, "to study English conversation" can be said in two ways:

英会話を勉強する / (Lit., "to study English conversation")

205

英会話の勉強をする   (Lit., "to do studies in English conversation")

3. カンパニーレに上がってみませ   How about going up to the top of the
     んか。   Campanile ?

に is used here instead of へ because the focus is on the result of the action, that is, being at the top of the tower.

あの山に登りましょう。   Let's climb that mountain.

4. あのう十セントは大きい方です   Is ten cents the bigger one?
     か。

方 literally means "side" or "direction," but it is often used for comparison (cf. L.11). In Okamura's mind, two coins, one larger and the other smaller, are being compared so she says 大きい方ですか。

Lesson 15   **Grammar Notes**

The main points of this lesson are:
  I. The pattern for saying "Let's do __ ."
 II. The pattern to indicate the purpose of "going" and "coming."
III. The pattern that conveys the meaning of "do __ and see."
IV. Another usage of から: "After <u>V</u>, <u>Y</u>"
 V. The use of でも in suggestion sentences meaning "<u>Noun</u> or something."

I. <u>Verb (pre-masu)</u> ましょう   Let's <u>V</u>

きょうは何をしましょうか。   What shall we do today ?

テニスをしましょう。   Let's play tennis.

日本語のクラスのパーティーを   Let's have a Japanese class party.
しましょう。

206

II. Verb (pre-masu) に { 行きます / 来ます / 帰ります }　I will { go in order to V / come in order to V / return in order to V }

英会話を勉強しに来ました。 | I came to study English conversation.

図書館へ本を返しに行きます。 | I am going to go to the library to return the books.

食事をしに帰りました。 | He went home to eat.

The purpose of "coming" or "going" is marked by に. The form that comes before に is the pre-masu form of the verb as seen in the above examples.

With compound verbs such as 勉強する (to study), 食事する (to eat a meal), and テニスする (to play tennis), する is optional.

山田さんは図書館へ勉強に行っています。 | Yamada has gone to the library to study.

サンフランシスコへ買物に行きませんか。 | Would you like to go shopping in San Francisco?

III. Verb (te-form) てみます | (I will) do V and see/try

これを食べてみてください。 | Please try this. (Lit., "Please eat this and see.")

アメリカ文学のクラスをとってみるつもりです。 | I am thinking of taking the course on American literature (and seeing how it is).

できるだけやってみます。 | I will do my best (and see), or I will try my best.

前に友達のうちで食べてみましたがあまり好きじゃありません。 | I tried it before (I ate it before to see what it was like) at my friend's house and I didn't like it very much.

レコードを買う前にきいてみたいんですが…… | I would like to listen to the record before I buy it.

207

IV. Verb (te-form) てから Y

After Verb, Y

大学を出てから日本へ行ってみるつもりです。

After graduating from college, I'm thinking of going to Japan (and seeing what it's like).

うちへ帰ってから宿題をしました。

After I got home, I did my homework.

コーヒーでも飲んでからあのカンパニーレに上がってみませんか。

After having some coffee (or something), Would you like to go up to (the top of) the Campanile?

V. コーヒーでも飲みませんか

Won't you have some coffee or something?

でも in suggestion sentences like the above literally means "Noun or something." It is attached to a noun which is given as a suggestion. This makes a statement polite by not confining the addressee to only the activity mentioned by the speaker.

テニスでもしませんか。

How about playing tennis or something?

ええ，そうしましょう。

Yes, let's do that.

カンパニーレにでも上がってみませんか。

How about climbing the Campanile (or something)?

いつ行きましょうか。

When shall we go?

日曜日にでも行きませんか。

How about Sunday?

208

第十五課　　漢字

単語
たん　ご
単　語

文法
ぶん　ぽう
文　法

意味
い　み
意　味

授業
じゅ　ぎょう
授　業

お茶
　　ちゃ
お　茶

週末
しゅう　まつ
週　末

終わる
お
終　わ　る

買物
かい　もの
買　物

入る
はい
入　る

先週
せん　しゅう
先　週

今週
こん　しゅう
今　週

来週
らい　しゅう
来　週

第 十 六 課

16 A   ジョンソン   どうしたんですか。顔色がよくありませんね。

岡村   ええ，昨日雨にぬれたので風邪を引いてしまったんです。

ジョンソン   それはいけませんね。で，何か薬を飲んでいるんですか。

岡村   アメリカの薬はよく分からないので今日病院へ行こうと思っています。

ジョンソン   病院もいいですが，この薬はどうですか。おなかが痛い時にはとてもよく効きますよ。

岡村   いえ，おなかはちっとも痛くないんです。

16 B   医者   岡村さんですね。熱がありますか。

岡村   いえ，熱はありませんからそう大したことはないと思いますが頭が痛いんです。

医者   じゃあ，そのままでいいですから上着だけ取ってください。(He holds up the stethoscope.) はい，深く息をしてください。

岡村   先生どうでしょうか。

医者   風邪ですね。ですから一週間ぐらいでよくなります。

① 例 T: 雨にぬれました，風邪をひいてしまいました
　　　S: 雨にぬれたので，風邪をひいてしまいました。

1. バスが来ませんでした，歩いて来ました
2. 事故がありました，遅刻しました
3. 寒いです，皆セーターを着ています
4. よく分かりません，薬は飲みませんでした
5. 風邪をひいていました，泳ぎ

ませんでした
6. よく勉強しませんでした，今日のクイズはだめでした
7. 今日は熱がありました，キャンパスへ行きませんでした
8. あの映画は評判がいいです，五か月も続いています
9. 昨日は大変疲れていました，すぐ寝ました

② 例 T: 熱はありません，大したことはないと思います
　　　S: 熱はありませんから大したことはないと思います。

1. 雨が降っています，車で行きましょう
2. 風邪をひいています，泳ぎません
3. アパートのほうが静かです，アパートにはいりたいです
4. うなぎはきらいです，さしみにします
5. 子供がねむっています，静かにしてください
6. お客さんが来ます，部屋をかたづけてください
7. あの人はカメラを持っています，たぶん日本人でしょう
8. 今日は寒いです，セーターを着ましょう
9. あのレストランはサービスがいいです，大好きです
10. 雨が降っています，行かないんです

③ 例 T: 明日学校へ行って勉強する
　　　S₁: 明日学校へ行って何をしますか。
　　　S₂: 勉強しようと思っています。

1. 来年日本へ行って日本語を習う

2. 明日試験が終わってから旅行する

3. 今日うちに帰ってから昼寝をする

4. 今晩宿題をしてからテレビを見る

5. 今晩日本町へ行ってから（お）すしを食べる

6. 金曜日食事をしてから映画を見に行く

7. 今日授業が終わってからコーヒーを飲みに行く

8. 明日手紙を書いてから日本語の予習をする

9. あさって公園へ行ってバスケットボールをする

10. 週末ロスへ行ってディズニーランドへ行く

4 例 T: ケーキはまだありますか。（食べる）
　　 S: いいえ，もう食べてしまいました。

1. ビールはまだありますか。（飲む）

2. スミスさんはまだいますか。（帰る）

3. 山田さんはまだ起きていますか。（寝る）

4. 本はまだ読んでいませんか。（読む）

5. 田中さんはまだいますか。（帰る）

6. スミスさんはまだいますか。（行く）

7. パイはまだありますか。（食べる）

8. まだお金がありますか。（使う）

9. まだ宿題をしていませんか。（する）

10. 彼女はまだ結婚していませんか。（結婚する）

5 例 T: この薬，おなかが痛いです，効きます
　　 S₁: この薬はどんなときに効きますか。
　　 S₂: そうですねえ，おなかが痛いときに効くと思います。

1. この薬，疲れています，効きます
2. この辞書，日本語を勉強します，便利です
3. アスピリン，熱があります，効きます
4. このペン，漢字を書きます，いいです
5. 「オニール」，漢字を調べます，便利です
6. この音楽，さびしいです，いいです
7. この辞書，日本語の意味を調べます，いいです
8. コーヒー，ねむいです，いいです
9. ウイスキー，　？　，いいです
10. アイスコーヒー，あついです，いいです

6 例 T: 風邪をひいています。
{S₁: どうしたんですか。顔色がよくありませんね。
S₂: ええ，風邪をひいているんです。
S₁: それはいけませんね。何か薬を飲んでいるんですか。
S₂: いえ，今日，病院へ行こうと思っています。

1. 頭が痛いです。
2. 熱があります。
3. おなかがいたいんです。
4. 歯が痛いです。
5. 腰が痛いです。

Lesson 16 Dialogues

16 A

Johnson: Are you all right? You look pale.

かおいろ 顔色	complexion, color
かおいろ 顔色がよくない	to look pale, colorless

Okamura: Well, I got caught in the rain yesterday and have come down with a cold.

ぬれる	to get wet

J: Gee, that's too bad... Are you taking anything for it?

くすり 薬	medicine
薬を飲む	to take (medicine)

O: Since I'm unfamiliar with the medicines here in America, I was thinking about going over to the clinic today.

びょういん 病院	hospital

J: Clinics are okay, but... How about trying some of this? This is great for stomachaches.

おなか	stomach
いた 痛い	painful
き 効く	to be effective, to work

O: Oh, but I don't have a stomachache.

16 B

Physician: You're Miss Okamura, aren't you? Do you have a fever?
Okamura: No, I don't have a fever, so I guess it can't be that bad. But I do have a headache.

そう	that much
たい 大したことはない	nothing serious
いた 頭が痛い	to have a headache

P: That's fine. Just take off your jacket. Okay, take a deep breath, please.

うわぎ 上着	jacket
だけ	just, only
取る	remove, take off
いき 息をする	to breathe

O: What do you think, Doctor?
P: Well, it looks like a cold. It should get better in about a week.

一週間   one week

よくなる   to get better, to improve

Lesson 16 Notes on Usage

16 A

1. どうしたんですか。顔色がよく
ありませんね。

What's the matter? You look pale.
(Lit., "the color of your face is bad.")

どうしたんですか "What's the matter with you?" is used when something is obviously wrong and the speaker thinks that the addressee has the explanation. In this case there is something wrong with the addressee himself. His 顔色 (face color) is bad (i.e. he looks pale or unwell).

2. 雨にぬれたので風邪を引いてし
まいました。

I got caught in the rain and (literally, "so") have come down with a cold.

雨にぬれる is a fixed expression that means "to get wet by the rain."

3. 何か薬を飲んでいるんですか。   Are you taking any medicine for it?

何か means "something" and "to take medicine" is 薬を飲む (to drink medicine) in Japanese.

4. アメリカの薬はよく分かりませ
んので。

Since I'm unfamiliar with the medicines here in America...

分かる here means "to know."

5. おなかが痛い時にはとてもよく
効きますよ。

It's very good (effective) when you have a stomachache.

216

おなかが痛い is a "stomachache" (lit., "(my) stomach hurts"). Likewise, 頭が痛い means "to have a headache" (lit., "(my) head hurts"). とても "very" is an informal variant of 大変 "very." 効きます means (the medicine or remedy) "works" or "is effective and is used in the following manner: X は Y に効きます "X is good (effective) for Y."

e.g. この薬は風邪によく効きます。　　This medicine is good for colds.

In the above sentence おなかが痛い時にはとてもよく効きます, however, the noun that corresponds to Y in the above pattern is missing because it is obvious from the context. The に after 時 is the marker for time (i.e. "When one's stomach hurts (for the stomachache), this medicine works well.")

6.　ちっとも痛くないんです。　　It doesn't hurt at all.

ちっとも means "not at all" and is used only in negative sentences.

あの映画はちっとも面白くありません。　This movie is not interesting at all.

16B

1.　熱はありませんからそう大したことはないと思います。　　I don't have a fever so I don't think it's serious.

大したことは {ないです / ありません} means "It's not so bad, great, etc." Depending on the situation 大したこと (lit., "great thing") can mean "great," "bad," "terrible" etc.

アリ：フレイザーなんて大したことはないよ。　　Ali: Fraser is nothing! (Lit., "That guy called Fraser or something is not that great.")

試験は難しかったですか。　　Was the exam hard?

…なあに，大したことはありませんでしたよ。　　Naa! (It was nothing.) (Lit., "No, it wasn't very difficult.")

2.　そのままでいいです。

まま means "as is" and the whole phrase means "You're fine the way you are."

きのう夜遅くうちへ帰りました。疲れていましたからそのままで寝てしまいました。　　Last night I returned home late and was so tired that I went to bed just as I was (without changing clothes).

3.　　上着だけ取ってください。　　　　Just take off your jacket, please.

取る can mean "to take, to pick up, to take off, etc." depending on context.

4.　　はい，深く息をしてください。　　Okay, now take a deep breath.

はい here does not mean "Yes." It is often used to call attention to what the speaker is going to do. It is also used as a signal to tell the adressee to begin something as in はい "Start." (when a teacher has the students repeat something one after another.)
息をする is a fixed expression meaning "to breathe."

5.　　先生どうでしょうか。　　　　　What do you think, Doctor?

Here 先生 means "Doctor,..." rather than teacher. Teachers, doctors, and statesmen are called 先生.

6.　　一週間ぐらいでよくなります。　　You'll be fine in a week.

よくなる means "to get well." (Likewise, 赤くなる is "to get red," 寒くなる, "to get cold," etc.) 一週間ぐらいで means "in a week or so" (lit., "with one week").

御飯は一時間ぐらいでできます。　　The meal will be ready in about an hour so. (できます here means "will be made.")

Lesson 16 **Grammar Notes**

The points of this lesson are:
 I. Two forms から and ので which are used to give reasons or explanation.
 II. Another way of saying "I'm thinking about doing ＿＿."
 III. A pattern that is used to express "completion" with a connotation of irreversibility.

I. から and ので

A. X から Y　　　　　　　　　　　　X therefore (so) Y; Because X, Y;
　　　　　　　　　　　　　　　　　　Y because X

218

| 熱はありませんから大したこと
はないでしょう。 | I haven't got a temperature, so I don't think it's serious. |
| あの映画はよかったからまた見
たいと思います。 | That movie was good, so I think I want to see it again. |

The same idea can be expressed using ですから (therefore) as in the following examples:

熱はありません。ですから	(See above)
大したことはないでしょう。	
あの映画はよかったです。	
ですからまた見たいと思います。	
風邪ですね。ですから一週間ぐ らいでよくなります。	It's (just) a cold so you'll get over it in a week.

With から, X may be a Verb, an Adjective, an Adjectival Noun, or a Noun. It may be either in the polite form or in the plain form.

B. X ので Y	X therefore (so) Y; Because X, Y; Y because X
朝寝坊をしたのでクラスに遅れ ました。	I overslept, so I was late for class.
店が遠いので買物に不便です。	The stores are far away so it's inconvenient (for shopping).
部屋が静かなので勉強ができま す。	The room is quiet, so I can study.

In many cases ので and から are used interchangeably and have the same meaning. The most significant differences are:

1. ので forms a stronger bond between X and Y. In other words, use X ので Y when Y is the obvious consequence of X or if one wishes to emphasize that there is no doubt about the causal relationship between X and Y.
2. ので is not used when the main clause contains だろう (plain form) or でしょう (polite form) which denotes probability.
3. ので is not used as a reason for prohibiting, giving an order (command) or making a request or suggestion to the addressee (i.e. sentences used to control the addressee).
4. With から, both X and Y can end with either the plain form or the polite form of a Verb, Adjective, Adjectival Noun, or Noun. With ので, however, only plain forms are used for Adjectives, Adjectival Nouns and Nouns, and both plain and polite forms

for Verbs. It should be noted that the plain forms of Adjectival Nouns and Nouns which precede ので and から are different.

	ので	から
V:	雨が降って いる (います) のでピクニックはできません。	雨が降って {いる / います} からピクニックはできません。
A:	新しいのできれいです。	新しい {—— / です} からきれいです。
AN:	立派(りっぱ)なので高いです。	立派 {だ / です} から高いです。
N:	学生なのでお金がありません。	学生 {だ / です} からお金がありません。

から can end a sentence (plain form からです) whereas ので cannot (cf. L. 11)

II. Verb (volitional form) と思っています   I am thinking about doing V

The form V (root) plus (y)oo is called the volitional form of the verb. RU-verbs are put into this form by adding <u>yoo</u> to the root of the verb and U-verbs, by adding <u>oo</u> to the root.

e.g. RU-verbs:　食べよう (to eat),　見よう (to see),　いよう (to stay), etc.

U-verbs:　買おう　(to buy),　使おう (to use),　待(ま)とう (to wait), etc.

Irregular Verbs:

する	しよう
行く	行こう
来(く)る	来(こ)よう

きょう 病院(びょういん)へ行こうと思っています。	I'm thinking of going to the hospital today
日本町(まち)でおすしを食べようと思っています。	I'm thinking of eating sushi in Japan town.
うちへ帰って昼寝(ひるね)をしようと思います。	I think I'll go home and take a nap.

III. <u>Verb (te-form)</u> てしまいました   finish doing <u>V</u>

This form emphasizes completion and irreversibility and is usually used with non-stative verbs.

ケーキは全部食べてしまいました。	We ate up the whole cake.
宿題をやってしまいました。	I finished my homework.
金魚が死んでしまいました。	My goldfish died.
きのう雨にぬれたので風邪を引いてしまいました。	I got wet (by the rain) yesterday so I caught a cold.
時計がこわれてしまいました。	My watch broke.

Since this pattern indicates finality, it is often used in sentences that indicate regret or undesirability as in examples 3), 4), and 5) above. <u>V</u> てしまう, therefore, has the nuance of "too bad" or "there is nothing that can be done about it now."

第十六課　漢字

頭	熱	薬	昼
あたま	ねつ	くすり	ひる
頭	熱	薬	昼

子供	仕事	持つ	調べる
こ ども	し ごと	も	しら
子供	仕事	持つ	調べる

返す	着る	歩く	取る
かえ	き	ある	と
返す	着る	歩く	取る

第 十 七 課

17 A 岡村　　　　ブラウンさんは週末にどこかへ行きましたか。

ブラウン　　リノへ行ってきました。

岡村　　　　リノですか。聞いたことはありますがどんな
所ですか。

ブラウン　　ばくちをしたり離婚をしたりする所です。

岡村　　　　ああ，ギャンブルですか。ブラウンさんはや
ったんでしょう。

ブラウン　　そりゃあもちろん。

岡村　　　　で，勝ったんですか。

ブラウン　　いや，全然。二晩寝ないでブラックジャック
をやりましたが……

岡村　　　　そうですか。ブラウンさんでもですか。

17 B ジョンソン　山田さんはスキーがお好きでしたね。

山田　　　　ええ，日本ではいつも蔵王へ行ったり白馬へ
行ったりしていたんですがアメリカではまだ
行っていません。

ジョンソン　一度も行ったことがないんですか。いいスキ
ー場がたくさんあるのに……

山田　　　　ええ，スキーは去年買ったんですが冬休みに
なっても雪がなかったんです。

ジョンソン　でもこの十日ばかり続けて雪が降っています
からスコーバレーなんかいいんじゃないん
ですか。

山田　　　　そうですね。あそこは近くて行きやすいです
ね。

1 例 T: 風邪をひいています，行った
　　S: 風邪をひいているのに行きました。

1. 雨が降っています，行った
2. 雨が降っていました，行った
3. 試験がありました，勉強しなかった
4. 寒いです，コートを着ていない
5. (お)すしを作りました，誰も食べなかった
6. 天気がよかったです，一日中うちの中にいた
7. 雨が降っていました，泳ぎに行った
8. あのアパートはせまいです，家賃が高い
9. 田中さんは頭がいいです，ぜんぜん勉強しない
10. 宿題がたくさんありました，飲みに行った
11. 週末じゃありません，十二時まで飲んだ
12. テキストを買いました，ぜんぜん読まなかった
13. スミスさんは話すことができます，話さない
14. 今日は金曜日です　約束がぜんぜんない

2 例1 T: お金がなかった，行った
　　　{ S₁: お金がありませんでしたか。
　　　{ S₂: ええ，お金がなかったんですが，行きました。
　例2 T: 薬を飲んだ，おなかがまだ痛い
　　　{ S₁: 薬を飲みましたか。
　　　{ S₂: ええ，飲んだんですがおなかがまだ痛いんです。

224

1. ギャンブルをした，負けた
2. スキーを買った，まだ行っていない
3. 読んだ，何もわからなかった
4. 車を買った，運転する時間がない
5. 日本語を勉強した，ぜんぜん使わない
6. 辞書を買った，使い方がわからない
7. アスピリンを飲んだ，頭がまだ痛い
8. 電話をかけた，いらっしゃらなかった
9. ロスへ行った，ディズニーランドへ行かなかった
10. 日本へ行ったことがある，京都は行かなかった
11. 山田さんは行った，田中さんは行かなかった
12. 結婚したことがある，離婚したことはない
13. ブラックジャックをやった，負けた
14. 聞いたことがある，行ったことはない
15. 漢字はあまり難しくない，文法は難しい
16. 頭は痛い，熱はない
17. 大きい方は五セントだ，小さい方は十セントだ
18. 映画を見る，時代劇は見ない
19. 薬を飲んだ，ぜんぜん効かない
20. いらっしゃった，おもしろくなかった

3 例 T: 雨が降ります，行きます
　　　S: 雨が降っても行こうと思っています。

1. お金がありません，行きます
2. 難しいです，日本語をとります
3. 高いです，タイプライターを買います
4. 遅れます，クラスへ行きます
5. 雨が降ります，ジョギングをします
6. 雨です，走ります
7. 高いです，アパートを借りま

す

8. 頭が痛いです，ラボへ行きま
す

9. 疲れています，彼女に電話し
ます

10. グレイドがCです，日本語を
続けます

11. 高いです，ポルシェを買いま
す

12. 冬になります，毎日泳ぎます

④ 例 T: 週末，映画を見る，散歩をする

  S₁: 週末はどんなことをしましたか。
  S₂: そうですねえ，週末には，映画を見たり散歩をしたりしま
  した。

1. 日曜日，せんたくをする，買
物をする

2. 冬休み，スキーに行く，本を
読む

3. 夏休み，旅行する，アルバイ
トをする

4. ヨセミテ，滝を見る，ハーフ
ドームを見る

5. リノ，飲む，ギャンブルをす
る

6. お金のあるとき，おいしい物
を食べる，芝居を見る

7. 週末，友達と会う，小説を
読む

8. 今週，試験の勉強をする，タ
ーム・ペーパーを書く

9. 今日，漢字の練習をする，ジ
ャズを聞く

10. きのう，テレビを見る，雑誌
を読む

11. 先週末，人と会う，そうじを
する

12. 去年，社会学の論文を書く，
ドイツ語をとる

⑤ 例 T: スコーバレー

  S₁: どこがいいでしょうか。
  S₂: そうですねえ，スコーバレーなんかいいんじゃありませんか。

1. ヨセミテ
2. カリフォルニアのワイン
3. 社会学〔しゃかいがく〕
4. スミスさん
5. ジョンソン先生
6. 図書館〔としょかん〕
7. 三島〔みしま〕の「金閣寺〔きんかくじ〕」
8. 今週の土曜日の夕方
9. 山田さん
10. この辞書

6 例1 T: その本は難しいですね。（分かる）
　　　 S: ええ，とても分かりにくいです。
　 例2 T: その本は難しくありませんね。（分かる）
　　　 S: ええ，とても分かりやすいです

1. そのペンはいいですね。
　 （書く）
2. この本の字は小さいですね。
　 （読む）
3. あの先生の講義〔こうぎ〕は難しいです
　 ね。（分かる）
4. 「アイビー・エム セレクトリッ
　 ク」はいいですね。（使う）
5. この辞書は，あまり良〔よ〕くあり
　 ませんね。（？）
6. 「ホンダ・シビック」はいい車
　 ですね。（運転〔うんてん〕する）
7. この万年筆〔まんねんひつ〕はだめですね。（書
　 く）
8. そのくつはいいですね。（は
　 く）
9. そのセーター，いいですね。
　 （着る）
10. この漢字，難しいですね。（覚
　 える）

7 例 T: 宿題をして寝ましたか。
　　　 S: いえ，宿題をしないで寝ました。

1. 本を読んでベッドに入りまし
　 たか。
2. お金をはらってレストランを
　 出ましたか。

227

3.　朝ごはんを食べて来ましたか。

4.　漢字を使って書きましたか。

5.　予習_{よしゅう}をして学校_{がっこう}へ行きますか。

6.　図書館_{としょかん}の本を調べてレポート

　　を書きましたか。

7.　薬を飲んで寝ましたか。

8.　歯_はをみがいて寝ましたか。

9.　辞書を使って書きましたか。

10.　宿題を出して帰りましたか。

Lesson 17 **Dialogues**

17 A

Okamura: Did you go somewhere over the weekend?

週末　　　　　　　　　　　　weekend

Brown: Yes, I went to Reno.

リノ　　　　　　　　　　　　Reno

行ってくる　　　　　　　　　Lit., "went and came back"

O: Reno? Well, I've heard the name before. What kind of a place is it?

聞く　　　　　　　　　　　　to hear

B: It's a place where you gamble and get divorced.

ばくちをする　　　　　　　　to gamble

離婚_{りこん}する　　　　　　　　　to divorce, to get divorced

O: Oh, you mean gambling? You did, didn't you?

ギャンブル　　　　　　　　　to gamble (has a better sense than ばくちをする)

やる　　　　　　　　　　　　to do, a variant of する. Here it means "to gamble."

B: Well, of course!

O: And did you win?

勝_かつ　　　　　　　　　　　to win

228

B: Not one red cent! I played blackjack for two solid nights without sleeping, but...
no luck!

全然（ぜんぜん）   not at all

二晩（ふたばん）   two nights

ブラックジャック   blackjack

O: You too, huh?

でも   even

17 B

Johnson: If I remember correctly, you're fond of skiing, aren't you?

Yamada: Yes. In Japan, I always used to go to Zaoo and Shirouma, but I haven't been
yet here in America.

蔵王（ざおう）⎫
白馬（しろうま）⎭   Ski areas near Tokyo

J: You mean you've never been here? When there are so many good ski spots...

スキー場（じょう）   skiing spots

Y: Yes, I know. I bought skis last year, but there wasn't any snow, not even at winter
break, so...

去年（きょねん）   last year

冬休み   winter vacation

J: But it's been snowing pretty much continuously for the last ten
days or so, so wouldn't the skiing be great at places like Squaw Valley?

続ける（つづ）   to continue

なんか   (places) like

Y: Yes, I imagine so. Squaw Valley's close and easy to get to, isn't it?

近い   near, close

Lesson 17 Notes on Usage

17 A

1. The verb やる (to do) is an informal variant of する (to do). Somehow when talking about gambling, the verb やる sounds better—probably because gambling is generally looked down upon. Strangely enough when one talks about movies, やる is used instead of する.

「スターウォーズ」はどこでやっ　　Where is <u>Star Wars</u> playing?
ていますか。

やる should be used only in the cases described above until one becomes familiar with the implications of this verb.

2. そりゃあもちろん　　　　　　　　of course

そりゃあ is a contracted form of それは "That's" and もちろん mean "of course" or "without saying." Together the phrase means "Of course" or "That goes without saying."

3. いや全然　　　　　　　　　　No, not at all.

いや is contracted form of いいえ (another variation is いえ). 全然 means "not at all" and it is usually used in negative sentences.

今日は全然調子が出ない。　　　　I just can't get it together at all today.
あの人を知っていますか。　　　　Do you know that person?
いや全然(知りません)。　　　　　…No, I don't know him at all.
あの映画は全然面白くありませ　　That movie is not interesting at all.
ん。

4. 二晩　　　　　　　　　　two nights

晩 is a classifier used to count "nights" or "evenings." It is used with the Japanese number system for counting from one up to three nights. For counting four nights, we say 四日間毎晩 "Every night for four days."

1.　一晩　　　2.　二晩　　　3.　三晩　　　4.　幾晩

230

17 B

1. 一度^{いちど}も行ったことがないんです。　　I haven't gone even once.

一度 is "once" and 度 is a classifier used to count "times," up to three "times." Thereafter 回^{かい} is more commonly used.

　　1.　一度　いちど　　　2.　二度　にど　　　3.　三度　さんど

回^{かい} is a classifier used to count "turn" or "time." 回^{かい} and 度^ど can be used interchangeably.

　　何回　　　　　　　　　　　　how many times.

1.	一回　いっかい		6.	六回　ろっかい
2.	二回　にかい		7.	七回　ななかい
3.	三回　さんかい		8.	八回　はちかい
4.	四回　よんかい		9.	九回　きゅうかい
5.	五回　ごかい		10.	十回　じゅっかい

2. スキー場^{じょう}　　　　　　　　　　ski resort

スキー "ski" + 場 "place." This usually refers to ski slopes with facilities such as lifts, lodges, restaurants, etc.

3. 冬休み　　　　　　　　　　　　winter vacation

冬 "winter" plus 休み "vacation, holiday(s)"

4. 冬休みになっても雪がなかった　　There wasn't any snow even at winter
　　んです　　　　　　　　　　　　break so...

Because からです is used to give straightforward, cause-and-effect type of reasons to explain a given situation, it may sound too strong or aggressive in some cases. To soften this, an explanation using のです "the fact (explanation) is..." can be used.

5. 十日^{とおか}ばかり　　　　　　　　for about ten days
　　How to count days:

231

1.	一日 いちにち	9.	九日 ここのか
2.	二日 ふつか	10.	十日 とおか
3.	三日 みっか	11.	十一日 じゅういちにち
4.	四日 よっか	12.	十二日 じゅうににち
5.	五日 いつか	13.	十四日 じゅうよっか
6.	六日 むいか	14.	二十日 はつか
7.	七日 なのか	15.	二十四日 にじゅうよっか
8.	八日 ようか		

Number (w/classifier) + ばかり   _____ or so (about _____)

ばかり basically means "exclusively" or "only," but when it follows immediately after numbers or numbers with classifiers it means "about _____" or "_____ or so."

昨日のパーティーには三十人ばかり来ましたよ。	About thirty people came to the party yesterday.
山田さんと五分ばかり話しました。	I talked to Yamada about five minutes or so.
田中さんに十ドルばかり貸しました。	I lent Tanaka about $10.

6. 続けて	continuously
続けてください。	Please go on.
十日ばかり続けて雪が降りました。	It snowed continuously for about ten days.
四日間毎晩続けてブラックジャックをやりました。	I played blackjack for four nights straight.

7. スコーバレーなんかいいんじゃありませんか。	Wouldn't something like Squaw Valley be good? (Lit., "Isn't it the case that Squaw Valley, for example, is good?")

なんか is an informal variant of など (and so on, and such) and is used to give some possible suggestions or examples. いいんじゃないんですか "isn't it good?" is in the form of a question, but it is used when making a suggestion to someone.

232

住むところを探しているんです
が。

I'm looking for a place to live.

ああそうですか。コープなんか
いいんじゃないんですか。

...Oh, I see... Wouldn't some place like
the Co-ops be good?

いいんじゃありませんか。 can also be used.

Lesson 17 Grammar Notes

The main points of this lesson are:
 I. Two patterns used to express "even though" or "although."
 II. A pattern used to express "even."
 III. A pattern used to express more than two activities that are done A) by one person
  one after another within a limited period of time or B) by two or more people, one
  doing one thing and another doing something else at the same time.
 IV. A pattern used to express "easy to do ____" and "difficult to do ____."
 V. A pattern used to express "without doing ____."

I. のに and が

A.　X のに Y

Even though/Although X, Y.

山田さんは風邪をひいているの
に学校へ行きました。

Yamada went to school even though
he has a cold.

寒いのにコートを着ないんです
か。

You're not wearing a coat even though
it's cold?

花子さんはきれいなのに誰もデ
ートに誘いません。

Even though Hanako is pretty, no one
asks her out (Lit., "dates her").

このアパートは狭いのに家賃が
高いんです。

Although it's small, the rent (of this apartment) is high.

せっかくおすしを作ったのに誰(だれ)
も食べていません。

Even though I went to all the trouble of making sushi, no one is eating any (or no one has eaten any.)

B. Sentence₁ が Sentence₂   Sentence₁ but Sentence₂

This is the same が that was introduced in Lesson 2 (さあよく分(わ)かりませんが図書館(としょかん)でしょう "Well, I don't know. I guess it's a library.")

お金があまりありませんでした
が買いました。

I didn't have much money but I bought it.

パーティーへ行きましたが面白(おもしろ)
くありませんでした。

I went to the party but it wasn't much fun.

In X のに Y it is implied that under normal circumstances, if X then something other than Y was expected to take place but for some reason Y occurred. が, on the other hand, does not necessarily have this implication. For instance, in the example above, if someone has a cold one would normally expect the person to stay at home. Yamada, however, does not stay at home but goes to school. The speaker expresses this occurrence of something contrary to his expectations by using のに. If, on the other hand, が were used, it would indicate that the speaker does not particularly consider Yamada's behavior as contrary to what is normally done. Thus, のに carries a stronger connotation of a contradiction of expectations and is translated into English as "even though" or "although."

いいスキー場(じょう)がたくさんあります。(There are many good ski resorts.) Since Yamada likes skiing, one would expect that she goes to ski at these resorts very often, but contrary to our expectations, she does not. Thus, のに is used in this sentence: いいスキー場がたくさんあるのに… Similarly, in 高いのに買いました (I bought it even though it was expensive.), a poor student who does not have much money usually does not buy expensive things, but in the example above, he does buy it.

With のに only plain forms are used. The polite form is more commonly used with が。

	のに	が
V	降っているのに行(い)きます。	降って{いる / います}が行きます。
A	高いのによくありません。	高い{ / です}がよくありません。
AN	立派(りっぱ)なのに安いです。	立派{だ / です}が安いです。
N	先生なのに何も知りません。	先生{だ / です}が何も知りません。

234

II. Verb (te-form) A/AN/N ても   even/even if

雨が降ってもやります。   We'll do it even if it rains.

お金があっても買いません。   I won't buy it even if we have money.

高くてもいいです。   It's all right even if it's expensive.

辞書をひいても分かりません。   I can't understand it even if I use a dictionary.

冬休みになっても雪がありませんでした。   Even during the winter holidays (Lit., "even after it became winter vacation"), it didn't snow.

ブラウンさんでも勝つことができません。   Even Brown can't win.

これは日本人でも分かりませんよ。   Even a Japanese wouldn't understand this.

The form is the same as the one in _____ てもいいです。 "You may _____."

III. V₁ たり V₂ たりする (Verb (plain past form) + り)

This pattern can mean a) the same person sometimes does A and sometimes B within a limited period of time or b) in a given group, some people are doing one thing and others another. (This pattern corresponds to the pattern for the partial listing of nouns, ~や~や~など.)

A. 日曜日には洗濯したり部屋を掃除したり，テレビを見たりします。   On Sundays I do the laundry, clean my room, and watch TV.

日本ではいつも蔵王へ行ったり白馬へ行ったりしました。   In Japan I went to Zaoo and Shirouma (both ski resorts).

勉強ばかりしないで時々泳いだり走ったりしなければいけませんよ。   You shouldn't just study; you should go swimming and jogging sometimes.

235

きょうは一日中降ったりやんだりするでしょう。

It will probably rain off and on all day today.

B. 子供たちはテレビを見たり昼寝をしたりしています。

Some children are watching TV and others are taking naps.

リノは（人々が）ばくちをしたり，離婚をしたりする所です。

Reno is a place where people make bets and get divorced. (Lit., "where some people make bets and others get divorced).

学生たちは図書館で勉強したりベアーズレアーでビールを飲んだりしています。

Some students study at the library and others drink beer at Bear's Lair.

The second V- たり can be left out when its implication is obvious.

日曜日には洗濯したりします。

I do the laundry (and other things) on Sundays.

IV. A. V(pre-masu form) + やすい   easy to V

B. V(pre-masu form) + にくい   difficult to V

スコーバレーは近くて行きやすいですね。

Squaw Valley is close by and easy to get to, isn't it?

「暖かい」は発音しにくいですね。

The word "atatakai" is hard to pronounce, isn't it?

このペンは書きやすいですね。

This pen is easy to write with, isn't it?

この活字は小さくて読みにくいです。

This typeface is so small that (literally, "and") it's hard to read.

山川先生の講義は分かりにくいです。

Professor Yamakawa's lectures are hard to understand.

V. Verb (Plain Non-Past Neg.) ないで   without doing _____

236

This is the same form as the one used in <u>V</u>– ないでください (L. 8)。

二晩寝ないでブラックジャックをやりました。

I played blackjack for two nights without sleeping.

花子さんはこのごろ仕事をしないで酒ばかり飲んでいますよ。

Nowadays Hanako doesn't work but (literally, "and") only drinks (sake).

毎朝御飯を食べないで学校へ行きます。

Every morning I go to school without eating breakfast.

第十七課　漢字

毎　日
まい　にち

毎　日

毎　朝
まい　あさ

毎　朝

毎　晩
まい　ばん

毎　晩

夕　方
ゆう　がた

夕　方

休　み
やす

休　み

小　説
しょう　せつ

小　説

運　転
うん　てん

運　転

結　婚　する
けっ　こん

結　婚　する

歌　う
うた

歌　う

復　習　する
ふく　しゅう

復　習　する

練　習　する
れん　しゅう

練　習　する

勉　強　する
べん　きょう

勉　強　する

第　十　八　課

18 A　スミス　　　明日ラグビーの試合を見に行きませんか。

　　　　岡村　　　　見ても分からないんじゃないかと思いますが
　　　　　　　　　　……

　　　　スミス　　　岡村さんは「スポーツが好きです」と言ってい
　　　　　　　　　　たでしょう。

　　　　岡村　　　　ええ，でもラグビーは見たことがないんです。
　　　　　　　　　　ここは強いんですか。

　　　　スミス　　　ええ，しかし明日の相手はサンノゼのはずです
　　　　　　　　　　から勝てるかどうか分かりません。

18 B　ブラウン　　　みんなが渡辺さんはピアノが得意だと言ってい
　　　　　　　　　　ますがいつか聞きたいですね。

　　　　渡辺　　　　何かの間違いでしょう。まだバイエルを始めた
　　　　　　　　　　ばかりです。ブラウンさんは何か……

　　　　ブラウン　　私は音楽は苦手で何もできません。第一あの音
　　　　　　　　　　符が読めないんです。

　　　　渡辺　　　　でも歌は歌えるでしょう。

　　　　ブラウン　　ええ，あまり上手なので隣の人がすぐ窓を閉め
　　　　　　　　　　ます。

239

1 例 T: 漢字を書く

  {S₁: 漢字が書けますか。

  {S₂: いいえ，書けません。

1. 日本語を話す
2. 車を運転する
3. ピアノをひく
4. テニスをする
5. フランス語を話す
6. 図書館を使う
7. 明日のパーティーに来る
8. 新しい車を買う
9. この漢字を読む
10. 歩いてサンフランシスコへ行く

11. 寮で勉強する
12. 「バンカメリカード」を使う
13. 今日，クイズを受ける
14. ここでタバコをすう
15. 教室でビールを飲む
16. 三時までに来る
17. さしみを食べる
18. はしを使う
19. 三十ページ予習する
20. 英語を教える

2 例 T: 行く

  {S₁: 行きますか。

  {S₂: さあ，行くかどうかわかりません。

1. 買う
2. 見る
3. 買える
4. 書ける
5. 食べる
6. 卒業できる
7. 日本語で話せる
8. スーツを着て行く
9. ビールを飲む
10. クラスに出る

11. 田中さんは帰った
12. あのレストランは高い
13. スミスさんは結婚している
14. 試験は難しい
15. 先生は研究室にいらっしゃる
16. これは先生の本だ
17. 山田さんはきれいだ
18. 山田さんは英語ができる
19. 来年日本へ行ける
20. 田中さんはピアノが上手だ

240

③　例　T: 行く
　　　　　 { S₁: 行きましたか。
　　　　　 { S₂: いいえ。行こうと思っていたんですが，行けませんでした。

1.　行く	11.　中国語，とる
2.　読む	12.　漢字，練習する
3.　見る	13.　宿題，する
4.　来る	14.　論文<ruby>(ろんぶん)</ruby>，書く
5.　予習<ruby>(よしゅう)</ruby>する	15.　日本，行く
6.　持って来る	16.　大学，卒業<ruby>(そつぎょう)</ruby>する
7.　作る	17.　先生，質問<ruby>(しつもん)</ruby>する
8.　コピーする	18.　先生，お会いする
9.　質問<ruby>(しつもん)</ruby>する	19.　新しい車，買う
10.　着る	20.　セミナー，出る

④　例1　T: 山田さんは来ますね。
　　　　　 S: ええ，来るはずです。
　　　例2　T: 山田さんは来ませんね。
　　　　　 S: ええ，来ないはずです。

1.　山田さんは行きますね。	6.　スミスさんは日本へ行きませんね。
2.　カーターさんは来ますね。	
3.　スミスさんは来ていますね。	7.　山田さんの部屋<ruby>(へや)</ruby>は広いですね。
4.　山田さんは英語を勉強していますね。	8.　渡辺<ruby>(わたなべ)</ruby>さんの部屋<ruby>(へや)</ruby>はきれいですね。
5.　船<ruby>(ふね)</ruby>はフィッシャーマンズウォーフから出ますね。	9.　山田さんは「ルーツ」を読んでいませんね。

241

10. 小山さんはサンフランシスコ
  へ行っていますね。
11. 今日はだれも来ませんね。
12. カーターさんはアパートです
  ね。
13. 山田さんの専門は社会学です
  ね。
14. ブラウンさんは日本へ行きま
  したね。
15. ビールは飲んでしまいました
  ね。

16. 飛行機は，午後一時の日航で
  すね。
17. スミスさんはさしみが好きじ
  ゃありませんね。
18. ジョンソンさんはヨーロッパ
  へ行ったことがありますね。
19. ルームメートはもう寝ました
  ね。
20. ブラウンさんはギャンブルを
  しますね。

5 例 T: 山田さん，「行きます」
  S₁: 山田さんが「行きます」と言いました。
  S₂: 本当ですか．山田さんが行くと言ったんですか。

1. 田中さん，「来ます」
2. スミスさん，「今晩は勉強しま
  せん」
3. カーターさん，「手紙を書きま
  す」
4. 小山さん，「結婚します」
5. 山田さん，「専門は社会学で
  す」
6. ベラーさん，「クラシックが好
  きです」

7. スミスさん，「日本語はおもし
  ろいです
8. ジョンソンさん，「スコーバレ
  ーがいいです」
9. ブラウンさん，「リノでブラッ
  クジャックをしません」
10. 山田さん，「日本へ帰ります」
11. 先生，「明日クイズをします」
12. ブラウンさん，「渡辺さんはピ
  アノが得意です」

242

6　例 1　T:　田中さんは行きますね。

　　　　　S:　いえ，行かないんじゃないかと思いますが……

　　例 2　T:　田中さんは行けませんね。

　　　　　S:　いえ，行けるんじゃないかと思いますが……

1.　スミスさんは来ませんね。

2.　山田さんは，図書館にいますね。

3.　先生はいらっしゃいますね。

4.　田中さんは結婚していますね。

5.　ブラウンさんは，ロシア語ができますね。

6.　スミスさんは，フランス語が話せますね。

7.　明日の試合は勝てますね。

8.　渡辺さんはピアノが得意ですね。

9.　ブラウンさんは，大学院の学生ですね。

10.　岡田さんは，日本人ですね。

11.　分かりますね。

12.　日本のスキーは，いいですね。

Lesson 18　**Dialogues**

18A

Smith: Would you like to go and see a rugby match tomorrow?

試合　　　　　　　　　　　　　　　　match, game

Okamura: Gee, I wonder if I'd know what was going on even if I went.

S: But you said you like sports, didn't you?

O: Yes, but I've never seen rugby. Is the team here good?

S: Yes, but I think tomorrow we're playing San Jose, so I don't know if we can beat them or not.

相手　　　　　　　　　　　　　　　　opponents, opposing team

Brown: Everyone says you're great on the piano. I'd like to hear you sometime?

得意　　とくい　　　　　　　　　　　　　　forte, specialty

Watanabe: There must be some mistake. I've only just begun <u>Beyer</u>. Do you play an instrument?

バイエル　　　　　　　　　　　　　　Beyer, a widely used piano exercise book for beginners (Ferdinand Beyer, 1803–1863)

B: I'm really terrible at music. I can't play a thing. In the first place I can't even read those notes.

音楽　　おんがく　　　　　　　　　　　　music
苦手　　にがて　　　　　　　　　　　　　a weak point
音符　　おんぷ　　　　　　　　　　　　　musical notes

W: But surely you can sing.

B: Oh, yes, I've got such a great voice that the people next door slam their windows shut whenever I sing.

隣　　となり　　　　　　　　　　　　　next door, neighbor

すぐ　　　　　　　　　　　　　　　　　right away

閉める　　し　　　　　　　　　　　　　to close (something)

Lesson 18 **Notes on Usage**

(nothing on 18A)

18B

1. ピアノが得意です。　とくい　　　(You) are good at piano.

音楽は苦手です。　にがて　　　　　(I) am not good at music

得意 means "one's forte" and 苦手, "one's weak point." Both words indicate one's subjective judgment. Thus, 得意 has the sense of "I think I am good at _____," or "He thinks that he is good at _____," etc. One can say, 私は歌が得意です。(I am good at singing.) even though other people unanimously disagree with him.

得意 means that the person feels good about his performance. Usually it is the case that his subjective judgment and other's objective judgment agree, so in most cases, 山田さんは歌が上手です and 山田さんは歌が得意です mean the same thing.

苦手 means that a person feels uneasy about his performance. It is a subjective judgment. Very often the person is not skilled at the thing in question, and therefore, feels uneasy about it. Normally, 私は音楽が苦手です and 私は音楽が下手です mean the same thing. 苦手 can also be used in the following manner;

私は山田さんが苦手です。　　　　I can't deal with Yamada.

上手 means that one is good at performing a skill. So, it is fine to say, 山田さんは英語が上手です。This means that Mr. Yamada is good at speaking English. For less kinesthetic activities, such as mathematics, 上手 cannot be used.

In such a case, one must say 山田さんは数学が得意です When 得意 means "one's forte" 上手 and 下手 indicate objective judgments. Therefore, they are usually used to refer to someone else. e.g. ジョンは歌が上手です。私は歌が上手です sounds extremely arrogant, and is best avoided. 私は歌が下手です on the other hand, sounds humble and is a good sentence. 山田さんは歌が得意ですが，下手です。Mr. Yamada's specialty is singing but he's not very good. (He thinks that he is good but he's really not.)

2.　何かの間違いでしょう。　　　　It must be a mistake of some kind.

　　間違い　　　　　　　　　　　　mistake

3.　始めたばかりです。

Verb (Plain, Past) + ばかり "just V (-ed)"
So, the sentence means, "I have just started now." Lesson 21 will deal with this pattern.

4.　ブラウンさんは何か……　　　　How about you, Brown? (Do you play) anything...?

5.　第一あの音符が読めないんです。　First of all I cannot read music (lit. sound symbols)

　　第一 "first of all" (第一 literally means "the first," or "the number one" of a series of items.)

　　あの音符，あの means "that (one that you know)," 音符，音 means "sound" and 符 "symbol." It is colloquially referred to as おたまじゃくし "a tadpole" because of its shape.

6.　でも歌は歌えるでしょう

しょう is pronounced with a rising intonation because it is a question.

7.　ええ，あまり上手なので隣の人がすぐ窓をしめます。

あまり上手なので "because I am too good" Usually, あまり takes a negative predicate such as ──ません, ─ないでしょう, etc. In this case, the negative is covertly implied, just like the English "too" as in "too good", etc.

隣の人 "nextdoor." すぐ "immediately," "as soon as." Altogether, the sentence means "Since I am too good (at singing), the people nextdoor shut their windows as soon as (I start singing)."

Lesson 18　**Grammar Notes**

The main points of this lesson are:
  I. Another pattern to express "potentiality." Unlike the form introduced in Lesson 6 (＿＿ことができる), this pattern attaches an affix to the root of a verb.
 II. The pattern used for quotations: direct quotes, and indirect quotes.
III. Three useful expressions:
  A. A pattern to express notions such as "It is presumably ＿＿," "It would normally be assumed that ＿＿," "I feel sure that ──," or "It is supposed to be that ＿＿."
  B. A pattern to express one's opinion without committing oneself as in "I have a feeling that ＿＿."
  C. A pattern expressing uncertainty as in "I don't know whether or not ──."

I. Potential expression

Potentials are formed by attaching an affix to the verb root:
rare-ru to RU-verbs and e-ru to U-verbs. This form is used much more widely than ことができる.

RU-verbs	Plain form	Polite form
食べる	食べられる	食べられます
起きる	起きられる	起きられます
いる	いられる	いられます
U-verbs	Plain form	Polite form
書く	書ける	書けます

246

飲む	飲める	飲めます
泳ぐ	泳げる	泳げます
Irregular verbs	Plain form	Polite form
する	できる	できます
来る	来られる	来られます
行く	行ける（行かれる）	行けます（行かれます）

できる is used as the potential form of する.

勉強する	(to study)	勉強できる
掃除する	(to clean up)	掃除できる

Verbs such as できる and わかる do not have a potential form because they are already potential in meaning.

Both 行く and 来る have two potential forms.

The object marker in this pattern is が instead of を just as with 好き, きらい, 欲しい, etc.

RU-verbs:	歯が痛いので何も食べられません。	(I) have a toothache so I can't eat anything.
	時間がなくて映画が見られませんでした。	I didn't have time so I couldn't go to (see) the movie.
U-verbs:	日本語で歌が歌えますか。	Can you sing in Japanese (lit. sing a song in Japanese)?
	私は音符が読めません。	I can't read music (lit. musical notes).

Irregular verbs:

何ができますか。	What can you do?
何もできません。	I can't do anything.
明日は来られないんですが。	I cannot come tomorrow, but...
明日は｛行　け／行かれ｝ないんですが。	I cannot go tomorrow, but...

Two verbs 見える and 聞こえる are similar to potential verbs. They are intransitive verbs, and are used in the following ways.

見える：きょうは天気がいいので富士山が見えます。	It's clear today so we can see Mt. Fuji. (lit. Mt. Fuji is visible (to us)).
聞こえる：あの家からねこの声が聞こえます。	From that house, a cat's meow can be heard.

II. Quotations

A. Direct quotation: 「_____」と言う
B. Indirect quotation: <u>Sentence (plain form)</u> と言う

と is a quotation marker used for both direct and indirect quotes. When in written form, direct quotations are marked by another set of markers: 「私は」 (for horizontal writing) or 「私は」 (for vertical writing). Indirect quotes do not have such markers. Instead the plain form of the verb is used for the quoted passage and, as in English, adjustments are made in tense and person (e.g. 1st person··· 3rd person) to coincide with the time and location of the utterance.

昨日山田さんは「明日オフィスに行きます」と言いました。	Yesterday Yamada said, "I'll go to the office tomorrow."
昨日山田さんはきょうオフィスに来ると言いました。	Yesterday Yamada said that she would come to the office today.
山田さんは「行きません」と言いました。	Yamada said, "I won't go."
山田さんは行かないと言いました。	Yamada said that she would not go.
山田さんは「見ました」と言いました。	Yamada said, "I saw it."
山田さんは見たと言いました。	Yamada said that she saw it.

Some verbs used in quotes: 言う to say, 話す to speak, 聞く to ask, inquire, 答える to answer

Verbs of thinking such as 思う to think, 考える to consider, etc. also take と, but they are never used with direct quotations.

雨が降ると思いますか。   Do you think that it'll rain tomorrow?

いいえ，降らないと思います。   No, I don't think it will (rain).

III. Three Useful Expressions

A.   <u>Sentence (plain form)</u> はずです   I expect that/I feel sure that _____, <u>X</u> is supposed to be _____.

    V （行く/行った）
    A （高い/高かった）
  AN （元気な/元気だった）
    N （先生の/先生だった）
  Neg （—ない/—なかった）

はずです means "What a speaker has every reason to believe/expect," "What ought naturally to be true."

きょうの相手はサンノゼのはずです。   We're supposed to play San Jose today. (Lit. Today's opponent is supposed to be San Jose.)

山田さんはきょう来るはずです。   Yamada is supposed/expected to come today.

山田さんはもううちに帰っているはずです。   Yamada is probably home by now. (Lit. Yamada is supposed to be home (already) by now.)

スミスさんは日本へ行かないはずです。   I expect that Smith won't be going to Japan. (Lit. "It's expected that Smith won't go to Japan.")

はず behaves like a noun.

死んだはずの人に会いました。   I met a person who was supposed to be dead.

Note the difference in nuance in the following negative sentences:

山田さんはきょうは来ないはずです。   (I) expect that Yamada won't come today. (definite expectation of Yamada's not coming)

山田さんはきょう来るはずはあ   There is no way that Yamada will come

りません。

today. (my conjecture)
(lit. "the expectation that Yamada will come does not exist.")

The form はずがある does not occur in declarative sentences. The affirmative form can only be はずです.

B. Sentence (Plain form) んじゃないか
　　　　　　　　　と思います

I have a feeling that____ (Lit. "I (think that) wonder if it is not the case that ____ "

V　（書く/書いた）
A　（高い/高かった）
AN　（元気な/元気だった）
N　（先生な/先生だった）
Neg　（―ない/―なかった）

ラグビーの試合(しあい)は見ても分から

ないんじゃないかと思います。

I have a feeling that I wouldn't understand a rugby match even if I (went to) see one.

雨が降るんじゃないかと思います。

I have a feeling that it will rain today.

This form sounds more modest than the straight forward ____ と思います because the speaker leaves a possibility that his opinion may be wrong.

C. Sentence (Plain form) かどうか分かりません

V　（行く/行った）
A　（高い/高かった）
AN　（きれい/きれいだった）
N　（学生/学生だった）
Neg　（―ない/―なかった）

I don't know whether or not ____

きょう行きますか。

Are you going today?

さあ，行くかどうか分かりません。

Gee, I don't know whether I will go or not.

あのレストランは高いですか。

Is that restaurant expensive?

さあ，高いかどうか分かりません。

Gee, I don't know whether or not it is expensive.

音楽
おん　がく
音　楽

専門
せん　もん
専　門

今　度
こん　ど
今　度

店
みせ
店

お酒
さけ
お　酒

和英辞典
わ　えい　じ　てん
和　英　辞　典

図書館
と　しょ　かん
図　書　館

言　う
い
言　う

受ける
う
受　け　る

強い
つよ
強　い

去年
きょ　ねん
去　年

今　年
こ　とし
今　年

来年
らい　ねん
来　年

19 A　ベイリー　　　札幌へ行きたいんですが，あのう，予約はまだなんですけど……

ぜんにっくう
全日空　　　あのう，申し訳ございませんが札幌は霧が深いために，今のところ欠航になっておりますが……

ベイリー　　　あ，そうですか。あのう，一日中だめですか。

ぜんにっくう
全日空　　　はあ。申し訳ございませんが……天気予報では一日中霧だそうですから……

ベイリー　　　でも，天気予報はあまり当たらないんじゃないんですか。

19 B　ブラウン　　　山田さんは明日何か予定がありますか。

山田　　　明日は……もしいいお天気になれば近くの公園へ散歩に行こうと思っていますが……

ブラウン　　　そうですか。でも天気予報によると明日も雨だそうですよ。

山田　　　そうですか。ところで，ねえブラウンさん，変な物を食べた時おなかが痛くなるでしょう。こういうことを何と言うか知っていますか。

ブラウン　　　「あたる」でしょう。山田さんのあげたてんぷらにあたったとか……

山田　　　まあ，じゃ食べ物にあたらないおまじないを教えましょうか。

ブラウン　　　そんなものあるんですか。

山田　　　　　　　天気予報，天気予報，天気予報って三遍言うんです。

1　例　T：明日，散歩に行きますか。（天気がいい）
　　　　S：ええ，もし天気がよければ行きます。

1. テニスをしますか。（時間がある）
2. 日本へ行きますか。（お金がある）
3. カメラを買いますか。（安い）
4. その本を買いますか。（分かりやすい）
5. 朝，早く起きられますか。（早く寝る）
6. その車を買いますか。（高くない）
7. 山田さんに会えますか。（早く行く）
8. 宿題をしますか。（時間がある）
9. 予習をしますか。（友達が来ない）
10. 映画に行きますか。（おもしろい）
11. セーターを買いますか。（いい）
12. パーティーへ行きますか。（宿題がない）
13. 泳ぎに行きますか。（宿題が終わる）
14. パーティーへ行きますか。（スミスさんが行かない）

2　例　T：あした雨が降ります。
　　　　S：あした雨が降るそうです。

1. 行きます。
2. 食べます。
3. 読みます。
4. アメリカ人です。
5. 社会学です。
6. 美しいです。

254

7. きれいです。
8. 立派（りっぱ）です。
9. おもしろいです。
10. 忙（いそが）しいです。
11. 上手です。
12. 話せます。
13. 大きいです。
14. 卒業（そつぎょう）しました。
15. 札幌（さっぽろ）は霧（きり）が深（ふか）いです。
16. 長崎（ながさき）は雨です。
17. その本は10ドルです。
18. 田中さんが結婚しました。
19. スミスさんはきれいです。

20. 来週，試験があります。
21. 北海道（ほっかいどう）の冬は寒いです。
22. 田中さんはソニーが好きです。
23. 先生はあしたいらっしゃいません。
24. あの店はてんぷらがおいしいです。
25. あの講義（こうぎ）はおもしろくありません。
26. 東京はきれいじゃありません。
27. 東京はあぶなくありません。
28. あしたは天気になります。

③　例1　T: 部屋，明るい，なる
　　　　　S: 部屋が明るくなりました。
　　例2　T: 部屋，明るい，する
　　　　　S: 部屋を明るくしました。

1. 空（そら），明るい，なる
2. かべ，明るい，する
3. 天気，よい，なる
4. 氷（こおり），水，なる
5. 部屋，あたたかい，する
6. 暑い，なる

7. 寒い，なる
8. ガソリン，高い，なる
9. 日本語，やさしい，なる
10. 部屋，きれい，する
11. いい，天気，なる

④　例　T: 天気予報，雨が降ります。

　　　　{S₁: 雨が降るでしょうか。
　　　　{S₂: 天気予報によると降るそうです。

1. テレビのニュース，ガソリンが高くなります。
2. 天気予報，来週から寒くなります。
3. 山川さん，あの映画はおもしろいです。
4. 田中さん，スミスさんは結婚します。
5. スミスさんの話，大学の寮はうるさいです。
6. ブラウンさん，あのバーはいいです。
7. 今日の新聞，モンデイルがバークレーに来ます。
8. 先生のお話，漢字は難しくありません。
9. 山田さん，スミスさんは結婚しています。
10. 新聞，また石油が高くなります。
11. 小山さん，山田さんは卒業しました。
12. 「ニューズ・ウイーク」，レーガンは新しいプランを作っています。

⑤　例　T: 事故がありました，遅くなりました。
　　　　S: 事故のために，遅くなったんです。

1. 試験がありました，手紙がおくれました。
2. 風邪をひいていました，泳ぎに行けませんでした。
3. 古い魚を食べました，おなかが痛くなりました。
4. 霧が深いです，飛行機がおくれました。
5. 強い風です，飛行機がおくれました。

256

6. 今朝4時まで飲んでいました，朝8時のクラスへ行けませんでした。

7. 友達が来ました，宿題ができませんでした。

8. お金を落としました，歩いて帰りました。

9. 友達が病気でした，自分のアパートに帰りませんでした。

10. 貯金がありました，勉強を続けることができました。

6 例1 T： 山田さん，先生です，学生です
　　　　{S₁： 山田さんは先生でしょうか。
　　　　{S₂： いえ，学生なんじゃないですか。

　　例2 T： 山田さん，行きます，行きません
　　　　{S₁： 山田さんは行くでしょうか。
　　　　{S₂： いえ，行かないんじゃないですか。

1. この車，安いです，高いです
2. 明日，雨が降ります，降りません
3. 明日，雨です，雨じゃありません
4. 田中さん，います，帰りました
5. あした，クイズがあります，ありません
6. あの方，先生です，大学院生です
7. 鈴木さん，卒業できません，できます
8. 渡辺さん，ピアノが上手です，下手です
9. 岡田さん，日本人です，日本人じゃありません
10. 札幌は，雨が降っています，雪が降っています

Lesson 19 **Dialogues**

19 A

Bailey: I'd like to go to Sapporo, but I haven't made any reservations yet. I wonder if (I could make some now)...

予約 — reservation

けど — variation of けれども however

Clerk: At the Zennikkuu (All Nippon Airlines) counter:
I'm sorry, but because of the heavy fog all flights to Sapporo have been cancelled for the time being.

霧 — fog

欠航 — no flights, flight is cancelled

B: Is that right? Well, will it be that way all day?

一日中 — all day long

だめ — no good

C: Yes, unfortunately..., according to the forecast, it looks like fog all day.

申し訳ございません — I am sorry

天気予報 — weather report

B: But weather reports aren't very reliable, are they?

でも — however, but

当たる — to be accurate

19 B

Brown: Do you have any plans for tomorrow?

予定 — plan

Yamada: Tomorrow.... Well, if the weather's nice, I am thinking about going for a walk in the park (close to my house).

もし   if

散歩（さんぽ）   a walk

B: I see. But according to the weather report, it's supposed to rain tomorrow, too.

Y: Is that right? By the way,... you know when you eat something bad and get a stomachache? Do you know what you call that?

変（へん）な物（もの）   something weird, bad

こういうこと   this sort of thing

B: It's "to get sick to your stomach," right? Like, "the tempura that you made made me sick to my stomach..."

〜にあたる   to get sick to one's stomach from eating something

Y: Well, really!... Shall I teach you an incantation so you won't get any upsets?

おまじない   an incantation, a magical charm

教えましょうか   shall I teach you

B: You mean there's such a thing?

Y: You say weather report, weather report, weather report three times.

三遍（さんべん）   three times

Lesson 19 **Notes on Usage**

19 A

1. あのう "Ummm..."

Though it is a meaningless and logically unnecessary form, it is very necessary in conversation. Without it the content of the sentence is exposed too directly, and the sentence sounds too bare.

2. けど

けど is a contracted form of けれど or けれども (Lit. "but"). が (but) is also used in this sense especially in a formal situation. けど is an informal counterpart of が.

259

3. 申し訳ございません   I am sorry.

It is a very humble form of apology. (Lit., "there is no excuse.")

4. 今のところ   for now

5. はあ   Yes.

A colloquial humble form of はい. Usually it is used by an inferior to a sperior. Some people use this form to exhalt the addressee to a higher status in conversation.

6. 天気予報では一日中霧だそうですから

天気 (てんき) (weather), 予報 (よほう) (forecast). で (in, by means of) Thus, it means, "According to the weather forecast, it will be foggy all day." では can only be used with an inanimate source of information.

この本では田中は何も知らなかったそうです。	According to this book (Lit. "In this book it says") Tanaka did not know anything.
あの映画ではその時山本は死にませんでした。	According to that movie (Lit. in that movie) Yamamoto didn't die at that time.

7. 当たらないんじゃないですか。

当たる is an intransitive verb, which means "to hit". The phrase 天気予報が当たる is an idiom, which means "the weather forecast is right."

19 B

1. 変な物を食べた時
変な物 literally means, "strange things," but here it means, "rotten, bad food."

2. こういうこと   this sort of thing

3. あたる as introduced in 19A 7, means "to hit" (or the weather forecast is right.)

Here in this case, however, the verb means "to be struck (by bad food)," i.e. "have stomach poisoning."

山田さんはふぐを食べて，あたって，すぐ死にました。

Yamada ate a globefish, had stomach poisoning and died right away.

The particle used in this usage of あたる is に as in てんぷらにあたる or ふぐにあたる.

4. 山田さんのあげたてんぷら

The verb to "deep fry" is あげる.

5. 食べ物にあたらないおまじない。

an incantation that makes one immune to food poisoning.

6. 教えましょうか

Shall I teach you?

7.   遍 "＿＿ times"
    一遍 いっぺん
    二遍 にへん

It is more common to use 〜回 after three. Cf. Lesson 17, Notes on Usage.

    三遍 さんべん

This classifier is often used in saying two or three times, four or five times, etc.

二，三遍，四，五遍

Lesson 19   Grammar Notes

The main point of this lesson are:
I. Conditional expression.
II. An expression of "hear-say."
III. Other expressions:
  A. Source of information: "according to ＿＿," as in "according to the newspaper, it will rain tomorrow."
  B. A pattern used to express cause or reason, "due to ＿＿."

C. The expression, "to become,"
   The expression, "to make," "to change."
D. An expression used to elicit confirmation of what the speaker believes to be true, "Isn't it the case that ____?"

I. Conditional expression with ば

$$\underline{\text{Sentence}_1} + ば \ \underline{\text{Sentence}_2} \qquad\qquad \text{If } \underline{S_1,} \text{ then } \underline{S_2}$$

The form preceding ば is called the ば form or the conditional form. The ば form is made by the following rules:

U-verbs: V(root) + eba	書けば，読めば，<ruby>歩<rt>ある</rt></ruby>けば
RU-verbs: V(root) + reba	食べれば，見れば
Irregular verbs:	すれば，<ruby>来<rt>く</rt></ruby>れば，<ruby>行<rt>い</rt></ruby>けば
Negative forms: Verbs: V-(a)nakereba	読まなければ，食べなければ
Adjectives: A(root) + kereba	大きければ，安ければ，よければ
Negative forms: A-kunakereba	大きくなければ，よくなければ
Adjectival Nouns: AN+nara(ba)	静かなら(ば)，きれいなら(ば)
Nouns: N+nara(ba)	男の子なら(ば)，車なら(ば)

In the case of Adjectival Nouns and Nouns, in the affirmative, ば is often deleted.

Negative forms: AN + denakereba	静かでなければ
N + denakereba	男でなければ

In this pattern, the condition S_1 should be satisfied first. Then, on that condition, S_2 takes place.

今日時間があれば<ruby>昼寝<rt>ひるね</rt></ruby>をします。	Today if I have time, I'll take a nap.
安ければ買いますが高ければ買いません。	If it's inexpensive, I'll buy it, but if it's expensive, I will not buy it.
部屋がきれいなら(ば)借りたいです。	If the room is clean, I want to rent it.
男の子なら(ば)<ruby>太郎<rt>たろう</rt></ruby>という名前にします。	If the baby is a boy, I'll name him Taro.
お<ruby>急<rt>いそ</rt></ruby>ぎなら(ば)すぐにしますよ。	If you are in a hurry, I'll do it right away.

部屋が広ければ借りたいです。	If the room is spacious, I want to rent it.

The form can be used both in generic statements and in statements of specific events.

Generic: 時間があれば昼寝をします から元気です。	Whenever I have time I take a nap, so I'm in good health.
Specific: きのう一晩中起きていた のできょう時間があれば昼 寝をします。	Since I was awake all night last night, I'll take a nap if I have time today.

Often the word もし (if) is used with S_1 ば.

もし雨が降ればピクニックは中 止します。	If it rains, (we'll) cancel the picnic.
もしその話が本当なら（ば）これ は大変です。	If the story (what you say) is true, it's remarkable (how fantastic/it's a disastrous situation).

II. そう (hear-say)

Sentence (Plain form)	I hear that ____ They say that ____
V （書く/書いた）	
A （大きい/大きかった）	
AN （きれいだ/きれいだった）	そうです
N （学生だ/学生だった）	
Neg （―ない/―なかった）	

The pattern is used when the speaker reports what he heard or read. The speaker is merely giving an objective report, i.e. he makes no committment regarding the truthfulness of the content of the sentence preceding そう.

新聞によるとあしたは雨だそう です。	According to the newspaper, it will rain tomorrow.
山田さんがつったさかなは大き かったそうです。	I hear the fish that Yamada caught was very big. （つる to fish）
山田さんはピアノが上手だそう です。	Yamada is good at piano, they say.

III. Other Expressions:

A.

$$\underline{\text{(Source of information)} \atop \text{Noun}} \begin{cases} \text{によれば} \\ \text{によると} \end{cases}$$

According to ____
(Lit. "If we depend on ____")

This pattern is used to indicate the source of information. It is often used in combination with the "hear-say" pattern introduced above.

天気予報によるとあしたは雪だ そうです。

According to the weather report, it will snow tomorrow.

田中さんによると山田さんはニューヨークへ行ったことがない そうです。

According to Tanaka, Yamada has not been to New York.

B. Sentence₁ ために Sentence₂
   (Past, state)

Due to S₁, S₂

S_1 is usually in the past tense or in a form that indicates a state.

車の事故があったために遅れました。

Due to a car accident, (Lit. "Because there was a car accident,") I was late.

霧が深いために欠航になっております。

Due to heavy fog, (Lit. "Because the fog is deep,") the flight has been cancelled.

山田さんがいなかったために困りました。

Due to Yamada's absence, (Lit. "Because Yamada was not there,") we were in trouble.

大風のために木が倒れました。

Due to the strong winds, the tree fell.

C.

1. (X が) ____ Y ____ なる   X becomes Y

A	く	(大きくなる, 赤くなる)
AN	に	(きれいになる, 元気になる)
N	に	(先生になる, 病気になる)

Verbs cannot be used in the Y slot.

264

A	変な物を食べた時，おなかが痛くなりますね。	When you eat bad food, you get a stomachache. (lit. "Your stomach becomes painful.")
AN	おたくのお子さんは立派になりましたね。	What a fine person he/she has become! (lit. "Your child has become splendid.")
N	霧のために欠航になっています。	Due to the fog, flights have been cancelled.
N	私は医者になるつもりです。	I intend to become a doctor.

2. (Xが) Y を ___Z___ する   (Agent X) makes Y into Z
          A. く   (X makes Y) Z
          AN に
          N に

A	このくつはきついんですが少し大きくしてくださいませんか。	These shoes are tight. Will you please make them a little larger (i.e. make them loose)?
AN	静かにしてください。	Please be quiet!
N	私は子どもを弁護士にします。	I will make my child a lawyer.

D. <u>Sentence (Plain form)</u> んじゃ {ありませんか / ないんですか}   Isn't it the case that ____?

This pattern is used when asking if what the speaker thinks correct is in fact correct or not.

What speaker thinks is true

（山田さんはパリへ行きました。）	山田さんはパリへ行ったんじゃないんですか。	Isn't it the case that Yamada went to Paris?
（田中さんは今日山田さんに会います。）	田中さんはきょう山田さんに会うんじゃないんですか。	Isn't it the case that Tanaka will meet Yamada today.
（田中さんは山田さんに会いません。）	田中さんは山田さんに会わないんじゃないんですか。	Isn't it the case that Tanaka is not going to meet Yamada.

265

（山田さんはパリへ行きませんでした。）	山田さんはパリへ行かなかったんじゃないんですか。	Isn't it the case that Yamada did not go to Paris?
（あの部屋は静かです。）	あの部屋は静かなんじゃありませんか。	Isn't it the case that the room is quiet?
（あの人はフランス人です。）	あの人はフランス人なんじゃありませんか。	Isn't it the case that the person is French?

第十九課　漢字

部屋
へ　や
部屋

今朝
け　さ
今朝

夜
よる
夜

事故
じ　こ
事故

病気
びょう き
病気

顔
かお
顔

旅行
りょ こう
旅行

乗る
の
乗る

待つ
ま
待つ

赤い
あか
赤い

天気
てん き
天気

第 二 十 課

20 A 　山田　　　　スミスさんのお姉さんはこの大学を卒業なさったそうですね。

　　　スミス　　　ええ，去年の六月でした。

　　　山田　　　　アメリカでは卒業のお祝いにどんなものをもらうんですか。

　　　スミス　　　いろいろありますよ。香水とか，ネーム入りの万年筆とか，腕時計とか，自動車とか…

　　　山田　　　　スミスさんもお姉さんに何かさしあげたんですか。

　　　スミス　　　ええ，真珠のイヤリングを買ったんですが…

　　　山田　　　　まあ，真珠のイヤリング。じゃあ，お姉さんはお喜びになったでしょう。

　　　スミス　　　いいえそれが，何かのまちがいで，箱の中に一個だけしか入っていなかったので，あまり喜ばなかったんです。

20 B 　魚屋　　　　らっしゃい。

　　　ベイリー　　えーっと，このえびとかいをください。

　　　魚屋　　　　これでいいすか。

　　　ベイリー　　もう少し多い方が…

　　　魚屋　　　　もっとね。じゃ，いくつずつですか。

　　　ベイリー　　友達が五人来るんだけどどのぐらいあればいいですか。

　　　魚屋　　　　五人ねえ，一人に十もあればいいんじゃありませんか。かいもえびも五十ですね。

　　　ベイリー　　はい，五十ずつおねがいします。

　　　魚屋　　　　はい，毎度ありい。

267

1 例 T: ブラウンさんに車をもらいました。

T: テ レ ビ S: ブラウンさんにテレビをもらいました。

T: 田中さん S: 田中さんにテレビをもらいました。

T: 本田（ほんだ）先生 S: 本田（ほんだ）先生にテレビをいただきました。

1. スミスさん
2. テキスト
3. 古い辞書
4. ブラウンさん
5. 先生
6. 教科書
7. 日本語の本

8. 田中さん
9. 先生
10. 東京の地図
11. 岡村（おかむら）さん
12. ブラウンさん
13. テキスト
14. 自転車

2 例 T: ブラウンさんが時計をくれました。

T: テ レ ビ S: ブラウンさんがテレビをくれました。

T: 田中さん S: 田中さんがテレビをくれました。

T: 本田（ほんだ）先生 S: 本田（ほんだ）先生がテレビをくださいました。

1. スミスさん
2. 古いテキスト
3. 辞書
4. ワイン
5. 音楽会（おんがくかい）のキップ
6. 先生

7. 渡辺（わたなべ）さん
8. レコード
9. 日本語のテープ
10. 先生
11. Ａプラス
12. 教科書

13. ブラウンさん　　　　　　　14. 花

3 T: ブラウンさんが切手をくれました。
　 T: もらう　　S: ブラウンさんに切手をもらいました。
　 T: テレビ　　S: ブラウンさんにテレビをもらいました。
　 T: 先生　　　S: 先生にテレビをいただきました。
　 T: 山田さん　S: 山田さんにテレビをもらいました。
　 T: くれる　　S: 山田さんがテレビをくれました。

1. 田中さん　　　　　　　　11. ジョンソン先生
2. 古いカメラ　　　　　　　12. 30ページのハンドアウト
3. 日本の雑誌_{ざっし}　　　　　13. 漢字のリスト
4. 本田先生_{ほんだ}　　　　　　14. 古いテキスト
5. 岡村さん_{おかむら}　　　　　　15. ブラウンさん
6. もらう　　　　　　　　　16. くれる
7. 田中さん　　　　　　　　17. 先生
8. 東京の地図　　　　　　　18. ブラウンさん
9. スミスさん　　　　　　　19. 教科書
10. ヨセミテの写真　　　　　20. もらう

4 例1 T: スミスさん，万年筆
　　　　S₁: スミスさんに何をあげましょうか。
　　　　S₂: そうですね。ああ，万年筆はどうですか。
　 例2 T: 本田先生，万年筆
　　　　S₁: 本田先生に何をさしあげましょうか。
　　　　S₂: そうですね。ああ，万年筆はどうですか。

269

1. 山田さん，レコード
2. スミスさん，ワイン
3. 岡村さん，英語の本
4. スミスさん，レコード
5. 山田さん，辞書
6. 先生，自転車
7. ジョンソンさん，川端の小説

8. 田中先生，カリフォルニアのワイン
9. 岡村さん，英語のテープ
10. ブラウンさん，香水
11. レーガンさん，ゼリービーンズ
12. ニクソン，？

5　例1　T:　レコード，ブラウンさんに
　　　　　{S₁:　いいレコードですねえ。
　　　　　{S₂:　ええ，ブラウンさんにもらったんです。
　　例2　T:　レコード，先生が
　　　　　{S₁:　いいレコードですねえ。
　　　　　{S₂:　ええ，先生がくださったんです。

1. タイプライター，父に
2. ステレオ，父が
3. テレビ，兄が
4. レコード，兄に
5. ペン，昔のガールフレンドが
6. 辞書，ルームメートが
7. 自転車，ともだちに
8. イヤリング，姉が
9. 写真，スミス先生が
10. テープレコーダー，兄が
11. テキスト，一年生の日本語の

先生に
12. ポスター，日本へ行った昔の友だちが
13. 車，バークレーを卒業した日本人のともだちが
14. カード，先生が
15. ハンドアウト，先生に
16. 犬，ジョンソンさんに
17. 写真，ニューヨークにいる兄が
18. ピアノ，母に

270

19. 犬，隣の人が　　　　　　　　　　　　シコ人のボーイフレンド
20. ペンダント，高校の時のメキ

6　例1　T: 30ドル，10ドルもらう
　　　　S: 30ドルだと思っていましたが，10ドルしかもらいませんでした。
　　例2　T: 5ドル，10ドルもらう
　　　　S: 5ドルだと思っていましたが，10ドルももらいました。

1. 50ドル，10ドルかかる
2. 10ドル，50ドルかかる
3. 1時間，3時間かかる
4. 30分，3時間かかる
5. 5時間，3時間かかる

6. 30人，10人来る
7. 6人，10人来る
8. 100点，40点とれる（←とる）
9. Aプラスもらえる（←もらう）
10. 私 一人，三人集まる

7　例　T: 少ない
　　　{S₁: あのう，すこし少ないでしょうか。
　　　{S₂: ええ，もうすこし多いほうがいいと思いますが…

1. 高い
2. 大きい
3. 難しい
4. きたない
5. 小さい

6. うるさい
7. 暗い
8. 短い
9. 重い
10. 遠い

8 例 1 T: 先生，来る

  S₁: 先生がいらっしゃいましたか。

  S₂: ええ，いらっしゃったと思います。

  例 2 T: 山田さん，行く

  S₁: 山田さんが行きましたか。

  S₂: ええ，行ったと思います。

1. 友だち，あの映画を見る   を見る

2. 田中先生，言う   8. スミス先生，いる

3. 先生，すしを食べる   9. 田中さん，来る

4. 先生，本を買う   10. ブラウン先生，来る

5. ブラウンさん，ヨセミテの滝（たき）   11. ルームメート，手紙を書く

  を見る   12. 先生，この本を書く

6. 山田さん，朝ごはんを食べる   13. 田中さん，言う

7. 山田先生，ゴールデンゲート   14. 先生，行く

Lesson 20 **Dialogues**

20 A

Yamada: I heard that your (older) sister graduated from this college.

  ——を卒業する   to graduate (from)...

  なさる   honorific form of する

Smith: Yes, last June.

Y: What sort of gifts do you get for graduation here in America?

  どんな   what kind, what sort

272

もらう	to receive

S: There's all kinds; perfume, engraved fountain pens, wrist-watches, and cars...

香水	perfume
ネーム入り	engraved (with one's name)
腕時計	wrist-watch
自動車	car

Y: Did you also give your sister something?

S: Yes, I bought pearl earrings for her but...

真珠	pearl

Y: Oh, pearl earrings! She was delighted, wasn't she?

お喜びになる	to be delighted, (an honorific form of 喜ぶ) to be happy

S: No, there was some mistake and there was only one earring in the box so she wasn't very happy.

箱	box

20 B

Fish Market

Employee: What'll it be today?

らっしゃい	＝ いらっしゃい, Welcome.

Bailey: Let's see... Please give me some (of these) shrimp and clams.

えーっと	umm..., Let's see, etc.
えび	shrimp
貝	clams

F: About this much?

いいすか	Lit., Will this (much) be okay? ←いいですか To be okay, all right.

B: Maybe a little more...

もう少し	a little more

F: Some more...About how many of each?

もっと   more

ずつ   each

B: I've got five friends coming over, (so) how much should I get?

どのぐらいあればいいか   Lit., "About how much should there be to be okay/enough?"

F: Five people...hmm...I think ten of each per person would be enough. So that's fifty each of the shrimp and the clams, right?

B: Yes, fifty of each, please.

F: Thanks. Come again.

毎度   every time.

ありい   ありがとうございます.

Lesson 20 **Notes on Usage**

20 A

1.　大学を卒業なさった   (She) graduated from college.

Verbs of "leaving" such as 出る (to leave) and 卒業する (to graduate) take を to mark the point of departure.

寮を出た時に雨が降っていました。	It was raining when I left the dorm.
学校を出てからもう三年になります。	It's been three years since I left (graduated from) school.
いつ大学を卒業するつもりですか。	When are you planning to graduate from college?

卒業なさる なさる is an honorific verb that means "to do," so the regular form is 卒業する。

274

2. 卒業のお祝いにどんな物をもらうんですか。

お祝い means "congratulatory gift." お祝いに (for a felicitous occasion), "in honor of."

Another example of this usage of に：

お礼に	as a show of gratitude
いろいろお世話になったお礼に歌を歌います。	I'll sing a song to show my gratitude for having been taken care of in many ways.

3. ずい分違いますね，日本とは。

This is an emphatic sentence. (Cf. Notes on Usage for L. 3) The normal word order is

日本とはずい分違いますね。	It's quite different from Japan.

4. お姉さんはどんなものをおもらいになったんですか。   What kinds of things did your sister receive?

5. たとえば   for example

6. 箱に一個だけしかはいっていなかった。
Often だけ and しか are used together to intensify the feeling of deficiency as in the above example. The word order is だけしか and not the other way around.

20 A

Colloquial Dialogue

山　田　お姉さんはこの大学を卒業したの。

スミス　うん，去年の六月。

山　田　アメリカじゃ卒業のお祝いにどんなものをもらうの。

スミス　いろいろ。香水とか，ネーム入りの万年筆とか，腕時計とか，自動車とか…

山田　スミスさんもお姉さんに何かあげたの。

スミス　ええ真珠のイヤリングをね。

山田　まあ，真珠のイヤリング。

スミス　うん。

山田　じゃ，お姉さんは喜んだんじゃない。

スミス　いや，それが箱に一個だけしかはいっていなかったんであまり喜ばなかった。

20 B

1. らっしゃい

When いらっしゃい is uttered very fast the initial い gets dropped. It sounds energetic and lively, and is often used by fish shop clerks, green grocers, sushi store clerks, etc., who deal in fresh commodities.

Throughout the dialogue, the fish store clerk uses a special style of language peculiar to the profession. The style is rather blunt, so it is advisable not to use the forms used by him.

2. えーっと

A variation of あのう... ("Umm...") This sounds much more informal than あのう.

3. いいすか

A contracted form of いいですか. It's a very loose form and students are advised not to use it.

4. もっとね

A contracted form of もっとですね。
"More, huh?"

5. いくつずつですか。　　　　　　How many of each?

五十ずつお願いします。　　　　Fifty of each please.

$$\frac{X}{\text{(number)}}$$ ずつ "X of each kind"

276

6. 五人ねえ。

Five people (you say),...let's see...

7. 一人に十もあればいいでしょう。

If there are ten per person, it will be all right.

一人に   per person

一日に   per day

一時間に   per hour

8. 毎度ありい。

A contracted form of 毎度ありがとうございます。(Thank you for your continued patronage). 毎度 means "every"(毎) "time" (度)

Lesson 20 **Grammar Notes**

The main points of this lesson are:
 I. Verbs of Giving and Receiving.
 II. Honorific forms of certain verbs.
 III. Miscellaneous expressions:

A. "only" (しか ＿＿＿ ない) with the implication of "less than I expected."
B. "as much as" (＿＿＿ も) with the implication of "more than I expected."
C. "a little more" (もう少し ＿＿＿).

 I. Verbs of Giving and Receiving:

There are three pairs of words to describe the concept of giving and receiving. They are さしあげる (RU)／あげる (RU)， くださる (irreg.)／くれる (RU)， and いただく (U)／もらう (U). The relation between the words in each pair is a matter of the superior-inferior relationship between the giver and the receiver.

A. Verbs of Giving:

 The pairs さしあげる／あげる and くださる／くれる can both be translated into English as "to give."

277

The pair さしあげる／あげる is used when someone (he can be the speaker himself) gives something to someone who is not the speaker himself. さしあげる (lit., "to raise high") is used when the receiver is superior (or equal) to the giver, and あげる is used when the receiver is equal or inferior to the giver.

$$\underline{\text{Giver}} \begin{Bmatrix} \text{は} \\ \text{が} \end{Bmatrix} \underline{\frac{\text{Receiver}}{\text{(2nd/3rd person)}}} \text{に } \underline{\text{Object}} \text{ を} \begin{Bmatrix} \text{さしあげる} \\ \text{あげる} \end{Bmatrix}$$

さしあげる	Giver ↗ Receiver (2nd/3rd person)
先生に何をさしあげましょうか。	What shall we give our teacher?
そうですねえ，ボールペンをさしあげましょう。	Let's see, let's give him a ball-point pen.
カーターさんに何をさしあげましょうか。	What shall we give Mr. Carter?
そうですね，ピーナッツはどうですか。	Let's see,...how about some peanuts?
上げる	Giver ↘ Receiver (2nd/3rd person)
山田さんは青山さんにレコードを上げました。	Yamada gave Aoyama some records.
(私は)山田さんに本をあげました。	I gave Yamada a book.

Note: Traditional people still use another form やる, when giving something to an inferior. They would say, for example,

山本さんは子どもに本をやりました。	Yamamoto gave the child a book.
(私は)ねこにさかなをやりました。	I gave the cat some fish.
(私は)弟にレコードをやりました。	I gave some records to my younger brother.

The pair 下さる／くれる is used when someone gives something to the speaker. Also, it is used when the giver is an outsider and the receiver is someone who is close to the speaker.

$$\underline{\text{Giver}} \begin{Bmatrix} \text{は} \\ \text{が} \end{Bmatrix} \underline{\frac{\text{Receiver}}{\text{(1st person or in-group)}}} \text{に } \underline{\text{Object}} \text{ を} \begin{Bmatrix} \text{下さる} \\ \text{くれる} \end{Bmatrix}$$

278

下さる   Giver ↘ Receiver (1st person)

青木さんは私にレコードを下さ   Aoki gave me a record.
いました。

田中さんは父に本を下さいまし   Tanaka gave my father a book.
た。

川田さんは弟と私にボールペン   Kawada gave my younger brother and me
を下さいました。   some ball-point pens.

くれる   Giver —→ Receiver (1st person)
                                                   ↗

田中さんは私にカメラをくれま   Tanaka gave me a camera.
した。

森田は妹に花をくれました。   Morita gave my younger sister some flowers.

森本さんは私に何もくれません   Morimoto did not give me anything.
でした。

B. Verbs of Receiving

The pair いただく／もらう is the Japanese equivalent of "receive." In this pattern, the particle に marks the agent (or the giver), not the receiver. The particle から "from" can also be used in place of に.

$$\underline{\text{Receiver}} \left\{\begin{matrix} は \\ が \end{matrix}\right\} \underline{\text{Giver}} \left\{\begin{matrix} に \\ から \end{matrix}\right\} \underline{\text{Object}} \text{ を} \left\{\begin{matrix} いただく \\ もらう \end{matrix}\right\}$$

いただく   Giver ↘ Receiver

青山さんは山田先生 $\left\{\begin{matrix} に \\ から \end{matrix}\right\}$ レコ   Aoyama received some records from
ードをいただきました。   Professor Yamada.

279

（私は）田中さん｛に／から｝本をいただきました。

I received a book from Tanaka.

妹は川上<ruby>川上<rt>かわかみ</rt></ruby>さん｛に／から｝何もいただきませんでした。

My younger sister did not receive anything from Kawakami.

父は森川<ruby>森川<rt>もりかわ</rt></ruby>さん｛に／から｝テレビをいただきました。

My father received a TV from Morikawa.

もらう

Giver ⟶ Receiver

金森<ruby>金森<rt>かなもり</rt></ruby>さん｛に／から｝カメラをもらいました。

I received a camera from Kanamori.

安田<ruby>安田<rt>やすだ</rt></ruby>さんは川本さんから時計をもらいました。

Yasuda received a watch from Kawamoto.

妹は早川<ruby>早川<rt>はやかわ</rt></ruby>さんから何ももらいませんでした。

My younger sister did not receive anything from Hayakawa.

When both the giver and the receiver are familiar to the speaker (e.g. the giver is the speaker's older brother and the receiver is his younger brother), the pattern (1) or the pattern (3) is used. If the pattern (2) is used, the implication is that the speaker feels closer to his younger brother than to his older brother.

cf. (1) 兄は弟に本をあげました。

(2) 兄は弟に本をくれました。

(3) 弟は兄に本をもらいました。

母は私に何もくれませんでした。

My mother gave me nothing (speaking to an outsider).

このカメラは父にもらいました。

As for this camera, I received it from my father (to an outsider).

母に花を上げました。

I gave my mother some flowers (to an outsider).

II. Honorific forms of certain verbs.

おもらいになる   is an honorific form of   もらう

In general a verb of Japanese origin can be made into the honorific form by this rule:

お ＋ <u>Verb(pre-masu)</u> ＋ になる

書く　(to write)：　　お書きになる

買う　(to buy)：　　お買いになる

喜ぶ<ruby>喜<rt>よろこ</rt></ruby>　(to feel glad)：　お喜びになる

見せる　(to show)：　お見せになる

Basic verbs like 行く (to go), 来る (to come), いる (to be), 食べる (to eat), 見る (to see), etc. have their own honorific forms rather than the forms derived by the above rule.

行く ⎫
来る ⎬ ：いらっしゃる
いる ⎭

食べる：めしあがる

見る　：ごらんになる

言う　：おっしゃる

Verbs of the form <u>Chinese word (written in kanji)</u> ＋ する are changed into their honorific form by following another rule:

ご ＋ <u>Chinese word</u> (＋ なさる)

ご結婚なさる

III. Miscellaneous

<u>X</u> しか ＿＿＿ない   only <u>X</u> (with implication of less than expected)

しか always takes a negative predicate and the particles が and を are deleted before しか。

山田さんはジーンズしかはいていません。

a) Yamada is only wearing jeans (and nothing else)! (disapproval)
b) Yamada should be wearing something dressier but is only wearing jeans.

太郎はジーンズだけはいています。	Taroo is only wearing jeans. (Neutral description).
スカートばかりはいています。	Yamada (habitually) wears skirts. (As opposed to pants, for example).
一年生の学生しか来ませんでした。	Only the first year students came.
十ドルしかもらいませんでした。	I received only $10. (I expected to get more.)
ヨセミテへしか行きませんでした。	I didn't go anywhere but Yosemite.
安い物しかもらいませんでした。	I didn't receive anything but inexpensive things.
$\underline{X}$ も (number, quantity)	as much as $\underline{X}$ (with implication of more than expected)
私は何もしなかったのに十ドルももらいました。	I didn't do anything but received as much as $10.
十ドルぐらいだと思っていましたが五十ドルもかかりました。	I thought it would cost about $10, but it (actually) cost (as much as) $50 (which was more than I had expected).

C. もう少し $\dfrac{\underline{X}}{\begin{array}{c}V\\A\\AN\end{array}}$ a little more $\underline{X}$

As a rule, Nouns cannot be used in the X slot.

もう少しお願いします。	A little more please.
もう少し多い方がいいと思います。	I think that a little more is better.
私のアパートの方がここよりもう少し静かです。	My apartment is a little more quiet than it is here.

282

第二十課　漢字

花
はな

花

魚
さかな

魚

枚
まい

枚

個
こ

個

写真
しゃ　しん

写　真

地図
ち　ず

地　図

切手
きっ　て

切　手

学期
がっ　き

学　期

時計
と　けい

時　計

教科書
きょう　か　しょ

教　科　書

自転車
じ　てん　しゃ

自　転　車

卒業
そつ　ぎょう

卒　業

第二十一課

21 A 　大山　　　　　ベイリーさんは九州へ行ったことがありますか。

　　　ベイリー　　　いえ，まだです。実はこの次の休みに伊万里へ
　　　　　　　　　　行くことにしています。

　　　大山　　　　　そうですか。で，新幹線でですか，飛行機でで
　　　　　　　　　　すか。

　　　ベイリー　　　飛行機はいっぱいだそうですから新幹線にしま
　　　　　　　　　　した。

　　　大山　　　　　ところで切符は買えましたか。

　　　ベイリー　　　まだなんですが今日藤原さんという友達が買っ
　　　　　　　　　　てきてくれることになっています。

　　　大山　　　　　だれかに案内してもらうんですか。

　　　ベイリー　　　いえ，一人で行くのでさっき佐賀県の地図を買
　　　　　　　　　　ってきたばかりです。

21 B 　　　(a few days later)

　　　大山　　　　　伊万里へ行く準備はできましたか。

　　　ベイリー　　　ええ，どうにか。この間大学の赤木先生にこん
　　　　　　　　　　どの旅行について話をしました。

　　　大山　　　　　赤木先生ってあの新しい本をお書きになったば
　　　　　　　　　　かりの先生ですか。

　　　イベリー　　　ええ，「伊万里に友達がいますから紹介状を書
　　　　　　　　　　いてあげましょう」と言ってくださいました。

　　　大山　　　　　ああ，それはよかったですね。

　　　ベイリー　　　ええ，それから藤原さんも伊万里にいるお母さ

んに電話をかけてくれました。

大山　　　　　じゃ，おみやげが大変^{たいへん}ですね。

1　例　T：藤原^{ふじわら}さんが買ってきてくれました。

T：案内する　　S：藤原さんが案内してくれました。

T：先生が　　　S：先生が案内してくださいました。

T：書く　　　　S：先生が書いてくださいました。

T：スミスさんが　S：スミスさんが書いてくれました。

T：スミスさんに　S：スミスさんに書いてもらいました。

T：先生に　　　S：先生に書いていただきました。

1.　ブラウンさんに　　　16.　先生が

2.　案内する　　　　　　17.　先生に

3.　電話をかける　　　　18.　田中先生が

4.　スミスさんが　　　　19.　教える

5.　山田さんが　　　　　20.　田中先生に

6.　説明する　　　　　　21.　スミスさんに

7.　ピアノをひく　　　　22.　スミスさんが

8.　日本語を教える　　　23.　英語を教える

9.　すしを作る　　　　　24.　ブラウンさんに

10.　岡村^{おかむら}さんに　　　25.　タイプを打^うつ

11.　日本語を教える　　　26.　スミスさんが

12.　切符^{きっぷ}を買う　　　　27.　説明する

13.　ブラウンさんが　　　28.　赤木先生に

14.　教える　　　　　　　29.　赤木先生が

15.　説明する　　　　　　30.　紹介状^{しょうかいじょう}を書く

286

② 例　T: 藤原さんが読みました
　　　　{ S₁: 誰かに読んでもらいましたか。
　　　　{ S₂: ええ，実は，藤原さんに読んでもらったんです。

1. スミスさんが説明しました
2. ブラウンさんが教えました
3. 田中さんが読みました
4. 先生が書きました
5. 先生が説明しました
6. 山田さんがピアノをひきました
7. ベイリーさんが買ってきました
8. 友達が写真をとりました
9. 山田さんが漢字の読み方を教えました

10. 先生がその意味を説明しました
11. 岡村さんが日本語で手紙を書きました
12. スミスさんがその言葉の意味を教えました
13. 本田先生が紹介状を書きました
14. ルームメートが郵便局へ行ってきました
15. 妹が銀行へ行ってきました

③ 例　T: 藤原さんが説明しました
　　　　{ S₁: 誰かが説明してくれましたか。
　　　　{ S₂: ええ，実は，藤原さんが説明してくれたんです。
　　　　{ S₁: ああ，それはよかったですねえ。

1. スミスさんが説明しました
2. 田中さんが教えました
3. 田中さんがビールを買ってきました
4. 田中さんが調べました

5. 先生が説明しました
6. スミスさんがその英語の意味を説明しました
7. 山田さんが日本語で手紙を書きました

8. ブラウンさんが英語を教えま
した

9. スミスさんがいっしょに行き
ました

10. 赤木先生が紹介状を書きまし

た

11. スミスさんが買ってきました

12. 姉が図書館へ行って来ました

13. 先生が調べました

4 例 T: 新聞，読む
S: あのう，新聞を読んでいただきたいんですが……。

1. 日本語，教える
2. この字，読む
3. これ，読む
4. これ，コピーする
5. この漢字，読む
6. 写真，とる
7. 住所，書く
8. これ，タイプする
9. これ，チェックする
10. その文，もう一度言う

11. スペル，この紙に書く
12. この言葉の意味，説明する
13. その本の名前，教える
14. 銀行，行ってくる
15. この漢字の読み方，教える
16. お金，少し，貸す
17. この漢字の書き方，教える
18. 田中さん，電話をかける
19. タバコ，すわない
20. 帰る

5 例 T: 次の休み，九州，行く
S₁: 次の休みに九州へ行くんだそうですね。(← L.18)
S₂: ええ，行くことにしていますが，実はまだいつかはっきり決
めていないんです。

1. 来年，ヨーロッパ，行く

2. 来年，日本，行く

3. 次の休み，メキシコ，行く
4. 夏休み，中国語，勉強する
5. 来年，結婚する
6. 冬休み，スキー，行く
7. 週末，ヨセミテ，行く

8. 夏休み，アルバイト，する
9. 卒業してから，銀行，働く
10. 次の休み，伊万里，行く
11. 来年，日本語10A，とる
12. 来年，大学，卒業する

6 例 T: あした，パーティー，ある
S_1: あした，パーティーがあるんだそうですね。
S_2: ええ，あることになっていますが，実は，私はあまりよく知らないんです。

1. 来週，クイズ，ある
2. 今週の土曜日，パーティー，する
3. 明日，みんなで，サンフランシスコ，行く
4. 明日，スミスさんの家，集まる
5. 今日の午後，会議，ある
6. 来月，ガソリンの値段，高く

なる
7. 今晩，飲みに行く
8. 来週，試験，ある
9. 来週，セミナー，ある
10. 来学期の中国語の先生，スミス先生だ
11. あした，クイズ，ない
12. ターム・ペーパーのしめきり，明日だ

7 例 T: 書く
S_1: 書きましたか。
S_2: ええ，書いたばかりです。

1. 食べる
2. 練習する

3.　宿題，する　　　　　　　　12.　田中さん，来る

4.　クラス，終わる　　　　　　13.　山田さん，帰る

5.　スミスさんに会う　　　　　14.　銀行，行ってくる
　　　　　　　　　　　　　　　　　　ぎんこう

6.　この本，読む　　　　　　　15.　試験，受ける

7.　ひるごはん，食べる　　　　16.　パンナム002便，着く
　　　　　　　　　　　　　　　　　　　　　　びん　っ

8.　薬，飲む　　　　　　　　　17.　サンフランシスコ，見る

9.　この漢字，調べる　　　　　18.　「…てもらう」，勉強する

10.　切符，買う　　　　　　　　19.　先生，説明していただく
　　　きっぷ

11.　この漢字，習う　　　　　　20.　先生，お帰りになる

Lesson 21 **Dialogues**

21A

Ooyama: Have you ever been to Kyushu?

九 州　　　　　　　　　　　　　southernmost island of 4 main islands in
きゅうしゅう　　　　　　　　　　Japanese archipelago.

Bailey: No, not yet. But I've decided to go to Imari during the next vacation.

この次の　　　　　　　　　　　the next, following
　　つぎ

休み　　　　　　　　　　　　　vacation, holiday

O: Is that so. Are you going by train (Shinkansen) or by plane?

伊万里　　　　　　　　　　　　a city famous for its pottery
い　ま　り
新幹線　　　　　　　　　　　　bullet train
しんかんせん

B: I understand that all flights are booked, so I decided on the train (Shinkansen).
O: Have you been able to buy a ticket?
B: No, not yet, but my friend (by the name of) Fujiwara is going to go and buy it for
　me.

買ってきてくれる　　　　　　　Lit., is going to buy it for me

290

O: Are you having someone show you around?

案内する   to guide

案内してもらう   to have someone guide

B: No. Since I'm going by myself, I just bought a map of Saga Prefecture (a little while ago).

さっき   a little while ago

佐賀県   prefecture in N.W. Kyushu, where Imari is located

地図   map

21B

Ooyama: Have you made all your arrangements to go to Imari yet?

準備   preparations

Bailey: Yes, I managed somehow or other. I talked to Prof. Akagi about my (up coming) trip the other day.

どうにか   somehow

O: By Professor Akagi, you mean the teacher who just wrote that new book?

お書きになる   an honorific form derived from 書く

B: Yes. He said that he has a friend in Imari, so he would write me a letter of introduction.

紹介状   a letter of introduction

This should be a direct quotation, i.e., "He (kindly) said (to me), 'I have a friend in Imari, so I will write a letter of introduction for you.'"

O: Well, that's nice.

B: Yes. And Ms. Fujiwara (too) called her mother in Imari and told her I was coming.

O: You'd better take a lot of presents then!

おみやげ   gifts

大変   to be a problem, to be terrible

Lesson 21   Notes on Usage

21A

1. 九州 is one of the four large islands that comprise Japan. It is the one which lies off the southern tip of Honshu. See the map.

伊万里 and neighboring 唐津 are famous for two distinctive types of ceramics.

日本の地図

2. この次の休みに

この "this" + 次 "next," "the next in a series."
休み "vacation, holiday, rest period"
に time marker

エンバーカデロはどこですか。	Where's the Embarcadero?
次の駅ですよ。	It's the next station
（次ですよ）	(It's next)
（この次ですよ）	(It's the one after this)

3. 新幹線 新 "new" + 幹線 "trunk line." Using the famous Bullet trains, the line connects major cities throughout the country, or at least that is the ultimate plan. At present, it runs between Tokyo and Hakata (one of the major cities in Northern Kyuushuu). Two more lines connect Tokyo and Niigata, and Tokyo and Morioka.

4. いっぱい "full." Note the accent difference between いっ￣ぱい "full" and ￣いっ｜ぱい "one cup, one glass, of ____."

$\overline{も}|うい\overline{っ}|ぱいで\overline{す}|か$ Is it full already?

and $\overline{も}|うい\overline{っ}|ぱいです|か$ Do you want another cup/glass of ____ ?

5. 切符（きっぷ）   ticket

    新幹線（しんかんせん）の切符（きっぷ）   tickets for the Shinkansen

    伊万里（いまり）までの切符（きっぷ）   tickets to Imari

    映画の切符（きっぷ）   tickets for a movie

    スターウォーズの切符（きっぷ）   tickets for Star Wars

6. 買って来てくれる

Literally, "buy and come." In English, one would more naturally say "go and buy," and imply the "coming" part. In Japanese, however, the "going" part is implied, and the "coming" part is expressed. Other examples of this pattern:

玄関（げんかん）で何か音（おと）がしましたね。   There was a noise at the front door.

ちょっと見て来てください。   Please (go and) see. (Lit. "see and come").
音がする is an idiomatic phrase meaning "there is a noise."

7. 案内する   to show (someone) around (a place)

    案内   a guide, "information

8. さっき   "a short while ago", "just now".

This form is often used with _____ たばかりです as in さっき地図（ちず）を買ってきたばかりです, or 山田さんにはさっきお会いしたばかりです (I met Yamada just now).

9. 佐賀県（さがけん）   県 is a prefecture. Altogether there are one 都（と）(Tokyo), one 道（どう）(Hokkai-doo), two 府（ふ）(Oosaka and Kyooto), and forty-three 県 in Japan. 佐賀県 is located in the northwestern part of 九州.

21B

1. 準備はできましたか

準備 "preparation." できる here means "to be completed," rather than "to be able to." Other examples of できる used in this sense:

食事ができました。 The meal is ready.

(At a laundry):

あのう、広瀬ですが、ワイシャ
ツはできていますか。

Ummm, my name is Hirose. Are my shirts ready?

はい、できております。 Yes, they are.

2. どうにか "somehow." Often used in the longer phrase, どうにかこうにか "one way or another," "somehow or other." Here it implies that Bailey somehow managed to complete preparations for the trip.

3. 今度の旅行について話をしました。

今度の "this next ____." 今度 literally means "this time." "this round." Sometimes, however, it means "this next," "the coming ____." The distinction is usually clear from the context.

(before leaving on a trip):

今度の旅行はお金がかかります
ねえ。

This (coming) trip is going to cost a bundle, isn't it?

(during the trip):

今度の旅行はお金がかかります
ねえ。

This (current) trip is costly, isn't it?

(also during the trip):

今度の旅行はもっと安くしまし
ょう。

Let's make our next trip cheaper.
(coming)

(right after the trip):

今度の旅行はとても楽しかった
ですよ。

This last trip was really a lot of fun.

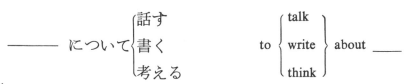

_____ について 話す / 書く / 考える   to talk / write / think about ____

話をする is another way of saying 話す "to talk."

4. お書きになる is an honorific form of 書く "to write". (Cf. L. 20, Grammar Notes II, for the rule for making honorific forms.)

5. 紹介状   letter of introduction

紹介する means "to introduce"; 状 is a suffix that means "a letter."

推薦状 letter of recommendation

6. それはよかったですね。   That's good/great

The past tense form よかった is used because it became "good" in the past and is still good. Here are similar examples of the past tense form:

(When one finds, after some searching, a pen thought to be lost):

      あった，あった。   Here it is! (It was here the whole time I was looking for it.)

(When one suddenly understands something):

      あ，わかりました。   So that's it!

7. 電話をかける "to make a phone call"; a variation of 電話をする. The basic meaning of かける is "to hang." By extension, it also means "to operate something which involves a 'hanging' condition, as in レコードをかける "to play a record."

8. おみやげ or みやげ has two meanings: 1) a souvenir; and 2) a present for a person one visits. (It is customary to take gifts along when visiting someone.) In the dialogue, the word is used in the second sense. A different word おくりもの (lit. "sending thing") is used when referring to gifts one gives for Christmas, New Years, birthdays, wedding, and other special occasions. おみやげ can also refer to little things (toys, candies, etc.) that a parent might bring home for his/her children.

9. 大変ですね。 大変 literally means "big change/difference", though the word is no longer used this way. Its basic meaning is "unusual(ly)," hence, "very much," "remarkable," "exceedingly," or "extraordinarily." Here it has the sense of "a big hassle," "a pain in the neck," etc.

Lesson 21 **Grammar Notes**

The main points of this lesson are:
I. An extended usage of the verbs of Giving and Receving.
II. Other expressions:
  A. To be decided.
  B. To decide on doing Verb.
  C. To have just Verb-ed.

I. In Lesson 20 various forms of giving and receiving things were introduced. The present lesson will introduce the various forms for the giving and receiving of an action.

$$
\text{A. Verb て form} + \begin{cases} くださる \\ くれる \end{cases}
$$

$$
\text{B. Verb て form} + \begin{cases} いただく \\ もらう \end{cases}
$$

$$
\text{C. Verb て form} + \begin{cases} さしあげる \\ あげる \\ (やる) \end{cases}
$$

The action indicated by the verb in the て form is performed for someone else's benefit when used with verbs of giving: さしあげる, あげる, (やる), くださる, くれる. The action which is indicated by the verb in the て form is received as a favor from someone else when used with verbs of receiving：いただく, もらう. The rules governing particles used with these giving and receiving verbs and the choice of verbs are exactly the same as described in Lesson 20.

Special care is required, however, when using pattern c.) as it may sound too aggressive, or seem as though the speaker is insinuating that the addressee is incapable of performing the action in question, the addressee may resent being told "V てあげます." It is best, therefore, to do what thoughtful Japanese would do and avoid using this pattern, particularly when speaking to an adult, and to use some other expression such as 買ってきましょうか ("Shall I go buy it?") which in effect is the same as 買ってあげましょうか ("Shall I buy it for you?"). For the same reason, even when one actually has taught something to one's teacher one would not say 教えてさしあげました, but rather お教えしました, or better yet, お伝えしました (伝える："to relay a message"), or お話ししました.

The てあげる pattern is necessary, however, to express what happened to a third party; for example, 山田さんはブラウンさんに漢字を教えてあげました "Yamada taught Brown kanji."

Pattern A	先生が町を案内してくださいました。	My teacher showed me around town.
	藤原さんが切符を買ってきてくれました。	Fujiwara bought some tickets for me.
Pattern B	先生に絵をかいていただきました。	I had my teacher draw a picture for me.
	スミスさんに絵をかいてもらいました。	I had Smith draw a picture for me.
Pattern C	山田さんはブラウンさんに漢字を教えてあげたそうです。	I hear that Yamada taught Brown kanji.

Note: When it is necessary to clearly mark the person on whose behalf the action is performed, ＿＿ のために is used. (ため means "for the sake of")

| 先生はブラウンさんのために駅へ電話をかけてくださいました。 | The teacher made a telephone call to the station on behalf of Brown. (for the sake of)(This implies that the speaker is close to Brown). |
| 藤原さんはわたしのために切符を買ってきてくれました。 | Fujiwara went and bought the tickets for me. |

II. A. Verb (plain, non-past)

It will be decided X will V.	ことになる
has been decided ＿＿	ことになっている
was decided ＿＿	ことになった

The agent, or decision maker is not specified in the ことになる pattern. This implies that the decision was made by someone else or by an unavoidable circumstance.

来週パーティーがあることになっていますね。	It's been decided that there will be a party next week, right?
来週わたしが大阪へ行くことになりました。	It so happens that I'm going to Osaka next week.
学生達は制服を着ないことになるでしょう。	It'll most likely be that students will not have to wear uniforms.

297

B. Verb (Plain, Non-Past)

X will decide to V	ことにする
X has decided	ことにしている
X decided	ことにした

Unlike pattern 2. a), above, this pattern clearly indicates the agent who does the decision making.

今度のピクニックはエンジェル
アイランドへ行くことにしまし
た。

We decided to go to Angel Island for the next picnic.

スミスさんに大阪の支店_{してん}に行っ
てもらうことにしましょう。

Let's (decide to) have Smith go to the Osaka branch office.

買うことにしましたがお金がな
いのでまだ買っていません。

I decided to buy it, but I haven't yet because I don't have any money.

C. Verb (Plain, Past) + ばかり   X (have/has) just V-ed

This pattern is used for an action/event which took place only a short time before.

これは買ったばかりです。

I just bought this.

これは買ったばかりの万年筆_{まんねんひつ}で
す。

This is the fountain pen that I just bought.

第二十一課　漢字

説 明	案 内	紹 介	教 える
せつ めい	あん ない	しょう かい	おし
説　明	案　内	紹　介	教　え　る

走 る	作 文	次	食 堂
はし	さく ぶん	つぎ	しょく どう
走　る	作　文	次	食　堂

駅	飛 行 機	食 事
えき	ひ こう き	しょく じ
駅	飛　行　機	食　事

第 二十二 課

22 A	岡村	あれは何ですか。
	スミス	ベイブリッジです。
	岡村	いえ，橋じゃなくてすぐそこの…
	スミス	ああ，あれは何と言うんでしょうか。彫刻のようなものですね。
	岡村	流木や古タイヤを使っているんですね。
	スミス	ええ。あそこにあるのは竜のようですよ。
	岡村	右の方にはピラミッドのような形をしたのがありますね。
	スミス	そう言えばその隣のはスフィンクスのようなかっこうをしていますね。
	岡村	もっと近くまで行けるんですね。
	スミス	ええ，行けますよ。用事が済んだあとで行ってみましょうか。

22 B	スミス	山田さん映画に行きませんか。
	山田	ええ，何か面白そうなのがありますか。
	スミス	ええ，「スターウォーズ」っていうのが面白いそうですよ。
	山田	「スターウォーズ」って何ですか。
	スミス	新聞には科学小説の映画化だって書いてありました。
	山田	わたしSFは大好きです。ところで，スミスさんはおなかがすいていませんか。

スミス　　　　ええ，映画に行く前に何か食べて行きましょうか。
何かラーメンのようなにおいがしますね。
山田　　　　鼻がいいんですね。ちょうど作っていたところな
んです。じゃ，のびないうちに食べましょうか。

① 例　T:　あの映画はおもしろいです。
{ S₁:　あの映画はおもしろそうですね。
{ S₂:　ええ，おもしろいそうですよ。(第19課の復習)

1.　山田さんのお弁当はおいしい
です。
2.　あのレストランは高いです。
3.　今日はクラスがないです。
4.　この宿題はやさしいです。
5.　お天気が悪くなります。
6.　二年生の日本語はやさしいで
す。
7.　雨が降ります。
8.　このネクタイはいいです。
9.　あの子は悲しいです。
10.　あの車はいいです。
11.　このお菓子は甘いです。
12.　スミスさんのおばあさんは元

気です。
13.　この小説はおもしろくありま
せん。
14.　日本語は簡単です。
15.　あの映画はあまりおもしろく
ありません。
16.　今日うちのチームは勝ちます。
17.　ここは夏もあまり暑くありま
せん。
18.　この試験は難しいです。
19.　おじいさんはあまり元気じゃ
ありません。
20.　この部屋は昼間も明るくあり
ません。

② 例 1　{ T:　まだ雨が降っていますか。(ええ)
{ S:　ええ，まだ降っているようです。
　　2　{ T:　まだ雨が降っていますか。(いいえ)
{ S:　いいえ，もう降っていないようです。

302

1. 岡村さんは風邪を引いていますか。（ええ）

2. この薬はよく効きますか。（ええ）

3. 山田さんはもう来ましたか。（いいえ）

4. ブラウンさんは歌が歌えますか。（いいえ）

5. 先生はもうお帰りになりましたか。（ええ）

6. この辞書は高いですか。（いいえ）

7. 雨がもう止みましたか。（ええ）

8. あのアパートは広いですか。（いいえ）

9. スミスさんはうなぎが好きですか。（いいえ）

10. あの映画はおもしろいですか。（ええ）

11. 先生はまだ研究室にいらっしゃいますか。（いいえ）

12. 渡辺さんはピアノが上手ですか。（ええ）

13. あれは山田さんの和英辞典ですか。（ええ）

14. ベイリーさんはさしみが好きですか。（いいえ）

15. このカメラは日本製ですか。（ええ）

16. スミスさんのうちは学校から近いですか。（いいえ）

17. あの建物は寮ですか。（ええ）

18. スミスさんは疲れていますか。（いいえ）

19. 山田さんは来ますか。（いいえ）

20. ブラウンさんはもうベッドに入りましたか。（ええ）

③ 例　T：あれ，彫刻
$\begin{cases} \text{S}_1：あれは彫刻ですか。\\ \text{S}_2：彫刻じゃあないんですが…まあ，彫刻のようなものですね。\end{cases}$

1. あれ，てんぷら
2. これ，名詞
3. あれ．空手
4. あれ，スープ

303

5. これ，バーベキュー

6. これ，オレンジ

7. あれ，SF

8. これ，万年筆

9. あれ，ブラックジャック

10. あれ，スパゲッティ

4 例 T: オレンジ・ジュースを買う

$\begin{cases} \text{S}_1: & \text{オレンジ・ジュースを買いましたか。} \\ \text{S}_2: & \text{ええ，もう買ってあります。} \end{cases}$

1. 買物をする
2. 部屋を片付ける
3. 宿題をする
4. 手紙を書く
5. 庭を掃除する
6. 窓を開ける
7. ごはんを作る
8. 勉強をする
9. ビールを買う
10. 戸をしめる

11. ストーブに火をつける
12. 電気をつける
13. 電気を消す
14. 明日の用意をする
15. スミスさんに電話をかける
16. ビールを冷やす
17. フットボールの切符を買う
18. クイズの勉強をする
19. 地図を買う
20. 手紙に住所を書く

例 5 T: うちへ帰ります，食べます

$\begin{cases} \text{S}_1: & \text{うちへ帰る前に食べますか。} \\ \text{S}_2: & \text{いいえ，帰った後で食べるんです。} \end{cases}$

1. 食べます，勉強します
2. 休みます，部屋を片付けます
3. 学校が終わります，旅行します

4. うちへ帰ります，本を読みます
5. 食べます，休みます

6. スミスさんが来ます，食べます

7. 昼寝をします，泳ぎに行きます

8. 勉強します，御両親に手紙を書きます

9. 学校（がっこう）へ行きます，朝ごはんを食べます

10. うちへ帰ります，テープを聞きます

11. 日本へ行きます，日本語を習います

12. スミスさんと相談（そうだん）します，カメラを買います

13. サンフランシスコへ行きます，食べます

14. 勉強します，テレビを見ます

15. ブラウンさんと会います，テニスをします

6 例1 T: 雨が降る，帰る
       S: 雨が降らないうちに帰りましょう。
    2 T: コーヒーがさめる，コーヒーを飲む
       S: コーヒーがさめないうちに飲みましょう。

1. ラーメンがのびる，食べる
2. 暗（くら）くなる，帰る
3. 暑くなる，庭（にわ）を掃除（そうじ）する
4. 遅（おそ）くなる，ペーパーを書く
5. 子供が大きくなる，ディズニーランドへ行く
6. 車が高くなる，車を買う
7. ごはんがさめる，ごはんを食べる
8. 山田さんが帰って来る，勉強してしまう
9. 遅（おそ）くなる，スミスさんに電話をかける
10. 母が言う，部屋を片付（かたづ）ける
11. お金がなくなる，本を買う
12. 田中さんが来る，このワインを飲む
13. 寒くなる，ヨセミテへ行く
14. 先生がいらっしゃる，宿題をする
15. FBI が来る，うちを出る

Lesson 22 Dialogues

22 A

Okamura: What's that over there?

Smith: The Bay Bridge.

O: No, not the bridge, but right over there.

S: Oh, that. I wonder what you call that. It's sort of like sculpture, I guess.

彫刻 (ちょうこく)   sculpture

O: It's made of driftwood and old tires, isn't it?

流木 (りゅうぼく)   driftwood

古タイヤ   old tire(s)

S: Yes. The one over there looks like a dragon.

竜 (りゅう)   dragon

O: Over there to the right is one shaped like a pyramid, huh?

ピラミッド   pyramid

形 (かたち)   shape, form

S: Yes, and right next to that is one that's sort of like the Sphinx, isn't it?

そう言えぼ   now that you mention it

スフィンクス   sphinx

かっこうをする   to have the appearance of

O: Can we go closer?

S: Yes, we can. Shall we go take a look after we finish our work?

用事   errands, business

済む (す)   to finish, complete

22 B

Smith: Would you like to go to the movies?

Yamada: Yes, is there something good (playing)?

<ruby>面白<rt>おもしろ</rt></ruby>い   interesting

S: Yes, I hear that the movie <u>Star Wars</u> is good.

<ruby>科学小説<rt>か がく</rt></ruby>   SF

Y: <u>Star Wars</u>? What sort of a movie is it?
S: In the paper it said that it's a movie based on a science novel.

    science (科学) ＋ novel (小説)

Y: I'm crazy about Sci-Fi! By the way, are you hungry?

<ruby>S F<rt>エスエフ</rt></ruby>   Sci-Fi

S: Yes, Shall we eat something before we go? Hmm, I smell something like <u>ramen</u>.

    ラーメン   Chinese style noodles in a soup

Y: You sure have a good nose! I was just fixing some. Shall we eat it before the noodles get soggy?

鼻   nose

ちょうど   just (now)

のびる   basic meaning is "to stretch," or "to get long"

Lesson 22 **Notes on Usage**

22 A

1. すぐそこ   すぐ means "immediately," and そこ usually would mean "there (close to you)," but in the dialogue すぐそこに means "right over there." Since the object is somewhat removed from both the speaker and the addressee, logically, the speaker should have used あそこ. By using すぐそこ, he implies that the object is relatively close to where they are.

2. 何というんでしょうか   "What do you call those?" This phrase is used when the speaker cannot think of or does not know the right word to describe an object.

3. <ruby>流木<rt>りゅうぼく</rt></ruby>や古タイヤを使っているんですね。

流 "drifting" + 木 "wood, log"; 古 "old"; タイヤ "tires"; 使っている "have used": "They have used drift wood and old tires." The subject of the sentence, "they," is not directly stated.

4. 右の方に   to the right. Here 方 means "toward" or "direction."

5. ピラミッドのような形をしたのがあります。

形をする "to be shaped (in the form of ____)"...lit. "to do a shape." The construction is similar to other idiomatic phrases such as かっこうをする "to be in the shape/style of ____," においがする "to have the smell of ____," and 音がする "there is a sound"

6. その隣に   next to it

7. 用事が済んだ後で

用事 means "business to take care of," "an errand." It does not mean "business" in the sense of "enterprise." Chores such as babysitting, shopping, going to a dentist, etc. qualify as 用事, but recreational activities such as going to the movies, or on picnics do not.

ちょっと用事があってそこまで来たものですから，およりしました。	I had some business to take care of and happened to be in the neighborhood, so I dropped by. （およりする is a humble form of よる (to drop by).)

(____ものですから, "because ____," is a polite form of ____ ので or ____から)
用事が済む literally means "business ends"; in other words, it means that "one is done with one's errands."

22 B

1. おもしろい   has two meanings: interesting and funny

2. スターウォーズっていうの

"____っていう Noun" is a contracted form of "____という Noun," which means "the N called ____." Often, いう is further contracted to ____って Noun with no

308

change in meaning. Note that ＿＿＿＿ って may appear before verbs such as 書く (to write) as in 科学小説の映画化だって書いてありました。 "It's been written that it is a movie version of a scientific novel."

3. 科学小説の映画化

科学小説 "scientific novel." 科学 "science" ＋ 小説 "story, novel."
映画化 "make into a movie." 映画 "motion picture" ＋ 化 "change/transform into ＿＿＿．"

4. SF, pronounced エスエフ, stands for "science-fiction."

5. 大好き like very much. Similarly, 大嫌い means "dislike very much" or "hate." Both words behave like adjectival nouns: e.g., 大好きなおかし "my favorite cake," and 大嫌いな人 "my least favorite person."

6. ラーメン Chinese-style noodles in Japan. **The word also refers to a popular** Chinese dish consisting of noodles in a soy sauce based soup with slices of pork and vegetables.

7. 鼻がいい literally means, "nose is good," i.e., "One has a good sense of smell." Likewise,

耳がいい   have good ears

頭がいい   head is good or smart

Lesson 22 **Grammar Notes**

The main points of this lesson are:
I. A pattern to express judgment. "It looks (to me)" This judgment is based on the speaker's subjective feeling, impression, inspiration, etc.
II. Another pattern to express judgment, "looks (like,)" "seems," "looks as if," etc. This judgment is based on informed information so is more objective.
III. A pattern to express the notion that something has been done for a certain purpose by an unspecified agent.

IV. "Before" and "after"

    Two expression of the notion of "before":

    A. A neutral "before" as in "I will go to the barber's before I attend the wedding ceremony." and

    B. a "before" used in a sentence to mean either 1. "do something before an undesirable event happens" as in "Before it starts raining, let's go home." or "undesirable event happens before doing something" as in "Before I finished eating, a guest arrived."

    C. One expression of "after."

I. Use of そう

A. <u>X</u> そうです   It looks <u>X</u>
       でした

    Non Stative (pre-masu from)

This expression represents the speaker's subjective judgment concerning an event or situation based on appearances or intuition rather than on objective, factual information. そう behaves like an adjectival noun.

天気が悪くなりそうですね。	It looks like the weather is going to turn bad, doesn't it.

(At the racetrack)

あの馬が勝ちそうです。	I have a hunch that horse is going to win.

When this pattern is used with <u>non-stative verbs</u>, it can also mean something like "about to ____," "on the verge of ____," etc. The following are examples of sentences that can mean either "looks" or "about to" depending on the context.

雨が降りそうです。	It's going to start raining (any minute). or, It looks like it's going to rain. (The second sentence does not contain as great a sense of imminency as the first.)
あの人は馬から落ちそうです。	That person is about to fall off of the horse. or, I think that he is going to fall off of the horse.
あの子は泣き出しそうです。	That child is about to burst into tears. or, I think that the child is going to cry.

Negative form for non-stative verbs:

Verb (pre-masu) ＋ そう ＋ にもありません。	It does not look like <u>V-ing</u> takes place.

バークレーは勝ちそうにもありません。	It does not look like Berkeley is going to win.
あの人は帰りそうにもありません。	It does not look like that person is going to go home.

B. <u>X</u> そうだ
      です
      でした
                                   It looks <u>X</u>

Stative verb (pre-masu)
A (root form)
AN (root form)

Nouns are not used with this pattern with the exception of Noun + negative (e.g. 学生じゃなさそうだ). Some Adjectival Nouns, that are considered too noun-like are also not used with そう.

このお菓子はおいしそうです。	This cake looks good.
あの店は高そうです。	That store looks expensive.
親切そうな人に会いました。	I met a person who looked kind.

When いい (or よい) and ない are followed by そう, they become よさそう (not いさそう) and なさそう, respectively.

このレストランはよさそうです。	This restaurant looks good.
この本屋にはいい本はなさそうです。	It looks like there aren't any good books in this bookstore.

Stative words: (Stative verbs, Adjectives. Adjectival Nouns and Nouns) <u>Stem + Neg.</u> そうです. なさそうです.

(V: わかる)

色々説明したんですが 山川さんはまだわからなさそうです	I explained it to Yamakawa in many ways, but he still looks puzzled.

(A: いい)

これはあまりよくなさそうですね。	This doesn't looks very good, does it? (Lit. "This looks not too good.")

(A: 安い)

あの時計はあまり安くなさそうです。	That watch doesn't look very cheap. (Lit. "That watch looks not too cheap.")

311

(AN: 静か)

あそこはあまり静かじゃなさそうです。

That place doesn't look very quiet.

(AN: 嫌い)

山田さんは酒が嫌いじゃなさそうです。あんなに飲んでいますよ。

It doesn't look like Yamada dislikes sake. Look how much she's drunk.

(N: 病気)

田中さんは病気じゃなさそうです。今朝走っていましたよ。

Tanaka doesn't look sick. He was running this morning.

(N: 日本人)

あの人は，何人でしょう。
——さあ，よくわかりませんが，あの歩き方は日本人じゃなさそうですね。

What (nationality) is he, I wonder. …Well I'm not sure, but he doesn't look Japanese from the way he walks. (Lit. "As for his way of walking, it does not look Japanese.")

II. Sentence (Pre-noun form) + ようだ   It looks like, seems, appears
                                 です   It looks as if
                                 でした

(V   行く/行った)
(A   高い/高かった)
(AN 静かな/静かだった)
(N   学生の/学生だった)
(Neg ない/なかった)

よう conjugates like an Adjectival Noun. Adjectival nouns preceding よう take な, and nouns take の, when in the non-past.

よう is used in two distinctive ways: 1) to mean something like "It looks like," "It appears," or "It seems," to express the speaker's judgment, and 2) to mean "looks as if," to express the fact that something is like X though it is not quite X.

1) よう is used to make statements of objective judgment based on direct experience or a sufficient amount of first hand information. The information is acquired through the senses, usually sight. そう is also used to make statements of judgment based on information acquired through the senses, but unlike よう, the judgment is arrived at intuitively rather than rationally.

By using よう the speaker does not imply that he is committed to his judgement; i.e., he leaves the way open for other possibilities.

1) (Yamada has the air of a person who understands French.)

山田さんはフランス語がわかり
そうです。

It seems to me (I sense) that Yamada understands French.

(A Frenchman is talking to Yamada. She is nodding.)

山田さんはフランス語がわかる
ようです。

It looks like Yamada understands French.

(The Frenchman has finished talking. Now Yamada is pointing toward the station.)

山田さんはフランス語がわかっ
たようです。

It looks like Yamada has understood (his) French.

(Now the Frenchman is shaking his head. He looks hopelessly frustrated.)

山田さんは，わかったようでし
たが，ほんとうはわからなかっ
たようです。

It looked like Yamada understood, but actually it looks like she did not, doesn't she?

あれは何でしょう。
——竜<ruby>竜<rt>りゅう</rt></ruby>のようですね。

What do you think that is?
...It looks like a dragon, doesn't it?

あそこにはピラミッドのような
<ruby>形<rt>かたち</rt></ruby>をしたのがありますね。

There's one shaped like a pyramid over there.

——その<ruby>隣<rt>となり</rt></ruby>のは，スフィンクス
のようなかっこうをしています
ね。

...The one next to it has the form/shape of a sphinx.

The よう construction is sometimes used in situations where the speaker does not want to express his opinion too firmly, even though he may in fact be very confident of what he is saying, or the judgment is an obvious one.

e.g. (At a shirt section of a department store; a father is buying a shirt for his son, who is not with him):

これはちょっと小さそうですね。
この方がよさそうです。これに
します。

I guess (it seems to me) this one is a little (too) small. This one looks better. I'll take this one.

(At home, the father looks at his son who is wearing the shirt. The sleeves extend down to his fingers.):

父：あれ，これはちょっと大き　　　F: Oh, I guess it was a little (too) big.
かったかな。

母：そうですね．ちょっと大き　　　M: Well, (yes), it does look a little (too)
いようですね。　　　　　　　　　　big.

2) "As if": When よう is used in this sense, often, the word まるで ("as if" (Lit. "as if entirely") is used with it.

あの人の顔はずいぶん赤いです　　That man's face is bright red, isn't it?
ね。まるで，お酒を飲んだよう　　He looks just like (as if) he's had some
ですね。　　　　　　　　　　　　　sake. (he had not had any though.)

この本は飛ぶように売れていま　　This book is selling like hotcakes. (Lit.
す。　　　　　　　　　　　　　　　This book is selling as if it flew.)

ずいぶんたくさん水をまいたん　　You've sure sprinkled a lot of water,
ですね。まるで雨が降ったよう　　haven't you? It looks as if it's rained.
ですね。

あそこは東京のよう（な所）で　　That place is (a place) like Tokyo.
す。

あの子はいつも男の子のような　　That child is always dressed like a boy.
かっこうをしていますね。

あの二人はまるで兄弟のように　　Those two look so much alike it's as if
よく似ていますね。　　　　　　　they were brothers. (似る "to resemble")

あれは彫刻のようなものです　　　That thing over there looks like a sculpture.
ね。　　　　　　　　　　　　　　　(Lit. "It's as if it were a sculpture.")

Note: Adjectives and Adjectival Nouns are rarely used in the above sense.

III. V (te-form) てある　　　　　　V is done (and left/kept that way)

This is used as an impersonal construction where the agent is not stated. The purpose of this construction is to focus on what has been done and not on who has done it. This pattern is used to express the unchanged result of an action done by someone (unspecified) for a certain purpose. Although it is not a passive sentence construction this pattern is frequently used in situations expressed by a passive construction in English.

314

この部屋は掃除してあります。 | The room has been cleaned (by someone for a certain purpose).

窓があけてあります。 | The window has been opened.

Note the differences in the following patterns:

((Agent) が/は) (Object) を V-transitive ている
(Object) が V-transitive てある
(Object) が V-intransitive ている

Compare the following two sentences:

a) 御飯を作っています。 | I have made the meal. or,
I am making the meal.

b) 御飯が作ってあります。 | The meal has been made.

Sentence a) has two meanings: I have cooked the meal (and am waiting for you/ someone to eat it); and I am cooking the meal (now). Only the first meaning will be dealt with here.

Sentence b) means that someone has cooked the meal and it's ready to be served. The agent or the person who cooked the meal is not specified in this construction. The speaker does not need to specify the agent because it is irrelevant to the discussion, because it is clear from the context, or for some other reason.

Also compare the following three sentences:

c) (私は) 窓をしめていました。 | I kept the window closed. (for some reason/purpose)

d) 窓がしめてありました。 | The window had been closed. (somebody kept the window closed for some reason)

e) 窓がしまっていました。 | The window was closed. (しまる: intransitive verb)

What was said about sentences a) and b) in the previous examples applies to the above examples c) and d) as well. c) contains an agent; d), does not (leaves it unspecified). e) is a simple description of the situation. (Although the English equivalents of d) and e) are in the passive form, the Japanese sentences are not passive sentences. Japanese passive sentences will be introduced in Lesson 26)

IV. "before" and "after"

A. "before" <u>V (Plain, Non-Past)</u> + 前に   before <u>V</u>

映画に行く前に何か食べて行きましょう。 | Let's eat something before we go to the movie. (lit. "eat and go").

結婚式に出る前に，床屋に行きます。

Before I attend the wedding ceremony, I will go to the barber shop.

日本へ行く前に，日本語を勉強します。

I will study Japanese before I go to Japan.

B. "before" V (Plain Non-Past neg.) ないうちに before V takes place
(lit. "within/during the period of time in which V does not occur.")

This pattern is used to express either 1) something is done/occurs before some undersirable event takes place, or 2) some undesirable event happens before something else happens.

1) 雨が降らないうちに行きましょう。

Let's go before it starts raining.

ラーメンがのびないうちに食べた方がいいですよ。

It'll be better if you eat your ramen before it gets soggy.

お客様がいらっしゃらないうちに掃除をするつもりです。

I intend to clean up (the place) before the guests arrive.

2) 大学につかないうちに雨が降ってきました。

Before I got to the university it started to rain. (ふってくる to start raining)

食べないうちにラーメンがのびてしまいました。

Before I had eaten it, the ramen got soggy.

掃除をしないうちにお客様がいらしゃいました。

Before I had cleaned the place, the guests arrived.

C. "after" V (Plain, Past) あとで

after V takes/took place

用事が済んだあとで，行ってみましょう。

Let's go have a look after our business (errands) is (are) over.

フェントンズでバナナスプリットを食べたあとで，マッカラムズでナイトメアを食べました。きょうはおなかが痛いです。

After I had a banana split at Fenton's, I had a "nightmare" at McCallum's. I have a stomachache today.

316

第二十二課　漢字

親切
しん せつ
親切

質問
しつ もん
質問

用事
よう じ
用事

住所
じゅう しょ
住所

悪い
わる
悪い

木
き
木

右
みぎ
右

左
ひだり
左

前
まえ
前

飛ぶ
と
飛ぶ

落ちる
お
落ちる

第 二十三 課

23 A　　ベイリー　　　ワイシャツが買いたいんですがどこがいいでしょうか。

　　　　藤原　　　　　やっぱりどこかデパートがいいんじゃないですか。

　　　　ベイリー　　　デパートは高すぎるんじゃないですか。

　　　　藤原　　　　　いえ，伊勢丹なんかいいですよ。

　　　　ベイリー　　　簡単に行けますか，ここから…

　　　　藤原　　　　　ええ，地下鉄で十五分ぐらいですよ。もしよかったら一緒に行きましょうか。今日はひまなんです。

　　　　ベイリー　　　藤原さんがきょうひまだということは，また大山先生の講義をサボるということですね。

　　　　藤原　　　　　よく分かりますね。

　　　　ベイリー　　　サボりすぎるとあとが大変なんじゃありませんか。

23 B　　店員　　　　　いらっしゃいませ。

　　　　ベイリー　　　このシャツを見せてください。

　　　　店員　　　　　お客様のですか。

　　　　ベイリー　　　ええ，私が着るんですが…

　　　　店員　　　　　これではいかがでございましょう。

　　　　ベイリー　　　これじゃちょっと小さすぎるかもしれませんね。

　　　　藤原　　　　　LLですよ，ベイリーさん。

　　　　ベイリー　　　でも洗うと小さくなるでしょう。

319

店員　　　　　　　さようでございますねえ。お客様の場合ですと両国あたりが…

① 例　T: サボります，後が大変だ
　　　　S: サボると後が大変です。

1. 新しいシャツを洗います，小さくなる
2. 春になります，桜が咲く
3. 新しいジーンズを洗います，小さくなる
4. 夏になります，暑くなる
5. 勉強しません，試験の時大変だ
6. 夕方になります，涼しくなる
7. 薬を飲みません，風邪が直らない
8. 一に二をたします，三になる
9. 朝起きます，ジュースを飲む
10. 授業が終わります，コーヒーを飲みに行く
11. 食べます，少し散歩する
12. 二から一をひきます，一になる
13. 図書館へ行きます，いつもスミスさんに会う
14. ストーブに火をつけます，あたたかくなる
15. 九に一をたします，十になる
16. 十三から五をひきます，八になる
18. 字引を引きません，分からない
19. 冬になります，いつもスキーに行きます
20. 毎晩八時間寝ません，翌日は大変だ

② 例　T: 窓を開けました，鳥が飛んで来ました
　　　　S: 窓を開けると鳥が飛んで来ました。

1. うちへ帰りました，スミスさんが待っていました
2. 朝起きました，電気がまだついていました

320

3. ドアを開けました，変な人が
   いました
4. 箱<ruby>箱<rt>はこ</rt></ruby>の中を見ました，何も入っ
   ていませんでした
5. <ruby>電車<rt>でんしゃ</rt></ruby>が駅に<ruby>着<rt>つ</rt></ruby>きました，人が
   <ruby>大勢<rt>おおぜい</rt></ruby><ruby>降<rt>お</rt></ruby>りました

6. 部屋の中を見ました，子供が
   寝ていました
7. <ruby>窓<rt>まど</rt></ruby>の外を見ました，スミスさ
   んが<ruby>立<rt>た</rt></ruby>っていました
8. <ruby>冷蔵庫<rt>れいぞうこ</rt></ruby>を開けてみました，何
   もありませんでした

③ 例　T: 高いです
　　　　　{S₁: あの…すこし高すぎるんじゃないでしょうか。
　　　　　{S₂: いえ，そうでもないんじゃないですか。

1. 小さいです
2. <ruby>甘<rt>あま</rt></ruby>いです
3. 難しいです
4. <ruby>簡単<rt>かんたん</rt></ruby>です
5. 大きいです
6. 遠いです
7. 飲みます
8. します
9. 飲みました
10. 働きました

11. 早いです
12. 食べました
13. 早かったです
14. <ruby>辛<rt>から</rt></ruby>いです
15. 長いです
16. 読みました
17. 難しかったです
18. 遊びました
19. 長かったです
20. きたないです

④ 例　T: これ，私，小さい。
　　　　　S: これは，私には，少し小さすぎるかもしれませんね。

1. この本，子供，難しい
2. このお肉，おばあさん，かたい

321

3. このキムチ，スミスさん，辛い
4. このお菓子，先生，甘い
5. このスーツ，上田さん，大きい
6. この本，木村さん，やさしい
7. この練習，一年生，やさしい
8. あのアパート，バークレーの学生，いい
9. あの映画の英語，岡村さん，難しい
10. テレビの日本語放送，ブラウンさん，難しい

5 例　T：今日，暇です，講義をサボります
　　　S：今日暇だということは講義をサボるということですね。

1. 先生が今日いらっしゃいません，休講です
2. 山下さんの部屋が暗いです，もう寝ました
3. ブラウンさんがまだ部屋にいます，クラスをサボっています
4. うちの子供が泣いています，また隣の子供とけんかをしました
5. 頭が痛いです，ゆうべ飲みすぎました
6. 山田さんの部屋の電気がついています，まだ勉強しています
7. ブラウンさんが山田さんをいつもからかっています，山田さんが好きです
8. ブラウンさんが歌っています，シャワーを浴びています
9. スミスさんがにこにこしています，試験でいい点をとりました
10. 山中さんが（御）両親に手紙を書いています，お金を送ってもらいたいです

Lesson 23 Dialogues

23 A

Bailey: I want to buy a dress shirt. Where do you think would be good?

ワイシャツ   dress shirt

Fujiwara: Wouldn't some department store be right for that?

…なんかいいですよ   an idiom: Don't you think a department store would be best?

Baily: But aren't they expensive?

Fujiwara: No, places like Isetan are pretty good, you know.

伊勢丹   one of several large department stores in Japan.

Baily: Can I get there easily from here?

Fujiwara: Yes, it's about fifteen minutes by subway. If it's okay with you, shall I come with you? I'm free today (anyhow).

地下鉄   subway

Baily: Your being free today means that you're cutting Prof. Ooyama's class, right?

サボる   to cut class

Fujiwara: How'd you know?

よく分かりますね   lit., "You know everything, don't you?"

Baily: But if you cut too much, won't it be rough (on you) later?

23 B

Clerk: May I help you?

いらっしゃいませ   lit., "Welcome!"

Baily: May I see this shirt, please?

Clerk: Is it for you?

お客様のですか   lit., "Is it for (you), sir?"

Baily: Yes, it's for me.

着る   to wear

Clerk: How about this one?

でござる   humble form of です

Baily: This one looks like it might be a little too small.
Fujiwara: But that's an LL, Bailey.
Baily: (Yes, I know,) but it'll shrink when I wash it, won't it?

洗う   to wash

Clerk: Let's see. Perhaps (in your situation) you should try (going to) Kuramae...

場合   circumstance, situation

両国   place in Tokyo, where the Sumo arena is
                                        located.

あたり   area, vicinity

Lesson 23 **Notes on Usage**

23 A

1. ワイシャツ   men's dress shirts. The word is said to be a corrupted form of the
English, "white shirts". It is usually written in katakana, but sometimes, especially in
advertisements for bargain sales, it is written Y シャツ. ワイシャツ no longer refers only to
shirts that are white.

Here are words for other articles of clothing:

男 性 用 (for men)		女 性 用 (for women)	
スポーツシャツ	(sport shirts)	ブラウス	(blouse)
ズボン	(trousers)	スラックス	(dress slacks)
靴下 (くつした)	(socks)	ソックス	(socks)
パンツ	(underpants)	パンティ	(underpants)

| シャツ | (undershirts) | スカート | (skirt) |
| ネクタイ | (necktie) | ストッキング | (nylons) |

男性用と女性用

ベルト	(belt)
くつ 靴	(shoes)
セーター	(sweater)
レーンコート	(raincoat)
コート	(overcoat)

2. どこがいい   Here どこ means "what store," "which store."

3. やっぱりどこかデパートがいいんじゃないですか。

やっぱり "as anyone would suggest," "as one might expect"; どこか "somewhere"; デパート "department store."

4. 伊勢丹   One of the major department stores in Tokyo. The main store is located in the 新宿 district, which is one of the cultural centers of Tokyo.

なんか When written in hiragana and used after a noun, it is a colloquial form of など "etc.", and is used when citing examples. The sentence means "Isetan, for example, is good." 何か written with the kanji for <u>nan</u> and the hiragana <u>ka</u> is a different word which is a contracted form of なにか. It is also pronounced なんか but it means "something," and never follows a noun.

5. 簡単に easily   簡単 ("simple") is an adjectival noun.
簡単に行けますかここから The normal word order for this sentence would be ここから簡単に行けますか.

6. 地下鉄 subway   地下 "underground," derives from 地 (earth) and 下 (under). 鉄 "iron," "steel," is short for 鉄道 "railway" (iron + way).

7. もしよかったら   The expression means "if you don't mind," or "if it is all right with you."
一緒に行きましょうか "Shall I go with you?" Notice that Fujiwara does not say 一緒に行ってあげましょうか to Bailey, even though, given the situation, she could have. She shows sensitivity and tact by not using the てあげる form.

8. きょうは暇なんです。　暇 means "free time."

9. 講義をサボる　サボる "to cut class," "to be idle (ie., to not be doing work one is supposed to do)"
　　As the katakana indicate, the word is of foreign origin. It is a contracted form of サボタージする, which derives from "sabotage." The Japanese word, originally used by students to mean "to cut class", is also used generally to mean that one is being idle when one should be working. Its connotations are not as strong as the English word "to sabotage."

10. あとが大変　あと "later"; 大変 "troublesome." The phrase means, "one will pay for it (one's idleness) later when one tries to catch up (in class)."

23 B

1. このシャツを見せてください。　"Please show me this shirt." Here Bailey is pointing to a shirt in the showcase. シャツ here means ワイシャツ.

2. お客様のですか　Is it (what you are looking for) for you?
　　お客様　お is an honorific prefix; 客 "customer"; 様 an honorific form of さん.

3. これではいかがでございましょう。
　　これで Lit., "with this". いかがでございましょう is a more polite way of saying どうですか "How is it?", or "How do you like it?"

4. LL (エルエル). Clothing sizes in Japan are indicated in various ways. One way is by using the series "SS, S, M, L, LL," which can be found on shirts, underwear, etc. Another way is by using the series" "小 (しょう), 中 (ちゅう), 大 (だい), 特大 (とくだい) (extra large)," which is reserved for Japanese style clothes such as ゆかた. Usually, shirt sizes are given in cm. (centimeters). A typical size would look something like, 40–80, which means that the collar size is 40 cm., and that the sleeve length is 80 cm. Shoe sizes are given in cm. as well, the width being indicated by a letter: A, B, C, etc. It is difficult to find a pair of shoes in Japan to fit American feet.

5. 洗うと小さくなるでしょう。　It will probably become small when you wash it. Another way of saying the above is 洗うとちぢむでしょう.
　　(ちぢむ to shrink)

326

これ洗うとちぢみますか。

そうですね…少しはしかたが
ありませんがそんなにちぢみ
ませんよ。

Will this shrink when I wash it?

...Let's see... You can't help it shrinking a little, but it won't shrink all that much.

6. さようでございますねえ   A humble form of そうですねえ "Let's see."

7. お客様の場合（ばあい）ですと

場合 means "in the case of," thus the phrase means "in the case of you," or "in your case." Note that the clerk says お客様 instead of あなた.

8. 両国（りょうごく）あたりが…

両国 is a section of Tokyo where 国技館 （こくぎかん）, the Sumo (Japanese wrestling) arena, is located. Many of the giant Sumo-wrestlers live in the area, and the clerk is suggesting that someone as big as Bailey might do well to go to Ryoogoku to find a shirt that would fit him. The full sentences including the part left unsaid would go something like,

（両国あたりが）お客様に合（あ）うシャツを置（お）いている店がある所だろう

と思いますが。

..."I think that the area (around Ryoogoku) is the place where there would be stores that have shirts that would fit you."

Lesson 23   Grammar Notes

The main points of this lesson are:
I. A pattern to express
  A. the idea of "whenever."
  B. the idea of "when/if."
II. Miscellaneous expressions
  A. A pattern to express the idea of "too much."
  B. A pattern to express <u>X</u> means, in other words, <u>Y,</u> as in "When you say that you have free time, it means that you are cutting classes, right?"

I. Sentence₁ と Sentence₂

A. Whenever S₁, S₂
    (generic situation)
B. If/When S₁ is the case, then
    (unexpected) S₂ (past).
    (a temporal expression describing a
    specific event)

Generally speaking と serves to connect an action or situation with its results. <u>Sentence₁</u> is always in the non-past tense regardless of the tense of <u>Sentence₂</u>. In addition, <u>Sentence₂</u> represents something that the speaker cannot control. It cannot contain a command, a request, or some form of determination.

There are two ways to use the S₁ と S₂ construction: (a) in a generic situation-- "Whenever S₁, S₂". Generic situations are those in which whenever <u>Sentence₁</u> is the case, <u>Sentence₂</u> will inevitably follow, or will be a predictable result; e.g. 一に二をたすと三になります "1＋2＝3" (or 一たす二は三です): and (b) a description of one specific event-- "If/When S₁ (is the case), then S₂" e.g. ドアをあけると変な人が寝ていました "When I opened the door, (to my surprise) there was a strange man lying (there)."

In usage (b), no logical antecedent-consequence relationship is implied between S₁ and S₂, and thus S₂ often presents a situation that is surprising to the speaker.

と is also used when S₁ ends in an adjective, adjectival noun, or noun, generally with the generic meaning.

広いと掃除（そうじ）がたいへんです。	If it is spacious, it is hard to clean up.

A. Generic situation:

一に二をたすと三になります。	When(ever) you add 2 to 1, it becomes 3. (2 added to 1 makes 3).
私が去年田中先生のオフィスに行くといつもいらっしゃいました。	Last year, whenever I went to Professor Tanaka's office he was always there.
夏になると暑くなります。	When(ever) it becomes summer, it gets hot.
山川（やまかわ）さんはお金がはいるといつもすぐ飲みに行ってしまいます。	Whenever Yamakawa gets some money, he always goes out drinking right away.

B. Specific event:

うちへ帰るとスミスさんが待っ	When I went home, Smith was waiting

328

ていました。

「いかがですか」と言うと「ま
あまあです」と言いました。

電車がマッカーサー駅に着くと
人が大勢降りました。

for me. (implication: I did not know that
he would be there.)

(When) I said, "How are you?," (then)
he said, "Not bad. (So so.)"

When the train (electric train) arrived at
MacArthur station, many people got off.

II Miscellaneous expressions:

A. _____X_____ すぎる

V   (pre-masu)
A   (root)
AN   (な is dropped)

too X (Lit. "exceedingly X")

Nouns cannot be used in this pattern except those nouns which denote quality, such as
美人 (beautiful woman), 金持 (rich person), etc., can be used in the pattern. See example
below).

V

山田さんはちょっと飲みすぎて
いるんじゃないですか。

Hasn't (isn't it the case that) Yamada
drunk a little too much?

A

ちょっと高すぎますねえ。わた
しには…

That's a little too expensive for me.

AN

この本はまじめすぎておもしろ
くありません。

This book is so serious that it's not interesting.

B. Sentence₁ (Plain form) ということは Sentence₂ (Plain form) ということです

と言う事 means "to say that," "the fact that." The construction can be taken to mean
"The fact that S_1 is the case, means that S_2 is the case," in other words, "What S_1 means
is S_2, or By S_1 (you/they/etc.) mean S_2."

暇だということは講義をサボる
ということですね。

When you say that you (the fact that you)
are free today, it means that you are
cutting classes, right?

329

山田さんが御両親に手紙を書い
ているということはお金がなく
なったということですね。

The fact that Yamada is writing her parents means that she has run out of money (now), doesn't it?

ブラウンさんの部屋が暗いとい
うことはもう寝たということで
しょうか。

Does the fact that Brown's room is dark (it is dark in B's room) mean that he has gone to bed?

さあ，部屋に居ないということ
かも知れませんよ。

Well, It may (also) mean that he is not in his room. (lit. it may also be a fact of his not being in his room)

第二十三課　漢字

働く
はたら

働　く

洗う
あら

洗　う

長い
なが

長　い

大変
たい　へん

大　変

問題
もん　だい

問　題

電気
でん　き

電　気

お客様
きゃく　さま

お　客　様

地下鉄
ち　か　てつ

地　下　鉄

学校
がっ　こう

学　校

貯金
ちょ　きん

貯　金

肉
にく

肉

330

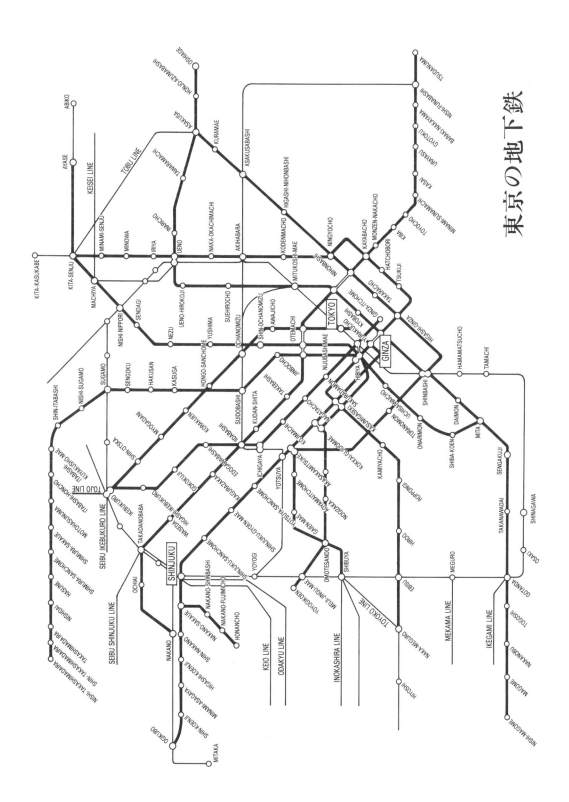

東京の地下鉄

第 二十四 課

24 A　ベイリー　　　もうすっかり春らしくなりましたね。

　　　　藤原　　　　本当に今日は春らしいお天気ですね。桜も満開
　　　　　　　　　　ですね。

　　　　ベイリー　　桜といえば下宿のおばさんに桜もちというも
　　　　　　　　　　のをもらいましたが，あれは何でできているん
　　　　　　　　　　ですか。

　　　　藤原　　　　あれは小麦粉とあんです。小麦粉を焼いてその
　　　　　　　　　　中にあんを入れて作るんです。

　　　　ベイリー　　なかなか詳しいんですね。

　　　　藤原　　　　それから桜の葉で包むんです。

　　　　ベイリー　　ああ，そうですか。それで桜もちって言うんで
　　　　　　　　　　すか。いかにも春らしいお菓子ですね。

24 B　ベイリー　　　ゆうべ初めて焼酎というものを飲みました。

　　　　藤原　　　　そうですか。私は飲んだことがないんです。ど
　　　　　　　　　　うでしたか。

　　　　ベイリー　　なかなか面白い味でしたよ。あれは何から作る
　　　　　　　　　　んですか。

　　　　藤原　　　　さあ，あまりよくは知りませんが沖縄などでは
　　　　　　　　　　さつまいもから作るらしいですよ。

　　　　ベイリー　　ははあ，そうですか。結局いもですか。なか
　　　　　　　　　　なか効きますね。飲みはじめて三十秒ぐらい
　　　　　　　　　　で頭がボーッとしてしまいました。

　　　　藤原　　　　ベイリーさんらしくありませんね。でも今日は

何ともないんでしょう。

ベイリー　　　　いや，まだ何だかボーッとしているんです。

① 例1　T:　このおかし，春
　　　　 {S₁:　このおかしは春らしいですね。
　　　　 {S₂:　ええ，ほんとうに春らしいおかしですね。
　　　　　　　　（いかにも）

　　　例2　T:　今日，春
　　　　 {S₁:　今日は，春らしいですね。
　　　　 {S₂:　ええ，ほんとうに春らしい日ですね。
　　　　　　　　（いかにも）　　　　（天気）

1.　ブラウンさん，男　　　　　　9.　ハンフリー・ボガード，男
2.　カーター，大統領　　　　　　10.　スミスさん，学生
3.　山田さん，女　　　　　　　　11.　タコ，メキシコ
4.　本田先生，先生　　　　　　　12.　「ナポレオン」，フランス
5.　テレグラフ，バークレー　　　　　　（ブランデー）
6.　ハンバーガー，アメリカ　　　13.　「フィアット」，イタリア
7.　岡村さん，日本人　　　　　　14.　フットボール，　？
8.　ベラー先生，学者　　　　　　15.　ジャズ，　　　　？

② 例　T:　このお酒は米から作るんですか。（さつまいも）
　　　　 S:　（いえ，）さつまいもから作るらしいです。

1.　スミスさんは今日来ますか。　　　　　（来ません）

334

2. 山田さんは来ましたか。（来ま
   せんでした）

3. このバスはどこへ行きますか。
   （オークランド）

4. あのレストランは高いですか。
   （安いです）

5. あのレストランは高いですか。
   （あまり高くありません）

6. 明日の試験は難しいでしょう
   か。（やさしいです）

7. 山田さんはまだいますか。（も
   う帰りました）

8. スミスさんは日本語を勉強し
   ますか。
   （中国語）

9. ブラウンさんはまだ寝ていま
   すか。（もう起きました）

10. ベイリーさんは日本でカメラ
    を買いますか。（もう買いまし
    た）

11. 酒は何から作るんですか。
    （米）

12. 岡村さんは元気ですか。（あま
    り元気じゃありません）

13. この薬はよく効くでしょうか。
    （よく効きます）

14. 田中さんは卒業できるでしょ
    うか。（できません）

15. ブラウンさんは，中国語を勉
    強していますか。（日本語）

16. スミスさんは，日本語を勉強
    しましたか。（韓国語）

17. ジョンソンさんは，まだひと
    りですか。（結婚しています）

18. 田中さんはバスで通っていま
    すか。（車）

19. 桜もちは何で作るんですか。
    （小麦粉とあん）

20. 「スターウォーズ」はどうで
    しょう。（おもしろいです）

③ 例

T: このお酒は何からつくるんですか。（いも）

S: さあ……詳しいことは知りませんが，沖縄などではいもから
   つくるらしいですよ。

1. しょうゆは何からつくるんですか。（大豆）

335

2. おせんべいは何でつくるんですか。（米）

3. あんは何からつくるんですか。（あずき）

4. 桜もちは何でつくるんですか。（小麦粉とあん）

5. みそは何からつくるんですか。（大豆）

6. あれは何でできているんですか。（流木や古タイヤ）

7. チーズは何からつくるんですか。（牛乳）

8. ミルクセーキは何でつくるんですか。（？）

9. テキーラは何からできているんですか。（？）

10. バーボンは何からつくるんですか。（？）

11. ウォッカは何からつくるんですか。（？）

④ 例1　T：もう食べたんですか。（ええ）
　　　　　S：ええ，食べ終わったばかりです。
　　例2　T：もう食べたんですか。（いえ）
　　　　　S：いえ，食べはじめたばかりです。

1. もう勉強したんですか。（いえ）

2. もう書いたんですか。（ええ）

3. テープはもう聞いたんですか。（ええ）

4. 手紙はもう書いたんですか。（ええ）

5. 論文はもう書いたんですか。（いえ）

6. 宿題はもうしたんですか。（いえ）

7. 晩ごはんはもう作ったんですか。（いえ）

8. 新聞はもう読んだんですか。（ええ）

9. もう夕ごはんを作ったんですか。（ええ）

10. タームペーパーはもうタイプしたんですか。（いいえ）

336

⑤　例　T：下宿のおばさん，桜もち，もらった

S：下宿のおばさんに桜もちをもらいました。（動詞の復習）

1. ゆうべ，焼酎，飲んだ
2. 焼酎，飲んだことがある
3. 焼酎，さつまいも，作る
4. デパート，ワイシャツ，買った
5. きのう，大山先生の講義，サボった
6. 洗う，小さい，なる
7. ラーメンのようなにおい，する
8. スミスさんと山田さん，映画，行く
9. あの流木，竜のような形，している
10. もっと近く，行ける
11. 赤木先生，紹介状，書く，くれた
12. 藤原さん，切符，買う，もらった
13. 来年，大学，卒業する
14. 日本，白馬，行く
15. リノ，ブラックジャック，する
16. 週末，リノ，行く
17. きのうの夜，熱，ある
18. きのう，雨，ぬれる
19. カンパニーレ，上がる，十セント，いる
20. 日本語，勉強する，日本，行く
21. この単語，どんな辞書，ない
22. きのう，クイズ，ある
23. 単語の意味，分からない
24. きのう，アパート，出る，雨，降っている
25. 東京の友達，万年筆，送る
26. 日本，中国語，勉強する
27. 先週，サンフランシスコ，行く
28. 先週，サンフランシスコ，映画，見る
29. 日本語，手紙，書く
30. 友達のアパート，カリフォルニア・ワイン，飲む

Lesson 24 **Dialogues**

24 A

Bailey: It's sure gotten to look a lot like spring, hasn't it?

すっかり   completely

Fujiwara: Yes, the weather is really like spring today, huh? And the cherry blossoms are in full bloom, aren't they?

春らしい   seems like spring
桜 (さくら)   cherry blossoms
満開 (まんかい)   to be in full bloom

Bailey: Speaking of cherry blossoms, I got some <u>sakuramochi</u> from the landlady at my boarding house. What's it made of?

下宿 (げしゅく)   boarding house

おばさん   lady, aunt

もち   a dumpling made of pounded steamed rice.

Fujiwara: That's basically made of wheat flour and a bean filling. You make it by toasting the wheat flour and putting the bean filling inside.

小麦粉 (こむぎこ)   wheat flour
あん   bean filling
焼く (や)   to bake, roast, fry

Bailey: You sure do know a lot!

なかなか   considerably, fairly, quite
詳しい (くわ)   detailed, to know the particulars

Fujiwara: And then you wrap it in a leaf from the cherry tree.

葉 (は)   leaf

Bailey: I see. So that's why it's called <u>sakuramochi</u>. It really is a spring confection, isn't it?

それで   thus, therefore

いかにも truly, really, indeed

菓子 <ruby>菓<rt>か</rt></ruby><ruby>子<rt>し</rt></ruby> confection

24 B

Bailey: Last night I drank syootyuu for the first time.

ゆうべ last night

<ruby>初<rt>はじ</rt></ruby>めて for the first time

<ruby>焼酎<rt>しょうちゅう</rt></ruby> a strong, low-grade liquor distilled from sweet potatoes, potatoes, or other grains.

Fujiwara: You did? I've never drunk it. How was it?
Bailey: It really had an interesting taste. What's it made of?

<ruby>味<rt>あじ</rt></ruby> flavor, taste

Fujiwara: Gee, I'm not really sure, but in Okinawa it seems that they make it from sweet potatoes.

<ruby>沖縄<rt>おきなわ</rt></ruby> now comprising a prefecture of Japan, the Ryukyus were returned by the U.S. in 1972

さつまいも sweet potatoes

らしい to seem

Bailey: Is that right. Potatoes, huh? It really has a kick, doesn't it. About thirty seconds after I took a drink, my head got all fuzzy.

<ruby>結局<rt>けっきょく</rt></ruby> after all, finally

<ruby>効<rt>き</rt></ruby>く to be effective

<ruby>秒<rt>びょう</rt></ruby> second(s)

Fujiwara, That's not like you at all! You're okay today though, aren't you?

何ともない nothing at all

Bailey: No, my head's still kind of funny.

何だか somewhat, somehow

Lesson 24   Notes on Usage

24 A

1. もうすっかり春らしくなりましたね。

もう "already," すっかり "totally, entirely," 春らしくなる "become typical of spring." すっかり is often used in the ___ らしくなる construction.

2. 桜も満開ですね。

桜 "cherry," 満開 "in full bloom, (満 full, 開 open), も after 桜 implies "among those things that herald the arrival of a typical spring season, I can also include cherry (blossoms)."

3. 桜と言えば "Speaking of cherry blossoms," "Now that you mention cherry blossoms." (cf. そう言えば "Now that you mention it," "Come to think of it" in L. 3 NU B2)

4. 下宿のおばさん

下宿 "rooming house." It is different from an apartment, an inn or a hotel by virtue of its being, in most cases, a part of an ordinary house; i.e., a room for rent. Some include kitchen privileges, and some offer board. College students who come from distant places often settle into a 下宿.

5. 桜もちと言うもの   (Lit. "thing called <u>sakuramochi</u>")

もち are pounded rice cakes.
桜もち are <u>mochi</u> wrapped in cherry leaves. The delicate fragrance of the leaf blends with the <u>mochi</u>, and enhances its flavor.

6. 何でできているんですか   What is it made of?

<u>X</u>でできている be made of/with <u>X</u>

桜もちは小麦粉とあんでできています。   <u>Sakuramochi</u> are made with wheat flour and <u>an</u> (sweet red bean paste).

昔の車は鉄と木でできていまし   Long ago cars were made of steel and

340

たがこのごろのは鉄とプラスチックでできています。

wood, but recent ones are made of steel and plastic.

<u>X</u> で <u>Y</u> を作る

to make <u>Y</u> with <u>X</u>

ぎょうざは豚肉^{ぶたにく}で作るんですよ。

(They) make potstickers with pork. (Lit. "As for potstickers, they make them with pork.")

折紙^{おりがみ}で鶴^{つる}を作ってください。

Please make a crane with the <u>origami</u>. (おりがみ thin, square sheets of colored paper one uses to make various figures.)

The particle で is used when the material used in making something is still identifiable in the finished product.

7. 小麦粉^{こむぎこ} "flour." 小麦 "wheat" (小 "small" 麦 "wheat, oats, barley") 粉 "powder" あん "sweet red bean paste."

8. 小麦紛を焼^やいて……

焼く has many meanings: "to burn," "to broil," "to bake," etc. Here it means "to bake."

9. なかなか詳^{くわ}しいんですね。

You are quite well versed in it, aren't you?

なかなか "quite (well, much, etc.)" (adverb), 詳しい "detailed," "knowledgeable."

なかなか面白^{おもしろ}い味^{あじ}です。

It has quite an interesting taste.

10. それで桜もちって言うんですか。

それで "thus, therefore, that's why, etc."

11. いかにも春らしいお菓子^{かし}ですね。

いかにも "indeed," "truly." This word is often used with ____ らしい。
お菓子 "cakes," "candies," "sweets."

24 B

1. ゆうべ "last night". This form is less formal than 昨夜^{さくや}, which also means "last night." The latter is of Chinese origin.

2. 初めて for the first time. Notice that the kanji for hajimete, when used in this sense, is 初 not 始.

3. 焼酎 a strong distilled liquor. Recently it is sometimes referred to as ホワイトリカー (white liquor). It is also used to make homemade plum wine.

4. 何から作るんですか。

   X から作る

      焼酎はさつまいもから作るらしいです。

      ナイロンは石炭と水と空気から作るのだそうです。

   X からできる

      石油からどんなものができますか。

What is it made from
(Lit. "From what do they make it?")
to make from X
(から is used when the original material is changed into something else.)

It seems that they make shoochuu from sweet potatoes.

I hear that nylon is made from coal, water and air.

be made from X

What kind of things are made from petroleum?

5. あまりよくは知りませんが…   I don't know much about it, but...

知る means "to get to know," "to have knowledge of."
Note that "I know" is 知っています <u>not</u> 知ります, but that "I don't know" is 知りません.
分かる means "to understand," "to figure out."
Note that in the situations that follow, 分かりません is used rather than 知りません because the speaker has not figured out what he is going to do.

      来学期は何を取るつもりですか。   What are you going to take next semester?

      まだ分かりません。   I don't know yet.

      日本ではどこに住むんですか。   Where are you going to live in Japan?

      さあ，まだ分かりません。   Gee, I don't know yet.

Also, note the difference in usage of the words:

      山田さんの誕生日はいつですか。   When is Yamada's birthday?

(without checking anything)

      さあ知りません。   Gee, I don't know.

(checked Yamada's file, but still don't know)

分かりません。 I don't know.

6. 沖縄<ruby>沖縄<rt>おきなわ</rt></ruby>などでは

沖縄 Name of a prefecture. It is located to the south of Kyuusyuu, and is made up of several islands. など means "etc." It follows a noun or a series of nouns mentioned as an example. Here the phrase means "In Okinawa, for example."

7. さつまいも sweet potato

さつま is the name of a region of Kagoshima prefecture in Kyuusyuu. いも "potatoes."

8. ははあ，そうですか。 Oh, I see.

ははあ is uttered when the speaker has figured out a problem, or when someone explains a problem to him and he finally understands it. The English equivalent would be "Oh!"

9. 結局<rt>けっきょく</rt> in the end, finally at last

In the dialogue, Bailey had been wondering what shoochuu was made from. Now his curiosity is finally satisfied. In his mind the origin of shoochuu has been made clear at last (ie., it is made from potatoes), thus he uses 結局.

10. 効<rt>き</rt>きますね。

効く means "be effective," and is usually used for medicines. When the word is used to refer to alcohol, it means "strong."

11. 三十秒<rt>びょう</rt>ぐらいで in thirty seconds or so

秒 means "seconds," ぐらい "about," で "in" (cf. L. 16 Notes on Usage B6 for で).
cf. 時間 hour 分 minutes 秒 seconds (duration of time)
時 o'clock 分 minutes 秒 seconds (point in time)

12. ボーッとしてしまいました。

ボーッとする become absentminded, semi-conscious
V てしまう indicates that an action/event has taken place and there is nothing that anyone can do about it. (cf. L. 16, GN III.)

13. 何ともない no problem, nothing at all

This phrase is used when something undesirable happens, or is supposed to happen to a person, yet that person himself thinks that everything is all right. "I'm all right, so don't worry," or "This is not bad at all, so don't worry," etc.

e.g. (A stumbles and falls)

B: おけがはありませんか。   B: Are you hurt?

A: ええ，おかげさまで，大丈夫
です．何ともありません。   A: Thanks. I'm all right.
          It was nothing at all.

14. 何だかボーッとしています。

    何だか   somehow

e.g. (talking to oneself):

何だか変だな   Somehow something's wrong.
                           (Somehow it's strange)

あなたを見ていると何だかうれ
しくなるんです。   When(ever) I look at you, I become
happy (for some reason).

Lesson 24 **Grammar Notes**

The main points of this lesson are:

I. A. Another pattern to express judgment: "look like" "seem" etc., as in "It seems that he understood the problem." This form らしい differs from the previously introduced forms そう and よう in that the speaker makes his judgment on objective evidence and/or rational deduction.

  B. 'X is a model X' (a typical X), and X is typical of Y.

II. Miscellaneous expressions:

  A. "To begin V -ing"

  B. "To finish V-ing"

I. A. <u>Sentence (Plain form)</u> らしい
                              らしいです   It seems that ____

    (V   行く/行った)
    (A   高い/高かった)
    (AN 静か/静かだった)
    (Neg ない/なかった)

344

The negative form らしくない is not used in this sense.

らしい behaves like an adjective.

らしい is used when the speaker makes a judgment based on some kind of evidence, either first, or second hand (if the source is reliable). The speaker must have arrived at his judgment rationally rather than intuitively. He has good reason to believe that what he concludes is in fact the case, although he may not be completely sure of it.

その薬はよく効くらしいです。	That medicine seems to work quite well.
まだ雨が降っているらしいです。	It seems still to be raining.
あの映画は面白いらしいです。	That movie seems to be interesting.
あの人は親切らしいです。	He seems to be kind.
あの人は金持ちらしいです。	It seems that he is rich.
雨はまだやまないらしいです。	It seems that the rain hasn't stopped yet.
焼酎はさつまいもから作るらしいです。	It seems that they make shoochuu from sweet potatoes.

Some differences between そう, よう, and らしい.

あの店は高そうです。	(From what I've seen....) The store looks expensive to me. (subjective opinion)
あの店は高いようです。	(Based on mainly visual evidence.) The store looks expensive. (objective opinion)
あの店は高いらしいです。	(I have read about the high prices the store charges and have also heard about the store from other sources, and judging from all this...) That store seems to be expensive.
このお菓子は甘そうです。	(I have not tried it yet, but judging from it's appearance...) I believe this confectionery looks sweet. (subjective opinion)
このお菓子は甘いようです。	(I have not tried it yet, but based on mainly visual evidence...) This confectionery looks swect. (objective opinion)
このお菓子は甘いらしいです。	(I have not tried it yet, but based on mainly hear-say evidence, and also other facts...) This confectionery looks sweet.

345

Since そう does not follow nouns, the next examples will be confined to よう and らしい.

(A person is holding a branch of a cherry tree. He asks someone to identify it.)

これは何の花ですか。	What kind of flower is this?
よく分かりませんが桜のよう ですね。	…I'm not sure, but …it looks like a cherry blossom, doesn't it.

(A person describes a flower to someone. He then asks what the name of the flower is.)

よく分かりませんが桜らしい ですね。	…I'm not sure, but it sounds like a cherry blossom. (Lit. "Judging from what you have said, I would conclude that it is a cherry blossom.")

Since そう does not follow words that are in the past tense, the next example is also confined to よう and らしい.

説明した時には分かったようで したが本当は分かっていません でした。	When I explained (it) (to him), he looked like he understood, but actually he didn't.

らしい cannot be used in this sentence because, in order to use らしい, the speaker must be fairly sure that the person in question has understood his explanation. Thus, the speaker would be contradicting himself if he were to say, "but actually he did not understand."

B. Noun₁ らしい (N₂).

When N_1 and N_2 are the same noun, or have the same meaning, the pattern means that N_2 is a model, typical N_1.

男らしい男	A manly man. (a man who matches the stereotypical image of what a man ought to be)
あの人はちっとも男らしくあり ません。	That guy is not at all manly. (ちっとも, 少しも Not at all)
医者らしい医者	A doctorly doctor, A doctor-like doctor. (A doctor who possesses those qualities/virtues most often associated with doctors.)

The same pattern is also used to indicate that N_2 is something that's typically associated with N_1.

346

アメリカ人らしい考え方	a way of thinking that is typical of Americans
春らしいお天気	weather that is typical for spring
春らしいお菓子	a kind of cake that is typically associated with spring
ベイリーさんらしい答え	an answer that's typical of Bailey
ベイリーさんらしくない答え	an answer that's not typical of Bailey

本当に ("truly") いかにも ("indeed")

ブラウンさんはいかにも男らしい人ですね。	Brown is indeed a manly man.
本田先生は本当に先生らしい先生ですね。	Mr. Honda is truly a model (teacher-like) teacher.
きょうはいかにも春らしいお天気ですね。	It is indeed a typical spring day, isn't it?

The pattern N₁ らしい is ambiguous. For example, あそこにいる人は男らしい can mean either "The person over there seems to be a man, (but you are not certain)," or "The person over there is a manly man." N₁ らしい N₂ is not ambiguous; 男らしい男 can only mean "a manly man."

男じゃないらしい means "doesn't seem to be a man." (the meaning here is the same as the meaning of らしい with verbs, adjectives and adjectival nouns.)

男らしくない means "not manly."

II. Miscellaneous Expressions

Verb (pre-masu form) はじめる	begin V-ing
Verb (pre-masu form) おわる	finish V-ing

では書きはじめてください。	Now then, please start writing.
主人はもう食事を作りはじめました。	My husband has already started cooking.
きょうは彼の番なんです。	It's his turn today. (番 "turn," "round")
もう読みおわったんですか。はやいですね。	Have you finished reading (it) already? You're quick, aren't you?

347

書きおわった人は静かに出てく
ださい。

Those who have finished writing, please
go out quietly.

第二十四課　漢字

最 近
さい きん

最 近

午 後
ご ご

午 後

午 前
ご ぜん

午 前

教 室
きょう しつ

教 室

数 学
すう がく

数 学

上 着
うわ ぎ

上 着

大 学 院
だい がく いん

大 学 院

味
あじ

味

米
こめ

米

始 め る
はじ

始 め る

受 か る
う

受 か る

第 二 十 五 課

25 A 岡村　　　あーあ。

　　　スミス　　どうしたんですか。ため息なんかついて。

　　　岡村　　　英語がちっともうまくならないんです。

　　　スミス　　そんなことないでしょう。来た時よりずっとうまくなりましたよ。

　　　岡村　　　でもまだほんとうに分からないんです。

　　　スミス　　岡村さんの弱いのは文法ですか。語彙ですか。

　　　岡村　　　みんなです。でも特に語彙が弱いんです。文法の方は日本で勉強しておいたので少しはいいんですが…

　　　スミス　　英語で考えるようにするために英英辞典を使ったらどうですか。今使っているのは英和でしょう。

　　　岡村　　　ええ，じゃそうしてみようかしら。買うのはどこがいいでしょうね。

　　　スミス　　大学の近くの本屋にいいのがあるかどうか聞きましょうか。

　　　岡村　　　ええ，じゃお願いします。

25 B 　スミス　　近ごろ英語の勉強はどうですか。

　　　岡村　　　それが全然前と変わりません。この前，スミスさん「英英辞典を使ったらどうですか。」と言ったでしょう。

　　　スミス　　ええ，あっ，本屋に聞くのを忘れてしまいました。

　　　岡村　　　もういいんです。大学の前の本屋に行ったら，ち

349

ょうど一冊ありました。

スミス	それはよかったですね。どうですか。
岡村	分からない単語が多すぎてだめです。
スミス	分からないのはひけばいいでしょう。
岡村	そんなことしていたら予習に何時間あっても足りませんよ。

① 例　T：大学の前の本屋に行く，一冊ある。

　　　　S：大学の前の本屋に行ったら，一冊ありました。

1.　見る，分かる

2.　スミスさんに聞く，分かる

3.　辞書を引く，意味が分かる

4.　図書館へ行く，スミスさんに会う

5.　Safeway へ行く，日本製のラーメンがある

6.　サンフランシスコへ行く，雨が降っている

7.　山田先生のクラスに出る，漢字のクイズがある

8.　文法の説明を読む，よく分か

る

9.　春休みにヨセミテへ行く，観光客がいっぱいいる

10.　赤木先生に電話する，いらっしゃらない

11.　きのう，アイスクリームを四つ食べる，おなかをこわす

12.　「スターウォーズ」を見に行く，満員で見られない

13.　その箱を開ける，水着が入っている

② 例　T：予習しますか。（時間がある）

　　　　S：時間があったら予習するつもりです。

1.　カメラを買いますか。（日本へ行く）

350

2. ピクニックに行きますか。(天気がいい)

3. 先生に質問しますか。(分からない)

4. 日本へ行きますか。(お金がある)

5. アパートを借りますか。(奨学金がもらえる)

6. 図書館で勉強しますか。(寮がうるさい)

7. 映画を見に行きますか。(暇だ)

8. 週末パーティーをしますか。(忙しくない)

9. 明日は家にいますか。(雨だ)

10. バスで通いますか。(ガソリンが上がる)

11. あしたの朝早く出ます。(雨が降らない)

12. 泳ぎますか。(水がつめたくない)

13. アパートを借りますか。(安くていいアパートがある)

③　例　T: いつも英語で考えていますか。
　　　　S: ええ，できるだけ英語で考えるようにしています。

1. 毎日，スポーツをしますか。

2. 毎日，ラボでテープを聞きますか。

3. いつも，十二時前に寝ますか。

4. よく野菜を食べますか。

5. バスに乗らないで歩きますか。

6. 日本語で質問しますか。

7. クラスで英語を話しませんか。

8. 授業に遅刻しませんか。

9. クラスをサボりませんか。

10. いつも散歩をしますか。

11. よくテープを聞きますか。

12. 彼に会いませんか。

④　例　T:「買ってください」と言ったんですか。
　　　　S: いいえ，買いなさいと言ったんです。

1. 「行ってください」と言ったんですか。

2. 「もう一度言ってください」と言ったんですか。

3. 「会ってください」と言ったんですか。

4. 「日本語で話してください」と言ったんですか。

5. 「帰ってくださいと」言ったんですか。

6. 「休んでください」と言ったんですか。

7. 「名前を書いてください」と言ったんですか。

8. 「来てください」と言ったんですか。

9. 「コピーしてください」と言ったんですか。

10. 「もっと大きな声で言ってください」と言ったんですか。

11. 「よく聞いてください」と言ったんですか。

12. 「早く行ってください」と言ったんですか。

13. 「もういっぱい飲んでください」と言ったんですか。

14. 「シャツを着てください」と言ったんですか。

5 例 T： あしたロスへ行く，切符を買う

S： あしたロスへ行きますから，切符を買っておいてください。

1. 夜友達が来る，そうじをする

2. あした友達が来る，買物をする

3. 今晩，友達が来る，ビールを冷蔵庫へ入れる

4. 先生がいらっしゃる，いいワインを一本冷やす

5. 来週クイズをする，復習する

6. 週末にパーティーをする，現金を作る

7. 大切なことだ，メモをとる

8. あしたは友達が来るかもしれない，今日洗濯する

9. すきやきを作るつもりだ，いい牛肉を三ポンド買う

10. 風邪をひくかもしれない，薬を飲む

11. タホ湖に行く，ホテルを予約する

12. コロンボが来るかもしれない，ピストルを捨てる

6 例1 T: スミスさんは行きません。
　　　　S: 行ったらどうですか，スミスさん。
　　例2 T: 先生はいらっしゃいません。
　　　　S: いらっしゃったらいかがですか，先生。

1. ブラウンさんは勉強しません。
2. 赤木(あかぎ)先生はお飲みになりません。
3. 赤木先生はお休みになりません。
4. スミスさんはクラスに出ません。
5. 山田さんは寮(りょう)に入りません。
6. 本田先生は病院へいらっしゃいません。
7. ブラックさんは離婚(りこん)しません。
8. 岡村(おかむら)さんは手紙を書きません。
9. 山田さんはスポーツをしません。
10. ベイリーさんは新幹線(しんかんせん)を使いません。

7 例1 T: 分かりませんでした，答(こた)えませんでした。
　　　　S: 分からなかったので答えられませんでした。

1. かぜをひきました，行きませんでした。
2. お金がありませんでした，帰りませんでした。
3. 寒かったです，泳ぎませんでした。
4. 静かじゃありませんでした，ねむりませんでした。
5. 言ってくれませんでした，しませんでした。
6. まずかったです，飲みませんでした。
7. 歩いて来ませんでした，見ませんでした。
8. 辛(から)すぎました，食べませんでした。
9. 雨がふりました，テニスをしませんでした。
10. 相談(そうだん)してくれませんでした，貸してあげませんでした。

Lesson 25 Dialogues

25 A

Okamura: Boy oh boy...
Smith: What's up? How come you're sighing?

ため息（をつく）	to sigh

Okamura: I'm just not getting any better in English.

ちっとも	not at all, not in the least
うまい	to be good at, synonymous with 上手だ
うまくなる	to get better, to get good at.

Smith: That's not really so, is it? You're a lot better than when you first came.
Okamura: But really, I still don't understand it.
Smith: Is it grammar or vocabulary that you're poor in?

弱い	weak
文法	grammar
語彙	vocabulary

Okamura: Everything! But I'm particularly bad in vocabulary. Since I studied grammar in Japan it's sort of okay, but...
Smith: How about using an English dictionary to make yourself think in English? The one you're using now is an English-Japanese dictionary, right?

考える	to think
ために	in order to
英英辞典	English-English dictionary
英和辞典	English-Japanese dictionary

Okamura: Hmm... maybe I'll try that. Where would be a good place to get one?

してみる	I'll try it (and see)
かしら	I wonder...

Smith: Shall I ask if the bookstore near campus has a good one?
Okamura: Yes, please.

354

25 B

Smith: How are your English studies going these days?

Okamura: It hasn't gotten any better. You said to get an English dictionary, right?

変わる <small>か</small>　　　　　　　　　　　to change

Smith: Oh! I forgot to ask at the book-store.

Okamura: Don't bother. When I checked at the bookstore in front of the university, they just happened to have a copy.

Smith: Well, that's good. And how is it?

Okamura: There are so many words that I don't know that it's no use.

Smith: Well, how about looking up the ones you don't know?

Okamura: If I did that, there wouldn't be enough hours (in the day) to get all my work done!

足りる　　　　　　　　　　　to be enough, adequate

そんなことしていたら予習に何　　Lit., "If I did that, no matter how many
時間あっても足りませんよ。　　hours I spend for preparation, there wouldn't be enough time."

Lesson 25　**Notes on Usage**

25 A

1. あーあ　A sound uttered in desperation, or disgust; a sigh.

2. ため息<small>いき</small>なんかついて

　ため息 "sigh." The verb is ため息をつく "to (emit a) sigh." なんか is an informal colloquial form of など "such things as..., "etc."

3. 英語がうまくならない

　うまい An informal colloquial form of 上手 "be good at." It is also used sometimes by men to mean "tasty," "delicious."

355

4. そんなことないでしょう

そんなこと "such a thing," "a thing such as that." The sentence literally means "(That is) not such a case, is it?"

5. でもまだ本当に分からないんです。

The object missing in this sentence is 英語が "English" or いろいろなことが "various things."

6. 岡村さんが弱いのは… The thing that you (Okamura-san) are weak in is

弱い "weak," in the sense of "a weak point."

7. みんな everything, all, the whole thing.

8. 特に語彙が弱いんです。

特に "especially," 語彙が弱い "(I am) weak in vocabulary"

9. 少しはいいんですが…

Often は is used to indicate contrast. Here 少しは is contrasted with とても or 大変 "a lot" i.e., "I'm a little better (in contrast to much);" and with 全然 （ぜんぜん） or 少しも "not at all" i.e., "I'm a little better (in contrast to not at all)." The form without は would be a neutral description of a situation.

たくさんはありませんが少しはありますから安心してください。	I don't have much, but I do have a little, so please relax.

10. cf.

英英辞典	an English-English dictionary
英和辞典	an English-Japanese dictionary,
和英辞典	a Japanese-English dictionary

11. 英英辞典を使ったらどうですか。

V たらどうですか。'Why don't you V ?' The pattern is used to offer a suggestion. A more polite form is V たらいかがですか.

こうしたらどうですか
こうなさったらいかがでしょう

Why don't you (what if you) do it this way, and see (what it's like)?

12. そうしてみようかしら　I wonder if I should do so (and see).

かしら indicates uncertainty ("I wonder if..."). It is usually used by women. The equivalent form that would be used by man is かな. In either case, the form is used in the manner of a monologue (talking to oneself).

Other examples:

山田さんはどこへ行ったの{かな / かしら

I wonder where Yamada has gone.

どこを探してもどこにもいないんですが。国へ帰ってしまったの{かな / かしら

No matter where I look for her, she is not around. I wonder if she has returned to her home town.

(探す "to search"; 国 here means one's home town/country)

13. 本屋にいいのがあるかどうか聞いておいてあげましょうか。

Shall I ask the bookstore (for you) whether or not there is a good one (so that next time you see me I can let you know about it)?

The phrase 本屋に can be interpreted in two ways: 1) as a location of existence, "Shall I ask someone (including someone at the bookstore) if there is a good book at the store;" and 2) as the indirect object of the verb 聞く "to ask" "Shall I ask the bookstore if there is a good one (at the store, in the world, etc.)?"

25 B

1. 全然前と変わりません

全然 "(not) at all," 前 "before," ＿＿＿と変わらない "is not different from ＿＿＿." 変わる "to change" here means "be different (as a result of some change)." It takes the particle と before it when used in this sense, and is similar in this respect to 同じ "same" and 違う "different."

2. この前 "the other day" (Lit. "before this"). Sometimes the phrase means "last time." この間 ("the other day") cannot be used if the interval is too long, but この前 can

be used regardless of how much time has elapsed.

この前お会いしたのはいつだっ   When was the last time we met?

たでしょうか。

そうですね。大分前ですね。   ...Let's see ...It was rather a long time ago, wasn't it?

十年ぐらい前じゃありませんか。   Wasn't it about ten years ago?

3. あ Oh!, My goodness!

4. 本屋に聞くのを忘れてしまいました。

I have (completely) forgotten to check with the bookstore (about it).

$$\underline{\underset{\text{(forms which occur before のです)}}{\text{Sentence}}}のを\begin{cases}\text{忘れる} & \text{to forget } \underline{S} \\ \text{おぼえている} & \text{to (still) remember that } \underline{S}\end{cases}$$

5. もういいんです。   Don't bother (any more), You can forget it. (Lit. "It's all right now.")

6. 本屋に行ったらちょうど一冊ありました。

ちょうど (Lit. "just," "exactly") here means just happen to ____.

7. 分からない単語が多すぎてだめです。

     It's no use; there are too many words I don't know."

（意味が）分からない単語 (Lit. "words (whose meaning) I cannot figure out.")
だめ means "no way, "no good," "no use."

8. ひけばいい   if you consult (it) it will be OK.

Lesson 25   Grammar Notes

The main points of this lesson are:
  I. Another pattern to express "when/if S_1, S_2"

II. A pattern to express the notion of doing something in advance in anticipation of some future situation, as in "I will go to Japan. So I will study Japanese beforehand so that I can use it then."

III. A pattern to express the situation "make/arrange things so that (a desired result takes place), as in "I'm making myself think in Japanese." (Lit. "I'm making it so that...")

IV. A pattern to express the situation "it's gotten so that," as in "It's gotten so that we can drink liquor on campus."

I. <u>Sentence₁</u> たら <u>Sentence₂</u> 　　　　　　　　When/if S₁, S₂ (Specific event)

The たら form is made by adding ら to the plain past form of verbs, adjectives, adjectival nouns and nouns.

V	書いたら，買ったら，見たら	(Negative　書かなかったら，買わな
		かったら見なかったら)
A	小さかったら	(Neg. 小さくなかったら)
A.N	静かだったら	(Neg. 静かでなかったら)
N	学生だったら	(Neg. 学生でなかったら)

S₁ takes place first (the た form implies completed action), and then S₂ follows; i.e., the event in S₁ occurs first. Unlike と and ば, たら cannot be used in a generic sense. The basic meaning of the pattern is "When S₁, then S₂."

If the statement is about some future event, then the pattern is

　A. a suppositional sentence.

If the statement refers to some past event, the pattern means either

　B. a situation is "contrary to fact"

　C. a simple "temporal expression," "S₁, then S₂" (i.e., S₁ happened and then S₂ happened. In this last case, S₂ must be an event that the speaker cannot control. See examples below.)

A	日本へ行ったらカメラを買ってください。	When you go to Japan, please buy me a camera.
	時間があったらコーヒーでも飲みませんか。	If you have time, would you like some coffee or something?
	アイスクリームがいいです。なかったら紅茶にします。	I'd like some ice cream. If they don't have any, I'll have a cup of tea. (紅茶 "black (Lit. 'red') tea" as opposed to "green tea")
	あした晴れていたらテニスをするつもりです。	If the weather is fine tomorrow, I intend to play tennis.

359

少し休んだらどうですか。	Why don't you rest a while? (Lit. "If you rest a little, then how would it be?")
いらっしゃったらいかがですか、先生。	**Why don't you go? (Lit. "If you were to go, how would it be?")**
B. お金があったら貸したんですが…	If I had had money (at the time), I would have loaned it (to you/him). (one specific occasion)
お金があれば貸しました。	(either specific or generic)
お金があると貸しました。	(と in the sense of "whenever")
C. 山田さんを見たら寝ていました。	When I looked over at Yamada, he was sleeping. (Lit. "I looked at Yamada, and (I found) him sleeping.")
山田さんを見ると寝ていました。	(same as the above) (See the usage of と described in L. 23)
スミスさんに聞いたら分かりました。	When I asked Smith, I then understood.
サンフランシスコへ行ったら雨が降っていました。	When I went to San Francisco, it was raining.

II. <u>Verb (te-form)</u> ておく | to do <u>V</u> (for future purpose) (Lit. "to do <u>V</u> and set aside (for the future)")

The action (indicated by the verb in the て form) is performed (taken) ahead of time in preparation for (or in anticipation of) some future situation.

今日切符を買っておきます。	I'll buy the ticket today.
考えておきます。	I'll think it over. (I'll think about it.)
夕食の用意はもうしておきました。	I have already made preparations for dinner.
今晩友達が来ますからビールを冷やしておきましょう。	Friends are coming this evening, so let's cool some beer (in advance).
日本へ行きますから日本語を勉強しておくんです。	I'll be going to Japan, so (the fact is that) I'm going to study Japanese (beforehand).

III. Verb (Plain, Non-past) ようにする

1) to make/arrange things so that V
2) to make an effort to V (often used with words like "as much as possible")

Verb (Neg. Non-past) ようにする

not to V (with both 1) and 2) above)

A. (to a store clerk, asking for a delivery):

あさってまでに着くようにしてくださいませんか。

Would you make sure it arrives by the day after tomorrow? (Lit. Would you arrange things so that it will arrive by the day after tomorrow?)

この窓が開かないようにしてください。

Please make it so this window does not open.

どろぼうがはいったらベルがなるようにしましょう。

Let's make it so that an alarm sounds if a thief enters.

B. できるだけ日本語で話すようにしています。

I'm making an effort to speak in Japanese as much as possible.

できるだけ生野菜を食べるようにしています。

I'm making an effort to eat raw vegetables as much as possible
(生 "raw", 野菜 "vegetable")

できるだけ遅れないようにしているんですか…

I'm trying as much as possible not to be late, but...

Note the difference between ようにする and ことにする, the latter meaning "to decide to do V." (See L. 21, GN 2b)

IV. Verb (Plain, Non-past) ようになる

It's gotten so that V

Verb (Neg., Non-past) ようになる

It's gotten so that not V

ようになる is different from ことになる in that the latter is restricted to situations where a "decision" is involved while the former is not. In other words, for ようになる it is the result itself that is at issue rather than how the result was obtained. Thus, while ことになる implies a sudden shift in a situation, ようになる may imply either a sudden or a gradual shift. Compare the following examples.

(Due to passage of a bill, drinking on campus is now legal—result of a "decision" by the legislature)

キャンパスでお酒が飲めることになりました。

It's been decided that we can drink liquor on campus.

361

キャンパスでお酒が飲めるよう It's gotten so that we can drink liquor
になりました。 on campus.

(I used to get sick whenever I drank sake, but now I can drink a lot.)

わたしはこのごろ酒が飲めるよ Lately, it's gotten so that I can drink
うになりました。 liquor.
(ことになる cannot be used in this case)

(The police have issued an order that no one can walk alone at night.)

夜一人で歩けないことになりま It has been decided that persons cannot
した。 walk alone at night.

(The place has become so dangerous that no one dare walk alone at night.)

夜一人で歩けないようになりま It's gotten so that persons cannot walk
した。 alone at night.

(It was decided to send Yamada to the bar.)

山田さんはバーへ行くことにな It's been decided that Yamada go to the
りました。 bar.

(Yamada has started frequenting bars; somehow, it's gotten to be a habit with him.)

山田さんはバーへ行くようにな It's gotten so that Yamada goes to the
りました。 bar.

山田さんはバーへ行くようにな It's gotten so that Yamada goes to bars,
りました。そして，学校へは行 and doesn't go to school.
かないようになりました。

第二十五課　漢字

晴 は	れ	る	変 か	わ	る	手 て	伝 つだ	う
晴	れ	る	変	わ	る	手	伝	う

足 た	り	る	冷 ひ	や	す	冷 つめ	た	い
足	り	る	冷	や	す	冷	た	い

予 よ	習 しゅう		本 ほん	当 とう		本 ほん	屋 や	
予	習		本	当		本	屋	

弱 よわ	い		水 みず			公 こう	園 えん	
弱	い		水			公	園	

第 二十六 課

26 A　藤原　　　　びっこをひいていますね。どうなさったんです
　　　　　　　　　か。

ベイリー　　犬にかまれたんです。

藤原　　　　どうして犬なんかにまた。

ベイリー　　ゆうべ隣の奥さんに「玄関の戸をこじあけてく
　　　　　　ださい」とたのまれたんです。

藤原　　　　お隣の玄関ですね。

ベイリー　　ええ，奥さんはかぎをうちの中に置き忘れて入
　　　　　　れなくなってしまったんです。

藤原　　　　まあ。

ベイリー　　ですから「じゃ，やってみましょう」と言わな
　　　　　　いわけにはいかないでしょう。

藤原　　　　そりゃあそうですよ。お隣の人なんですから…

ベイリー　　で，ねじ回しで開けようとしたんです。

藤原　　　　その時ですか，犬にかまれたのは。

ベイリー　　ええ，一生懸命にあけようとしていた時です。

藤原　　　　お医者さんに見てもらわなくてもいいですか。

ベイリー　　ええ，ですからけさ病院へ行ってペニシリン
　　　　　　をもらってきました。多分大丈夫でしょう。

藤原　　　　とんだ災難でしたね。

26 B　(Brown shows up 40 minutes late huffing and puffing.)

ブラウン　　どうもすみません。遅くなりました。

山田　　　　いいえ。

ブラウン	ちょうど出ようとした時に友達に来られてしま ったんです。
山田	ああ，そうですか。
ブラウン	それが小学校の時の友達でカリフォルニアは 初めてなんです。
山田	ええ，ええ。
ブラウン	それでバートに乗ったら持っていたお金とクレ ジットカードを全部すられてしまったんだそう です。
山田	まあ。
ブラウン	それで，すまないが二十ドルばかり貸してくれ って言うんです。
山田	まあ，それじゃ，ブラウンさんも大変ですね。
ブラウン	でも，とにかく貸さないわけにはいかないでし ょう。
山田	そりゃあそうですよ。昔のお友達なんですか ら…
ブラウン	ところが僕は二ドルしかないんです。 山田さん少し貸してやってくれませんか。
山田	まあ。

1　例　T：犬が私をかみました。

　　　　S：私は犬にかまれました。

1.　スミスさんが私を呼びました。　　　した。
2.　先生は私をしかりました。　　4.　山田さんはブラウンさんを招
3.　ルームメートが私を起こしま　　　　待しました。

366

5. オズワルドがケネディーを殺しました。
6. 風がその建物を倒しました。
7. みんながその本を読みました。
8. 友達がわたしを笑いました。
9. みんながその小説を知っています。
10. ねこがねずみを食べました。
11. ジョンはメリーを愛しています

12. 学生達は，本田先生を尊敬しています。
13. 小鳥の声が私を起こしました。
14. スミスさんは私の論文を批判しました。
15. ブラウンさんは私に皮肉を言いました。
16. 田中さんが私に反対しました。

2 例1 T: 友達が来ました。
　　　S: （私は）友達に来られました。
　例2 T: 誰かが（私の）クレジットカードをすりました。
　　　S: （私は）誰かにクレジットカードをすられました。

1. 雨が降りました。
2. 父が死にました。
3. スミスさんが来ました。
4. 母が（私の）日記を読みました。
5. 友達が（私の）ウイスキーを飲みました。
6. 犬が大きな声でなきました。
7. 誰かが（私の）くつをまちがえました。
8. 子供が（私の）タイプライターをこわしました。
9. 誰かが（私の）車のガラスを

こわしました。
10. ガールフレンドが朝まで泣きました。
11. スミスさんは（私の）論文を批判しました。
12. 山田さんは（私の）発音をなおしました。
13. 母は笑いました。
14. そのウエイトレスは（私の）スーツをよごしました。
15. ねこが（私の）金魚を食べました。
16. ルームメートが朝までピアノ

367

をひきました。

17. 誰かが(私の)足を踏みました。

18. スミスさんは（ブラウンさんの）カメラをこわしました。

③　例　T: 歩く

　　　　{ S₁: 歩きましたか。

　　　　{ S₂: 歩こうとしましたが，歩けませんでした。

1. 食べる

2. 歌う

3. 書く

4. 立つ

5. 飲む

6. 起きる

7. 入る

8. 翻訳する

9. 着る

10. 出る

11. 読む

12. 日本語で話す

13. 復習する

14. 眠る

15. なっとうを食べる

16. 助ける

17. 作る

18. 上がる

19. 持って来る

20. 笑う

④　例　T: 出る，友達が来る

　　　　S: ちょうど出ようとしたとき友達が来たんです。

1. アパートを出る，スミスさんが来る

2. うちを出る，雨が降りはじめる

3. クラスへ行く，ブラウンさんに会う

4. 帰る，先生にお会いする

5. ベッドに入る，宿題を思い出す

6. 車から降りる，コンタクトレ

ンズをおとす

7. 食事を始める，山田さんから電話がある

8. 寝る，ルームメートが帰って来る

9. 泳ぎに行く，雨が降りはじめる

10. バスを降りる，さいふをすられる

⑤ 例　T：貸します
　　　⎧S₁：貸すんですか。
　　　⎨S₂：ええ，本当は，貸したくないんですが，貸さないわけにはいかないんです。

1. 行きます
2. 読みます
3. 買います
4. 予習します
5. クイズを受けます
6. ミルクを飲みます
7. ネクタイをしめます
8. お金を借ります
9. アルバイトをする
10. 覚えます
11. サンフランシスコへ行きます

12. 車を買います
13. ブラウンさんと会います
14. ブラウンさんと飲みに行きます
15. パーティーに行きます
16. 大学院に行きます
17. アメリカへ帰る
18. あの人にお金を借ります
19. 案内します
20. 先生に手紙を書きます

⑥ 例　T：三十ドル貸す
　　　S：あのう，三十ドルばかり貸していただきたいんですが…。

1. 十五分待つ
2. 二時間後で来る
3. ビールを五十本注文する

4. ボールペンを二十本用意する
5. 牛肉三ポンド買ってくる
6. 十五分早く来る

369

7. ワインを三本持ってくる
8. 五十ドル現金にする
9. 本を三冊貸す
10. オレンジを十買って来る

Lesson 26 **Dialogues**

26 A

Fujiwara: I see you're limping. What happened?

びっこをひく   to limp

Bailey: I got bitten by a dog.

かまれる   to get bitten, passive form of かむ, to bite.

Fujiwara: Bitten? How?

なんか   such as (a dog)

また   again, on top of that

Bailey: Last **night, I was asked by the lady next door (who was locked out of her house)** to open her **front door.**

ゆうべ   last night

隣の奥さん   the (married) lady next door

玄関の戸   front door

こじあける   to try to open

Fujiwara: I see, your neighbor's front door,
Bailey: Yes. She'd left her keys inside and couldn't get back in.

かぎ   key(s)

置き忘れる   to leave and forget

Fujiwara: My goodness!
Bailey: So I couldn't say no, could I?

「じゃ，やってみましょう」と言   Lit., "So you see, I had no choice but to say, 'Well, let's give it a try.'"
わないわけにはいかないでしょ
う。

370

Fujiwara: Of course. Her being your neighbor and all.
Bailey: And so I tried to open it with a screwdriver.

ねじ回し   screwdriver

Fujiwara: Was it then that you got bitten?
Bailey Yes, just when I was working at opening it.

一生懸命に   with all one's might, energy, etc.

開けようとする   to try to open

Fujiwara: Shouldn't you have the doctor take a look at it?

見てもらう   Lit., "To have it looked at, to have it examined"

Bailey: Yes, so I went to the hospital this morning, and got some penicillin. It should be okay.

ペニシリン   Penicillin

Fujiwara: What a drag!

とんだ   unexpected, awful, terrible
災難   misfortune, calamity

26 B

Brown: I'm sorry to be so late!
Yamada: That's okay.
Brown: Just when I was about to leave, a friend dropped in on me.

来られる   Lit., "I was visited by a friend of mine."

Yamada: I see.
Brown: You see, this fellow is a friend from my elementary school days, and this is his first trip to California.

初めて   for the first time

Yamada: I see.
Brown: And when he was riding on BART, he got all his money and credit cards ripped off.

すられる   to be pickpocketed

Yamada: Good heavens!
Brown: And so he wanted to know if he could borrow $20.

「すまないが二十ドルばかり貸

してくれ」

すまないが	to be sorry to cause an inconvenience
二十ドルばかり	about $20 or so
貸す	to lend

Yamada: Gee, then that must have been tough on you too, huh?
Brown: But I couldn't not lend it to him, right?

とにかく	anyway

Yamada: Well, of course you had to. After all, he is an old friend and everything.

そりゃあ	それは

Brown: But... the only thing is that I've only got $2. Would you mind lending him some money?

僕 ぼく	"I" used exclusively by men in informal situations.

Yamada: What!

Lesson 26 **Notes on Usage**

26 A

1. どうなさったんですか。　　　　**What happened to you?**

なさる is an honorific verb of する "to do."

2. どうして犬なんかにまた。

また literally means "again," but when it is used together with なんか as "N なんか (particle) また" in a question, it means "why on earth?" or "of all things, people, places, etc." to indicate the speaker's surprise, disappointment, and/or accusation (to a person who let such an event to take place).

どうして佐藤さんなんかにまた
ノーベル賞をあげたんでしょう。

Why on earth did they give a Nobel Prize to Mr. Sato (of all people)?

(The speaker is surprised at the announcement. He is disappointed in the Nobel Prize Committee's selection because in his judgment Sato does not deserve the prize, and he accuses them for having chosen the least qualified person.)

372

山田さんはどうして太郎さんなんかがまた好きになったんでしょう。

Why on earth did Yamada fall in love with Taro (of all men)?

(The speaker is surprised at the fact that Yamada is in love with Taro. He is disappointed in the fact because, in his opinion, Yamada could have done better. And, he is accusing Yamada for having carelessly fallen in love with the least qualified man.)

どうしてキャデラックなんか買ったんですか。

Why in the world did you buy a Cadillac (of all cars)?
(The connotation is similar to the sentences above.)

When an action or event is at issue the pattern V たりなんかまた is used.
(Situation: Knowing Yamada, I could imagine her doing lots of weird things, but I would never have expected her to hit someone.)

どうして山田さんになぐられたりなんか（したんですか）また。

Why in the world were you hit (of all the things that she might have done to you) by Yamada?

(There may be others who would have hit you, but I wouldn't have expected Yamada to do that.)

どうして山田さんなんかにまた（なぐられたんですか）。

Why in the world were you hit by Yamada (of all people)?

どうしたんですか。
今ちょっと泳いだらくたびれてしまったんです。

What's the matter?

I swam a little just now, and I feel wiped out.

どうして泳いだりなんかまた（したんですか）。

Why on earth did you swim?

26 B

1. いいえ

Here means "That's all right."
(Lit. "No, (that's all right.)")

2. ええ，ええ

"Uhuh, Uhuh…"
(cf. L. 2, NU 2A, 1)

Lesson 26 **Grammar Notes**

The main points of this lesson are:
I. Passive sentences. There are two types of passive sentences in Japanese:
   A. A simple passive sentence, such as, "My mousse was eaten by a mouse," as opposed to the active sentence, "A mouse ate my mousse."
   B. The so called "indirect passive." sometimes called the "adversative" or "affected" passive sentence. The pattern is so called because it carries with it a nuance of being adversely affected by the event. There is no English equivalent for this pattern, although certain English sentences, such as, "It rained on me," or "I was robbed of my money," approach the force of the Japanese.
II. A pattern that expresses either a) "to try to do V," as in "I tried to walk, but I couldn't." or b) "be about to do V," as in "Just as I was about to leave, a friend came by."
III. An expression which means "cannot very well not V," "be obliged to V," "be forced by circumstances to V," "can't get out of V-ing," etc., as in "My mother is coming tomorrow so I cannot very well not clean my place."

I. Passive sentensce

active sentence: $\underline{A}$ が $\underline{B}$ を V (transitive).
passive sentence: $\underline{B}$ が $\underline{A}$ に V (transitive passive).

A. Simple passive sentence

A) 犬がベイリーさんをかみました。

A dog bit Bailey.

B) ベイリーさんが犬にかまれました。

Bailey was bitten by a dog.

The above situation can be described in two ways: in terms of either a) what the dog did, or b) what Bailey had done to him. If the speaker wants to say what the dog did, he would choose sentence A). If he wants to say what happened to Bailey, he would choose B). Sentence B) is an example of a simple passive sentence.

Verbs are changed into the simple passive form either by adding -rare (RU-verbs), or

374

-are (U-verbs) to the verb stem. See the chart below.

RU-verbs (+rare-ru)		U-verbs (+are-ru)		Irregular verbs	
食べる	食べられる	書く	書かれる	する	される
見る	見られる	持つ	持たれる	来る	来られる
着る	着られる	買う	買われる	行く	行かれる

The resulting passive forms behave like RU-verbs: V-(r)are-ru

In passive sentences, the agent (the dog in sentence B) above) of the action is marked by the particle に.

ブラウンさんは先生にほめられ ました。	Brown (subject) was praised by the teacher (agent).
私は社長にしかられました。	I (subject) was scolded by the company president (agent).

An inanimate noun can become the subject of a passive sentence.

私の論文がスミスさんに批判さ れました。	My thesis (subject) was criticized by Smith (agent).

The agent is often omitted when it is obvious from the context, or when it does not need to be specified.

明日新しい切手が売り出されま す。	Tomorrow new stamps will be issued. (The agent, post office, is omitted) (売り出す "to start selling")
聖書はいつごろ書かれたんです か。	When was the Bible written? (The agent is irrelevent to the question) (いつごろ "around when".)
さあ，知りません。昔です。	Well, I don't know. A long time ago.

B. Indirect passive sentences (affected passive).

Active Sentence:	A が B の C を V transitive.
Indirect Passive Sentence:	B は C を A に V transitive, passive.
Active Sentence:	A が V intransitive
Passive Sentence:	A に V intransitive passive

Passive forms of verbs are also used to indicate that the subject of the sentence is adversely affected by a situation. That is why the pattern used to express such a situation is often called the "affected" or "adversative" passive.

In this structure, intransitive verbs as well as transitive verbs can be used.

1.

    a. 雨が降りました。   It rained. (Intransitive verb, active sentence).

    b. 雨に降られました。   It rained on me. (I got rained on—adversative passive)

Sentence a) is a simple description of a situation; b) suggests that the situation adversely affected the subject of the sentence.

2.   **a.** あの人はお父さんが死にました。   (As for that person), his father died. (active sentence)

    b. あの人はお父さんに死なれました。   (As for that person), his father died. (Implies that he is now in a state of grief)

3.   **a.** 山田さんがわたしのラブレターを読みました。   Yamada read my love letter. (active sentence)

    b. （わたしは）山田さんにラブレターを読まれました。   I got my love letter read by Yamada. (I was adversely affected by Yamada's reading my letter: i.e., she now knows everything, I feel mortified, etc.)

    cf. わたしのラブレターは山田さんに読まれました。   My love letter was read by Yamada. (simple passive sentence)

4.   **a.** 山田さんはブラウンさんの大事なウイスキーを全部飲んでしまいました。   Yamada drank up all of (finished the whole bottle of) Brown's treasured whiskey. (大事な "important") (active sentence)

    b. ブラウンさんは大事なウイスキーを山田さんに全部飲まれてしまいました。   Brown had all of his treasured whiskey drunk up by Yamada (and he is furious). (indirect passive)

    cf. ブラウンさんのウイスキーが山田さんに全部飲まれてしまいました。   All of Brown's whiskey was drunk by Yamada. (simple passive)

As the last example shows, てしまう is often used in adversative passive sentences.

376

II. Verb-(y)oo とする

A) try to do V
B) to be about to do V

The volitional form of a verb (See Lesson 16), followed by とする, may mean either A) or B) depending on the context.

A) 歩こうとしましたが歩けませんでした。

I tried to walk, but I couldn't.

眠^{ねむ}ろうとしているんですがちっとも眠れません。

I'm trying to sleep, but I can't at all.

サンフランシスコへ行って飲もうとしたんですがお金がなかったのでやめました。

We thought of (tried to) going to San Francisco and having a few drinks, but since we didn't have any money, we gave it (the idea) up.

ドアを開けようとしていた時に犬^{いぬ}にかまれました。

When I was trying to open the door, I was bitten by a dog.

B) ちょうど出ようとした時に友達^{だち}が来たんです。

When I was just about to leave the house, a friend of mine came.

ああ，山田さん今日^{こんにち}は，今ちょうどあなたに御電話しようとしていたところです。

Oh, Yamada-san. I was just going to telephone you.
(Note: ところ in this example refers to a point in time, not a place.)

バスから降りようとした時にコンタクトレンズを落^おとしてしまいました。

When I was just about to get off the bus, I lost a contact (lens).
(Lit. "I dropped a contact lens.")

III. Verb (Plain, Non-Past Neg.) ないわけにはいかない

can't very well not V, be obliged to V,
be forced by circumstances to V, can't get out of V-ing

The construction introduced here is an idiomatic phrase which expresses the fact that one is obliged to do something as a result of inescapable circumstances, when there is just no way of getting around it.

あまり貸したくないんですが貸さないわけにはいかないんです。

I don't want to lend it (to him/anyone), but it wouldn't be right not to (lend it).

きょうは風邪で熱があるんです
が行かないわけにはいかないん
です。

Today I have a cold and a fever, but I can't very well not go.

どうしてこんな物を買ったんで
すか。

Why did you buy a thing like this?

友達にたのまれたので買わない
わけにはいかなかったんですよ。

It was a favor for a friend (Lit. "I was asked by a friend"), so there was nothing I could do but buy it.

第二十六課　漢字

笑う　　　泣く　　　眠る
わら　　　な　　　　ねむ

死ぬ　　　大事　　　用意
し　　　だい じ　　　よう い

初めて　　　戸　　　全部
はじ　　　　と　　　ぜん ぶ

小学校　　医者　　病院
しょう がっ こう　い しゃ　びょう いん

378

第 二十七 課

27 A　藤原　　　交通公社へ行ったんですが切符は買えませんでした。

ベイリー　　あ そうですか。

藤原　　　私では分からないことをいろいろ聞かれたんです。

ベイリー　　というと。

藤原　　　周遊券を買った方がいいんじゃないかとか，ユースには泊まらない方がいいんじゃないかとか…

ベイリー　　ユースはどうしていけないんですか。

藤原　　　安いことは安いんですが，門限があったり男女別別の部屋でなくてはいけなかったり，いろいろ制限があるんだそうですよ。

ベイリー　　ははあ，私が行った方がいいですね。

藤原　　　でも一人で行って分かるでしょうか。

ベイリー　　ええ，英語の分かる人がいるから大丈夫ですよ。

藤原　　　でも，何だか心配ですねえ。

ベイリー　　何とかなりますよ。

藤原　　　じゃ，今日の三時すぎならあいていますから一緒に行ってみましょうか。

ベイリー　　どうもたびたび申し訳ありません。一緒に行ってくださるんなら晩御飯をおごりますよ。

27 B　ベイリー　　九州へ行きたいんですが周遊券というのが

	あるんだそうですね。
JTB	目的地はどちらですか。
ベイリー	伊万里です。そのほか二三か所行ってみたいんですが…
JTB	二三か所おいでになるのなら周遊券の方が便利です。
ベイリー	普通の切符より安いんですか。
JTB	はい，一割ばかり安くなります。
ベイリー	そんなに安くなるんならそちらにしましょう。何か制限があるんですか。
JTB	二つあります。指定の場所，これは周遊地と言っておりますが， 周遊地を二か所以上回って出発地にもどること，それにJRを二百一キロ以上利用すること，この二つです。
ベイリー	九州まで何キロですか。
JTB	博多まで片道千百七十六キロです。
ベイリー	じゃあ，二百一キロ以上ですね．で伊万里は周遊地なんですか。
JTB	いえ，でも近くの唐津が周遊地になっております。
ベイリー	Far out!
JTB	は。ファーアウト…あ，九州は遠いですね。

1　例　T：サンフランシスコへ行きます，バートのほうが早いですよ。
　　　　S：サンフランシスコへ行くんなら，バートのほうが早いですよ。

1.　寒いです，ストーブをつけたらどうですか

2.　四か所へ行きます，周遊券のほうが便利ですよ

380

3. 三十パーセントも安くなります，日本製（せい）にします
4. オークランドへいらっしゃいます，私の車をお使いください
5. ブラウンさんが来ます，私は帰ります
6. 頭がいたいです，早く帰ったらどうですか
7. タイプライターがあります，

タイプしてください
8. 宿題がありません，映画でも見に行きませんか
9. 山田さんと岡村（おかむら）さんが行きます，私も行きたいです
10. ギャンブルをします，ラスベガスが一番ですね
11. グレイドが心配です，もう少し勉強したらどうですか

② 例 1. T： 行きます
　　　S： 行ったほうがいいんじゃないですか。
　　例 2. T： 行きません
　　　S： 行かないほうがいいんじゃないですか。

1. 食べます
2. サボりません
3. 復習します
4. 運動します
5. 覚えます
6. 飲みます
7. 書きます
8. 書きません
9. 行きます
10. ゆっくり言（い）います
11. 本を読んでおきます
12. 先生と相談します
13. 大学院へ行きます
14. 病院でよく調べてもらう
15. タバコを吸（す）いません
16. 歩いて通（かよ）います
17. 奨学金（しょうがくきん）を探（さが）します
18. 行く前に電話します
19. たまにスポーツをします
20. 夜ひとりで歩きません

③ 例 T: 頭が痛い，アスピリンを飲んで早く休む

$\begin{cases} S_1: & どうしたんですか。 \\ S_2: & 実は，頭が痛いんです。 \\ S: & ああ，それはいけませんね。アスピリンを飲んで早く休んだ \\ & ほうがいいんじゃないですか。 \end{cases}$

1. 熱がある，すぐに医者に行く
2. チェックブックをおとした，すぐ銀行に電話する
3. 父が入院した，一度日本へ帰る
4. アパートがうるさくて勉強ができない，新しいアパートを探す
5. 漢字がぜんぜん覚えられない，先生と相談する
6. お金がなくて大学をやめなけ
ればならない，もう一度，奨学金を探してみる
7. 時々，腰が痛くなる，病院でよく調べてもらう
8. 風邪をひいて少し熱がある，今日はクラスを休む
9. 風邪をひいて少し熱がある，今日はクラスに出ない
10. 胃が少し痛い，あまり食べない

④ 例 T: 安い，あまりよくない

$\begin{cases} S_1: & 安いんですか。 \\ S_2: & ええ，安いことは安いんですが，あまりよくないんです。 \end{cases}$

1. 大きい，おいしくない
2. 早い，少し高すぎる
3. おもしろい，あまり役にたたない
4. 読める，書けない
5. 持っている，あまり運転しな
い
6. クラスに来る，ねてばかりいる
7. 食べる，あまり好きじゃない
8. 静かだ，キャンパスから少し遠すぎる

9.　難しい，とてもおもしろい　　　10.　読んだ，よく分からなかった

⑤　例　T：三時過ぎはあいていますか。
　　　　S：ええ，三時過ぎならあいています。

1.　あさっては大丈夫ですか
2.　コーヒーはありますか
3.　赤木先生はまだいらっしゃいますか
4.　アイスクリームはあの店がいいですか
5.　田中さんはできますか
6.　ひるごはんは食べましたか
7.　サンフランシスコはバートが一番はやいですか

8.　ブラウンさんは信頼できますね
9.　JTBは英語の分かる人がいますね
10.　あしたの午後はあいているでしょうか
11.　ブランデーは「ナポレオン」がいいですか
12.　それじゃあ…金曜日の夕方はどうでしょうか

Lesson 27　Dialogues

27 A

Fujiwara: Well, I went to the Travel Bureau, all right, but I couldn't get your ticket.

交通公社　　　　　　　　　　　　Travel Bureau

Bailey: Oh, I see.
Fujiwara: I got asked a lot of questions that I didn't know the answers to.
Bailey: Like what?

　　　というと　　　　　　　　　　Lit., "What do you mean?"

Fujiwara: Like wouldn't it be better to buy an excursion ticket, or wouldn't it be better not to stay at a youth hostel, and so on...

しゅうゆうけん 周遊券	excursion ticket
ユース	youth hostel
と 泊まる	to stay at

Bailey: How come a hostel's no good?

Fujiwara: Well, it's cheap all right, but there are hours, and men and women have separate accomodations, and anyway, I understand there are a lot of restrictions like that.

もんげん 門限	curfew
べつべつ 別別	separate
せいげん 制限	restriction, limitation

Bailey: I see. Then maybe it's better that I go myself.

Fujiwara: But I wonder if you'll be okay by yourself.

Bailey: There's someone who understands English there, so I'll be fine.

Fujiwara: Yes, but I'm still worried.

何だか	somehow, somewhat

Bailey: I'm sure it'll work out somehow.

何とかなる	somehow or other things will work out

Fujiwara: Well, I'm free after 3:00 today, so shall we go (there) together?

三時すぎ	after 3:00 o'clock
なら	if (you say)

Bailey: Thank you so much. You're always doing such nice things for me. If you're going to come with me, I'll buy dinner.

たびたび	so often, time after time
もう わけ 申し訳ありません	I can't possibly thank you enough...
いっしょ い （一緒に）行ってくださる	to do me the favor of going (with me).
おごる	to treat

27 B

Bailey: I want to go to Kyushu, and I understand that you have an excursion ticket?

JTB: Yes. What's your destination?

| もくてきち
目的地 | destination |

Bailey: Imari. And I am hoping to see two or three other places besides that...

JTB: If you're going to two or three other places, then the excursion ticket would be just right for you.

| 便利 | convenient |

Bailey: Is it cheaper than the regular ticket?

JTB: Yes, it's about 10% cheaper.

| いちわり
一割 | 10% |

Bailey: If it's that much cheaper, I'll take it. Are there any restrictions?

| ばかり | about, some, or so |

JTB: Yes, there are two: that you visit two or more designated areas, the so-called excursion spots, and return to your point of departure; and in addition, that you use the National Railroad for a distance over 201 km.

してい 指定の	designated
ばしょ 場所	place, area
周遊地	excursion area, spot
いじょう 以上	more than
まわ 回る	to go around, visit
しゅっぱつち 出発地	point of departure
りよう 利用	to use, employ

Bailey: How many kilometers is it to Kyushu?

JTB: It's 1176 km, one way (to Hakata).

| はかた
博多 | a city in northern Kyushu, |

Bailey: Well, that's more than 201 km, isn't it? And is Imari an excursion spot?

| かたみち
片道 | one way |

JTB: No, but nearby Karatsu is.

| からつ
唐津 | another city in northwest Kyushu famous for its pottery |

Bailey: Far out!

JTB: Pardon me? FAA-A U TO ...Ah! Kyushu's far, isn't it?

Lesson 27 **Notes on Usage**

27 A

1. 何とかなりますよ。

何とかなる is an idiom which means "One way or another/somehow things will get done."

お金がなくても大丈夫ですか。

Can you manage without money? (Lit. "Even if you don't have money, will it be okay?")

何とかなりますよ。 — Somehow, it'll work out, I'm sure.

ことばが分からなくても一人で 行って大丈夫でしょうか。 — Will it be all right for you to go alone, even if you cannot understand the language?

多分何とかなりましょう。 — I'm sure it'll work out one way or another.

2. どうも申し訳ありません is more formal than すみません。

晩御飯をおごりますよ。 — おごる means "to treat someone to (a meal, a drink, etc.)."

The form is used among students or friends. A more polite way of saying it would be 御馳走します, or 私が..., as in 晩御飯は私が ... or きょうは私が ...

"Go Dutch" in Japanese is 割り勘 (にする), which literally means "to divide the bill." This form is used only among students or friends.

27 B

1. 二, 三か所

The classifier for counting places is か所.

1.	一か所	いっかしょ		7.	七か所	ななかしょ
2.	二か所	にかしょ		8.	八か所	はっかしょ
3.	三か所	さんかしょ		9.	九か所	きゅうかしょ
4.	四か所	よんかしょ		10.	十か所	じゅっかしょ
5.	五か所	ごかしょ				じっかしょ
6.	六か所	ろっかしょ				

2. 一割
　いちわり

割 means 10%. The verb 割る means "to divide."
　　　　　　　　　　わ

10%	一割	いちわり		60%	六割	ろくわり
20%	二割	にわり		70%	七割	ななわり
30%	三割	さんわり		80%	八割	はちわり
40%	四割	よんわり		90%	九割	きゅうわり
50%	五割	ごわり		100%	十割	じゅうわり

分　　　1%
ぶ

e.g. 一割五分　15%
　　　いちわり ご ぶ

3. 二か所以上
　　　　　い じょう

X 以上	X or more
X 以下	X or less
三本以上	three or more (of cylindrical things)
五人以下	five or less (of people)

さんぼん 以上
ご にん 以下

Lesson 27 **Grammar Notes**

The main points of this lesson are:

I. Another conditional pattern: なら
II. Miscellaneous expressions:
    A. "It would be better if V"
    B. "It would be better if not V"

C. A pattern used when the speaker concedes the truth of a statement, but wishes to add restrictions or further comment.

I. <u>Sentence₁</u> なら <u>Sentence₂</u>　　　　　　　If (you say/think that) S₁, then S₂

V　行く　（の/ん）/行ったの

A　高い　（の/ん）/高かったの

AN　立派^{りっぱ}　　　　/立派だったの

N　本　　　　　/本だったの

Neg.　ない（の/ん）/なかったの

Note: The なら in this pattern is different from the one used with nouns and adjectives in S₁ なら S₂ pattern introduced in Lesson 19. (cf. L. 19 GN 1)

なら is used when the speaker receives information (S₁) from the addressee or someone else, either by direct statement (assertion) or by implication, that information then serving as the condition upon which the speaker bases S₂. To distinguish this meaning of なら from the one in Lesson 19, the pattern is translated literally (below) as "If (you say, think, mean) S₁, then S₂."

S₁ may be in either the non-past or the past tense. S₂ may occur before S₁ has actually occured or has been completed. なら is preceded by の/ん when it follows a past tense form, and optionally as indicated, in the non-past. S₂ may be a request, command or suggestion.

e.g. (At a restaurant)

(Before the waitress comes)

私はチーズケーキがいいですが　　　I would like some cheesecake, but if you
{なかったら / なければ} パイにします。　don't have any, I'll have some pie.

(The waitress says they don't have cheesecake)

なければパイにします。　　　　　If you don't have (there isn't) any (cheesecake), then I'll have pie.

ないんならパイにします。　　　　If (you say that) there isn't any cheesecake, I'll have some pie.

大木さんが来る（ん）ならわたし　If (you are saying that) Ooki is coming,
は帰ります。　　　　　　　　　　I'll go home.

大木さんが来ればわたしは帰り　　If Ooki comes (when he has come), I'll
ます。　　　　　　　　　　　　　go home.

388

奥さんがお作りになったんなら いただきます。	If (you are saying that) you (Mrs. X) made it, I'll take (Lit. 'receive") it. (S₁ may have been completed some time ago.)
奥さんがお作りになったらいた だきます。	I'll take it when you are through making it. (when S₁ is completed)
サンフランシスコへ行く (ん) な らバートの方が早いですよ。	If (you are saying that) you're going to San Francisco, (I would say that) BART is faster (than going by bus).
頭が痛い (ん) ならアスピリンを のんだらどうですか。	If (as you seem to indicate) you have a headache, why don't you take some aspirin? (Lit. "How about taking some aspirin?")
高い (の) なら買いません。	If (you are saying that) it is expensive, I will not buy it.

きらいなら食べなくてもいいで すよ。

This sentence is ambiguous; it may mean either:

> (I made this because I thought you would like it, but...)
> If you don't like it, you don't have to eat it.
> (ば, straightforward conditional).

> (I see you haven't tried to eat any)
> If (by your reluctance you are suggesting that) you don't like it, you don't have to eat it.
> (なら of this lesson)

あさってなら大丈夫です。

This sentence is also ambiguous:
> (I can't do it today, but)
> the day after tomorrow will be all right.
> (ば)

> (The addressee had asked if the day after tomorrow was okay)
> Oh, (if you mean/say) the day after tomorrow, that'll be fine.

ブランデーならナポレオンがい いですよ。

(If you are asking me about brandy) Napoleon is (a) good (one).

II. Miscellaneous Expressions:

A. Verb (Plain Past) 方がいい   It'd be better if one V-ed.

This is a pattern to express the fact that "doing V would be better" (cf. L. 11 GN 1 "comparison").

When it is used in making suggestions, it is followed often by んじゃないですか。 ("Isn't it the case that...?" cf. L. 17 GN III D)

説明を読んだ方がいいと思います。	I think you'd better (it'd be better if you) read the directions (explanations).
医者に見てもらった方がいいんじゃないですか。	Wouldn't it be better to have a doctor look at you?
少し運動をした方がいいんじゃないですか。	Wouldn't it be better to get a little exercise?

B. Verb (Plain Non-Past, Neg.) ない方がいい   It'd be better not to V

This is a pattern to express the fact that one is better off not doing V.

明日来ない方がいいでしょう。	You'd probably better not come tomorrow.
たばこを吸わない方がいいんじゃないですか。	Wouldn't it be better (for you) not to smoke?
夜一人で歩かない方がいいんじゃないですか。	Wouldn't it be better not to walk alone at night?
早く読む方がいいです。	It is better if you read fast. (emphasis on reading)
早く読んだ方がいいです。	It would be better if you read fast. (emphasis on finishing)

Note: If the speaker wants to say "It would have been better...," i.e. if he wants to say that it would have been better had a different situation been the case, he would use よかった instead of いい.

説明を読んだ方がよかったですね。	We should have read the directions shouldn't we (have)?
今日は来ない方がよかったようですね。	It looks like I shouldn't have come today, doesn't it?

390

来ない方がよかった can mean either a) "It would have been better if I/we hadn't come," or b) "It would have been better if I/we weren't coming..."

C. X ことは X んですが…

X: V, A, AN Plain forms (Affirmative and Negative), Non-past
This pattern is used when the speaker concedes the truth of a statement (X) but wishes to qualify it further.

山田さんはクラスに来ることは
来るんですが寝てばかりいます。

Yamada does come to class all right, but all he does is sleep (here).

面白いことは面白いんですがあ
まりやくにたたないんです。

It is interesting all right, but it is not that useful.

あそこは静かなことは静かなん
ですがちょっと遠すぎますね。

That place is quiet all right, but it's a little too far isn't it?

When a noun is used in the X slot, こと is deleted.

エリザベスさんは秘書は秘書な
んですがタイプはできないそう
です。

Elizabeth is a secretary all right, but I hear she can't type.

第二十七課　漢字

切	符	運	動	町
きっ	ぶ	うん	どう	まち
切	符	運	動	町

建	物	全	然	成	績
たて	もの	ぜん	ぜん	せい	せき
建	物	全	然	成	績

招	待	相	談	反	対
しょう	たい	そう	だん	はん	たい
招	待	相	談	反	対

第 二十八 課

28 A　　（伊万里の藤原さんのうちで）

　　ベイリー　　　　　はじめましてベイリーです。

　　藤原の母　　　　　よくおいでくださいました。いつも娘がお世話

　　　　　　　　　　　になっておりますそうで。

　　ベイリー　　　　　いいえ，　こちらこそお嬢様には御迷惑ばかり

　　　　　　　　　　　おかけしております。

　　藤原の母　　　　　これは末の息子の三郎です。

　　ベイリー　　　　　ベイリーです。どうぞよろしく。

　　三郎　　　　　　　どうぞよろしく。

　　藤原の母　　　　　お疲れでしょう。おふろでもいかがですか。汗

　　　　　　　　　　　をお流しになってゆっくりなさってください。

　　ベイリー　　　　　はい，ありがとうございます。それよりもまだ

　　　　　　　　　　　お嬢さんからお預かりした荷物が次の便で着き

　　　　　　　　　　　ますので…

　　藤原の母　　　　　じゃ，明日でも三郎に行かせましょう。

　　ベイリー　　　　　いえ，私が行きますよ。

　　三郎　　　　　　　ベイリーさん，そのあと，町の案内をさせてく

　　　　　　　　　　　ださいませんか。

　　ベイリー　　　　　でも〔藤原の母に〕お願いしてもいいんでしょ

　　　　　　　　　　　うか。

　　藤原の母　　　　　いいですとも，いつも遊んでばかりいるんです

　　　　　　　　　　　から案内させてやってください。

28 B　　山田　　　　　手紙ですか。

ブラウン	ええ，日本語のクラスで書かされたんです。
山田	今何を勉強してるんですか。
ブラウン	使役の形を復習させられているんです。
山田	使役って何だったかしら，文法は中学校の時に習ったんですけどもう忘れてしまいました。
ブラウン	「食べさせる」「飲ませる」というあれですよ。
山田	ああ，あれですか。
ブラウン	そんなこと忘れて，よく日本語が話せますね。
山田	でも，日本人はそんなもの普段あまり使わないんですよ。
ブラウン	そうですか。
山田	あらこの本面白そうですね。いつか読ませてくださいませんか。
ブラウン	あ，山田さん，今使ったじゃありませんか。

① 例　T：行く

S：（私は）忙しかったので弟に行かせました。

1. 荷物を取りに行く
2. 車を洗う
3. 買物をする
4. そうじをする
5. ベイリーさんを案内する
6. 洗濯する
7. 手伝う
8. 手紙を書く
9. タイプを打つ
10. 計画をつくる

② 例　T：弟さんが行きましたね。

S：ええ，実は，私が弟に行かせたんです。

394

1. 弟さんが車を洗いましたね。
2. 妹さんがさらを洗いましたね。
3. 妹さんが夕食を作りました
   ね。
4. ブラウンさんが飲みましたね。
5. ブラウンさんが歌いましたね。

6. 学生が漢字を覚えましたね。
7. 犬が新聞を持って来ましたね。
8. スミスさんが書きましたね。
9. 妹さんが洗濯しましたね。
10. 弟さんがタイプを打ちました
    ね。

3 例 T： 行く

　　S： あんなに行きたがっているんですからやっぱり行かせましょ
　　　　うよ。

1. 食べる
2. 飲む
3. 帰る
4. 勉強する
5. やめる
6. 働く
7. 泳ぐ
8. 教える
9. 歌う
10. 休む

11. 日本へ行く
12. 運転する
13. 書く
14. 読む
15. 入る
16. 出る
17. 一人で行く
18. 日本語で話す
19. 結婚する
20. 別れる

4 例 T： 町を案内する

　　S： あのう，町を案内させてくださいませんか。

1. ここで勉強する
2. ここで働く

3. セミナーに参加する
4. 講義を聞く
5. その本を読む
6. お手伝いする
7. 日本へ行く
8. 中国料理を作る
9. ごちそうする
10. 来週も出席する

⑤ 例 T: スミスさんは笑いました。（ブラウンさん）
　　　S: ブラウンさんはスミスさんを笑わせました。

1. 両親は心配しました。（ブラウンさん）
2. 山田さんは怒りました。（スミスさん）
3. 先生はがっかりしました。(山田さん)
4. 私は病院へ行きました。（母）
5. ボーイフレンドは困りました。（ジョンソンさん）
6. 子供は外で遊びました。（彼女）
7. スミスさんは待ちました。(ブラウンさん)
8. ジョンソンさんはよろこびました。（山田さん）
9. 山田さんは泣きました。(スミスさん)
10. 子供達は帰りました。（先生）

⑥ 例 T: 書きたかったんですか。
　　　S: いえ，書かされたんですよ。

1. 復習したかったんですか。
2. 行きたかったんですか。
3. 飲みたかったんですか。
4. 勉強したかったんですか。
5. 結婚したかったんですか。
6. 翻訳したかったんですか。
7. 買いたかったんですか。
8. 作りたかったんですか。
9. 手伝いたかったんですか。
10. 日本語で話したかったんですか。

Lesson 28 **Dialogues**

28 A

(At the Fujiwara's in Imari)
Bailey: I'm Bailey. I'm so pleased to meet you.
Fujiwara's Mother: Thank you for coming. I understand my daughter is much indebted to you.

娘	(my) daughter
お世話になる	to be much obliged to someone

Bailey: No, it's me who's always bothering her.

迷惑をかける	to cause inconvenience

Mother: This is our youngest son Saburoo.

末	the last, the final
息子	(my) son

Bailey: I'm Bailey. Pleased to meet you.
Saburoo: Pleased to meet you.
Mother: You must be tired. Please make yourself at home.

お疲れでしょう。おふろでもいかがですか。汗をお流しになってゆっくりなさってください。	Lit., "You must be tired. How about a bath or something? Then after your bath (after you rinse/wash off your perspiration), please relax."
汗	perspiration
お流しになる	an honorific form derived from 流す, "to rinse," "to wash off," etc.
ゆっくりする	to relax

Bailey: Thank you, but I have some things that your daughter asked me to bring that will be arriving on the next train, so...

預かる	to be entrusted with something
お預かりする	a humble form derived from 預かる
荷物	baggage, goods

397

次の便 (つぎ・びん)　　　　　　　　the next arrival/departure of (train, plane, etc.)

着く (つ・く)　　　　　　　　　　to arrive

Mother: Well, I'll have Saburoo get them sometime tomorrow.
Bailey: Oh, no, no, I'll go.
Saburoo: (Mr.) Bailey, after that, let me show you around town.
Bailey: But [turning to Fujiwara's mother] is it really all right?
Mother: Oh yes. All he's doing is playing anyway, so please let him show you around.

28 B

Yamada: Is that a letter (you're looking at)?
Brown: Yes. They made us write it in class.

日本語のクラスで書かされたんです。　　Lit., "We were made to write it in Japanese class."

Yamada: What are you studying now?
Brown: They're making us review the causative construction.

使役の形 (しえき・かたち)　　　　causative construction

Yamada: What was the causative construction anyway? I know we learned it (Japanese grammar) in junior high, but I've forgotten what it was.

中学校 (ちゅうがっこう)　　　　　Junior High School (in Japan, grades 7–9)

Brown: You know, it's like "tabesaseru" and "nomaseru."
Yamada: Oh, that...

Brown: I'm amazed that you can speak Japanese without knowing such an important thing!

忘れる (わす・れる)　　　　　　　to forget

Yamada: But we (Japanese) don't usually use it.
Brown: Is that right.
Yamada: Gee. This book looks really interesting. Will you let me read it sometime?
Brown: Hey, you just used it!

398

Lesson 28 **Notes on Usage**

28 A

1. よくおいでくださいました。

A variation of よくいらっしゃいました。 The former sounds more humble. いつも 娘 がお世話になっておりますそうで is a part of the exchange of greetings. Even if the statement contradicts the facts, this form will still be used.

2. いいえ，こちらこそお嬢様には御迷惑ばかりおかけしております。

This is also a part of the greetings exchanged. It is said even when the facts do not correspond to the literal meaning of the statement.

3. でもお願いしてもいいんですか。

Notice that Bailey is asking Mrs. Fujiwara rather than Saburoo, because she has the authority to decide in this situation.

27 B

1. 使役って何だったかしら。

The past tense is used because Yamada remembers that in the past she had learned the grammar. If she had never learned the grammar, she would have said, 何かしら, i.e. the present tense form.

Lesson 28 **Grammar Notes**

The main points of this lesson are:

I. Causative forms.
  A. A pattern to express "let someone do V (as he wishes)."
  B. A pattern to express "force someone to do V."
II. Passive causative sentences.
  A pattern to express "be made to V," as in "I didn't want to drink, but I was made to drink."

I. Causative sentences:

There are two kinds of causative sentences: A. "let causatives," and B. "make causatives." Both use the same causative forms of verbs.

Causative verb forms:

U-verbs:	-ase-ru	RU-verbs:	-sase-ru	Irregular verbs	
書く	書かせる	食べる	食べさせる	する	させる
泳ぐ	泳がせる	着る	着させる	来る	来させる
持つ	持たせる	見る	見させる		

When the verb is intransitive, i.e. in the pattern "A causes B to V(int.)," there are two particles that B can take, depending on the situation. One is に (the agent marker), and the other is を (the object marker).

A. A が B に V-(s)ase-ru   A lets B do V

The particle に is used when A (the causer) respects B's (the causee's) desire or will to perform the action. Accordingly, B must be a noun that has both the will and the ability to perform an action. Also, the verb must be a self-controllable action. This pattern is often called the "let" causative.

山田さんは前から行きたがっていますからこんどは彼に行かせましょう。	Yamada has been wanting to go for a long time, so let's let him go this time.
ぼくは仕事もあるし、貯金も少しできたから、お父さん、ぼくに結婚させてください。	I've got a job, and I've even saved some money, so please, Dad, let me get married.

400

B. A が B を V-(s)ase-ru   A makes/forces B to V

Generally speaking, the particle を is used when B does not want to perform an action or be in a situation of his own accord. In addition, B may be either human or non-human (including inanimate objects). This form is often called the "make" causative:

There are three ways to use the "make" causative:

1. When A intentionally makes (forces B to) perform an action regardless of (and sometimes against) his (B's) will.

山田を行かせましょう。	Let's make Yamada go.
ことしは花子を結婚させなければなりませんね。あの子もそろそろとしごろですから。	We've got to get Hanako married off this year, hadn't we. Now that she's of marriageable age and all.
社長は山田さんをやめさせました。	The (company) president made Yamada quit.

2. When an action cannot be controlled by B; emotional verbs such as 心配する, よろこぶ, おこる, 泣く, etc., belong to this class. In this case, A is the causer of the situation, regardless of whether or not he wanted to be.

ブラウンさんは病気がよくならないので両親を心配させました。	Because his illness does not improve, Brown was a cause of worry for his parents. (Lit. "Brown caused his parents to worry.")
ジョンソンさんはボーイフレンドをこまらせています。	Johnson is giving her boyfriend a hard time. (Lit. "Johnson is causing her boyfriend trouble.")
スミスさんは悲しい話をして山田さんを泣かせました。	Smith made Yamada cry by telling (her) a sad story.

3) Though it is not a major concern of this lesson, it might be mentioned that を is also used when <u>A</u> unintentionally allows a situation to occur in which <u>V</u> happens to B. In this case, <u>A</u> is not the one who causes the action, but the one who experience the situation.

山田さんはがんで子供を死なせました。	Yamada allowed his child to die of cancer.

When the verb is a transitive verb, the above distinctions disappear, resulting in ambiguous sentences. Context will distinguish one meaning from the other.

<u>A</u> が <u>B</u> に <u>C</u> を <u>V-(s)ase-ru</u>   <u>A</u> {makes/lets} <u>B</u> Verb <u>C</u>

わたしは子どもに日本語を勉強させるつもりです。

I intend to make/let my child study Japanese.

ムハメッド・アリにあんなことを言わせていいんですか。

Is it okay to make/let Muhammad Ali say a thing like that?

Notice that に is used even when the object does not appear in the object slot.

夕食は娘に作らせましょう。

I will (Let's) make/let our daughter make dinner.

この本は面白いですね。いつか読ませてくださいませんか。

This book looks interesting. Would you let me read it sometime?

Pragmatic applications of the basic rules for the causative form: The causative form is often used when an inferior speaks to his superior.

どうぞわたしにその仕事を
{させて
 やらせて} ください。

Please allow me to do the work (Lit. "Please let me do the work.")

お先に読ませていただきました。

I went ahead and read it (the book) before you did (read it). (Lit. "I received the favor of your allowing me to read it before you did.")

When a superior speaks about making someone who is inferior to himself do something, に is often used instead of を, as if the person who is made to perform the action were willing to undertake the task. For example, Fujiwara's mother in dialogue A in Lesson 27 says あしたでも三郎に行かせましょう, instead of 三郎を.

Also, even when B is willing to do the task (and therefore a case where に would normally be called for), if the final decision hinges on the superior's approval, を still tends to be used. For example, even when Hanako really wants to get married, her perents would still say, 花子を結婚させましょう (Let's make Hanako get married).

II. Passive causative sentences:

$$\underset{\text{(CAUSATIVE)}}{\text{Verb(root) - (s)ase}} + \underset{\text{(PASSIVE)}}{\text{rare - ru}} \quad \text{be made to V}$$

This pattern expresses the fact that someone is made to perform an action. The agent who causes the action is marked by the particle に.

A.　(causative sentence)

父はわたしを結婚させました。　Father made me get married.

(passive causative sentence)

わたしは父に結婚させられました。 — I was made to get married by my father.

B. 太田さんは田中さんに変な物を食べさせたそうです。 — I hear that Ota made Tanaka eat some strange things.

田中さんは太田さんに変な物を食べさせられたそうです。 — I hear that Tanaka was made to eat some strange things by Ota.

C. 先生は田中さんに英語で答えさせました。 — The teacher made Tanaka answer in English.

田中さんは先生に英語で答えさせられました。 — Tanaka was made to answer in English by the teacher.

Besides the structure introduced in Section 1 above, there is another way to form causatives; that is,

Verb(root) - s(as) - u   e.g. RU-verbs: 食べさす

U-verbs: 書かす

This causative form, when combined with the passive form-(r)are-ru, makes another passive causative form;

Verb (root) - (s)as - are-ru   (r of rare is dropped because of the preceding s.)
(As a rule of thumb, use this formula: -NAI stem of U-verb-sare-ru)

This passive causative form tends to be used with U-verbs, and the other passive causative form tends to be used with RU-verbs.

Thus,

U-verbs	RU-verbs	Irregular verbs
書く：書かされる	食べる：食べさせられる	する：させられる
飲む：飲まされる	着る ：着させられる	来る：来させられる
行く：行かされる	答える：答えさせられる	
(See the example sentences below.)	(See the example sentences above.)	

1) 山田さんは秘書にタイプをうたせています。 — Yamada is making the secretary do the typing.

秘書は山田さんにタイプをうたされています。 — The secretary is being made to do the typing by Yamada.

2) あのセールスマンはうまいで すね。とうとう山田さんに歯 ブラシを買わせてしまいまし たよ。

That salesperson is clever, isn't he? He's finally gotten Yamada to buy a toothbrush.

とうとう山田さんはあのセー ルスマンに歯ブラシを買わさ れてしまいましたよ。

Yamada was finally made to buy the toothbrush by the salesperson.

3) 山田さんに飲ませたんでしょ う。

You made Yamada drink, right?

…いいえ，山田さんに飲まさ れたんです。

...No, I was made to drink by Yamada.

Index to Notes (Lessons 2–27)

Grammatical forms and idiomatic phrases are listed in the index alphabetically either by the form itself (e.g. bakari), or, when appropriate, by general category (e.g. Honorifics). The references given are to the Grammar Notes (GN), or to the Notes on Usage (NU). The first number that appears represents the lesson from which the entry is taken, followed by GN or NU. The letter A or B following NU refers to the relevant dialogue. The last number represents the section within the notes where the entry appears. In other words, the citation 13NUA3, for example, would refer to Lesson 13, Notes on Usage, dialogue A, number 3. A number followed by D(A) or (B) refers to dialogue A or B in which the entry appears.

B

ba   X ba Y   "if X, then Y"   19GN1

bakari

    <u>N</u> bakari <u>V</u>   "V nothing but N."   9GN6 (See also DAKE and SHIKA____NAI)

    number + classifier + bakari   "about" 17NUB5

    <u>V</u>(plain, past) + bakari   "(X) has just V-ed"   18NUB, 21GN2C

    <u>V</u>-te bakari iru   11GN4

ban   classifier for "nights"   17NUA

Before

    mae ni   22GN4A

    nai uchi ni   22GN4B

byoo   "seconds"   24NUB11

C

Causatives   "let" and "make" causatives   28GN1

chitto mo   "not at all"   14NUA6

Classifiers/counters

    ri/nin, doru, sento, en, ji, jikan, nen, hon, mai   8GN1

    goo "issue"   13NUB2

satsu	13NUB4	ko "small objects"	20NUA6
kai "floor"	14NUA4	hen "times"	19NUB17
ban "nights"	17NUA7	kai "turn/fines"	17NUB4
do "times"	17NUB1		17NUB4

    nichi, ka   "days"   17NUB5

    sho   "places"   27NUB1

    wari   "10%"   27NUB2

Clothing   Various words for   23NUA1

Comparison

    Two things, three things   11GN1

    With gurai   "X is as____as Y"   14GN1a

    With hodo   "X is not as____as Y"   14GN1b

    V (plain, past)/(plain, neg.) + hoo ga ii 27GN2a, b

Conditionals   See BA, NARA, TARA and TO

D

dake "only" "nothing but" See also BAKARI and SHIKA____NAI

dakeshika   "only"   20NUA6

dare   "who"   2GN6B

dareka   "someone"   3GN7; 5GN7; 9GN5

de

    "according to"   19GN3a

    Contraction of sorede/tokorode   11NUA4

    Instrument marker   4GN1c

    Location marker (action verbs)   4GN1B

dekiru

    <u>X</u> de dekiteiru   "be made of/with X"   24NUA6

    <u>X</u> kara dekiru   "be made from X"   24NUB4

dekirudake yattemimasu   "I'll try my best"   12D(A)

406

hodo
     "approximately" (suffix)   5GN6
     In comparisons (negative)   14GN1
hokani   "other (than this/that) 4NUB1; 11NUA1
Honorifics and Humble Vocabulary
     irassharu "come, go, be"   15NUB1
     o + $\underline{V}$(pre-masu) + ni naru   20GN2
     go + Chinese word + nasaru   20GN2
hontoo wa   "the truth is"   11NUB9
hoo
     "direction"   22NUA4
     hoo ga ii $\underline{V}$(plain, past) + hoo ga ii   27GN2 (See also 'Comparison')
hoshii $\underline{N}$(object) ga hoshii; $\underline{N}$(obj.) o hoshigaru   13GN1

I

ieba   (See TO IEBA "speaking of")   3NUB2
ii   Used in idiomatic phrases such hana ga ii "have a good nose," mimi ga ii "have
     good ears"   22NUB4
ijoo   "$\underline{X}$ or more"   27NUB3
ika   "$\underline{X}$ or less"   27NUB3
ikaga de gozaimashoo   'how about (this one)'   10NUB1; 23D(B)
ikemasen   (See TE WA IKEMASEN)
ima no tokoro   "for now"   19NUA5
Indirect objects marked by NI (See NI)
ippai   "full" (contrast with 'one cupful')   21NUA4
irasshai   "welcome"   10NUA1
iroirona   "various"   5NUA2
iron na   Contraction of iroiro na   12NUB1
iru
     "need"   15DB   (See 'Necessity')
(See TE IRU)
itadaku   "(humbly) receive"   20GN1; 21GN1
itte kuru   "go and come"   17D(A)
iu
     _____to iu koto wa_____to iu koto desu   23GN2B
     _____to iu mono   "thing called_____"
     _____tte iu $\underline{N}$ "a $\underline{N}$ called_____"   22NUB2;
iya   Contraction of iie   17NUA3

J

ja "well" "then"   Contraction of dewa   11NUB3
ja nai ka to omoimasu   "I have a feeling that..."   18GN3(B)
jitsu wa   "actually"   11NUB5

K

ka
     Question marker   2GN6A
ka doo ka wakarimasen   "I don't know whether or not"   18GN3(C)

kakaru   "takes" (time, cost, manpower)   8GN7
kamo shiremasen   <u>X</u>(plain forms) + kamo shiremasen   8GN9
kara
      <u>X</u> <u>V</u>-te kara <u>Y</u>   "after doing <u>V</u>"   15GN4
      <u>X</u> kara <u>Y</u>   "because"   16GN1
kara____made   "from____to"   5GN1; 11NUB2
kare   "he" "sweetheart"   11NUB10
kashira   "I wonder if..."   28NUB1
katte kuru   "buy and come"   21NUA6
kedo   Contraction of keredomo; keredo   19NUA2
Kinship terms (immediate family)   8NUA3
kireteimasu   "out of stock"   10NUA5
koko   "here"   2GN2
kondo no   "the next"
kono   "this <u>N</u>"   2GN2
kono mae   "the other day"   25NUB2
kono tsugi   "next (in a series)"   21NUA2
koo iu koto   "this sort of thing"   19D(B)
kore   "this"   2GN2
koto
      ____to iu koto wa____to iu koto desu   23GN2B
      <u>X</u> koto wa <u>X</u> n desu ga...   27GN2c
      koto ga aru   <u>S</u>(plain, past) + koto ga aru   "have the experience of"   10GN5
      koto ga aru   <u>V</u>(dict. form) + koto ga aru   "there are times when..."   12GN4
      koto ga dekiru <u>V</u>(dict. form) + koto ga dekiru   6GN1 (See 'Potentials')
      koto ni naru <u>V</u>(plain, non-past) + koto ni   "be decided"   21GN2A
      koto ni suru <u>V</u>(plain, non-past) + koto ni suru   "decide to"   21GN2B
kudasai   For objects   "please give me____"   (See 'Requests')
kudasaimasen ka   (See "Requests")
kudasaru   "he (superior) gives"   20GN1 (See "Giving and Receiving")
kureru   "he (inferior) gives"   20GN1 (See "Giving and Receiving")

M

maa, hidoi desu nee   "What a thing to say!"   6NUA7
maa——ii desu   "oh, that's all right"   12D(A)
mada
      "not yet"   5GN4; 7GN8
      "still (more)"   4NUB1
mae ni   <u>V</u>(plain, non-past) + mae ni   "before <u>V</u>"   22GN4A
masen ka   Negative question   6NUB3
mashoo   "let's"   15GN1
mata
      "as usual"
      "of all things, people, places"   26NUA2
miru   <u>V</u>-te + miru   "try"   (See TE MIRU)
mo
      "also"   2GN4; 3GN6
      "as much as"   20GN3

Modification
    Multiple modifiers   6GN4
    Sentences modifying nouns (relative clauses)   7GN2;
morau   "receive (from inferior)"   20GN1
moo   "already"   5GN4; 8GN8;
mooshiwake gozaimasen   "I am sorry"   19NUA3
moo sukoshi   "a little more"   19GN2c
moshi yokattara   "if it's all right with you"   23NUA7

N
nagara V_1 (pre-masu) nagara V_2 "while"   12GN3
nai
    naide   V-naide   "without doing V"   17GN5
    naidekudasai   "please don't V"   8GN6 (See "Requests")
    nai tsumori   V(non-past, neg.) + tsumori   "no intention" 5GN2
    nai uchi ni   "before"   22GN4B
nakereba narimasen   "must" 14GN2
nakutemo ii desu   "all right if (you) don't"   12GN1B
nanda ka   "somehow"   24NUB14
nani/nan   "what"   2GN6B
nani ga ii desu ka   "What is good?"   1NUA2
nanika/nanimo   3GN4; 5GN7
/nanka   Informal variant of nado   17NUB7
nan to iu n deshoo ka   "What do you call that, I wonder?"   22NUA2
nan to ka narimasu yo   "It'll work out somehow or other"   27NUA1
nan tomo nai   "no problem"   24NUB13
naru
    X ga Y + naru   "become"   19GN3c
    V(plain, non-past) + koto ni naru   (See KOTO NI NARU)
    V(plain, non-past) + yoo ni naru   (SOO NI NARU)
ne   "isn't that right?"   3NUA1
Necessity   X ni(wa) Y ga iru   15DB
Negative forms
    Of the te-iru form   9GN2
    X wa Y dewa arimasen   2GN5
    Of existential sentences (arimasen/imasen)   3GN2
ni
    Absolute time marker   "at, in, on"   4GN1E
    Final destination marker   4GN1D
    V(pre-masu) + in + V(go/come/go home)   "for the purpose of"   15GN2
    Indirect object marker   8GN5
    Location marker   3GN1, 2
    ni suru   "decide on"   10GN2
nigate   "weak point"   18NUB1
n ja arimasen ka/n ja nai n desu ka   "isn't it the case that"   19GN3(D)
nikui   V(pre-masu) + nikui   "difficult to"   17GN4
no
    N no N (possessive, appositive, descriptive)   2GN3

410

dooshite (plain forms) no/n desu ka

Receiving   (See "Giving and Receiving")

rei no   "the one people are talking about"   9NUB1

Requests

    kudasai   Y o kudasai   "please give me X"   8GN4

    V-te kudasai   "please do V for me/him/them"   8GN6

    Negative   -naide kudasai   "please do not V"   8GN6

    Polite request V-te kudasaimasenka   "won't you please V?"   8GN6

    Polite negative request   V-naide kudasaimasenka   "please do not V"   8GN6

S

sa   Changes adjectives to nouns   A. (stem)/AN + sa   14GN4

sakki   "a short while ago"   21NUA8

sashiageru   "give (to superior)"   20GN1 (See 'Giving and Receiving')

sayoode gozaimasu nee   Humble form of soo desu nee   (23NUB6)

shika____nai   "only"   (See also BAKARI and DAKE)   20GN4

shimau   (See TE SHIMAU)

shitsurei shimasu   When entering/leaving a room   12NUA1

soko   "there"   2GN2

sono   "that N"   2GN2

shoochi itashimashita   "very well"   10NUB3

sono mama   16NUB2

sonna koto   "a thing like that"   25NUA4

sonna ni   "that much"   12NUB3

soo

    "hearsay"   19GN2

    V(pre-masu)/A(stem)/AN + soo   "looks (like)"   22GN1

soo desu ka   "I see"   4NUB4

soo desu nee   "hmmmm..."   4NUA2

soo ieba   "come to think of it"   3NUB2

soo ja arimasen   "that's not what I mean"   2NUA2

sore   "that"   2GN2

sore ga   Usually used with jitsu wa   11NUB4

soretomo   "or"   12NUA5

sore wa   "of course"   "needless to say"   11NUA5

Suggestions   V-tara doo desu ka   25NUA11

sugiru   X + sugiru   "too"   23GN2A

sugu soko   "right there"   22NUA1

sumimasen ga   "I'm sorry but..."   10NUB2

superlatives   11GN2

suru

    N ni suru   "decide on"   10GN2

    koto ni suru   "decide to"   21GN2B

    Z ga X o Y suru   "make"   19GN3c (cf.____ni suru)

    V(plain, non-past) + yoo ni suru   "make it so that V"   25GN3

    V(y)oo to suru   "try to do V"   26GN2

    In idiomatic phrases such as katachi o suru   "be shaped like____"   22NUA5

See also "Causatives," "Passive forms," "Passive-causatives," "Potentials," and "TE-forms"

W
wa

    Old information   "as for..." "speaking of..."   2GN1

wake   V-nai wake ni wa ikanai   "can't very well not V"   26GN3

wasureru   X no o wasureru   "forget to X"   25NUB4

Y
ya____ya-____nado   Random listing   4GN3

yappari   "just as one thinks/expects"   4NUA3; 23NUA3

yaru   Variant of suru   17NUA1

yasui V(pre-masu) + yasui   "easy to V"   17GN4

yo   Emphatic particle (sentence final)   2NUA3

yokatta   "that's wonderful"   21NUB6

yoku oide kudasai mashita   "Thank you for coming"   28NUA1

yoo

    "looks like" "looks as if"   22GN2

    yoo ni naru V(plain, non-past) + yoo ni naru "it's gotten so that"   25GN4

    yoo ni suru V(plain, non-past) + yoo ni suru "arrange things so that"   25GN3

yoroshii   15NUA1; 12D(A)

yoru   Source ni yoru to/ni yoreba   'according to'   19GN3

Z
zutsu   X zutsu   "X of each kind"   20NUB2

zutto

    "by far"   11NUA6

    "continuously"   14NUA3

一年生で勉強した漢字

あ　会う　（あう）
　　赤い　（あかい）
　　明るい　（あかるい）
　　秋　（あき）
　　開く　（あく）
　　朝　（あさ）
　　足　（あし）
　　味　（あじ）
　　明日　（あした）
　　遊ぶ　（あそぶ）
　　頭　（あたま）
　　新しい　（あたらしい）
　　暑い　（あつい）
　　兄　（あに）
　　姉　（あね）
　　雨　（あめ）
　　洗う　（あらう）
　　歩く　（あるく）
　　案内　（あんない）

い　言う　（いう）
　　行く　（いく）
　　医者　（いしゃ）
　　急ぐ　（いそぐ）
　　一　（いち）
　　一番　（いちばん）
　　犬　（いぬ）
　　今　（いま）
　　意味　（いみ）
　　妹　（いもうと）

う　上　（うえ）
　　受かる　（うかる）
　　受ける　（うける）
　　歌う　（うたう）
　　生まれる　（うまれる）

　　上着　（うわぎ）
　　運転　（うんてん）
　　運動　（うんどう）

え　映画　（えいが）
　　英語　（えいご）
　　駅　（えき）
　　円　（えん）

お　大きい　（おおきい）
　　多い　（おおい）
　　起きる　（おきる）
　　送る　（おくる）
　　教える　（おしえる）
　　落ちる　（おちる）
　　弟　（おとうと）
　　男　（おとこ）
　　同じ　（おなじ）
　　覚える　（おぼえる）
　　思う　（おもう）
　　泳ぐ　（およぐ）
　　終わる　（おわる）
　　音楽　（おんがく）
　　女　（おんな）

か　火　（か）
　　外国人　（がいこくじん）
　　買物　（かいもの）
　　買う　（かう）
　　返す　（かえす）
　　帰る　（かえる）
　　顔　（かお）
　　書く　（かく）
　　学生　（がくせい）
　　か月　（かげつ）
　　貸す　（かす）

家族　（かぞく）
月　（がつ）
学期　（がっき）
学校　（がっこう）
(お)金　（お)(かね）
借りる　（かりる）
変わる　（かわる）
考える　（かんがえる）
漢字　（かんじ）

き　木　（き）
　聞く　（きく）
　切手　（きって）
　切符　（きっぷ）
　昨日　（きのう）
　お客様　（お)(きゃくさま）
　九　（きゅう）
　今日　（きょう）
　教科書　（きょうかしょ）
　教室　（きょうしつ）
　兄弟　（きょうだい）
　去年　（きょねん）
　着る　（きる）
　金　（きん）

く　九　（く）
　薬　（くすり）
　口　（くち）
　国　（くに）
　来る　（くる）
　車　（くるま）

け　今朝　（けさ）
　月　（げつ）
　結婚　（けっこん）
　元気だ　（げんきだ）

こ　個　（こ）
　五　（ご）
　語　（ご）

午後　（ごご）
午前　（ごぜん）
今年　（ことし）
子ども　（こども）
米　（こめ）
今週　（こんしゅう）
今度　（こんど）

さ　最近　（さいきん）
　魚　（さかな）
　作文　（さくぶん）
　(お)酒　（おさけ）
　冊　（さつ）
　寒い　（さむい）
　三　（さん）

し　四　（し）
　時間　（じかん）
　試験　（しけん）
　事故　（じこ）
　仕事　（しごと）
　辞書　（じしょ）
　静かだ　（しずかだ）
　下　（した）
　七　（しち）
　質問　（しつもん）
　自転車　（じてんしゃ）
　死ぬ　（しぬ）
　字引　（じびき）
　十　（じゅう）
　住所　（じゅうしょ）
　週末　（しゅうまつ）
　授業　（じゅぎょう）
　宿題　（しゅくだい）
　紹介　（しょうかい）
　小学校　（しょうがっこう）
　上手だ　（じょうずだ）
　小説　（しょうせつ）
　招待　（しょうたい）
　食事　（しょくじ）

416

調べる　（しらべる）
知る　（しる）
人　（じん）
親切　（しんせつ）
心配　（しんぱい）
新聞　（しんぶん）

す　水　（すい）
　　数学　（すうがく）
　　好きだ（すきだ）
　　少し　（すこし）
　　住む　（すむ）

せ　成績　（せいせき）
　　説明　（せつめい）
　　千　（せん）
　　先週　（せんしゅう）
　　先生　（せんせい）
　　全然　（ぜんぜん）
　　専門　（せんもん）

そ　相談　（そうだん）
　　卒業　（そつぎょう）
　　外　（そと）

た　大学　（だいがく）
　　大学院　（だいがくいん）
　　大事　（だいじ）
　　大変だ　（たいへんだ）
　　高い　（たかい）
　　出す　（だす）
　　建物　（たてもの）
　　田中　（たなか）
　　楽しい　（たのしい）
　　食べる　（たべる）
　　足りる　（たりる）
　　単語　（たんご）

ち　小さい　（ちいさい）
　　近い　（ちかい）

地下鉄　（ちかてつ）
地図　（ちず）
父　（ちち）
お(茶)　（お)(ちゃ）
中国　（ちゅうごく）
貯金　（ちょきん）

つ　使う　（つかう）
　　次　（つぎ）
　　作る　（つくる）
　　冷たい　（つめたい）
　　強い　（つよい）

て　手　（て）
　　手紙　（てがみ）
　　手伝う　（てつだう）
　　出る　（でる）
　　天気　（てんき）
　　電気　（でんき）
　　電話　（でんわ）

と　戸　（と）
　　東京　（とうきょう）
　　遠い　（とおい）
　　時　（とき）
　　時計　（とけい）
　　所　（ところ）
　　図書館　（としょかん）
　　飛ぶ　（とぶ）
　　友だち　（ともだち）
　　取る　（とる）

な　中　（なか）
　　長い　（ながい）
　　泣く　（なく）
　　夏　（なつ）
　　七　（なな）
　　何　（なに）
　　名前　（なまえ）
　　習う　（ならう）

何　（なん）

に　二　（に）
　　肉　（にく）
　　日　（にち）
　　日本　（にほん）
　　人　（にん）

ね　お願い　（おねがい）
　　熱　（ねつ）
　　眠る　（ねむる）
　　寝る　（ねる）

の　飲む　（のむ）
　　乗る　（のる）

は　入る　（はいる）
　　始まる　（はじまる）
　　初めて　（はじめて）
　　始める　（はじめる）
　　走る　（はしる）
　　働く　（はたらく）
　　八　（はち）
　　花　（はな）
　　話す　（はなす）
　　母　（はは）
　　早い　（はやい）
　　春　（はる）
　　晴れる　（はれる）
　　半　（はん）
　　晩　（ばん）
　　反対　（はんたい）

ひ　飛行機　（ひこうき）
　　左　（ひだり）
　　百　（ひゃく）
　　冷やす　（ひやす）
　　病院（　びょういん）
　　病気　（びょうき）
　　昼　（ひる）

広い　（ひろい）

ふ　復習　（ふくしゅう）
　　不便だ　（ふべんだ）
　　冬　（ふゆ）
　　古い　（ふるい）
　　文法　（ぶんぽう）

へ　下手だ　（へただ）
　　部屋　（へや）
　　勉強　（べんきょう）
　　便利だ　（べんりだ）

ほ　方　（ほう）
　　本　（ほん）
　　本当　（ほんとう）
　　本屋　（ほんや）

ま　枚　（まい）
　　毎朝　（まいあさ）
　　毎日　（まいにち）
　　毎晩　（まいばん）
　　前　（まえ）
　　町　（まち）
　　待つ　（まつ）

み　右　（みぎ）
　　水　（みず）
　　店　（みせ）
　　耳　（みみ）
　　見る　（みる）

む　難しい　（むずかしい）

め　目　（め）

も　木　（もく）
　　持つ　（もつ）
　　問題　（もんだい）

や　安い　（やすい）
　　休み　（やすみ）
　　山田　（やまだ）

ゆ　夕方　（ゆうがた）
　　雪　（ゆき）

よ　用意　（ようい）
　　用事　（ようじ）
　　曜日　（ようび）
　　予習　（よしゅう）
　　読む　（よむ）
　　夜　（よる）
　　弱い　（よわい）
　　四　（よん）

ら　来週　（らいしゅう）
　　来年　（らいねん）

り　両親　（りょうしん）
　　料理　（りょうり）
　　旅行　（りょこう）

れ　練習　（れんしゅう）

ろ　六　（ろく）

わ　和英辞典　（わえいじてん）
　　分かる　（わかる）
　　私　（わたし）
　　笑う　（わらう）
　　悪い　（わるい）

Vocabulary List by Lessons

Before⌐ the pitch is high. When⌐ does not follow the first *kana*, the first *kana* is low. When there is no mark, all *kana* are high except the first.

第 二 課　（だ⌐いに⌐か）

2A.	あれ	are		pron. that
	りょ⌐う	ryoo	寮	n. dormitory
	そ⌐う	soo		that's right
	しょくどう	syokudoo	食堂	n. cafeteria
	な⌐ん	nan	何	pron. what
	たいいく⌐かん	taiikukan	体育館	n. gymnasium
	ここ	koko		pron. here
	ど⌐こ	doko		pron. where
	ば⌐あくれえ	baakuree	バークレー	n. Berkeley
	たて⌐もの	tatemono	建物	n. building
	としょ⌐かん	tosyokan	図書館	n. library
B.	わたし⌐たち	watasitati	私たち	pron. we
	だいがく	daigaku	大学	n. university
	しんぶん	sinbun	新聞	n. newspaper
	ひと	hito	人	n. person
	だ⌐れ	dare		pron. who
	しんり⌐がく	sinrigaku	心理学	n. psychology
	せんせ⌐い	sensee	先生	n. professor, teacher
	すた⌐んふぉおど	stanhuoodo	スタンフォード	n. Stanford
	せんもん	senmon	専門	n. major
	けいざ⌐いがく	keizaigaku	経済学	n. economics
	しゃか⌐いがく	syakaigaku	社会学	n. sociology
1.	これ	kore		pron. this
	それ	sore		pron. that
2.1.	かた⌐	kata		n. person (polite)
	がくせい	gakusee	学生	n. student
	て⌐きすと	tekisuto	テキスト	n. textbook
	じ⌐しょ	zisyo	辞書	n. dictionary
	にほんご	nihongo	日本語	n. Japanese (language)
	ぶ⌐んがく	bungaku	文学	n. literature
	あぱ⌐あと	apaato	アパート	n. apartment

2.	にね￢んせい	ninensee	二年生	n.	second year student
3.	だいが￢くせい	daigakusee	大学生	n.	university student
	だいがくい￢んせい	daigakuinsee	大学院生	n.	graduate student
	にほんじ￢ん	nihonzin	日本人	n.	Japanese (person)
	あめりか￢じん	amerikazin	アメリカ人	n.	American (person)
	さんふらんし￢すこ	sanhuransisuko	サンフランシスコ	n.	San Francisco
	れきし	rekisi	歴史	n.	history
4.	おとこ￢	otoko	男	n.	man
	おんな￢	onna	女	n.	woman
	ほ￢ん	hon	本	n.	book
	び￢る	biru	ビル	n.	building

第三課　（だ￢いさ￢んか）

3.A.	あそこ	asoko		pron.	that place
	しゃしん	syasin	写真	n.	picture
	あ￢る	aru		v.	there is/ are, exist
	がくちょう	gakutyoo	学長	n.	president (of university)
	むかし	mukasi	昔	n.	past time
	そ￢ふ	sohu	祖父	n.	grandfather
	こ￢ろ	koro		n.	(that) time
	おじ￢いさん	oziisan		n.	grandfather (honorific)
B.	いぬ￢	inu	犬	n.	dog
	たくさ￢ん	takusan		n.	many, much
	いる	iru		v.	there is/are, exist
	な￢か	naka	中	n.	in, at
	うち￢	uti		n.	house, home
	は￢は	haha	母	n.	mother (humble)
	いもうと￢	imooto	妹	n.	younger sister (humble)
	くに	kuni	国	n.	country

422

1.	べいぶり￢っじ	beiburizzi	ベイブリッジ	n.	Bay Bridge
	でゅらんと・ほ￢おる	dyuranto hooru	デュラントホール	n.	Durant Hall
	ちち￢	titi	父	n.	father (humble)
	あ￢に	ani	兄	n.	older brother (humble)
2.	きゃ￢んぱす	kyanpasu	キャンパス	n.	campus
	いらっしゃ￢る	irassyaru		v.	there is/are, exist/to come (polite)
	ね￢こ	neko		n.	cat
	そ￢にい	sonii	ソニー	n.	Sony
	て￢れび	terebi	テレビ	n.	television
	ひ￢っぴい	hippii	ヒッピー	n.	hippie
	ちか￢く	tikaku	近く		vicinity
	つくえ	tukue	机	n.	desk
	うえ	ue	上	n.	top
	にかい	nikai	二階	n.	second floor
3.2.	ばんく・おぶ・あめ￢りか	banku・obu・amerika	バンク・オブ・アメリカ		Bank of America
	となり	tonari		n.	nextdoor
	ゆうび￢んきょく	yuubinkyoku	郵便局	n.	post office
	きょ￢う	kyoo	今日	n.	today
3.	ど￢なた	donata		pron.	who (polite)
	ちゅうごくご	tyuugokugo	中国語	n.	Chinese (language)
	おれんじ・じゅ￢うす	orenzi・zyuusu	オレンジ・ジュース	n.	orange juice
	おと￢うさん	otoosan	お父さん	n,	father (polite)
	いもうとさん	imootosan	妹さん	n.	younger sister (polite)
4.	へや￢	heya	部屋	n.	room
	あね	ane	姉	n.	older sister (humble)
	ろさんぜ￢るす	rosanzerusu	ロサンゼルス	n.	Los Angeles
	そ￢と	soto	外	n.	outside
	くるま	kuruma	車	n.	car
	ぎんこう	ginkoo	銀行	n.	bank
	みなみ	minami	南	n.	south
	て￢れぐらふ	teregurahu	テレグラフ	n.	Telegraph (Avenue)

れ˥すとらん	resutoran	レストラン	n.	restaurant
5. すぺいんご	supeingo	スペイン語	n.	Spanish
び˥ざ	biza	ビザ	n.	Visa
ますたあ・か˥あど	mastaa・kaado	マスターカード	n.	Master Card
げんご˥がく	gengogaku	言語学	n.	linguistics
からあて˥れび	karaaterebi	カラーテレビ	n.	color TV
しろくろて˥れび	sirokuroterebi	白黒テレビ	n.	black & white TV
6. きた	kita	北	n.	north
せいふうえ˥い	seihuuei	セイフウェイ	n.	Safeway
しょうゆ	syooyu	しょう油	n.	soy sauce
せぶん いれぶん	sebun irebun	セブンイレブン	n.	7-Eleven
ぺえじ	peezi	ページ	n.	page
あるふぁべ˥っと	aruhuabetto	アルファベット	n.	alphabet
ほ˥んや	honya	本屋	n.	bookstore
も˥ふぃっと	mohuitto	モフィット	n.	Moffit Library
ひがしあ˥じあ	higasiazia	東アジア	n.	East Asia
てえぷれこ˥おだあ	teepurekoodaa	テープレコーダー	n.	tape recorder
たいぷら˥いたあ	taipuraitaa	タイプライター	n.	typewriter
よこ	yoko	横	n.	the side
ば˥んくろふと	bankurohuto	バンクロフト	n.	Bancroft (Avenue)
7. な˥にか	nanika	何か	pron.	something
だ˥れか	dareka	誰か	pron.	someone
ど˥こか	dokoka		pron.	somewhere
お˥ふぃす	ohuisu	オフィス	n.	office
く˥らす	kurasu	クラス	n.	class
8. おおぜ˥い	oozei		n.	many (people)

第 四 課 （だ˥いよ˥んか）

4.A. あした˥		明日	n.	tomorrow
く˥る		来る	v.	to come
ヨセミテ			n.	Yosemite
いく		行く	v.	to go
バ˥ス			n.	bus
み˥る		見る	v.	to see, watch, look at
たき		滝	n.	waterfall
ハーフド˥ーム			n.	Half Dome

B.	い˥つ		pron.	when
	はじまる		v.	(something) begins
	えいご	英語	n.	English
	ま˥だ		adv	still
	ほかに		adv.	other
	べんきょうする	勉強する	v.	to study
	アメリカぶ˥んがく	アメリカ文学	n.	American literature
	と˥る		v.	to take
	じゅうがつ˥	十月	n.	October
	ふつか	二日		second of the month
1.	か˥える	帰る	v.	to return (home)
	よ˥む	読む	v.	to read
	たべ˥る	食べる	v.	to eat
	かう	買う	v.	to buy
	はな˥す	話す	v.	to speak
	する		v.	to do
2.	ニューヨ˥ーク		n.	New York
	にほ˥ん	日本	n.	Japan
3.	え˥いが	映画	n.	movie
	ビ˥ール		n.	beer
4.	バ˥ー		n.	bar
	ウイ˥スキー		n.	whiskey
4.4	にほんぶ˥んがく	日本文学	n.	Japanese literature
5.	バ˥ート		n.	BART
	は˥し		n.	chopstick
	すきやき		n.	sukiyaki
	ナ˥イフ		n.	knife
	フォ˥ーク		n.	fork
	ビフテキ		n.	beefsteak
	ひらが˥な		n.	hiragana
	なまえ		n.	name
	か˥く	書く	v.	to write
	ローマ˥じ	ローマ字	n.	Romanized writing
	ボールペン		n.	ball-point pen
6.	あさご˥はん	朝ごはん	n.	breakfast
	コ˥ース		n.	course
	フランスご	フランス語	n.	French (language)
7.	ともだち	友達	n.	friend
	カ˥メラ		n.	camera
	ブック・スト˥アー		n.	book store

第 五 課 （だ￢いご￢か）

5.A.	にちよ￢うび	日曜日	n.	Sunday

5.A. にちよ￢うび　日曜日　n.　Sunday
　　 ゴールデンゲ￢ート　　　n.　Golden Gate
　　 はし￢　橋　n.　bridge
　　 こうえん　公園　n.　park
　　 ふ￢ね　船　n.　boat
　　 き￢れいだ　　an.　beautiful, clean
　　 で￢る　出る　v.　to leave (from)
　　 フィッシャーマンズ　　　n.　Fisherman's Wharf
　　　 ウォ￢ーフ
　　 した￢　下　n.　under
　 B. こちら　　n.　this person (polite)
　　 じゅうにがつ￢　十二月　n.　December
　　 じゅういちがつ￢　十一月　n.　November
　　 ハ￢ワイ　　n.　Hawaii
　　 いっか￢げつ　一か月　n.　one month's time
　　 ホノルル　　n.　Honolulu
　　 はじ￢めて　　n.　the first time
　　 おとうと￢　　n.　younger brother (humble)
　　 きょ￢ねん　　n.　last year
　 1. ばんご￢はん　晩ごはん　n.　dinner
　　 か￢いぎ, かいぎ￢　会議　n.　meeting
　　 しゅくだい　宿題　n.　homework
　　 きの￢う　昨日　n.　yesterday
　　 あそぶ　遊ぶ　v.　to play
　 2. かんじ　漢字　n.　Chinese characters
　 4. あさ￢って　　n.　day after tomorrow
　 5. リ￢ッチモンド　　n.　Richmond
　　 オ￢ークランド　　n.　Oakland
　　 イースト・ベ￢ー　　n.　East Bay
　　 デイリー・シ￢ティー　　n.　Daly City
　　 じっぺ￢ージ　十ページ　n.　ten pages, tenth page
　　 ひこ￢うき　飛行機　n.　airplane
　　 く￢じ　九時　n.　nine o'clock
　　 じゅ￢うじ　十時　n.　ten o'clock
　　 ティーダブリューエ￢ー　T.W.A.　n.　Trans World Airline
　　 げつよ￢うび　月曜日　n.　Monday
　　 きんよ￢うび　金曜日　n.　Friday

く￢がつ	九月	n.	September
ろくがつ￢	六月	n.	June
7. おさけ	お酒	n.	sake (rice wine), liquor
しけ￢ん	試験	n.	examination
8. がっこう	学校	n.	school
つく￢る	作る	v.	to make
すし￢		n.	sushi
ワ￢イン		n.	wine
てんぷら		n.	tempura
おとと￢い		n.	day before yesterday

第 六 課 （だ￢いろ￢っか）

6.A. りっぱだ	立派だ	an.	splendid, excellent
ひろ￢い	広い	a.	spacious, roomy
あかるい	明るい	a.	bright
うるさ￢い		a.	noisy
とき￢	時	n.	when
ルームメ￢ート		n.	roommate
まじめだ		an.	serious, earnest
ひど￢い		a.	terrible
6.B. あ￢さ	朝	n.	morning
し￢ずかだ	静かだ	an.	quiet
ゆうがた	夕方	n.	evening
ま￢え	前	n.	before, in front of
1. にぎ￢やかだ		an.	bustling
だ￢いろ￢っか	第六課	n.	sixth lesson
おもしろ￢い		a.	interesting
むずかしい	難しい	a.	difficult
やす￢い	安い	a.	inexpensive
い￢い		a.	good
2. おいしい		a.	tasty
こども	子供	n.	child
せま￢い		a.	not spacious
3. やさしい		a.	easy, kind
あたらし￢い	新しい	a.	new
ちいさ￢い	小さい	a.	small
ふる￢い	古い	a.	old
たか￢い	高い	a.	expensive, tall

おおき￢い	大きい	a.	big
4. べ￢んりだ	便利だ	an.	useful
おか￢し		n.	candy
まず￢い		a.	not good
5. ハンバ￢ーガー		n.	hamburger
アラビアご	アラビア語	n.	Arabic (language)

第 七 課 （だ￢いなな￢か）

7.A.	ウエ￢ートレス・ウ￢ェートレス		n.	waitress
	レモ￢ン・ティー		n.	lemon tea
	コーヒ￢ー		n.	coffee
B.	ちょ￢っと		adv.	a little
	で￢も		conj.	or something else
	ま￢あまあ		n.	so-so
C.	しょうかいする	紹介する	v.	to introduce
1.	ク￢イズ		n.	quiz
	ふ￢べんだ	不便だ	an.	not useful
2.	め￢	目	n.	eye
	はな	鼻	n.	nose
	みみ￢	耳	n.	ear
	て￢	手	n.	hand
	みせ￢	店	n.	store
	ま￢ど	窓	n.	window
	あし￢	足	n.	leg, foot
3.	ど￢んな		pron.	what kind
	あたま￢	頭	n.	head
	じょうず￢だ	上手だ	an.	skillful
	うた￢	歌	n.	song
	へた￢だ	下手だ	an.	not skillful
	テ￢ニス		n.	tennis
4.	ま￢いにち	毎日	n.	every day
	にく￢	肉	n.	meat
	じゅうじは￢ん	十時半	n.	ten thirty
5.	ど￢れ		pron.	which one
	な￢りた	成田	n.	Narita (airport)
	リ￢ノ		n.	Reno
6.	ペ￢ン		n.	pen

つかう	使う	v.	to use
えꜜ	絵	n.	drawing, painting
かꜜく	描く	v.	to draw
セꜜーター		n.	sweater
7. こꜜんばん	今晩	n.	tonight
アイスクリꜜーム		n.	ice cream
にほꜜんまち	日本町	n.	Japan Town
らいねん	来年	n.	next year
ちゅうかりょꜜうり	中華料理	n.	Chinese cuisine
こんしゅうまつ	今週末	n.	this weekend
ピꜜクニック		n.	picnic
プꜜール		n.	swimming pool
およꜜぐ	泳ぐ	v.	to swim
キꜜップス		n.	Kip's Pizza Parlor
ピꜜザ		n.	pizza
ワインカꜜントリー		n.	Wine Country

第 八 課 （だꜜいはꜜっか）

8.A. きょꜜうだい	兄弟	n.	siblings
なꜜんにん	何人		how many people
かꜜぞく	家族	n.	family
りょꜜうしん	両親	n.	parents
そꜜぼ	祖母	n.	grandmother
おばꜜあさん		n.	grandmother (polite)
めꜜいじ	明治	n.	Meiji period
げꜜんきだ	元気だ	an.	healthy, lively
はꜜ	歯	n.	teeth
しょくじ	食事	n.	meal
じかん	時間	n.	time
かかꜜる		v.	to take, require
B. なꜜんじ	何時		what time
ごꜜご	午後	n.	afternoon, P.M.
なんじꜜかん	何時間		how many hours
ぐꜜらい，ぐらい		n.	about, approximately
チャꜜーター		n.	charter (airplane)
にっこう	日航	n.	Japan Air Lines
おうふく	往復	n.	round trip
せꜜんドル	千ドル	n.	one thousand dollars

ひと˥りで		adv.	by oneself
ガールフレ˥ンド		n.	girlfriend
うめぼし		n.	pickled plum
おくる	送る	v.	to send
1. かみ˥	紙	n.	paper
——まい			(counter) for flat objects
——ほん			(counter) for cylindrica objects
——だい			(counter) for mechanical objects
えんぴつ		n.	pencil
チョ˥ーク		n.	chalk
シ˥ーツ		n.	sheets
まんね˥んひつ	万年筆	n.	fountain pen
タ˥オル		n.	towel
2. おかね	お金	n.	money
3. い˥くら			how much (does it cost)
カタリナ		n.	Catalina Islands
4. てがみ	手紙	n.	letter
5. レコ˥ード		n.	record
きく	聞く	v.	to listen, hear
かいもの	買物	n.	shopping
かす	貸す	v.	to lend
6. いう	言う	v.	to say
つつ˥む	包む	v.	to wrap
7. いそ˥ぐ	急ぐ	v.	to hurry
か˥もしれない		v.	might
9. あ˥め	雨	n.	rain
ふ˥る			to rain, to snow
こ˥んでいる	混んでいる	v.	to be crowded
すいている		v.	to be empty

第九課 （だ˥いきゅう˥か）

9.B. さいきん	最近	n.(adv.)	recently, these days
れ˥いの	例の		that (the one that you know)
ル˥ーツ		n.	Roots
お˥おい	多い	a.	plenty of,
パチンコ		n.	*pachinko*, a pinball game
ティービーガ˥イド	T.V. ガイド	n.	TV Guide
2. す˥む	住む	v.	to live (somewhere)

あく		v.	something opens
おなか		n.	stomach
けっこんする	結婚する	v.	to get married
かりる	借りる	v.	to borrow
3. れんしゅうする	練習する	v.	to practice
ジャ゚ズ		n.	jazz
テ゚ープ		n.	tape
ふくしゅうする	復習する	v.	to review
5. スコ゚ッチ		n.	Scotch
しょうせつ	小説	n.	novel
6. ラ゚ボ			lab
きょ゚うと	京都	n.	Kyoto
ゴールデンゲート ブリッジ		n.	Golden Gate Bridge
7. からて	空手	n.	karate
クリス゚マス		n.	Christmas
8. ノ゚ート		n.	notebook
ざっし	雑誌	n.	magazine
テーブル		n.	table
ケ゚ーキ		n.	cake
9.8. うたう	歌う	v.	to sing

第 十 課 （だ゚いじ゚っか）

10.A. うなぎ		n.	eel
すき゚だ		an.	to like
いちど	一度		once
あまり		adv.	not so much
さしみ゚		n.	sashimi
じょ゚う	上	n.	deluxe, on top
なみ	並	n.	regular
きれ゚る	切れる	v.	to be out of stock, to run out
B. てんいん	店員	n.	clerk
とうきょう	東京	n.	Tokyo
い゚っぽん	一本	n.	one cylindrical object
はや゚い	早い	a.	quick, early
2. パンサムだ		an.	handsome
3. きらいだ		an.	to dislike
うま゚い		a.	good at, tasty

431

ゴ⌐ルフ		n.	golf
にほんふう	日本風	n.	Japanese style
スポ⌐ーツ		n.	sport(s)
4. ゴールデンゲート パ⌐ーク		n.	Golden Gate Park
ちゅ⌐うごく	中国	n.	China
フランス		n.	France
ド⌐イツ		n.	Germany
5. ク⌐ールズ		n.	Coors
コ⌐ーラ		n.	cola
にほんちゃ	日本茶	n.	Japanese tea
ス⌐ープ		n.	soup
7. だ⌐いさ⌐んか	第三課	n.	lesson three
こんしゅう	今週	n.	this week
ことし	今年	n.	this year
8. ご⌐ぜん	午前	n.	morning, A.M.
ヨーロ⌐ッパ		n.	Europe

第十一課 （だ⌐いじゅうい⌐っか）

11.A. こうこう	高校	n.	highschool
ど⌐うして			why
メキシコ⌐じん	メキシコ人	n.	Mexican (person)
ど⌐ちら			which
ず⌐っと		adv.	by far, considerably
B. ちか⌐ごろ		adv.	these days, recently
もち⌐ろん		adv.	of course
ばん	晩	n.	late evening, night
じつ⌐は	実は		(to tell you) the truth
ほんとうは			actually
ホームシ⌐ック		n.	homesick
か⌐れ	彼	n.	he, boyfriend
1. たのし⌐い	楽しい	a.	enjoyable
キャ⌐デラック		n.	Cadillac
ベ⌐ンツ		n.	(Mercedes) Benz
すずし⌐い		a.	cool
おちゃ	お茶	n.	(Japanese) tea
やまの⌐ぼり	山登り	n.	mountain climbing
はや⌐い	速い	a.	fast

432

2. いちばん	一番	adv.	the most
にほんりょ゛うり	日本料理	n.	Japanese cuisine
フランスりょ゛うり	フランス料理	n.	French cuisine
スキ゛ー		n.	ski
ねる	寝る	v.	to sleep, to go to to bed
のんび゛りする		v.	to relax
3. バーボン		n.	Bourbon
パ゛ン		n.	bread
4. おき゛る	起きる	v.	to get up
ちこくする	遅刻する	v.	to be late
あさね゛ぼうする	朝ねぼうする	v.	to oversleep
かぜをひく	風邪を引く		to catch a cold
すうがく	数学	n.	mathematics
アスピリン		n.	aspirin
いた゛い	痛い	a.	painful
じ゛こ	事故	n.	accident
そうじする	掃除する	v.	to clean up (rooms)
おきゃく	お客	n.	guest
5. ゆうびん	郵便	n.	mail
かいわ	会話	n.	conversation
6. わえいじ゛てん	和英辞典	n.	Japanese-English dictionary

第十二課 （だ゛いじゅうに゛か）

12.A. しつ゛れいする	失礼する	v.	to be impolite, excuse oneself
すこ゛し	少し	adv.	a little
ねつ	熱	n.	fever
だ゛す	出す	v.	to turn in
それと゛も		conj.	or
しんぱいする	心配する	v.	to worry
らいしゅう	来週	n.	next week
できるだけ		a.	as much as possible
やる		v.	to do
む゛りをする	無理をする		to over do (work)
B. いろんな			various
じびき゛をひく	字引をひく		to look up something in a dictionary
サンスクリットご	サンスクリット語	n.	Sanskrit
いちにち゛	一日	n.	a day

すくな￢くとも	少なくとも		at least
ときどき	時々	adv.	sometimes
1. サンドイッチ		n.	sandwich
ふるほん	古本	n.	used book
2. たばこをす￢う	たばこを吸う		to smoke (cigarettes)
でんわ	電話	n.	telephone
3. (〜に)で￢る	出る	v.	to attend
4. タ￢イプする		v.	to type
4. シャ￢ワーをあびる	シャワーを浴びる		to take a shower
5. かたづけ￢る	片付ける	v.	to straighten up
ある￢く	歩く	v.	to walk
おぼえる	覚える	v.	to memorize
ご￢はん		n.	meal
うんてんする	運転する	v.	to drive
6. たまに		adv.	occasionally
め￢ったに		adv.	rarely
じゅ￢ぎょう	授業	n.	class
さむ￢い	寒い	a.	cold, chilly
ほと￢んど		adv.	almost, hardly
い￢つも		adv.	always
たべ￢もの	食べ物	n.	food, something to eat
ぜんぜん	全然	adv.	never

第十三課　（だ￢いじゅうさ￢んか）

13. A. しち￢にんのさむらい	七人の侍	n.	seven *samurai*
ま￢だ		adv.	not yet
ボーイフレ￢ンド		n.	boyfriend
いっしょに	一緒に	adv.	together
じだ￢いげき	時代劇	n.	samurai films, play with historical setting
ざと￢ういち	座頭市	n.	Zatoichi
B. ぶんげいしゅ￢んじゅう	文芸春秋	n.	*Bungeishunju* (magazine title)
にがつ￢ごう	二月号	n.	Febuary issue
ほし￢い		a.	to want
に￢さつ	二冊	n.	two copies
1. やっぱ￢り		adv.	after all
けいさ￢んき	計算器	n.	calculator

えいわじ⌐てん	英和辞典	n.	English-Japanese dictionary
かんわじ⌐てん	漢和辞典	n.	*Kanji* dictionary
2. もの⌐		n.	thing
ところ		n.	place
こと⌐		n.	thing, matter
なら⌐う	習う	v.	to learn
しゅうまつ	週末	n.	weekend
ステレオ		n.	stereo
3. ぜ⌐ひ		adv.	by all means
4. じて⌐んしゃ	自転車	n.	bicycle
5. パ⌐ーティー		n.	party
コ⌐ンサート		n.	concert
かいがん	海岸	n.	beach
ディズニーラ⌐ンド		n.	Disneyland
6. えは⌐がき	絵葉書	n.	picture postcard
セ⌐ント		n.	cent
ビッグマ⌐ック		n.	Big Mac

第十四課　（だ⌐いじゅうよ⌐んか）

14.A. ノースダ⌐コタ		n.	North Dakota
ほっか⌐いどう	北海道	n.	Hokkaido
ふゆ⌐	冬	n.	winter
しる	知る	v.	to know
れ⌐いか	零下	n.	below zero
さんじゅ⌐うど	三十度	n.	thirty degrees
ゆき⌐	雪	n.	snow
ふか⌐い	深い	a.	deep
で⌐はいりする	出入りする	v.	to go in and out
た⌐ぶん	多分	adv.	probably
B. あたたか⌐い	暖かい	a.	warm
あたた⌐かさ	暖かさ	n.	warmth
だいたい	大体	adv.	generally
おなじ	同じ		same
1. イタリアご	イタリア語	n.	Italian (language)
スモ⌐ッグ		n.	smog
ミ⌐シガン		n.	Michigan
ト⌐ヨタ		n.	Toyota (car)

	ニッサン			Nissan (car)
2.	ロシアご	ロシア語	n.	Russian (language)
	ハ⌐イニケン		n.	Heineken (beer)
	カリフォルニア		n.	California
	ほ⌐んしゅう	本州	n.	Honshu
3.	(〜に)のる	(〜に)乗る	v.	to ride
	(〜に)あ⌐う	(〜に)会う	v.	to meet, see
4.	スーツケ⌐ース		n.	suitcase
	ラ⌐ジオ		n.	radio
	デ⌐ートする		v.	to date
	め⌐がねをかけ⌐る			to put on eye glasses
	(でんわを)かけ⌐る		v.	to make a phone call
	ホ⌐ンコン		n.	Hong Kong
	(〜に)つ⌐く	着く	v.	to arrive
5.	ま⌐いあさ	毎朝	n.	every morning
	しごと	仕事	n.	work
	さがす	探す	v.	to look for
	せんたくする	洗濯する	v.	to wash, to do the laundry
	おや⌐	親	n.	parent(s)
	ろんぶん	論文	n.	thesis, term paper
	こうがい	公害	n.	pollution
	もんだい	問題	n.	problem
	かんがえ⌐る	考える	v.	to think
	か⌐えす	返す	v.	to return (something)
	エネ⌐ルギー		n.	energy
6.	とおい	遠い	a.	far
	やす⌐む	休む	v.	to rest
	(〜が)わか⌐る	分かる	v.	to understand
	ごかい	五階	adv.	fifth floor
	すてる	捨てる	v.	to throw away
	うご⌐く	動く	v.	(something) moves
	きたな⌐い		a.	dirty
	かきなおす	書きなおす	v.	to rewrite
14.6.	きる	着る	v.	to wear
	(〜に)きく	(〜に)聞く	v.	to ask
	わる⌐い		a.	bad
	やめる		v.	to quit

436

第十五課　（だ￢いじゅうご￢か）

15.A.	たんご	単語	n.	word, vocabulary
	い￢み	意味	n.	meaning
	さ￢んびゃく	三百	n.	three hundred
	だけ			only
	ミスプリ￢ント		n.	misprint
B.	えいか￢いわ	英会話	n.	English conversation
	カンパニ￢ーレ		n.	Campanile
	あがる	上がる	v.	to climb, rise
	いる		v.	to need
2.	でかける	出かける	v.	to go out
	きって	切手	n.	stamp
4.	はたらく	働く	v.	to work, labor
	ひるね	昼寝	n.	nap
	りょこうする	旅行する	v.	to travel
	マ￢スターする		v.	to master
	ビジネススク￢ール		n.	business school
	（〜に）は￢いる	（〜に）入る	v.	to enter
	ワシ￢ントン		n.	Washington
5.	おふ￢ろ	お風呂	n.	Japanese bath
6.	よみかた	読み方	n.	way of reading
	パ￢ラグラフ		n.	paragraph

第十六課　（だ￢いじゅうろ￢っか）

16.A.	かおいろ	顔色	n.	complexion, color
	（〜に）ぬれる		v.	to get wet
	くすり	薬	n.	medicine
	びょういん	病院	n.	hospital
	きく	効く	v.	to work, be effective
	ちっと￢も		adv.	not at all
	いしゃ	医者	n.	doctor, physician
B.	うわぎ	上着	n.	overcoat jacket
	い￢き	息	n.	breath
1.	みんな￢	皆	n.	everyone
	だめ￢だ		an.	no good
	ひょうばん	評判	n.	reputation

つづく	続く	v.	to continue
たいへん	大変	adv.	very much
つかれ⌐る	疲れる	v.	to be fatigued, tired
2. ねむる		v.	to sleep
も⌐つ	持つ	v.	to hold
サ⌐ービス		n.	service
だいすきだ	大好きだ	an.	to like a lot
3. よしゅう	予習	n.	preparation
バスケットボ⌐ール		n.	basketball
4. パ⌐イ		n.	pie
か⌐のじょ	彼女	n.	her, girlfriend
5. オニ⌐ール		n.	O'Neil ('s character dictionary)
お⌐んがく	音楽	n.	music
さびし⌐い		a.	lonely
しらべ⌐る	調べる	v.	to investigate, to look into
ねむい		a.	sleepy
アイスコ⌐ーヒー		n.	ice coffee
あつ⌐い		a.	hot
6. こし	腰	n.	lower back, loin, hips

第十七課　(だ⌐いじゅうなな⌐か)

17.A. ばくち		n.	gamble
りこん	離婚	n.	divorce
ギャ⌐ンブル		n.	gamble
か⌐つ	勝つ	v.	to win
ふた⌐ばん	二晩		two nights
ブラックジャ⌐ック		n.	blackjack
B. ざお⌐う	蔵王	n.	Zao
しろうま	白馬	n.	Shirouma
スキーじょう	スキー場	n.	ski resort
ふゆや⌐すみ	冬休み	n.	winter vacation
スコーバ⌐レー		n.	Squaw Valley
1. コ⌐ート		n.	coat
て⌐んき	天気	n.	weather
いちにちじゅう	一日中	adv.	all day long
や⌐ちん	家賃	n.	rent
やくそく	約束	n.	promise
2. まける	負ける	v.	to lose

つかいかた	使い方	n.	way of using
ぶんぽう	文法	n.	grammar
3. おくれる	遅れる	v.	to be late
ジョギング		n.	jogging
はし⌐る	走る	v.	to run
グレイド		n.	grade
ポ⌐ルシェ		n.	Porsche (car)
4. さんぽをする	散歩をする		to take a walk
なつや⌐すみ	夏休み	n.	Summer vacation
アルバ⌐イト		n.	part-time job
しばい	芝居	n.	play, drama
ターム・ペ⌐ーパー		n.	term paper
せんしゅ⌐うまつ	先週末	n.	last weekend
5. き⌐んかくじ	金閣寺	n.	Temple of the Golden Pavilion
6. こうぎ	講義	n.	lecture
アイ・ビ・ー・エ⌐ム		n.	I.B.M.
セレ⌐クトリック		n.	selectric
ホ⌐ンダ・シ⌐ビック		n.	Honda Civic
くつ⌐をはく			to put on shoes
7, ベ⌐ッド		n.	bed
はら⌐う		v.	to pay
レポート		n.	report
みがく		v.	to shine, to brush

第十八課　（だ⌐いじゅうは⌐っか）

18.A. ラ⌐グビー		n.	rugby
しあい	試合	n.	match, game
つよ⌐い	強い	a.	strong
あいて⌐	相手	n.	opponent
サンノゼ		n.	San Jose
B. ピアノをひく			to play the piano
とくいだ	得意だ	an.	forte, be good at
い⌐つか			sometime
まちが⌐い	間違い	n.	mistake
バ⌐イエル		n.	Beyer (piano primer)
にがてだ	苦手だ	an.	not good at
だ⌐いいち	第一	adv.	in the first place
おんぷ	音符	n.	musical note

	す￢ぐ		adv.	right away
	しめ￢る	閉める	v.	to close
1.	バンカメリカ￢ード		n.	Bank of America Card
	うけ￢る	受ける	v.	to take
	きょうしつ	教室	n.	classroom
	ま￢でに			by (three o'clock)
	おしえる	教える	v.	to teach
2.	そつぎょうする	卒業する	v.	to graduate
	ス￢ーツ		n.	suit
	けんきゅ￢うしつ	研究室	n.	(professor's) office
3.	も￢ってくる	持って来る	v.	to bring
	コ￢ピーする		v.	to copy
	しつもんする	質問する	v.	to ask (a) question('s)
	セ￢ミナー		n.	seminar
5.	クラシ￢ック		n.	classic

第十九課　（だ￢いじゅうきゅ￢うか）

19.A.	さっぽろ	札幌	n.	Sapporo
	よやく	予約	n.	reservation
	ぜんにっ￢くう	全日空	n.	All Japan Airlines
	きり	霧	n.	fog
	けっこう	欠航	n.	no flights
	てんきよ￢ほう	天気予報	n.	weather report
	あたる	当たる	v.	to be accurate
B.	よてい	予定	n.	plan
	へ￢んだ	変だ	an.	strange, bad, weird
	あげる		v.	to deep fry
	おまじない		n.	incantation
	さんべん	三遍	adv.	three times
2.	うつくし￢い	美しい	a.	beautiful
	いそがし￢い	忙しい	a.	busy
	なが￢さき	長崎	n.	Nagasaki
	あぶない		a.	dangerous
3.	そ￢ら	空	n.	sky
	かべ		n.	wall
19.3.	こおり	氷	n.	ice
	ガソリン		n.	gasoline
4.	ニュ￢ース		n.	news

はなし⌐	話	n.	story, talk
せきゆ	石油	n.	petroleum
ニューズウィ⌐ーク		n.	Newsweek
プ⌐ラン		n.	plan

5.
おそい	遅い	a.	late, slow
さかな	魚	n.	fish
かぜ	風	n.	wind
け⌐さ	今朝	n.	this morning
おと⌐す	落とす	v.	to lose, to drop
びょうき	病気	n.	sickness
じぶん	自分	n.	self
ちょきん	貯金	n.	saving(s)
つづける	続ける	v.	to continue

第二十課　（だ⌐いにじ⌐っか）

20.A.
おいわい	お祝い	n.	present, celebration
もらう		v.	to receive
こうすい	香水	n.	perfume
ネームいり	ネーム入り	n.	engraved with one's name
うでど⌐けい	腕時計	n.	wrist watch
じど⌐うしゃ	自動車	n.	automobile
ず⌐いぶん		adv.	a lot, considerably, very
ちがう	違う	v.	to be different, wrong
しんじゅ	真珠	n.	pearl
くれる		v.	to give (me)
よろこ⌐ぶ	喜ぶ	v.	to be pleased (with)
はこ	箱	n.	box
おこ⌐る		v.	to get angry

B.
さかなや	魚屋	n.	fish market
えび		n.	prawn
か⌐い		n.	clam
も⌐っと		adv.	more
い⌐くつ			how many
ず⌐つ			of each
おねがい	お願い	n.	request
まいど	毎度		every time

1.
いただく		v.	to receive (humble)
ち⌐ず	地図	n.	map

441

2. くださ⌐る		v.	to give (me) (hororific)
おんが⌐くかい	音楽会	n.	concert
きっぷ		n.	ticket
3. ハンドア⌐ウト		n.	handout
リ⌐スト		n.	list
あげる		v.	to give
さしあげる		v.	to give (humble)
4. ピ⌐ーナツ		n.	peanut(s)
5. ポ⌐スター		n.	poster
カ⌐ード		n.	card
ペ⌐ンダント		n.	pendant
6. ——てん	——点		(counter) point
あつま⌐る	集まる	v.	to assemble, gather
7. くらい	暗い	a.	dark
みじか⌐い	短い	a.	short
おもい	重い	a.	heavy

第二十一課　（だ⌐いにじゅうい⌐っか）

21.A. きゅ⌐うしゅう	九州	n.	Kyushu
つぎ⌐	次	n.	next
やすみ⌐	休み	n.	holiday, vacation
い⌐まり	伊万里	n.	Imari
しんか⌐んせん	新幹線	n.	New Trunk Line ("bullet train")
いっぱい		n.	full, (booked, as in reservations)
あんな⌐いする	案内する	v.	to guide
さが⌐けん	佐賀県	n.	Saga prefecture
B. じゅ⌐んび	準備	n.	preparation
このあいだ	この間	n.	awhile ago
こ⌐んど	今度	n.	this (time), next (time)
〜につ⌐いて			about (something)
しょうかいじょう	紹介状	n.	letter of introduction
おみやげ		n.	souvenir, gift
たいへんだ	大変だ	an.	terrible
1. せつめいする	説明する	v.	to explain
タ⌐イプをう⌐つ	タイプを打つ	v.	to type
2. ことば⌐	言葉	n.	word
4. じ⌐	字	n.	letter (character)
じゅ⌐うしょ	住所	n.	address

チェ￢ックする		v.	to check
ぶ￢ん	文	n.	sentence
もういちど	もう一度	adv.	again
スペ￢ル		n.	spell
5. はっき￢り		adv.	clearly
きめる	決める	v.	to decide
6. ねだん	値段	n.	price
らいが￢っき	来学期	n.	next semester
しめきり		n.	deadline
7. ——びん	——便	n.	(counter) for flights

第二十二課　（だ￢いにじゅうに￢か）

22.A. ちょうこく	彫刻	n.	sculpture
りゅうぼく	流木	n.	driftwood
タイヤ		n.	tire
りゅ￢う	竜	n.	dragon
みぎ	右	n.	right
ピラミ￢ッド		n.	Pyramid
かたち	形	n.	shape
スフィ￢ンクス		n.	Sphinx
かっこう		n.	appearance
ようじ	用事	n.	business, errands
す￢む	済む	v.	to end, complete
あ￢と	後	n.	after
B. スターウォ￢ーズ		n.	Star Wars
か￢がく	科学	n.	Science (fiction)
えいがか	映画化	n.	film adaptation
ラーメン		n.	*ramen*
にお￢い		n.	smell, scent
のび￢る		v.	to get soggy, stretch out
1. おべんとう	お弁当	n.	lunch
ネ￢クタイ		n.	(neck) tie
こ	子	n.	child
かなしい	悲しい	a.	sad
あまい	甘い	a.	sweet
かんたんだ	簡単だ	an.	simple, easy
チ￢ーム		n.	team
ひるま	昼間	n.	daytime

443

2.	やむ	止む	v.	(something) stops
	にほんせい	日本製	n.	made in Japan
3.	めいし	名刺	n.	namecard
	バーベ⌐キュー		n.	barbecue
	オレ⌐ンジ		n.	orange
	スパゲ⌐ッティ		n.	spaghetti
4.	にわ	庭	n.	yard
	あける	開ける	v.	to open
	と	戸	n.	door
	スト⌐ーブ		n.	stove, space heater
	ひ⌐	火	n.	fire
4.	つけ⌐る		v.	to turn on (lights, etc.)
	で⌐んき	電気	n.	electric light
	けす	消す	v.	to turn off
	よ⌐うい	用意する	v.	to prepare
	ひや⌐す	冷やす	v.	to cool
	フットボ⌐ール		n.	football
5.	そうだんする	相談する	v.	to consult
6.	さめ⌐る		v.	to get cold

第二十三課　(だ⌐いにじゅうさ」んか)

23.A.	ワイシャツ		n.	dress shirt
	デパ⌐ート		n.	department store
	いせたん	伊勢丹	n.	Isetan (dept. store)
	ちかてつ	地下鉄	n.	subway
	ひまだ		an.	free (not working), not busy
	サボ⌐る		v.	to cut (class)
B.	シャ⌐ツ		n.	shirt
	みせ⌐る	見せる	v.	to show
	あらう	洗う	v.	to wash
	ばあい	場合	n.	situation, circumstance
	りょうごく	両国	n.	Ryoogoku
	あ⌐たり		n.	around
1.	は⌐る	春	n.	spring
	さくら	桜	n.	cherry blossom
	さく	咲く	v.	to bloom
	ジ⌐ーンズ		n.	jeans
	なつ⌐	夏	n.	summer

444

なお￢る	直る	v.	to be fixed, to get better
たす		v.	to add
ひく		v.	to subtract
よくじつ	翌日	n.	the next day
2. とり	鳥	n.	bird
とぶ	飛ぶ	v.	to fly, jump
ま￢つ	待つ	v.	to wait
ド￢ア		n.	door
で￢んしゃ	電車	n.	train
え￢き	駅	n.	station
おり￢る	降りる	v.	to get off
た￢つ	立つ	v.	to stand
れいぞ￢うこ	冷蔵庫	n.	refrigerator
3. から￢い	辛い	a.	spicy, hot
なが￢い	長い	a.	long
4. (お)に￢く	(お)肉	n.	meat
かたい		a.	tough
キ￢ムチ		n.	kimchee (Korean pickles)
いちね￢んせい	一年生	n.	first year student
ほうそう	放送	n.	broadcast
5. きゅうこう	急行	n.	express
なく	泣く	v.	to cry
けんかする		n.	to fight, argue
ゆうべ		n.	last night
からか￢う		v.	to tease
に￢こにこする		v.	smile, look happy

第二十四課　（だ￢いにじゅうよ￢んか）

24.A. まんかい	満開	n.	in full bloom
げしゅく	下宿	n.	boarding house
おばさん		n.	middle aged woman
さくら￢もち	桜もち	n.	*sakuramochi*
でき￢る		v.	to be made
こむぎこ	小麦粉	n.	wheat flour
あ￢ん		n.	bean filling
やく	焼く	v.	to bake
くわし￢い	詳しい	a.	detailed

445

は	葉	n.	leaf
いか⌐にも		adv.	really
B. しょうちゅ⌐う	焼酎	n.	*shochu*
あじ	味	n.	taste
おきなわ	沖縄	n.	Okinawa
さつまいも		n.	sweet potato
けっきょく	結局	adv.	after all
いも⌐		n.	potato
びょ⌐う	秒	n.	(counter) second
ボーッとする		v.	to be fuzzy, out of it
1. ひ	日	n.	day
だいと⌐うりょう	大統領	n.	president (of a country)
がくしゃ	学者	n.	scholar
タ⌐コ		n.	taco (spanish)
ナポレオン		n.	Napoleon
ブラ⌐ンデー		n.	Brandy
フィ⌐アット		n.	Fiat
2. こめ⌐	米	n.	rice
かんこくご	韓国語	n.	Korean (language)
ひと⌐り		n.	single, bachelor
かよう	通う	v.	to commute
3. だいず	大豆	n.	soybean
(お)せ⌐んべい		n.	rice cracker
あず(づ)き		n.	*azuki*
み⌐そ		n.	miso (soybean paste)
チ⌐ーズ		n.	cheese
ぎゅうにゅう	牛乳	n.	milk
ミルクセ⌐ーキ		n.	milkshake
テキ⌐ーラ		n.	Tequila
ウォ⌐ッカ		n.	Vodka
4. ゆうご⌐はん	夕ごはん	n.	dinner

第二十五課 （だ⌐いにじゅうご⌐か）

25.A. ため⌐いきをつ⌐く	ため息をつく		to sigh
よわ⌐い	弱い	a.	weak
ご⌐い	語彙	n.	vocabulary
と⌐くに	特に	adv.	especially
えいえいじ⌐てん	英英辞典	n.	English-English dictionary

446

B.	かわる	変わる	v.	(something) changes
	わすれる	忘れる	v.	to forget
	たりる	足りる	v.	to be enough
1.	かんこ⌐うきゃく	観光客	n.	tourist
	こわ⌐す		v.	to break
	まんいん	満員	n.	to be full of people
2.	しょうがくきん	奨学金	n.	scholarship
	いえ⌐	家	n.	house
	つめたい		a.	cold (not weather)
3.	やさい	野菜	n.	vegetable
4.	お⌐おきな	大きな		big
	こ⌐え	声	n.	voice
	い⌐っぱい		n.	a cup of
5.	よ⌐る	夜	n.	night
	げんき⌐ん	現金	n.	cash, ready money
	たいせつだ	大切だ	an.	important
	メ⌐モをと⌐る			to take a memo
	ぎゅうにく	牛肉	n.	beef
	ポ⌐ンド		n.	pound
	タホ⌐こ	タホ湖	n.	Lake Tahoe
	ホ⌐テル		n.	hotel
	ピストル		n.	pistol
7.	こたえ⌐る	答える	v.	to respond, answer

第二十六課　（だ⌐いにじゅうろ⌐っか）

26.A.	び⌐っこをひく			to limp
	か⌐む		v.	to bite
	お⌐くさん	奥さん	n.	wife
	げ⌐んかん	玄関	n.	entrance
	こじあける		v.	to pry, force open
	たの⌐む		v.	to request
	かぎ⌐		n.	key
	おきわすれ⌐る	置き忘れる	v.	to misplace
	ねじま⌐わし	ねじ回し	n.	screw-driver
	いっしょうけ⌐んめい	一生懸命	adv.	with all one's effort
	おいしゃさん	お医者さん	n.	doctor, physician
	ペニシリン		n.	penicillin
	だいじょ⌐うぶ	大丈夫	n.	all right, fine

	とんだ			awful, shocking
	さいな⌐ん	災難	n.	misfortune, disaster
B.	しょうが⌐っこう	小学校	n.	elementary school
	クレジットカ⌐ード		n.	credit card
	ぜ⌐んぶ	全部	adv.	all
	す⌐る		v.	to pickpocket
	と⌐にかく		adv.	anyway, anyhow
	ところ⌐が		conj.	however, nevertheless
	ぼ⌐く	僕	n.	I (for male)
1.	よぶ	呼ぶ	v.	to call
	しかる		v.	to scold
	おこ⌐す	起こす	v.	to wake up
	しょ⌐うたいする	招待する	v.	to invite
	ころす	殺す	v.	to kill
	たお⌐す	倒す	v.	to knock over, down
	わらう	笑う	v.	to laugh
	ねずみ		n.	rat, mouse
	あいす⌐る	愛する	v.	to love
	がくせいた⌐ち	学生達	n.	students
	そんけいする	尊敬する	v.	to respect
	ことり	小鳥	n.	small bird
	ひはんする	批判する	v.	to criticize
	ひにく	皮肉	n.	sarcastic remarks
	はんたいする	反対する	v.	to oppose
2.	しぬ	死ぬ	v.	to die
	にっき	日記	n.	diary
	まちがえ⌐る		v.	to make a mistake
	ガラス		n.	glass
	はつおん	発音	n.	pronunciation
	よごす		v.	to soil
	き⌐んぎょ	金魚	n.	goldfish
	ふむ	踏む	v.	to step on
3.	ほんやくする	翻訳する	v.	to translate
	たすけ⌐る	助ける	v.	to help
4.	コンタクトレ⌐ンズ		n.	contact lens
	さいふ		n.	wallet
5.	ミ⌐ルク		n.	milk
	だいがく⌐いん	大学院	n.	graduate school
6.	ちゅうもんする	注文する	v.	to order

448

第二十七課　（だ¬いにじゅうなな¬か）

27.A.	こうつうこ¬うしゃ	交通公社	n.	Japan Travel Bureau
	しゅうゆ¬うけん	周遊券	n.	excursion ticket
	ユ¬ース		n.	youth hostel
	とまる	泊まる	v.	to stay at
	もんげ¬ん	門限	n.	curfew
	だ¬んじょべつべつ	男女別別	n.	men and women separate
	せいげ¬ん	制限	n.	restriction
	たびたび		adv.	often, repeatedly
	おごる		v.	to treat
B.	もくてき¬ち	目的地	n.	destination
	——か¬しょ	——か所		places
	おいでにな¬る		v.	to come (polite)
	ふつう	普通	n.	regular
	いち¬わり	一割	n.	10%
	してい	指定	n.	designation
	ばしょ	場所	n.	place
	い¬じょう	以上		more than
	まわる	回る	v.	to visit, go around to
	しゅっぱ¬つち	出発地	n.	starting point
	もど¬る		v.	to return
	ジェイアール	ＪＲ	n.	Japan Railroad
	キ¬ロ		n.	(counter) kilometer
	りようする	利用する	v.	to make use of
	はかた	博多	n.	Hakata
	かたみち	片道	n.	one-way
	しゅうゆ¬うち	周遊地	n.	excursion place
	か¬らつ	唐津	n.	Karatsu
	ファーア¬ウト			far out!
1.	パーセ¬ント		n.	percent
2.	ゆっく¬り		adv.	slowly
3.	チェックブ¬ック		n.	checkbook
	にゅういんする	入院する	v.	to be admitted to a hospital
	い	胃	n.	stomach
4.	やく¬にた¬つ	役にたつ		to be of use
5.	しんらいする	信頼する	v.	to trust

第二十八課　（に⌐じゅうは⌐っか）

28.A. むすめ⌐　　　　　　娘　　　　　n.　daughter
　　おせ⌐わ　　　　　　お世話　　　n.　to be indebted to (for many favors)

　　おじょ⌐うさま　　　お嬢様　　　n.　(your) daughter (polite)
　　ごめ⌐いわく　　　　御迷惑　　　n.　trouble
　　(め⌐いわくを)かけ⌐る　　　　　　v.　to cause trouble
　　すえ　　　　　　　　末　　　　　n.　the youngest
　　むすこ　　　　　　　息子　　　　n.　(my) son
　　あ⌐せ　　　　　　　汗　　　　　n.　sweat
　　なが⌐す　　　　　　流す　　　　v.　to shed (tears), to sweat
　　あずか⌐る　　　　　預かる　　　v.　to leave in someone's care
　　に⌐もつ　　　　　　荷物　　　　n.　luggage
　　び⌐ん　　　　　　　便　　　　　n.　(counter) the scheduled train (plane)

　B. しえき　　　　　　　使役　　　　n.　causitive
　　ちゅうが⌐っこう　　中学校　　　n.　high school
　　ふ⌐だん　　　　　　普段　　　　　　usually
1.　けいかく　　　　　　計画　　　　n.　plan
　　ゆうしょく　　　　　夕食　　　　n.　evening meal
3.　わかれ⌐る　　　　　別れる　　　v.　to part
4.　さんかする　　　　　参加する　　v.　to participate
　　ちゅうごくりょ⌐うり　中国料理　n.　Chinese cuisine
　　ごちそうする　　　　　　　　　　v.　to treat
　　しゅっせきする　　　出席する　　v.　to attend
　　がっか⌐りする　　　　　　　　　v.　to regret
　　こま⌐る　　　　　　困る　　　　v.　to be troubled

450

A Unified Vocabulary List (The numbers refer to lessons)

あ

アイスクリーム	ice cream　7
あいする　（愛する）　Nを・・・	to love　26
あいて　（相手）	opponent, opposing team　18
アイビーエム	IBM　17
あう　（会う）　Nに／と・・・	to meet (with), to see　14
あおい　（青い）	blue
あかい　（赤い）	red　19
あかちゅん　（赤ちゅん）	baby　13
あがる　（上がる）　Nに・・・	to ascend, to climb　15
あかるい　（明るい）	bright　6
あく　（開く）　Nが・・・	open, be opened (intrans.)　9
あける　（開ける）　Nを・・・	to open (trans.)　22
あげる　Nを・・・	to deep-fry　19
あげる　NにNを・・・	to give (something) to (someone)　20
あさ　（朝）	morning　6
あさごはん　（朝御飯）	breakfast　4
あさねぼう（を)する　（朝・・・）	to oversleep　11
あじ　（味）	flavor, taste　24
あじがする	to have flavor
あした　（明日）	tomorrow　4
あずかる　（預かる）	to be entrusted with　28
あずき	azuki beans　24
アスピリン	aspirin　11
あせ　（汗）	perspiration　28
あせをかく	to perspire
あそこ	that place　3
あそぶ　（遊ぶ）	to frolic, to play　5
あたたかい　（暖かい）	warm　14
あたたかさ	warmth　14
あたま　（頭）	head　7
あたまがいい	to have a good head, to be smart
あたらしい　（新しい）	new　6
あたり	around　23
あたる　（当たる）　Nが・・・	to be accurate　19

あたる　Nに・・・	to get hit by N
あつい　（暑い）	hot　16
アップルパイ	apple pie
あつまる　（集まる）	gather (intr.)　20
あと　（後）	after　22
あに　（兄）	older brother (self)　3
あね　（姉）	older sister (self)　3
アパート	apartment　2
あびる　（浴びる）　Nを・・・	to take (a shower)　12
シャワーをあびる	
あぶない	dangerous　19
あまい　（甘い）	sweet　22
あまり　　　・・・ない	(not) often, (not) much　10
・・・	
あめ　（雨）	rain　8
アメリカ	America
アメリカじん　（・・・人）	American
あらう　（洗う）　Nを・・・	to wash　23
アラビア語　（・・・語）	Arabic　6
ある　NがNに・・・	to exist　3
NがNで・・・	
あるく　（歩く）　Nを・・・	to walk　12
あるいて来る／行く	to come/go on foot
アルバイト	part-time work　17
アルファベット	alphabet　3
あれ	that　2
あん	sweet bean paste　24
あんないする　（案内する）　Nを・・・	to guide, to show arond　21

い

い(胃)	stomach　27
いい	good, alright　6
イースト・ベイ	East Bay　5
いう　（言う）　Nに　「　」と・・・	to say　8
いえ(家)	house　25
いき　（息）	breath　16
いきをする	to breathe
いき　（行き）　N・・・	bound (for N)
いく　（行く）　Nへ・・・	to go　4
Nに・・・	

452

いくつ	how many　20
いくら	how much　8
いけない	no good
いじめる　Nを・・・	to bully, to tease
いしゃ　（医者）	physician　26
いせたん　（伊勢丹）	Isetan　23
いそがしい　（忙しい）	busy　19
いそぐ　（急ぐ）	to hurry　8
いたい　（痛い）	painful　11
いただく　NにNを・・・	to receive　20
イタリア	Italy　14
いちにち　（一日）	a day　12
いちにちじゅう　（一日中）	all day long　17
いちばん　（一番）	the most　11
いつか	sometime　18
いっしょに　（一緒に）　Nと・・・	together　13
いっしょうけんめい　（に）　（一生懸命）	with all one's energy　26
いってくる　（行って来る）　Nへ／に・・・	to go and come back
いっぱい	full　21
いぬ　（犬）	dog　3
いびき	snore
いびきをかく	to snore
いま　（今）	now
いまのところ　（今・・・）	for now, for the time being
いまり　（伊万里）	Imari　21
いみ　（意味）	meaning　15
いも	potato　24
いもうと　（妹）	younger sister (self)　3
イヤリング	earring
いらっしゃる　　　　Nに・・・	to be　3
Nへ／に・・・	to come
Nへ／に・・・	to go
いる　　　NがNに・・・	to be, to stay　3
いる　　　Nに（は）Nが・・・	to be necessary　15
いろいろ	various　12
いろんな　　　　＝いろいろな	

う

ウイスキー	whiskey　4
うえ　（上）	top, above　3

\,

ウエイトレス	waitress 7
ウェスタン	Western
ウォッカ	vodka 24
うかる（受かる） Nに・・・	to pass, succeed in an examination 24
うける （受ける） Nを・・・	to take (an exam or class) 18
うごく （動く） Nが・・・	to move 14
うた （歌）	song 7
うたう （歌う）	to sing 9
うち	home 3
うつ （打つ） Nを・・・	to hit, to shoot
うでどけい （腕時計）	wristwatch 20
うどん	noodles
うなぎ	eel 10
うまい Nが・・・	to be good at 10
うまく	well
うまれ （生まれ） N・・・	birthplace
うまれる （生まれる）	to be born
うめぼし （梅干し）	pickled plum
うるさい	noisy, bothersome 6
うれしい	happy
うわぎ （上着）	jacket 16
うんてん	drive
うんてんする （運転する） Nを・・・	to drive 12
うんどう （運動）	exercise
うんどうする （運動する）	to exercise

え

え （絵）	picture, painting 7
えいえいじてん （英英辞典）	English dictionary 25
えいが （映画）	movie 4
えいかいわ （英会話）	English conversation 15
えいご （英語）	English 4
えいわじてん （英和辞典）	English-Japanese dictionary 13
えき （駅）	station 23
エネルギー	energy 14
えはがき （絵葉書）	picture postcard 13
えび	shrimp 20
えんぴつ	pencil 8

お

おいしい	delicious 6
おいでになる	be, come, go (polite) 27
おいわい （お祝い）	gift, present 20
おうふく （往復）	round trip 8
おおい （多い）	much, many 9
おおきい （大きい）	big 6
オークランド	Oakland 5
おおぜい （大勢）	many people 3
おかあさん （お母さん）	mother (other)
おかし （お菓子）	confection 6
（お）かね （お金）	money 8
おきなわ （沖）	Okinawa 24
（お）きゅく （お客）	guest, customer 11
おきゃくさま （お客様）	
おきる （起きる） Nが・・・	to wake up 11
おくさん （奥さん）	wife (other) 26
おくる （送る） Nを・・・	to send 8
Nを・・・	to take home
おくれる （遅れる） Nに・・・	to be late 17
おこす （起こす） Nを・・・	to awaken 26
（お）こめ （お米）	rice 24
おこる （怒る） Nが・・・	to get angry 20
おごる	to treat 27
（お）さけ （お酒）	rice wine, alcohol 5
（お）さら （お皿）	plate
おじいさん	grandfather (other) 3
おしえる （教える） NにNを・・・	to teach 18
おじょうさま （お嬢様）	daughter (other) 28
（お）すし	sushi
（お）せわになる （お世話になる） Nに／の・・・	to be cared for 28
おそい （遅い）	late, slow 19
（お）ちゃ （お茶）	green tea 11
（お）てんき （お天気）	weather
おとうさん （お父さん）	father (other) 3
おとうと （弟）	younger brother (self) 5
おとこ （男）	male person 2
おとこのひと （男の人）	
おとす （落とす） Nを・・・	to lose, to drop 19
おととい	day before yesterday 5

おなか	stomach 9
おなじ （同じ） Ｎと・・・	the same 14
おねがい （お願い）	request, favor 20
おねがいする （お願いする） ＮにＮ（のこと）を・・・	to ask a favor
（お）にく （お肉）	meat 23
おばあさん	grandmother (other) 8
おばさん	aunt (other) 24
オフィス	office 3
（お）ふろ （お風呂）	bath 15
おふろにはいる	to take a bath
（お）べんとう （お弁当）	lunch box 22
おぼえる （覚える） Ｎを・・・	to remember 12
おまじない	incantation 19
おみやげ	souvenir, gift 21
おもい （重い）	heavy 20
おもう （思う）　　　と・・・	to think
おもいだす （思い出す） Ｎ（のこと） を・・・	to recall
おもしろい	interesting 6
おや （親）	parent (self) 14
およぐ （泳ぐ） Ｎが・・・	to swim 7
おりる Ｎを・・・	to disembark 23
Ｎから・・・	
オレンジ	orange 22
オレンジ・ジュース	orange juice 3
おわる （終わる） Ｎが・・・	to end
おんがく （音楽）	music 16
おんがくかい （音楽会）	concert 20
おんな （女）	female 2
おんなのひと （女の人）	female person
おんぷ （音符）	musical note 18

か

カード	card
ガールフレンド	girlfriend
かい （貝）	shellfish 20
かい （階） ＃・・・	floor
かい （回） ＃・・・	time(s), occasion(s)
かいがん （海岸）	coast, beach 13
かいぎ （会議）	meeting 5
かいもの （買物）	shopping 8

456

かいわ　（会話）	conversation　11
かう　（買う）	to buy　4
かえす　（返す）　NにNを・・・	to return (an object)　14
かえり　（帰り）	return
かえる　（帰る）　NがNへ／に・・・	to return　4
かお　（顔）	face
かおいろ　（顔色）	complexion　16
かがく　（科学）	science　22
かかる　NにNが・・・	to take, to require　8
かぎ	key　26
かきなおす　（書きなおす）	to rewrite　14
かく　（書く）　Nを・・・	to write　4
がくせい　（学生）	student　2
がくちょう　（学長）	university president　3
かげつ　（か月）　♯・・・	months
かける，でんわをかける	to make a phone call　14
かさ	umbrella
かしょ　（か所）　♯・・・	places　27
かす　（貸す）　NにNを・・・	to lend　8
かぜ　（風)	wind　19
かぜ　（風邪)	cold　11
かぜをひく	to catch a cold
かぞく　（家族）	family (self)　8
ガソリン	gasoline　19
かた　（方）	person　2
かた　（方）　V(pre ます)・・・	way of V, method of V
かたい　（固い）	tough, stiff　23
かたち　（形）	shape　22
かたちをする	to have a shape
かたづける　（片付ける）　Nを・・・	to straighten up　12
かたみち　（片道）	one way　27
カタリナ	Santa Catalina　8
かつ　（勝つ）　Nに・・・	to win　17
がっき　（学期）	semester
がっこう　（学校）	school　5
かなしい　（悲しい）	sad　22
かね　（金）	money　8
かのじょ　（彼女）	she　16
かべ	wall　19
かみ　（紙）	paper　8

きょうしつ （教室）	classroom	18
きょうだい （兄弟）	siblings (self)	8
きょうと （京都）	Kyoto	9
きょねん （去年）	last year	5
きらい　Nが・・・	dislike	10
きり （霧）	fog	19
きる （着る）　Nを・・・	to wear	14
きれい	beautiful	5
キロ　♯・・・	kilometer	27
きんぎょ （金魚）	goldfish	26
ぎんこう （銀行）	bank	3

く

クイズ	quiz	7
くすり （薬）	medicine	16
くすりをのむ	to take medicine	
くださる　Nを・・・・	to give (to self)	20
くつ	shoes	17
くつをはく	to wear shoes	
くに （国）	country	3
くらい （暗い）	dark	20
クラス	class	3
クリスマス	Christmas	9
くる （来る）　Nへ／に・・・	to come	4
くるま （車）	automobile	3
グレイド	grade	17
クレジット・カード	credit card	26
くれる　Nを・・・	to give (to self)	20

け

けいかく （計画）	plan	28
けいざいがく （経済学）	economics	2
けいさんき （計算器）	calculator	13
ケーキ	cake	9
げしゅく （下宿）	boarding house	24
けす （消す）　Nを・・・	to turn off	22
けっこん （結婚）	marriage	9
けっこんする （結婚する）　Nと・・・	to marry	
げんかん （玄関）	entry way	26

げんき （元気）	healthy, good health 8
けんきゅうしつ （研究室）	research room, office 8
げんごがく （言語学）	linguistics 3

こ

ごい （語彙）	vocabulary 25
こういう	this sort of
こうえん （公園）	park 5
こうがい （公害）	pollution 14
こうぎ （講義）	lecture 17
こうこう （高校）	high school 11
こうすい （香水）	perfume 20
こうちゃ （紅茶）	black tea
こうつうこうしゃ （交通交社）	travel bureau 27
こえ （声）	voice 25
コース	course 4
コート	coat 17
コーヒー	coffee 4
コープ	CO-OP 3
コーラ	cola 10
こおり （氷）	ice 19
ゴールデンゲートブリッジ	Golden Gate Bridge 9
ゴールデンゲートパーク	Golden Gate Park 10
こくばん （黒板）	blackboard
ごご （午後）	afternoon (p.m.) 8
ござる	to be (humble)
こじあける　Ｎを・・・	to pry open 26
ごしゅじん （ご主人）	husband (other)
ごぜん （午前）	morning (a.m.) 10
ごちそうする　ＮにＮを・・・	to treat 28
こと	thing (intangible) 13
こども （子ども）	child 6
ことり （小鳥）	small bird 26
ことわる （断わる）　Ｎを・・・	to refuse
このあいだ （この間）	the other day 21
ごはん	meal, rice 12
コピーする　Ｎを・・・	to copy 18
こぼれる　Ｎが・・・	to overflow
こむ （混む）　Ｎが・・・	to get crowded
こむぎこ （小麦粉）	wheat flour 24

460

こめ　（米）	rice 24
（ご）めいわく　（ご迷惑）	trouble, bother 28
ゴルフ	golf 10
これぐらい	about this much
ごろ	about (time) 3
ころす　（殺す）　Nを・・・	to kill 26
こわす　Nを・・・	to break 25
こわれる　Nが・・・	to be broken
こんがっき　（今学期）	this semester
こんげつ　（今日）	this month
コンサート	concert 13
こんしゅう　（今週）	this week 10
コンタクトレンズ	contact lens 26
こんど　（今度）	upcoming, next 21
こんばん　（今晩）	this evening 7

さ

さあ	well, come on
サービス	service
さいきん　（最近）	recently, these days 9
さいなん　（災難）	misfortune 26
さいふ	wallet 26
ざおう　（蔵王）	Zao 17
さがす　Nを・・・	to look for 14
さがけん　（佐賀県）	Saga Prefecture 21
さく　（咲く）	to bloom 23
さくぶん　（作文）	composition
さくら　（桜）	cherry tree, blossom 23
さくらもち　（桜もち）	sakuramochi 24
さけ　（酒）	rice wine, alcohol 5
さしみ	raw fish 10
さつ　（冊）　♯・・・	book (counter)
さっき	a few minutes ago
ざっし　（雑誌）	magazine 9
さっぽろ　（札幌）	Sapporo 19
さつまいも	sweet potato 24
ざとういち　（座頭市）	Zatoichi 13
さびしい	lonely 16
サボる　Nを・・・	to play hookey 23
さむい　（寒い）	cold 12

さめる　Ｎが・・・	to get cold　22
さようなら	good-bye　12
さら　（皿）	plate
サラダ	salad
さんかする　（参加する）　Ｎに・・・	to participate
サンスクリットご　（・・・語）	Sanskrit　12
サンドイッチ	sandwich　12
サンノゼ	San Jose　18
サンフランシスコ	San Francisco　2
さんぽ　（散歩）	stroll　19
さんぽ（を）する　（散歩をする）	to take a walk

し

じ　（時）　♯・・・	o'clock
しあい　（試合）	tournament, game　18
ジェイアール　（ＪＲ）	Japan Railroad　27
しえき　（使役）	causative　28
しかる　Ｎを・・・	to scold　26
じかん　（時間）	time　8
じかん　（時間）　♯・・・	
しけん　（試験）	examination　5
じこ　（事故）	accident　11
しごと　（仕事）	work　14
じしょ　（辞書）	dictionary　2
じしょをひく	to look up in a dictionary
じしん　（地震）	earthquake
しずか　（静か）	quiet　6
した　（下）	under, below　5
じだいげき　（時代劇）	historical drama　13
じつは　（実は）	the truth is　11
しつもん　（質問）	question　18
しつもん（を）する　（質問をする）	to ask a question
しつれいする　（失礼する）	to be impolite　12
してい（指定）	designated　27
じてんしゃ　（自転車）	bicycle　13
じどうしゃ　（自動車）	automobile　20
しぬ　（死ぬ）	to die　26
しばい　（芝居）	play　17
じびき　（字引）	dictionary　12
じびきをひく	to look up in a dictionary

462

しろうま （白馬）	Shirouma 17
しろくろ （白黒）	black and white
しろくろテレビ （白黒テレビ）	black and white TV 3
しんがっき （新学期）	new semester
しんかんせん （新幹線）	Shinkansen 21
しんじゅ （真珠）	pearl 20
しんぞう （心臓）	heart
しんぱい （心配） Nが・・・	worry 12
しんぱいする （心配する） N(のこと)を・・・	to worry
しんぶん （新聞）	newspaper 2
しんらいする （信頼する） N(のこと)を・・・	to trust 27
しんりがく （心理学）	psychology 2

す

ずいぶん	considerably, quite 20
すう　たばこを・・・	to smoke 12
すうがく （数学）	mathematics 11
スーツ	suit 18
スープ	soup 10
すえ （末）	the end, close, the youngest 28
すき(好き) Nが・・・	likable, to like 10
スキー	ski 11
スキーじょう （スキー場）	ski resort 17
すきやき	sukiyaki 4
すく　Nが・・・	to be empty 8
すぐ	immediately 18
すくない （少ない）	few
すくなくとも （少なくとも）	at least 12
すこし （少し）	a little 12
スコッチ	Scotch 9
すし	sushi 5
すずしい	cool 11
スタンフォード	Stanford 2
ずつ　♯・・・	of each 20
すっかり	completely
ずっと	by far, considerably, continuously, the whole time 11
すてる （捨てる） Nを・・・	to throw 14
ステレオ	stereo 13
ストーブ	heater 22

スパゲッティー	spaghetti 22
スフィンクス	Sphinx 22
スペインご （・・・語）	Spanish 3
スポーツ	sports 10
すみません	excuse me
すむ　Nが・・・	to finish, complete 22
する　Nを・・・	to do, to play (sports), to wear (accessories) 4
Nが・・・	
する　Nを・・・	to pickpocket 26
すわる　（座る）　Nに・・・	to sit

せ

せ　（背）	the back, torso
せがたかい	to be tall
せいげん　（制限）	restriction 27
せいせき　（成績）	academic grade
せきゆ　（石油）	petroleum
せつめい　（説明）	explanation 21
せつめいする　（説明する）　Nを・・・	to explain
ぜひ	by all means 13
せまい	narrow 6
セミナー	seminar 18
せんがっき　（先学期）	last semester
せんげつ　（先月）	last month
せんしゅう　（先週）	last week
せんせい　（先生）	teacher 2
ぜんぜん　（全然）　・・・ない	not at all 12
せんたく　（洗たく）	laundry 14
せんたくき　（洗たく機）	washing machine
せんたくする　（洗たくする）　Nを・・・	to do laundry
セント　♯・・・	cent 13
ぜんにっくう　（全日空）	All Japan Airlines 19
ぜんぶ　（全部）	all, whole 26
せんもん　（専門）	major, specialization 2

そ

そう	so 2
そうじ　（掃除）	cleaning 11
そうじする　（掃除する）　Nを・・・	to clean up

そうだん（相談）	consultation 22
そうだんする（相談する）Nに／とNのことを・・・	to consult
そつぎょう（卒業）	graduation 18
そつぎょうする（卒業する）Nを・・・	to graduate
そと（外）	outside 3
そふ（祖父）	grandfather (self) 3
そぼ（祖母）	grandmother (self) 8
そら（空）	sky 19
そんけいする（尊敬する）Nを・・・	to respect 26

た

たいいくかん（体育館）	gymnasium 2
だいいち（第一）	in the first place 18
だいがく（大学）	university 2
だいがくいん（大学院）	graduate school 26
だいがくいんせい（大学院生）	graduate student 2
だいがくせい（大学生）	university student 2
たいした（大した）	grave, serious
だいじょうぶ（大丈夫）	all right 26
だいず（大豆）	soybean 24
だいすき（大好き）Nが・・・	to like a lot 16
たいせつ（大切）	important 25
だいじ（大事）	serious, important
おだいじに	take care of yourself
だいたい（大体）	generally 14
だいとうりょう（大統領）	president (country) 24
だいとうりょうふじん（大統領夫人）	president's wife
だいぶ（大分）	quite
タイプする　Nを・・・	to type 12
タイプライター	typewriter 3
たいへん（大変）	very much, problematical, terrible 16
たかい（高い）	high, expensive 6
たき（滝）	waterfall 4
たくさん	much, many 3
たす　NにNを・・・	to add 23
だす（出す）Nを・・・	to send, submit 12
たすける（助ける）Nを・・・	to assist. save 26
ただ	only
たつ（立つ）Nに・・・	to stand 23

ダットサン	Datsun
たてもの　（建物）	building　2
たてる　（建てる）　Nを・・・	to build
たとえば	for example
たのしい　（楽しい）	enjoyable　11
たのむ　（頼む）　Nに・・・	to ask (a favor of)　26
たばこ	cigarette　12
たばこをすう	to smoke cigarettes　12
たびたび	time after time, repeatedly　27
たぶん　（多分）	perhaps　14
たべる　（食べる）　Nを・・・	to eat　4
タホ	Tahoe　25
たまご　（卵）	egg
だます　Nを・・・	to deceive
たまに	occasionally　12
だめ	no good　16
ためいき　（ため息）	sigh　25
ためいきをつく	to sigh　25
たりる　（足りる）　Nが・・・	to be sufficient
たんご　（単語）	word　15
だんじょ　（男女）	men and women　27
たんじょうび　（誕生日）	birthday

ち

ちいさい　（小さい）	small　6
チーズ	cheese　24
チェックする	to check　21
ちがう　（違う）　Nと・・・	to differ　20
ちかい　（近い）　Nに／から・・・	near
ちかく　（近く）	nearby　3
ちかごろ	recently, lately　11
ちかてつ　（地下鉄）	subway　23
ちこくする　（遅刻する）　Nに・・・	to be late　11
ちず　（地図）	map　20
ちち（父）	father (self)　3
ちゃ　（茶）	tea
チャーター	charter　8
ちゅうがっこう　（中学校）	middle school　28
ちゅうかりょうり　（中華料理）	Chinese cuisine　7
ちゅうごくご　（中国語）	Chinese　3

ちゅうごくじん　（中国人）	Chinese (person)
ちゅうし　（中止）	cancellation
ちゅうしする　（中止する）　Ｎを・・・	to cancel
ちゅうもんする　（注文する）　Ｎを・・・	to order　26
ちょうこく　（彫刻）	sculpture　22
ちょうど	just
ちょきん　（貯金）	savings　19
ちょきんする　（貯金する）	to save (money)　19
ちょっと	a little　7

つ

つかう　（使う）　Ｎを・・・	to use　7
つかれる　（疲れる）	to get tired　16
つぎ　（次）	next, coming, following　21
つく（着く）　Ｎに・・・	to arrive (in)　14
つく　Ｎが・・・	to arrive
つくえ　（机）	desk　3
つくる　（作る）　Ｎを・・・	to make　5
つける　Ｎ・・・を	to turn on　22
つづく　（続く）　Ｎが・・・	to continue (intr)　16
つづける　（続ける）　Ｎを・・・	to continue (tr)　19
つつむ　（包む）　Ｎを・・・	to wrap　8
って　＝と，というのは	to say (that)
つめたい　（冷たい）	cold (to the touch)　25
つよい　（強い）	strong　18

て

て　（手）	hand　7
テープ	tape　9
テープレコーダー	tape recorder　3
でかける　（出かける）　Ｎに／へ・・・	to go out　15
てがみ　（手紙）	letter　8
テキスト	text book　2
できるだけ	as much as possible　12
てつだう　（手伝う）　Ｎを・・・	to help
テニス	tennis　7
テニスをする	to play tennis　7
デパート	department store　23
ではいりする　（出入りする）　Ｎから・・・	to go in and out　14
デュラントホール	Durant Hall　3

468

でる （出る） Nを・・・	to leave 5
Nに・・・	to attend 12
テレグラフ	Telegraph 3
テレビ	television 3
てん （点） ♯・・・	point 20
てんき （天気）	weather 17
でんき （電気）	electricity, electric light 22
でんきがつく	electricity is on
でんきをつける	to turn on electricity
てんきよほう （天気予報）	weather report 19
てんぷら	tempura 5
でんわ （電話）	telephone 12
でんわをかける／する	to make a phone call

と

と （戸）	door 22
ど （度） ♯・・・	degree time
ドア	door 23
ドイツ	Germany 10
どう （銅）	copper
とうきょう （東京）	Tokyo 10
どうぞ	please
どうにか	somehow or other
どうも	no matter how much I try
とおい （遠い） Nから・・・	far 14
ときどき （時々）	sometimes 12
とくい （得意） Nが・・・	forte 18
とくに （特に）	particularly, especially 25
とけい （時計）	watch
ところ （所）	place 13
ところで	by the way
としょかん （図書館）	library 2
とても	very
となり	next to, next door 3
とにかく	anyway 26
とまる （泊まる） Nに・・・	to stay at 27
とまる （止まる） Nが・・・	to stop
ともだち （友達）	friend 4
トヨタ	Toyota 14
とり （鳥）	bird 23

とる （取る）　Nを・・・	to take, to remove　4
ドル　♯・・・	dollar
どろぼう	thief

な

ナイフ	knife　4
なおす　Nを・・・	to correct
なおる　Nが・・・	to get well　23
なか （中）	in, at　3
ながい （長い）	long　23
ながす （流す）　Nを・・・	to wash away　28
なく （泣く）	to cry　23
なくなる　Nが・・・	to disappear
なぐる　Nを・・・	to hit
ナポレオン	Napoleon　24
なま （生）	raw, fresh
なまえ	name　4
なみ （並）	regular　10
ならう （習う）　NにNを・・・	to learn　13
なる	to become
なんだか （何だか）	somehow

に

におい	smell　22
にがて （苦手）　Nが・・・	weak point　18
にぎやか	bustling　6
にく （肉）	meat　7
にこにこする	to smile
に，さん （二，三）	two or three
にちようび （日曜日）	Sunday　5
にっき （日記）	diary
について　N・・・	concerning...
にっこう （日航）	JAL
にている （似ている）　Nに・・・	to resemble
にほん （日本）	Japan　2
にほんご （日本語）	the Japanese language　2
にほんじん （日本人）	Japanese (person)　2
にほんせい （日本製）	made in Japan　22
にほんちゃ （日本茶）	Japanese tea　10
にほんまち （日本町）	Japan Town　7

にほんりょうり　（日本料理）	Japanese cuisine　11
にもつ（荷物）	baggage　28
ニューズウィーク	Newsweek
ニューヨーク	New York　4
にわ（庭）	garden　22
にん　（人）　♯・・・	person
にんげん　（人間）	human being

ぬ

ぬすむ　（盗む）　Nを・・・	to steal
ぬれる　Nに・・・	to get wet　16

ね

ネクタイ	necktie　22
ねこ	cat　3
ねじまわし	screwdriver　26
ねずみ	rat　26
ねだん　（値段）	price　21
ねつ　（熱）	fever　12
ねむい	sleepy　16
ねむる　（眠る）	to sleep　11
ねる　（寝る）	to go to bed, to sleep
ネルソン	Nelson's (dictionary)
ねん　（年）　♯・・・	year
ねんせい　（年生）　♯・・・	school year

の

ノースダコタ	North Dakota　14
のびる	to get soggy, to be stretched　22
のむ　（飲む）　Nを・・・	to drink
のる　（乗る）　Nに・・・	to ride　14
のんびりする	to relax　11

は

は　（歯）	tooth　8
は　（葉）	leaf　24
バー	bar　4
パーセント　♯・・・	percent　27
パーティー	party　13
バーボン	bourbon　11

はれる （晴れる）	to be clear, to clear up
ハワイ	Hawaii 5
はん （半）	half
ばん （晩）	late evening, night 11
＃・・・	night(s)
パン	bread 11
ばら	rose
パンケーキ	pancake
ばんごう （番号）	number
ばんごはん （晩ごはん）	dinner 5
ハンサム	handsome 10
はんたいする （反対する） Nに・・・	to oppose 26
ハンバーガー	hamburger 6

ひ

ひ （火）	fire 22
ピアノ	piano 18
ピアノをひく	to play the piano
ビール	beer
ひく　Nを・・・	to catch (cold)
Nから Nを・・・	to subtract 23
ピクニック	picnic 7
ひこうき （飛行機）	airplane 5
ひしょ （秘書）	secretary
びっくりする	to be suprised
びっこ	limp 26
びっこをひく	to limp
ヒッピー	hippie 3
ひと （人）	person 2
ひどい	terrible 6
ひとりで （一人で）	alone, by oneself 8
ひはんする （批判する） Nを・・・	to criticize 26
ビフテキ	beefsteak 4
ひま	leisure, free time 23
ひやす （冷やす）	to chill 22
びょう （秒）	second (time) 24
びょういん （病院）	hospital 16
びょうき （病気）	illness, disease 19
ひらがな	Hiragana 4
ピラミッド	Pyramid 22

へた（下手）	unskillful, poor at 7
べつに　（別に）　・・・ない	not particularly
べつべつ　（別々）	separate
ペニシリン	penicillin 26
へや　（部屋）	room 3
ベル	buzzar, alarm
へん　（変）	strange, wierd
ペン	pen 7
べんきょうする　（勉強する）	to study 4
ペンダント	pendant 20
ベンツ	Mercedes Benz 11
べんとう	lunch box
べんり　（便利）	convenient, useful 6

ほ

ほう　（方）	side, the one
ボーイフレンド	boyfriend 13
ほうそう　（放送）	broadcast 23
ボーッとする	to get fuzzy 24
ボールペン	ball-point pen 4
ホームシック	homesick 11
ぼく	me, I (male) 26
ほしい　（欲しい）	to want, desirable (self) 13
ほっかいどう　（北海道）	Hokkaido 14
ほとんど	almost 12
ほめる	to praise 1
ポルシェ	Porsche 17
ほん　（本）	book 2
ほん　（本）	(counter) 8
ホンコン	Hong Kong 14
ほんしゅう　（本州）	Honshu 14
ポンド	pound 25
ほんとう	truth 11
ほんとうは	actually 11
ほんや　（本屋）	bookstore 3

ま

まあ	oh
まいあさ　（毎朝）	every morning 14
まいばん　（毎晩）	every evening

まいど　（毎度）	every time　10
まいにち　（毎日）	every day　7
まえ　（前）	before　6
まける　（負ける）	to lose　17
まじめ	consciencious, serious　6
まずい	not tasty　6
マスターする	to master　15
マスターカード	Master Card　3
また	again
まだ	not yet　4
まち　（町）	town
まちがい　（間違い）	mistake　18
まちがえる　（間違える）	to make a mistake　26
まつ　（待つ）	to wait　23
まったく	indeed
まで	unity, by　18
までに	until
まど　（窓）	window　7
まわる　（回る）	to go around　27
まんが　（漫画）	comics
まんかい　（満開）	full bloom　24
まんねんひつ　（万年筆）	fountain pen　8

み

みぎ　（右）	right　22
みじかい　（短かい）	short　20
ミシガン	Michigan　14
みしまゆきおのしょうせつ　（三島由紀夫の小説）	Mishima Yukio's novel(s)
みず（水）	water
ミスプリント	misprint　15
みせ　（店）	shop　7
みそ	fermented bean paste　24
みなみ　（南）	south　3
みる　（見る）	to see　4
ミルク	milk　26
ミルクセーキ	milk shake　24
みんな	everyone, everything　16

む

むかえる　（迎える）	to meet

476

むかえにくる　（迎えに来る）	to come to meet
むかえにいく　（迎えに行く）	to go to meet
むかし　（昔）	the past　3
むずかしい　（難しい）	difficult　6
むすこ　（息子）	son (self)　28
むすめ　（娘）	daughter (self)　28
むり　（無理）	impossible, unreasonable　12
むりをする　（無理をする）	to do to an unreasonable extent

め

め　（目）	eye　7
めいし　（名刺）	namecard　22
めいじ　（明治）	Meiji (era)　8
めがね	eye glasses　14
めがみ　（女神）	goddess
メキシコ	Mexico　11
めったに	rarely　12
メモ	memo　25

も

もう	already, any longer
もう	more
もうしわけ　（申し訳）	excuse
もくてきち　（目的地）	destination　27
もし，もしも	if
もち	rice cake
もちろん　（勿論）	of course　11
もつ　（持つ）	to hold　16
もっている　（持っている）	to have
もってくる　（持って来る）	to bring　18
もっと	more　20
もの　（物）	thing (tangible)　13
もらう	to receive　20
もんげん　（門限）	curfew　27

や

やく　（焼く）	to bake, to broil　24
やくそく　（約束）	promise　17
やくにたつ　（役にたつ）	to be useful　27
やさい　（野菜）	vegetables　25

やさしい	easy 6
やすい （安い）	inexpensive 6
やすみ （休み）	holiday 21
やすむ （休む）	to rest 14
やちん （家賃）	rent 17
やっぱり	as one may expect 13
やまのぼり （山登り）	mountain climbing 11
やむ （止む）	to stop (intrans.) 22
やめる （止める）	to stop (trans.) 14
やる	to do 12

ゆ

ゆうがた （夕方）	evening 6
ゆうしょく （夕食）	evening meal 28
ゆうめい （有名）	famous
ユース	youth hostel 27
ゆうびん （郵便）	mail 11
ゆうびんきょく （郵便局）	post office 3
ゆうべ	last night 23
ゆき （雪）	snow 14
ゆっくり	slowly 27
ゆっくりする	to take it easy
ゆびわ	ring

よ

ようい （用意）	preparation 22
ようじ （用事）	errands, business 22
ヨーロッパ	Europe 10
よく	well, often
よくなる	to get better
よくじつ （よく日）	following day 23
よこ （横）	side 3
よしゅう （予習）	preparation for class 16
よてい （予定）	plan
よぶ （呼ぶ）	to call 26
よみかた （読みかた）	how to read 15
よむ （読む）	to read 4
よやく （予約）	reservation 19
よやくをする （予約をする）	to make a reservation
よる （夜）	night 25

478

こ（に）よると	according to
よろこぶ（喜ぶ）	to be delighted, pleased 20
よろしい	all right
よわい（弱い）	weak 25
がよわい（が弱い）	to be weak at

ら

ラーメン	*ramen* 22
らいがっき（来学期）	next semester 21
らいげつ（来月）	next month
らいしゅう（来週）	next week 12
らいねん（来年）	next year 7
ラグビー	rugby 18
らっしゃい＝いらっしゃい	welcome
ラボ	language lab 9

り

りこん（離婚）	divorce 17
りこんする（離婚する）	to divorce
りっぱ	elegant, splendid 6
リノ	Reno 7
りゅう（竜）	dragon 22
りょう（寮）	dormitory 2
りょうしん（両親）	parents (self) 8
りようする（利用する）	to use 27
りょうりする（料理する）	to cook
りょかん（旅館）	Japanese style inn
りょこう（旅行）	travel 15
りょこうする（旅行する）	to travel

る

ルーツ	*Roots* 9
ルームメート	roomate 6

れ

れい（例）	example, the one we know 9
れいか（零下）	below 0° 14
レポート	report, term paper 17
れいぞうこ（冷蔵庫）	refrigerator 23
れきし（歴史）	history 2

Basic Structures
in Japanese
日本語の基本構造 © H. Aoki, M. Hirose,
J. Keller, K. Sakuma, 1984

1984年8月1日　初版発行　　　　　　　　本体価格3,800円
1989年1月10日　普及版第1刷発行
1994年9月1日　普及版第6刷発行

　　　　　　　　　　　　　　　青 木 晴 夫
　　　　　　　　　　　　　　　広 瀬 正 宜
　　　　　著　者　　　　　　Jean　Keller
　　　　　　　　　　　　　　　佐 久 間 勝 彦
　　　　　発行者　　　　　鈴 木 荘 夫

　　　発行所　株式会社　大 修 館 書 店
　　　　　(101) 東京都千代田区神田錦町3-24
　　　電話 03-3295-6231 販売部　03-3294-2356 編集部
　　　　　　　振替　00190-7-40504

　　印刷／横山印刷　製本／牧製本　装幀／近藤敬三
　　ISBN4-469-22062-0　　　　　Printed in Japan